# SANGHARAKSHITA

## A NEW VOICE IN THE BUDDHIST TRADITION

Dharmacari Subhuti (Alex Kennedy)

# Sangharakshita

•

## A New Voice

•

## in the Buddhist Tradition

•

Windhorse Publications

*Published by*
Windhorse Publications Ltd.
38 Newmarket Road
Cambridge
CB5 8DT, UK
email: info@windhorsepublications.com
web: www.windhorsepublications.com

First edition 1994
Reprinted with a new cover 2009

Cover design by Dhammarati
Front cover image © Clear Vision Trust Picture Archive
Back cover image © Diego Franssens
Printed by Bell & Bain Ltd., Glasgow

British Library Cataloguing in Publication Data:
A catalogue record for this book is available from the British Library

ISBN 9780 904766 68 4

# CONTENTS

## About the Author

Dharmacari Subhuti was born Alex Kennedy, in Chatham, England, in 1947. Since joining the Western Buddhist Order in 1973 he has been energetically concerned with its development and with that of the Friends of the Western Buddhist Order, the wider movement for which the Order provides a nucleus.

His fields of activity have been remarkably diverse. Among other things he established the London Buddhist Centre and the Guhyaloka Retreat Centre in Spain. He has written two books as well as the present volume, and an outline of the life of Sangharakshita, to be published in 1995. For eight years he served as Sangharakshita's personal secretary. As one of those responsible for the ordination of the Western Buddhist Order's new members, he developed and for some years directed the 'training process' for men preparing to join the Order.

He currently spends much of each year engaged in writing at Guhyaloka, but makes regular visits to England, India, and the USA, where he is much in demand as a speaker and retreat leader.

MANY YEARS AGO, I CONSTANTLY ASKED MYSELF: 'How does this teaching relate to one's actual spiritual experience, spiritual life, and spiritual development? Why did the Buddha say this? Why was the Buddha concerned with this? Where does it connect up with spiritual life?' But I found that very few scholars ever thought in these terms. In many cases, it didn't even seem to occur to them to do so—it didn't seem to occur even to many Buddhists to ask these questions. It was as though it was just a sort of game that had no relevance to life and no bearing on the spiritual life or on spiritual development as an individual.[1]

# PREFACE

SANGHARAKSHITA MERITS AN INTRODUCTION as one of the leading Buddhists of modern times. He is probably best known for his writings on Buddhist themes, which are widely read in the English-speaking Buddhist world. But he is no mere theoretician. He has played a key part in the revival of Buddhism in India, particularly through his work among the ex-Untouchables. Sangharakshita has been among the leaders of the movement of conversion of millions of these downtrodden people, which is one of the most significant events for Buddhism in the twentieth century. His most important contribution to modern Buddhism, however, is his creation, in 1967, of a new Buddhist movement, the Friends of the Western Buddhist Order (FWBO) and his establishment, the following year, of the Western Buddhist Order (WBO), the spiritual community at the heart of the FWBO. That movement now extends world-wide and has, under Sangharakshita's guidance, developed a new Buddhist way of life, applying basic Buddhist principles to the modern world.

An introduction is not only merited, it is also needed. Sangharakshita's writing and lecturing have been very extensive, both in quantity and range. However, he has not unfolded his thinking according to some grand and unifying scheme. His ideas have developed in relation to the problems and opportunities that have presented themselves to him as his own spiritual life has progressed. In a sense, they are rather untidy. Some overview is therefore called for, so that his thought can be comprehended in its breadth and in the context of his experience.

Sangharakshita's life and teaching will interest different people for different reasons, so an introduction must fulfil several functions. Members of the growing and international body of men and women for whom he is a principal guide and influence will want a presentation of his leading ideas. They will want to see how his teachings fit together to form a complete pattern. Many other Buddhists will want to know whether his thought has anything to offer them. They will be seeking principles by which to live the Buddhist life in the new circumstances of the modern world. Those many who find themselves drawn to Buddhism, but are not yet committed to it, will want to see what relevance a Westerner has made of that ancient spiritual tradition. Has it anything to offer the individual today? What can it contribute to modern society?

In presenting an overview of Sangharakshita's ideas, I am conscious of a problem. A summary must, in a sense, always falsify. It will sacrifice elegant subtlety of thought for the crude clarity of general outlines. It will miss much expressed not in the matter but in the manner of writing and speaking. And it will seem to fix a definition and finality not true to the intricate dialectic of growing ideas, particularly when their author is still alive and still thinking. An introduction must be taken as an introduction, a first meeting with its subject. It is no substitute for a deeper personal encounter through his own work. Nonetheless, an orientation and perspective may help those who have some inclination to discover more of his thought. Perhaps it will suggest a starting point for that encounter, so that they may engage more closely with the man himself.

I must, straight away, declare an interest: Sangharakshita is my own teacher and guide. He has influenced me far more than anyone else in my life and I cannot disguise my love and esteem for him. Nor do I wish to. I am convinced that his thinking is of the greatest importance to the future of Buddhism, perhaps of humanity in general, and to anyone who wants to make something of his or her own life. While I do not want to disguise my own conviction, I cannot expect my readers to share it from the outset. I hope that his ideas will speak for themselves and declare their own significance.

When I planned this book, I had intended to write a chapter on Sangharakshita's poetry, since poetry is, to him, a very important medium of communication. Somehow it did not work out. Instead I have prefaced each chapter with one of his poems, choosing one that, to me at least, seems to say something about the theme to be pursued. I have selected the poems both for this reason and because they are ones I particularly like. Not all of them are especially good poetry—or even Sangharakshita's best. My justification for including them is that they express a side of Sangharakshita that may be overlooked in the exposition of his ideas. As he himself writes of the poems included in *The Enchanted Heart*, from which those published here are all taken, 'They constitute a sort of spiritual biography, sketchy indeed, but perhaps revealing, or at least suggesting, aspects of my life which would not otherwise be known'.[2] In the references I have put the year of composition of each poem, since they come from all periods of Sangharakshita's life.

I have given quite a bit of thought to the much vexed issue of the 'gender inclusive' pronoun. Can 'he' be used as a generic pronoun, including women as well as men? Can one speak of 'the individual and his spiritual development' and still be understood as referring to a woman as much as to a man? Should one avoid that usage and if so how? My present conclusion is that there is a problem in the English language that, in general, we have to live with, for it has no easy solution. I have sympathy with those women who moderately inform me that they find themselves identifying more strongly with what is being written about if it explicitly mentions women. At the same time, there are points where one wants to, perhaps even has to, write about a hypothetical single individual, who could be either male or female. This is particularly the case in a didactic work of this kind. English offers only one way in which that can be done that is neither offensive to the eye nor ridiculously verbose. I do not mind the occasional 'him or her', but too many of them become obtrusive and ugly. I have therefore tried as much as I can to mention both men and women when I am talking about both—but where I think that it is clear I am talking about both and I need a generic singular pronoun, I have adhered to the standard English usage of 'he', 'his', and 'him' as referring to both men and women. Where I have done this, I am sure there will be no doubt that I am referring to both men and women. Sangharakshita himself follows that standard practice even more strictly. He especially believes that we should not allow the English language to be manipulated for purely ideological ends. I have therefore left quotations from him in the form he gave them. It should be understood that, unless he makes it clear that he is talking about only men or only women, he includes both. Neither Sangharakshita nor I have any doubts about the equal spiritual potential of men and women and want women, as much as men, to identify fully with what we say about the spiritual life in general.

I have tried always to base my presentation directly on Sangharakshita's own work. In general, all the ideas in this book are his and can be traced to him. Where possible, I have used his own words, weaving them into the text as smoothly as I can. This has sometimes entailed quite heavy editing when I am quoting from discussions and seminars. I have used the editing conventions established by Sangharakshita himself for translating his spoken word into written form, and have shown him all the edited passages.

Some people who read this book may have little or no knowledge of Buddhism. Though it is not intended as an introduction to Buddhism, I hope it has been written in such a way that newcomers will be able to follow all its main points. I have explained Buddhist terms as much as possible and hope that their meaning will be clear enough for the purpose of expounding Sangharakshita's ideas. I also hope that this work will encourage those new to Buddhism to read a general introduction to the subject.

Numbered references in the text refer to endnotes, which give the sources of quotations. Other references are to footnotes, which explain matters in the text. Most endnote references are to Sangharakshita's published works. Those few such references that are not to his writings are clearly attributed to their authors. Some references are to Sangharakshita's seminars and discussions that are in circulation in unedited form. I have given no page references for these, since their availability is very limited and I suspect that few of my readers will wish to look them up. Those who do will easily be able to trace the quotations using the table of contents at the beginning of each transcript. If necessary I can supply more detailed references. References to tape-recorded talks give their reference number in the latest catalogue of Dharmachakra Tapes, who distribute them. I have generally given Buddhist technical terms in Sanskrit, since that is the most widely applicable canonical language. Sometimes a term has become well-known in its Pali form, in which case I have used that form, making clear its Sanskrit equivalent.

Many people have contributed to the preparation of this work and I would like to acknowledge their contributions publicly. Silabhadra has for many years struggled to get all Sangharakshita's seminars transcribed and published. It is thanks to him and his transcribers that I have much of my material. I have had essential technical assistance from Shantavira, Sahamati, Sahananda, and Phil Woodward. The index was compiled by Vidyaratna and Shantavira. The Padmaloka community has supported me financially. The members of the Guhyaloka community have looked after all my material needs. Retreatants at Guhyaloka have cooked me supper every evening—and carried it down the hill to me every day, rain or shine. In particular I must thank Yashodeva for this service. I have showed an early draft of the book to my friends Dolf In'tveld, Xavi Alongina, Baukje Joustra, Kulananda, Srimala, Dhammadinna, Sona, Suvajra, Kovida, Julian Burgess, and Nagapriya. Reading a draft is work, not least because considerable tact has to be employed in giving comments! The observations they have all made have been very helpful—but most of all their encouragement has been indispensable. Without detracting from the contributions of these readers, I must particularly mention the detailed and very useful comments of Sagaramati, Saramati, Cittapala, Stephen Batchelor, Visvapani, and, of course, Nagabodhi—there is no doubt that they have considerably improved the book, and saved me from my own excesses. I hardly need say that the person I have most to thank is Sangharakshita himself, in the first place for giving me something to write about. He has, as always, been very encouraging and helpful, answering my questions and looking over my presentation of his ideas. There are many others who have helped in less direct ways—but I will not fill up space listing them all. I hope they will realise my gratitude to them.

I thank all these people for their contribution and hope that this work justifies their labours. As is usual, I must stress that though they have all helped me immeasurably, they cannot be held responsible for any deficiencies in my work.

*Chapter One*

# THE TRANSLATOR

*'Hammer your thoughts into a unity.'*
*This line once read*
*The sound came clangingly*
*Of golden hammers in my head*
*Beating and beating sheet on sheet*
*To make the figured foil complete.*

*Religion, friendship, art*
*Were hammered there*
*On the cyclopean anvils of my heart*
*Into an image bright and fair.*
*Under the strain the forge-floor split;*
*Nerveless the arms that fashioned it.*[3]

MODERN BUDDHISM IS IN CRISIS. The Buddhist tradition, like so many others, is being challenged by a world radically different from the one in which it has flourished for two-and-a-half millennia. Technological development is changing ever more drastically the way people live—even the way they think about their lives. In most of the lands where it has been established for centuries, Buddhism is in disarray and retreat, unable yet to adapt its old message to new circumstances. Curiously, it is in the West itself, the very heartland of technological development, that it is beginning to communicate itself most successfully to the modern world and is expanding most rapidly. But that too presents its problems. What should Buddhism in the West bring from Buddhism in the East? Which form of Buddhism is appropriate to the West? How is modern Buddhism to relate to Western culture? How is one to live the Buddhist life in the modern world? What really *is* Buddhism? More properly, as Buddhists themselves would prefer to say, what is the *Dharma*? What is the 'Truth', the 'Path', or the 'Teaching'?

Sangharakshita is one of those who has confronted these issues most directly. In a favourite image, he is a translator. He is a translator between the East and the West, between the traditional world and the modern.

> One who is a translator metaphorically brings a discipline, or set of
> ideas, or a culture, from the obscurity and darkness of unfamiliar terms
> into the light of terms that are familiar. I myself am a translator because I
> elucidate, that is, elucidate the Dharma.[4]

Above all, he is a translator between principles and practice. From his earliest contact with Buddhism, he has sought to discover its essential principles. It has been his life's work to give those principles expression, both in ideas and in institutions and practices.

For Sangharakshita, the essential insight of the Buddha is beyond words and finds expression in different forms in different circumstances. The many schools, formed in Buddhism's 2,500 years of history and its diffusion throughout Asia, have to a greater or lesser extent kept alive that original insight. Each has elaborated it further and explored its various aspects in diverse ways. Whether it is the rich exuberance of Tibetan Vajrayāna or the austere simplicity of Japanese Zen, all schools carry the same intrinsic message. Sangharakshita has striven to discern the fundamental Buddhist experience behind these many forms and to communicate it to the modern world. He has embodied his under-standing in the Friends of the Western Buddhist Order, the new Buddhist movement he has founded.

Since its initiation in 1967, Sangharakshita has devoted himself mainly to clarifying the many issues that have arisen during the establishment and growth of that movement. As his disciples have engaged more deeply with the Dharma, they have come up against innumerable problems and conflicts. What place does work have in spiritual life? Is homosexual activity a contravention of Buddhist ethics? How should Buddhists relate to the wider world? Do Western art and literature have anything to offer the Buddhist practitioner? How is one to work with the various feelings that arise in meditation? How should a residential community organise itself? As issues have arisen, Sangharakshita has elucidated the underlying principles on which a resolution depends. He has thus evolved a philosophy of active spiritual life, embracing every aspect of human affairs: community, work, sexuality, art and culture, social action, meditation, ceremony, personal relationships, and more. All have received his attention and, if he has not exhausted each topic, he has laid bare its essential principles so that his disciples can continue to live the Buddhist life in an ever-changing world.

Although Sangharakshita has devoted many years to the creation of an organised Buddhist movement, his ideas are relevant outside the circle of his own disciples. Buddhists everywhere, whether in the East or West, are moving into a new world, to which traditional forms are increasingly irrelevant. If they are not simply to become fossils, interesting relics of a bygone era, all Buddhists must look beyond the forms of their own schools. They must recognise the timeless core that each, perhaps, still conveys. They must let go of whatever in their own tradition is merely the unreflecting propagation of a culture long since dead or is simply of local significance. They must rely only on the essential Buddhist experience in their own spiritual lives. They must let the fundamental Buddhist message speak out to the men and women of the present. Since Sangharakshita has faced these issues in a particularly radical way, all Buddhists will find that he has something important to say to them. They will discover much in his teaching that will help them in their own task of spiritual renewal.

Sangharakshita's teaching has wider relevance yet. A great many people today sense that humanity has a higher purpose than mere material advancement. They are seeking some new vision to give their lives greater meaning and purpose. Many are strongly drawn to Buddhism's non-theism and to its teachings of nonviolence and of universal fellowship. However, they are not attracted to its present cultural forms. If they are to respond at all it will be to a presentation like Sangharakshita's: clear and intelligent, taking into account modern concerns and susceptibilities, and free from cultural anachronism. Sangharakshita's appeal is broad, for he points to something beyond type to be found in all human beings. His disciples already include people of very diverse backgrounds and temperaments: illiterate peasants and sophisticated professionals, ex-Christians and ex-communists, Indians and Americans, intellectuals and devotees, hermits and activists. Sangharakshita's ideas can surely help more people understand the real significance of their lives.

It is Sangharakshita's ideas that we will now set out to explore. While we are contemplating Sangharakshita's thought, we should not forget the perspective within which he himself functions. He is a bold and original thinker and, at the same time, a faithful follower of the Buddha. To some this has seemed paradoxical: I remember the poet Allen Ginsberg pondering, after a visit to Sangharakshita, why one so unconventional and revolutionary in his outlook should write poetry so traditional in form. When I reported this to Sangharakshita, he laughed and reflected that he is but a reluctant revolutionary. Really he is a complete traditionalist, forced by circumstances to take to revolution. His tastes are thoroughly traditional, and he says that, if circumstances had allowed it, he would have found fulfilment living in a very traditional Buddhist monastery in a very traditional Buddhist culture: studying, meditating, writing. But circumstances have not allowed it. He has been called upon to give new life to the old truths, not only through ideas but through practical guidance and new institutions. All his work is entirely fresh, revolutionary even, yet completely faithful to the original insight and teaching of the Buddha. His own teaching consists essentially of restating that insight within the modern context or else working out its unexplored implications.

So that we can better appreciate the significance of Sangharakshita's ideas, we must learn more about their author. It is, however, not easy to get a full impression of the man. Sangharakshita is a complex figure who has lived a singular life and has a very individual intelligence. He has formed himself under rather unusual conditions and speaks with a particular voice. Thinker, poet, communicator, mystic, organiser, scholar, guide: it is hard to comprehend so many-sided and unique a character.

> Who am I? I must confess I do not know. I am as much a mystery to myself as I probably am to you. Not that I am a mystery to everyone, apparently. Quite a lot of people know exactly who and what I am (I am speaking of people outside the [FWBO]). Quite a lot of people 'see' me. But they see me in different ways. This was very much the case when I lived in India. According to who it was that did the seeing, I was 'the English monk', 'a rabid Mahayanist', 'a narrow-minded Hinayanist', 'the Enemy of the Church', 'a Russian spy', 'an American agent', 'the Editor of the Maha Bodhi', 'an impractical young idealist', 'a good speaker', 'the invader of Suez', 'the guru of the Untouchables', and so on. More recently, here in England, I have been 'a good monk', 'a bad monk', 'the Buddhist counterpart of the Vicar of Hampstead', 'the author of [*A Survey of Buddhism*]', 'a crypto-Vajrayanist', 'a lecturer at Yale', 'the hippie guru', 'a first-class organizer', 'a traditionalist', 'a maverick', 'a misogynist', 'a sexist', 'a controversial figure', and 'An Enlightened Englishman'.
>
> All these different 'sightings' have at least some truth in them, even though the people doing the 'seeing' may have looked at me from the wrong angle, in the wrong kind of light, through tinted spectacles, or through the wrong end of the telescope. They may even have had spots floating before their eyes. The reason why all these different sightings have at least some truth in them is that I am a rather complex person.[5]

His life is immediately striking for the number of modern myths it embodies. To begin with, Sangharakshita is a 'self-made man'. He was born in relatively humble circumstances with few material or cultural advantages, without much benefit of formal education, and with little or no religious background and no effective spiritual mentors. Yet he has become a man of formidable learning, with a penetrating and creative mind, one of the leading Buddhist teachers of his age. Further, Sangharakshita made the 'journey to the East' and he made it well before the era of the package-deal spiritual trip. He did not merely drop in on oriental culture for a few weeks, but lived in the immemorial traditions of Indian asceticism and immersed himself in Indian culture. He met Indian gurus and Tibetan lamas and studied at first hand the great spiritual riches of the East. Sangharakshita made the 'return journey'. He 'came back home', bringing back to the land and culture from which he sprang the wealth that he had found while he was in India.

In India he began his career as 'helper of the oppressed'. He devoted himself to teaching hundreds of thousands of ex-Untouchables the true significance of the Dharma. Their recent conversion to Buddhism was of immense social significance since it gave them a basis for dignity and confidence. Later he encouraged his Western disciples to continue that work, supplementing the teaching of Buddhism with social action. Here, Sangharakshita reverses the modern myth: for he is a Westerner who brings wisdom to the East! In a certain sense, Sangharakshita is a 'rebel', the 'individual against the group', a gadfly to the herd. He has often found himself at odds with 'establishments', whether the authorities of the Maha Bodhi Society in India or the leaders of Buddhist organisations in London in the sixties. However, he has no psychological compulsion to rebellion: he has often shown he can co-operate well with others. The 'establishments' have found him inconvenient because of his fearless and uncompromising adherence to spiritual truth and his willingness to speak out when he sees hypocrisy and confusion.

The variety of the myths exemplified in his life illustrates the breadth and complexity of his character. He is a man with the inclinations of a hermit, preferring the peace of his hermitage and the company of a few close friends: yet he functions on an increasingly large stage, before the thousands of people who consider him their spiritual teacher and the many more who are interested in what he has to say. He is by nature a scholar and an artist: but he has shown himself to be a formidable organiser who has founded a movement of great flexibility and effectiveness. He is a witty and charming conversationalist, a sympathetic listener and counsellor, and a firm and faithful friend: yet he can be a fierce polemicist and a few of his works have aroused some controversy and even hostility.

Many who meet him for the first time are astonished that this man should be so 'ordinary' in appearance. His spiritual perspicacity shines out from his writing and speaking and he is honoured and respected by many—yet he is entirely lacking in 'charisma', as popularly understood. Several tell of first meeting Sangharakshita at an FWBO* centre without realising who he was. He lacks, even disdains, that animal magnetism that gains many a guru his following. Yet, if one attends closely when one is with him, one will feel the force of his presence. He has a great stillness and self-possession, a mindfulness of every movement. In his eyes there is an extraordinary watchfulness, betokening a deep awareness and an exceptionally penetrating mind. Yet those detached and watchful eyes that can make him seem somewhat Olympian can suddenly spark with humour, flash mischievously, or even blaze with a kind of angry fire. For, although he is invariably kindly and considerate in his dealings with people, and although he has always shown outstanding patience and perseverance in the face of some considerable difficulties, he has that underlying confidence, vigour, and determination that alone make possible the successful completion of worthwhile tasks.

## A SELF-MADE MAN

Sangharakshita's origins offer few clues to how he became what he now is. Dennis Philip Edward Lingwood, as he was first known, was born on 26 August 1925 in South London of working-class parents. Though his mother and father had little education themselves, they were upright and sensible people, providing a happy and loving home for the young Dennis and his sister. It was obvious from an early age that he was exceptionally intelligent, but life went on normally enough for him until he was eight years old. He was then diagnosed as having a serious heart condition that demanded he be kept completely immobile and calm at peril of his life. For two years he was confined to bed, seeing only his parents and the family doctor. What might have been an oppressive

---

* FWBO: Friends of the Western Buddhist Order—the name of the new Buddhist movement founded by Sangharakshita. WBO: the Western Buddhist Order.

disaster was, for so lively a mind, a singular opportunity. Guided by a surprisingly mature sensibility, the eight-year-old boy kept himself occupied by reading: mainly the classics of English literature and all sixty-one parts of Harmsworth's *Children's Encyclopaedia*, several of which he read many times. In this way he gained an introduction to literature, philosophy, religion, and art.

Two years later, the original diagnosis being overturned by a pioneering doctor, Dennis was liberated from bed and eventually allowed to return to school. However, he himself asserts that he never learned anything useful from his formal education, particularly as it was further interrupted by the outbreak of the Second World War. He has acquired his considerable learning almost entirely by his own efforts. From the time he was confined to bed he has read several books of solid merit every week, absorbing the contents of each with keen discernment and an excellent memory. From that time also dates his love of art: indeed, so great was his early ability that it was assumed he would become a painter. But painting gave way to a new and greater love. At the age of twelve, on reading Milton's *Paradise Lost*, he discovered a passion for poetry and began writing verse himself—as he has continued to do throughout his life.

With the coming of war and the threat of air raids, most of London's children were evacuated from the city. Dennis left for Devon in 1940, in the second wave of evacuations, where he continued his self-education, spending many hours in public libraries. As soon as he could persuade his parents, he left school and took a job in a coal merchant's office. During this period he came across Madame Blavatsky's *Isis Unveiled*, a seminal work of the Theosophical movement. Reading this convinced him that he was not a Christian 'and never had been'. He returned to London in 1941, for the next two years living at home with his parents once more and working as a clerk for the London County Council. This was a very turbulent period, during which he fell in love, began to have psychic and mystical experiences, composed much poetry, and wrote a novel—never published and now lost.

In 1942, in his insatiable scouring of the London bookshops, he purchased copies of two important works of Mahāyāna Buddhism: the *Vajracchedikā Prajñāpāramitā* or *Diamond Sūtra* and the *Sūtra of Wei-lang* (otherwise known as the *Sūtra of Hui-neng* or the *Platform Sūtra*). These had a decisive impact, convincing him that he was a Buddhist—and that he 'always had been'. He became a member of the London Buddhist Society, contributing an article to its journal, *The Middle Way*, and attending its meetings. Here he encountered Christmas Humphreys and most of the leading figures in English Buddhism of that time. The full-moon day of May 1944 saw his formal accession to Buddhism, during the Society's celebrations of Wesak—the anniversary of the birth, Enlightenment, and *parinirvāṇa* of the Buddha. On that occasion, he recited for the first time the Refuges and Precepts after the Burmese *bhikkhu*, U Thittila.

## THE JOURNEY TO THE EAST

By this time, he had been conscripted into the army and had been trained as a signalman in the Royal Corps of Signals. In August 1944, he was sent with his unit to Delhi in India. He could hardly believe his good fortune, for here he was in the land of the Buddha, which he had never expected to see. However, there being little Buddhism to be encountered there, he secured a transfer to Colombo in Sri Lanka. Though now in a 'Buddhist country', he made no effective contact with Buddhists. It was among the Hindu swamis of the Ramakrishna Mission that he found some genuine spiritual companionship. Indeed, with the strong encouragement of the swamis, he discovered an urgent desire to renounce the world and become a monk. On his next transfer, to Calcutta, he continued his association with the Mission, without ever losing his basic loyalty to Buddhism. In 1946 a final transfer took him to Singapore and here he did make contact with Buddhists and began the practice of meditation. Hearing that his unit was to be demobilised in England, he checked in his equipment and left camp, technically a deserter.

Back in Calcutta he worked briefly with the Ramakrishna Mission and then with the Maha Bodhi Society, the leading Buddhist organisation in India. Both these experiences convinced him of the corruption of religious bodies and strengthened his determination to renounce the world. In August 1947, at the age of twenty-two, he took one of the most important steps of his life. With a young Indian friend he burned his identification papers, gave away his possessions, and, dressed in an orange robe, 'went forth' as a wandering ascetic, as the Buddha had done before him. He even left behind his name, from now on calling himself Anagarika Dharmapriya. The two friends spent the next two years mainly in South India. For periods they settled in one place, meditating and studying. At other times they wandered, always depending on alms for their food and shelter. They also visited the ashrams of various Hindu teachers, such as Anandamayi, Swami Ramdas, and Ramana Maharshi.

While staying in a cave near the Maharshi's ashram he had a powerful vision of the Buddha Amitābha. This he took as confirmation that he should now seek ordination as a Buddhist monk.

Ordination did not however prove easy to come by. Their first request received a rather unceremonious rejection from the monks of the Maha Bodhi Society's *vihāra* or monastery at Sarnath. The two friends next approached the Burmese *bhikkhu*,* U Chandramani, then the seniormost monk in India, and with some difficulty persuaded him to give them the *sāmanera*, or novice, ordination. It was at this ceremony, in May 1949, that he received the name Sangharakshita: 'Protector of (or Protected by) the Spiritual Community'. His full ordination as a *bhikkhu* took place at Sarnath in November of the following year, with another Burmese *bhikkhu*, U Kawinda, as *upādhyāya* or preceptor, and Ven. Jagdish Kashyap as his *ācārya* or teacher. After their *sāmanera* ordinations, he and his friend travelled briefly into Nepal to minister to the disciples of U Chandramani, begging all the way. He then spent seven months living with Ven. Jagdish Kashyap, one of the foremost Indian Buddhist monks of the twentieth century, studying the Pali language, the *Abhidhamma*, and Logic. This idyllic period ended when he and his teacher went on pilgrimage through the Buddhist sites of Bihar and up into the Himalayas. In the small hill-station of Kalimpong, on the borders of India, Nepal, Bhutan, Sikkim, and Tibet, Ven. Kashyap requested him to stay and 'work for the good of Buddhism'. In fulfilment of his teacher's wishes, Kalimpong was to be his base for the next fourteen years.

From his arrival in Kalimpong at the age of twenty-five, Sangharakshita worked very actively for the revival of Buddhism in the border regions, which contained a large proportion of nominally Buddhist peoples. Finding the existing Buddhist groups too factious and sectarian, he started a new organisation, the Young Men's Buddhist Association. The Association not only offered Buddhist teaching and practice but also cultural and social activities—even tutorial classes to help the young men pass their all-important examinations. It quickly established itself as a valued part of the life of the town, appreciated alike by young and old, Buddhist and non-Buddhist. Three years later, it became a branch of the

---

* *Bhikkhu*: a fully ordained Buddhist monk. There are two phases in the ordination of a Buddhist monk: first one becomes a *sāmanera* and then a *bhikkhu*.

Maha Bodhi Society, gaining thereby a small grant and affiliation with the major Buddhist organisation in India. Sangharakshita was however careful to ensure that it lost none of its autonomy.

During his first seven years in Kalimpong, Sangharakshita lived and worked in rented or borrowed accommodation. Despite the small grant from the Maha Bodhi Society for the branch's activities, he himself had no regular income. He lived entirely from the donations of well-wishers, small payments for articles and poems published in various journals, and fees for English lessons—many of which, however, he gave free of charge. There were times when he quite literally had no money at all—although he says that this never worried him. In 1957, through the generosity of the King of Sikkim and of an English Buddhist friend, he was able to purchase his own *vihāra*.

A few months after his first arrival in Kalimpong, he commenced the publication of *Stepping-Stones*, 'a bimonthly journal of Himalayan Buddhism'. This very soon attracted an impressive list of contributors such as Lama Govinda, Dr Herbert Guenther, Dr Edward Conze, and Prince Peter of Greece. Although the journal had to cease publication after two years through lack of funds, it had achieved a wide circulation, bringing the young English *bhikkhu* to the notice of many in the English-speaking Buddhist world and introducing him to some prominent scholars and teachers.

Over the years he spent in the town Sangharakshita managed to unite the Buddhist community in a quite unprecedented way. He arranged the joint celebration by all local Buddhist groups of various important Buddhist festivals. He even organised the commemoration of Tsongkapa's birthday by all the Tibetan Buddhists in the town together— a feat that brought the Dalai Lama's personal congratulations. His activities were not confined to the town: he gave lectures and held meetings all over the region. During regular visits to Sikkim at the personal request of the royal family and of the Indian Government's representative, he did what he could to revitalise the rather degenerate Buddhism of the kingdom, drawing up a scheme of studies for the monks of the royal monastery. So much a leader of the Buddhists in the region did he become that the Indian Government specifically asked him to stay on in the town, at a time when there were rumours of a Chinese invasion of the border regions, to help discourage the mass flight of its Buddhist inhabitants.

His association with the Maha Bodhi Society began in 1952 when he was invited by its General Secretary, Devapriya Valisinha, to write a biographical sketch of the Society's great founder, Anagarika

Dharmapala. Through this work, he came to have great admiration for Dharmapala and sympathy for Valisinha, his dedicated, if less capable, successor. He had, however, serious criticisms of the Society's present organisation: its governing body was dominated by caste Hindus, one member being openly hostile to Buddhism. He therefore took care never to compromise himself by becoming a member. Nonetheless, he was for many years the principal editor of its organ, *The Maha Bodhi*, and often lectured at its premises in Calcutta and elsewhere.

HELPER OF THE OPPRESSED

Though Kalimpong was his base from 1950 to 1964, he had a much wider sphere of operation. Most years he would spend some months away from the hills, lecturing in many parts of India. A very able speaker, he was much in demand at branches of the Maha Bodhi Society, as well as at various non-Buddhist organisations. He came to know a great variety of people: Buddhist monks of many different nationalities and schools, Western scholars who flocked to the Himalayas to study Tibetan culture and religion, Theosophists, Christian missionaries, politicians, even Raj Kapoor, the 'Clark Gable of India'. One of his most significant encounters was with Dr Bhimrao Ambedkar. This formidable man was among the foremost Indian politicians of the day: it was he who had headed the commission that drafted the constitution of independent India. Himself born an Untouchable, he had become the unrivalled leader of his people in their struggle for social justice. Dr Ambedkar eventually concluded that the only way out of the oppression of the Hindu caste system lay in leaving Hinduism altogether. After long and careful deliberation, he decided to become a Buddhist. This was to be one of the most significant events for Buddhism in the twentieth century, initiating the conversion of millions of people. Sangharakshita was able to advise him what conversion really meant and how it was undertaken. At Dr Ambedkar's invitation, he began teaching his followers the significance of the religion they were about to espouse.

Sangharakshita was not able to attend the ceremony in October 1956 at which Dr Ambedkar converted to Buddhism with nearly 400,000 of his followers. However, six weeks later he visited Nagpur, the city where the conversions had taken place, to be greeted with the news that the great leader had died just a few hours before. He had arrived at exactly the time he was most needed. Over the next few critical days he worked tirelessly to rally the grief-stricken multitudes, earning himself a secure place in their affections. Nearly every year from then until he left India he would spend several months touring among the new Buddhists of Western India, teaching them the tenets of their religion. He personally conducted the conversion ceremonies of more than 200,000 people.

Active as he was, both in Kalimpong and beyond, Sangharakshita did not neglect spiritual practice. He meditated at least every morning and evening, continued with his studies, and reflected on the Dharma. Each year he would observe the traditional 'rains retreat', remaining within his vihara compound for three months and devoting himself entirely to meditation, study, and writing. His situation in the border region gave him the opportunity to study Tibetan Buddhism at first hand. Many leading lamas were now escaping the Chinese invasion of their country and Kalimpong was often their first stopping-place. In 1956 he received initiation from Chetul Sangye Dorje, a highly respected, if rather unconventional, lama. He later received initiations and teachings from Jamyang Khyentse Rimpoche, Dilgo Khyentse Rimpoche, Dudjom Rimpoche, and Khachu Rimpoche, all of whom functioned within the Nyingmapa tradition, and from Dhardo Rimpoche, a Gelugpa whose previous 'incarnations' had all been Nyingmapas. From Dhardo Rimpoche, who became a close friend, he received, in October 1962, the Bodhisattva ordination, thus giving him ordination and initiation within all three *yānas* of Buddhism.

Throughout his stay in India he continued to write. Despite burning most of his poetry in 1949, he continued to pour forth verse, some of which appeared in various journals, including the widely-circulating *Illustrated Weekly of India*. In 1954 a volume of his poems was published, *Messengers from Tibet and other Poems*. Besides many articles and editorials for *Stepping-Stones, The Maha Bodhi*, and other periodicals, he wrote *Flame in Darkness: A Biographical Sketch of Anagarika Dharmapala*, and his major work, *A Survey of Buddhism*, both of which were published while he was in India. Two other works written at this time, *The Three Jewels*, an introduction to Buddhism that began life as contributions to an encyclopaedia, and *The Eternal Legacy*, a survey of Buddhist canonical literature, were not published until some years later.

## THE RETURN JOURNEY

He had followed with sympathy the fortunes of the Buddhist movement in the West, particularly through correspondence with some of his English Buddhist friends. In 1964 he was invited to London for six months to help restore harmony in the already factious British Buddhist world. Realising that, for many reasons, he could do little more for Buddhism in India, he decided to see what opportunities awaited him in the West and accepted the invitation. He soon breathed new spirit into the rather staid atmosphere of English Buddhism, plunging into a vigorous round of classes, lectures, and meetings. He was clearly very popular and numbers at meetings began to mount. It was obvious that Buddhism had great potential in the West. Six months stretched to eighteen, and finally he decided that he would say farewell to his friends in India and then return permanently to London.

While he was in London he had been incumbent of the Hampstead Buddhist Vihara, and it was to the Vihara that he intended to return. However, his nonsectarian approach and refusal to fit narrow expectations of what a Buddhist monk should and should not do turned some of the Vihara's trustees against him. While he was on his farewell tour of India he received notice that he would not be allowed to take up his former post. Despite the outcry of the greater part of those attending the Vihara, by a narrow majority the trustees had voted to exclude him. Sangharakshita's first response was one of relief. He was free to start again, free from the confusion and disharmony of the present British Buddhist world. With the full blessings of his teachers and friends in India, he returned to England. Just a few days after his arrival, in April 1967, he founded the Friends of the Western Buddhist Order with a small band of his disciples from the Vihara. One year later he ordained the first thirteen men and women into the Western Buddhist Order itself.

The rest of Sangharakshita's life is so closely bound up with the development of the FWBO that it is difficult to reduce it to a simple account. Broadly, he completely devoted himself to the movement, which grew, on the whole, very steadily and surely. The first five years or so proved intensely creative. He had, so to speak, served his apprenticeship in the traditional Buddhist world: he had thought deeply about the Dharma and had practised it intensively. He was now on his own and must bring Buddhism to life in an entirely new environment, basing himself only on its fundamental principles. Step by step, Sangharakshita formed his new Buddhist movement.

Each week there would be three or four classes. At first activities were held in a rented basement in central London, then in borrowed rooms at a macrobiotic restaurant and 'new age' centre, and finally in a disused factory in an area of North London scheduled for redevelopment. Not only was Sangharakshita taking all the classes but he personally did much of the organisational work, gradually training his disciples in the tasks of running a Buddhist movement. He gave several important lecture series in which he set out the essential teachings of Buddhism, drawing on all schools and traditions. Twice a year he led major retreats, and throughout the year there were weekend or day seminars and workshops. Much of his time was spent in personal interviews with the many people who wished to see him—for he was not merely a teacher and leader to his disciples but a friend.

By 1973 it seemed that the new Buddhist movement was firmly enough established for its founder to withdraw from daily involvement. Not only was it possible, it was desirable. Order members needed the opportunity to take more responsibility themselves, and Sangharakshita himself needed to function in new ways. The movement now had two centres in London and two in New Zealand, besides substantial groups in Glasgow and Brighton and smaller ones elsewhere. Sangharakshita was the leader of a growing movement and could not remain involved in one centre alone. He moved first to a small chalet overlooking the sea in Cornwall and then to various cottages in East Anglia. He completed the first part of his memoirs, published in two volumes as *Learning to Walk* and *The Thousand-Petalled Lotus*, and wrote several articles and papers.

Although he was no longer involved in daily organisation, he still kept a close eye on everything that happened, being particularly concerned with new developments. As the movement expanded and deepened, he elaborated his teaching ever more fully, thinking out the principles that underlay its evolution at every stage. He continued, over the next fifteen years, to give several important lectures, and conducted seminars for small groups of his disciples on various Buddhist texts, modern accounts of the Dharma, and a few works from other sources.

Each year he would visit several centres and groups, both in Britain and abroad, meeting people, giving lectures, and talking with Order members. London was still the main focus and here he was a frequent visitor, particularly after the opening in 1979 of the large London Buddhist Centre, where he had a small flat. In 1977 he had shifted his principal residence to a country house in Norfolk, which became the Padmaloka Men's Retreat Centre. Here he gathered around him a small community, some of whom functioned as his secretaries, forming the nucleus of the Office of the Western Buddhist Order. By the end of the seventies the movement consisted of some fifteen centres, several of which had communities and businesses attached to them. The FWBO no longer offered only teachings and practices but a new and radical way of life, developing under the personal guidance of the founder.

In 1977 one of Sangharakshita's leading disciples made contact with some of his followers in India and, with their help, began to establish the FWBO there—where it was known as the Trailokya Bauddha Maha-sangha Sahayak Gana (TBMSG).* It was soon clear that Sangharakshita was not forgotten and that the principles of his new Buddhist movement were as applicable in India as in the West. Very quickly many thousands of people became involved with the movement. Sangharakshita himself visited India two years later, and conducted the first ordinations of Indians into the Order. He has visited India periodically since then and has interested himself closely in activities there, which are growing far more rapidly than anywhere else in the world. At his urging, his disciples in the West began to raise money for social projects among the new Buddhists of India. They formed what has now become a substantial fund-raising charity, the Karuna Trust.

By now Sangharakshita had an extremely heavy workload. Simply keeping himself informed of what was happening and maintaining contact with all those he had ordained occupied much of his time. By virtue of strong self-discipline, he kept at his literary work while also visiting centres, giving personal interviews, lecturing and leading semi-nars, and dealing with the many questions and problems that flowed in from all parts of the movement. In 1981 he instituted an annual three-month-long retreat for men who were nearing ordination in a former Catholic monastery in Italy, himself leading many activities and super-vising study. For the next eight years these retreats, though still demand-ing, were an opportunity to stand back from the regular duties of the ever-expanding movement. He also spent some time each year attending women's ordination retreats.

Fortunately, his senior disciples were maturing. In 1985 and 1986 he delegated the conferring of ordinations in India to teams of men and women Order members, and in 1989 he handed on responsibility for ordinations in the West. There were by now some capable teachers and leaders among Order members, well imbued with the principles he had been clarifying over the last twenty years. He decided that he needed to

* 'The Community of Helpers of the Buddhist Order of the Three Worlds'—the three worlds being an allusion both to the three worlds of Buddhist cosmology and to the First, Second, and Third Worlds of modern politics.

concentrate yet more on his literary work, as much as possible leaving others to direct the movement. Since 1989 he has been living in his flat at the London Buddhist Centre, paradoxically finding seclusion in the midst of the city. He retains several important central responsibilities, although he is in the process of handing these over. Besides his writing and organisational responsibilities, Sangharakshita keeps contact with his many disciples, seeing several each day and corresponding with others. From time to time he visits FWBO centres, taking a particular interest in places where the movement is newly taking hold.

The movement has grown now to the point at which the great majority of those involved have had little or no personal contact with its founder. Whilst there is no 'cult of personality' in the FWBO, Sangharakshita is very much appreciated and his influence pervades every aspect of the movement. But he has always been keenly aware that his disciples must learn to carry on the work without him. From the outset he has engaged in a conscious process of stepping back, so that others have to take up the responsibilities he leaves behind. As he approaches his seventieth year he hopes to hand over his final duties to his senior disciples. He will then devote himself fully to his writing, through which he can clarify the principles and practice of the spiritual life to future generations.

Such is the bare outline of Sangharakshita's life. Perhaps one of the most remarkable things about it is that he has seldom premeditated what he is going to do. Opportunities have simply arisen and he has taken them. His thinking too, as perhaps all thought should, has arisen in relation to his experience. He himself has come to the conclusion

> that the course of my life has been determined by impulse and intuition rather than by reason and logic and that, for me, there could be no question of first clarifying an idea or concept and then acting upon it, i.e. acting upon it in its clarified form. An idea or concept was clarified in the process of its being acted upon.[6]

The circumstances of his thinking are therefore important if we are to gain a full understanding of his ideas. We must then look more closely now at some aspects of his life as we explore the leading themes of his thought.

Chapter Two

# THE UNITY OF BUDDHISM

*They carved Him out of sandal, chipped from stone*
*The Ever-moving, cast in rigid bronze*
*Him Who was Life itself, and made Him sit,*
*Hands idly folded, for a thousand years*
*Immobile in the incensed image-house;*
*They gilded Him till He was sick with gold.*

*And underneath the shadow of the shrine*
*They sauntered in their yellow silken robes,*
*Or—lolled replete on purple-cushioned thrones—*
*In sleepy stanzas droned His vigorous words*
*To gentle flutterings of jewelled fans...*

*Arise, O Lord, and with Thy dust-stained feet*
*Walk not the roads of India but the world!*
*Shake from the slumber of a thousand years*
*Thy dream-mazed fold! Burn as a Fire for men!*[7]

IN THE LATE SUMMER OF 1942, at the age of sixteen, Sangharakshita had the
decisive experience of his life. On reading the *Diamond Sūtra* he knew for
the first time that he was a Buddhist. Sublime as was the teaching of the
*Sūtra*,

> I at once joyfully embraced it with an unqualified acceptance and assent.
> To me the *Diamond Sūtra* was not new. I had known it and believed it
> and realized it ages before and the reading of the *Sūtra* as it were awoke
> me to the existence of something I had forgotten. Once I realized that I
> was a Buddhist it seemed that I had always been one, that it was the
> most natural thing in the world to be, and that I had never been
> anything else.[8]

He had a similar response to the *Sutra of Hui-neng*, a translation of which he discovered at the same time as the *Diamond Sūtra*. Whenever he read it, he was thrown into a 'kind of ecstasy'. The impact of these two spiritual masterpieces has continued to affect him. Recently he has said that he has never seen any reason to doubt the initial insight they precipitated in him. Indeed, it has been the basis for his whole life, from that moment on.

Sangharakshita's discovery that he was a Buddhist and that he had always been one came through direct contact with the inspired utterance of the Enlightened mind, for, although the *Diamond Sūtra* is almost certainly not a literal record of the historical Buddha's teaching, its words clearly emanate from a very high level of spiritual experience. The *Sūtra*, through paradox and counter-paradox, systematically negates all the categories of Buddhist thought. It leaves nothing for the rational mind to grasp, particularly a mind almost entirely unfamiliar with Buddhist doctrine. The *prajñā-pāramitā* or 'Perfection of Wisdom', which is the subject of the *Sūtra*, reveals itself not to the intellect, but only to the uplifted spiritual imagination. It is all the more remarkable that the sixteen-year-old youth should have responded as he did.

Before encountering the *Sūtra*, he knew little of Buddhist teaching. He had had no contact with Buddhist culture and he was not to meet another Buddhist for a further two years. For him, Buddhism was therefore nothing but the supra-rational insight to which the *Diamond Sūtra* had introduced him. Buddhism was the Dharma: the pure and undiluted truth about the nature of reality, communicated from the lips of the Buddha of the *Sūtra* who himself embodied that truth. The Dharma was, for Sangharakshita, beyond all thought and all culture. In a sense, it was therefore eternal and omnipresent. This is perhaps partly what he means when he says that the *Diamond Sūtra* was not new to him when he first heard it.

Sangharakshita's insight into the meaning of the *Diamond Sūtra* enabled him to see from the outset the underlying unity of Buddhism. Extraordinary though it may seem, he first perceived the truth of the Dharma at the point where words dissolve into paradox and the rational intellect is confounded. He saw, from the first, the entirely transcendental nature of the Buddha's Enlightenment—transcendent, that is, over all our normal ways of knowing, accessible only to the eye of Wisdom. If the Dharma is, by its very nature, beyond all thinking, then no one expression of it can claim to be exhaustive. Words and concepts can only be 'fingers pointing to the moon', as the Zen saying has it: they can only indicate a higher truth that they can never fully capture. Sangharakshita has therefore always seen the various schools and traditions as so many attempts to express that single transcendent experience that he first encountered in the *Diamond Sūtra*. Indeed, his first published work on Buddhism, written at the age of eighteen, was an article on 'The Unity of Buddhism', published in June 1944 in *Buddhism in England* (now *The Middle Way*), the journal of the London Buddhist Society.

> Buddhism ... is not one road to Enlightenment but many—although in a deeper and more hidden sense all ways (*dharmas*) are one. It is therefore suited to all sorts and conditions of minds; the youthful and the aged, the melancholy and the joyful, the simple and the profound; it is the universal way of salvation. In its all-embracing unity all the polarities which our arbitrary habits of discrimination have built up since [the] beginning of time, all distinctions of colour, creed, and social position, of ignorant and learned, even of Enlightened and Unenlightened—all these are utterly obliterated.[9]

An understanding of this would seem to be integral to Buddhism itself, yet it has not always been unequivocally shared by all Buddhists. This is not, in a sense, surprising. In the elaboration of the Buddha's original teaching by the different schools, quite diverse, even contrary, teachings and practices arose. Those divergences were then compounded by transmission through the various cultures of Asia. It has not been easy to see all Buddhism's many manifestations as equally striving for the same transcendental goal. Buddhists have therefore often identified the Dharma with their own particular brand. Fortunately, such Buddhist sectarianism has been altogether of a milder kind than is often found in Christianity, yet ignorance of other schools or indifference to them is widespread.

From the very outset of his career as a Buddhist, Sangharakshita did not identify with any particular school, nor did he conceive of Buddhism in terms of any one of its many cultural forms. This perspective gave him the freedom of the entire Buddhist tradition. He could draw sustenance and inspiration from whatever source was available to him, according to his unfolding spiritual needs. Before we examine his idea of the unity of Buddhism in more detail we must follow him in his encounters with its various manifestations.

He had begun early on the road to that crucial experience brought to him by the *Diamond Sūtra*. It was principally his reading that guided him to Buddhism. At the age of eight he was confined to bed for two years and launched into the world of literature and art. Among other books, he read Charles Kingsley's *Hypatia*, a historical novel about the last of the Neoplatonists in Christian Alexandria. He was deeply impressed by

Kingsley's description of the trance into which the beautiful Hypatia falls as her soul flies 'alone to the Alone'. This was his first encounter with the mystical and it made a lasting impression. In Harmsworth's *Children's Encyclopaedia* he read the lives of the world's great religious leaders. The Buddha must have made a particular impression on him, even at this age, for he wrote a life of the great sage, which he copied in purple ink on his best notepaper. He learnt of Plato too, when he was about ten, and sent his mother to the local public library for a copy of the *Republic*, the first work of philosophy he read.

Although baptised into the Church of England, Sangharakshita received little formal religious education and his parents put him under no pressure to attend services. Indeed, they themselves showed decidedly heterodox tendencies and dabbled in some of the more obscure popular religious movements of the time, such as spiritualism, the Rechabites, the Druids, and Coué's New Thought. When he was eleven, mainly for social reasons, he joined the Boy's Brigade—a quasi-military organisation similar to the Boy Scouts, formed to encourage the leading of a Christian life. His company was attached to the local Baptist church and so he began attending Bible classes and Sunday services. Although he did experience some temporary fervour for the person of Christ, the simple emotionalism of the Baptists made little lasting impression on him. He was, even then, already thinking for himself on religious matters and said his daily prayers to the Buddha, Christ, and Mohammed in turn,

> it being my naïve conviction that by this means I should be sure of
> gaining the ear of whoever happened to be the true saviour.[10]

When he was evacuated to Devon at the age of fourteen to avoid the London Blitz, the young Dennis read more deeply in the great philosophical and religious classics of the West: the works of Plato, Aristotle, and Longinus, for instance. It was however those of Seneca and of the emperor Julian 'the Apostate' that most deeply impressed him. He began also to read some of the classics of the East: the *Vedas* and *Upanishads*. Sir Edwin Arnold's *The Song Celestial*, a verse translation of the *Bhagavad Gītā*, he read 'in a state bordering on ecstasy'. However, the book that most deeply affected him at this period was Madame Blavatsky's *Isis Unveiled*. Reading this convinced him

> that *I was not a Christian*—that I never had been, and never would
> be—and that the whole structure of Christian doctrine was from
> beginning to end thoroughly repugnant to me. This realization gave me
> a sense of relief, of liberation as from some oppressive burden, which
> was so great that I wanted to dance and sing for joy. What I was, what I

believed, I knew not, but what I was not and what I did not believe, that
I knew with utter certainty, and this knowledge, merely negative though
it was as yet, gave me a foretaste of that freedom which comes when all
obstacles are removed, all barriers broken down, all limitations
transcended.[11]

The fifteen-year-old boy who returned to London in 1940 was in a state
of intense fervour. He was liberated from the oppressive influence of
Christianity. The words of the great masters of philosophy and literature
rang in his ears. Moreover, his senses were stirring with the onset of
puberty. At this time, he had various spontaneous psychic experiences in
which he would foresee a sequence of events that would take place half
an hour or an hour later. He also began to have what can only be described
as mystical experiences. These were of two principal kinds: he would
experience in one 'the complete absurdity of the mind being tied down
to a single physical body'[12] and in the other the total unreality of the
ordinary world. It was at this time of turbulence and heightened intensity
that he encountered the *Diamond Sūtra* and that it made its profound and
decisive impact upon him.

Although his first encounter was with the Mahāyāna tradition as
expressed in the *Diamond Sūtra*, he read as widely in all schools of
Buddhism as was then possible. Books on the subject and translations of
scriptures were, however, still comparatively rare. The most accessible
texts were those of the Pali Canon, the greater part of which had early
been translated into English. This was the scriptural collection of the
Theravāda and it was this South-east Asian school, with its yellow-robed
monks, that was most well known in the West. Until he settled in
Kalimpong almost all the Buddhists he met in India and Sri Lanka were
Theravadins. When he came to seek ordination, without really considering the matter, it was to the Theravāda that he looked. This was not
because he especially wanted to identify himself with that school. He
took ordination from Theravadins because they were the ones who
happened to be accessible to him in India. However, he had also unquestioningly imbibed the popular image of the Buddhist monk as yellow-
robed. It was therefore a yellow-robed monk he became. For him,
however, ordination represented renunciation of the world, complete
dedication to the Buddhist path, and acceptance into the Buddhist community *as a whole*. Perhaps somewhat naïvely, he had not thought about
which school he was being ordained into.

From his arrival in the East, he had begun to form considerable reservations about the Theravāda School. He certainly had a great love and

respect for the Pali Canon, which it had successfully preserved. However he saw that modern Theravadins, with a few notable exceptions, showed little spiritual vitality. Buddhism in Sri Lanka 'seemed dead, or at least asleep'.[13] He encountered among many Theravadins a strong conviction that theirs was the only true and pure form of Buddhism, all others being degenerations and distortions. His own first teacher, Jagdish Kashyap, though himself a Theravadin, confirmed him in his reservations. The Indian monk openly acknowledged the shortcomings of the school to which he belonged. While he taught Sangharakshita much about the Pali scriptures, he never denigrated other schools or claimed any special place for his own. Throughout his time in India, Sangharakshita constantly found himself confronted by the arrogance, narrow-mindedness, and literalism of many Theravadins. In his editorials for *Stepping-Stones* and the *Maha Bodhi* he continuously drew attention to these failings.

In Kalimpong, Sangharakshita wore the yellow robe and was in friendly contact, through the Maha Bodhi Society, with many Theravadin monks from various countries. He was forced, however, to look to other sources for his principal spiritual inspiration. His first years on his own, 'working for the good of Buddhism', were exceptionally difficult. He faced lack of co-operation and occasionally outright opposition, even from those who were nominally helping him. He derived no support from the order to which he belonged. Indeed, it was from some members of that order that he experienced the most open hostility. His guidance and support were to come not from any earthly agency but from that sublime ideal of the Bodhisattva, which is the very heart of the Mahāyāna schools of Buddhism. The Bodhisattva, who dedicates him or herself for countless existences to the spiritual welfare of all beings,

> provided me with an example, on the grandest possible scale, of what I was myself trying to do within my own infinitely smaller sphere and on an infinitely lower level.[14]

From the time of discovering that he was a Buddhist this ideal had inspired him, central as it is to both the *Diamond Sūtra* and the *Sūtra of Hui-neng*. It came now to have a deeper and more powerful influence on him in his present spiritual isolation. Nonetheless, it was several years before he felt himself ready to take the Bodhisattva ordination, thus formally espousing the Bodhisattva Ideal and adding Mahāyāna ordination to his 'Hīnayāna' ones as a *sāmanera* and *bhikkhu*. In 1962 he took from Dhardo Rimpoche the sixty-four Bodhisattva vows that constitute the ordination. This Gelugpa 'incarnate lama' had become his close friend and teacher and Sangharakshita had come to revere him as himself a living Bodhisattva.

In Kalimpong Sangharakshita could meet many Tibetan teachers and study Tibetan Buddhism at first hand. He was impressed by the Tibetans' acceptance of all three *yānas* or 'paths', the three major currents in the development of Buddhism: Hīnayāna, Mahāyāna, and Vajrayāna. He also found himself deeply moved by the intense but simple faith of ordinary Tibetans and the great learning and obvious spiritual stature of several of their leading teachers. Above all he was strongly attracted to the rich symbolic world of Tibetan Buddhism. He came to see Tantric initiation as preserved in the Tibetan tradition as a way of contacting the highest dimension of reality. From 1956 onwards he received several Tantric initiations and practised Vajrayāna meditation, as well as studying the Vajrayāna extensively. Besides receiving initiation and teaching from a number of prominent Tibetan lamas, Sangharakshita gained considerable guidance in this field from Mr C.M.Chen, a Chinese hermit living in Kalimpong. Yogi Chen was a very learned man who had practised the Vajrayāna intensively for many years. He was also well versed in Ch'an, the Chinese antecedent of the Japanese Zen School, thus giving Sangharakshita first hand knowledge of that important tradition.

Sangharakshita's openness to the entire Buddhist tradition found expression in his personal practice of meditation techniques derived from different schools. Reading as widely as he could, he kept abreast of most new Buddhist publications in English, whether translations of scriptures or works on all aspects of Buddhism, including those of scholarly research. He also took every opportunity to discuss the Dharma with scholars and monks from various traditions. His nonsectarianism was also manifest in his work for the good of Buddhism. When he came to found his own *vihāra* in 1957, it was given the name Triyana Vardhana Vihara, 'the Abode Where the Three Yānas Flourish', by his first Tibetan teacher, Chetul Sangye Dorje.* In a report on the Vihara's first five years of existence, Sangharakshita made clear its commitment to nonsectarian Buddhism:

> One of the greatest needs of the Buddhist world today is unity. Not,
> indeed, unity in the sense of uniformity, much less still in that of
> centralisation of authority, but in the sense of a deeper and more

* This lama, whose name is variously spelt, is well known for the impression
he made on the American Trappist monk, Thomas Merton, who mentions
him in his *Asian Journals*.

effective recognition of the basic fact that despite differences, even
divergencies, of Doctrine and Method, all Buddhist traditions have for
their ultimate goal that state of Bodhi or Enlightenment whence the very
name of their religion derives. The Triyana Vardhana Vihara has
therefore been dedicated by its founder to the study, practice, and
dissemination *of the total Buddhist tradition*.[15]

His friend and 'kindred spirit', Lama Govinda, who shared his vision
of Buddhism as transcending school and *yāna*, wrote of the Vihara,
'Probably for the first time in the history of Buddhism the Hīnayāna,
Mahāyāna, and the Vajrayāna have found a common centre in the Triyana
Vardhana Vihara. This is an important step forward on the road towards
the unification of Buddhist tradition.'[16] Modest as were the facilities of
the Vihara, its aspiration and its significance were great indeed.

His return to England in 1964 brought him up against sectarianism
again. There were two principal Buddhist organisations in London at that
time: the Buddhist Society and the Hampstead Buddhist Vihara. Considerable tensions had arisen between them and it was to help resolve these
that Sangharakshita had been invited to visit. The Society, under its
well-known president, Christmas Humphreys, was in principle open to
all Buddhist schools. However, some of the trustees of the Hampstead
Buddhist Vihara, which was to be Sangharakshita's base, tended to
support a particularly narrow and puritanical brand of Theravāda
Buddhism. Already, in British Buddhism generally, there was a marked
tendency to espouse one or other Eastern school and to ignore—even
reject—all others. Sangharakshita did what he could to promote an
understanding of the entire tradition, giving notable series of talks on
Tibetan Buddhism and on Zen. Above all, in his teaching he emphasised
the core of doctrines that all schools hold in common, such as conditioned
co-production, the Four Noble Truths, and the Noble Eightfold Path.

However, he had, in all innocence, antagonised some of the trustees of
the Vihara. He taught from the entire Buddhist tradition and not exclusively from the Theravāda. He banned a form of meditation, dear to
a leading trustee, when he saw that it was causing some people severe
mental disturbance. He did not keep austerely aloof, but valued
friendship and intimacy. He went to the theatre and the opera a few times.
He did not keep his hair completely shaved but let it grow an inch or two,
in the fashion of Tibetan monks. He even did not always wear his robes!
His failure to operate within the narrow confines of what some of the
trustees thought a Theravāda monk should teach and do led to his being
excluded from the Vihara in 1967.

In many ways, as we have seen, his exclusion was a relief: he was free to start afresh. Almost from his first arrival in 1964 he had doubted whether the Buddhist movement as it was in England at that time could be brought to any health and vitality. He had wanted then to start a new movement. Some of his friends and disciples had persuaded him that it was his duty to work within the existing framework and not cause more division. Now however a new movement could be started that was simply *Buddhist*: based on the fundamental principles of the Dharma and open to the entire Buddhist tradition. To emphasise its nonsectarian character, Sangharakshita invited some Buddhists from other traditions to be present at the first ordinations into the Western Buddhist Order. A Shin priest, a Zen monk, and two Theravadin *bhikkhus*, one from Sri Lanka and one from Thailand, attended the ceremony.

In this new phase of his work, no doubt the most important of his life, Sangharakshita was free to embody his vision of the Dharma fully and without compromise. He no longer had to fit into other people's expectations or follow outworn cultural patterns. The movement he set out to create would be the direct expression of his own understanding of Buddhism's essential principles. One of the most important of those principles is the unity of Buddhism. This we must therefore now explore in greater detail. The unity of Buddhism is a complex notion that can be viewed from several different perspectives: historical, methodological, doctrinal, metaphysical, ethical, social, and, most significantly of all, as a personal spiritual act. In the first place, Sangharakshita's vision of the unity of Buddhism rests upon his understanding of what Buddhism most fundamentally is.

## THE TRANSCENDENTAL UNITY OF BUDDHISM

Buddhism is founded on the Buddha's experience of Enlightenment or *bodhi*, his direct understanding of the true nature of things. All Buddhists accept that the Buddha attained Enlightenment. All accept that he taught the path to Enlightenment. All Buddhists of all schools ultimately derive their own particular doctrines and methods from the Buddha's Enlightened vision of reality: all those doctrines and methods are ultimately directed to the attainment of Enlightenment. It is in this common recognition of the Buddha's Enlightenment experience as the source and goal that the *transcendental unity* of Buddhism lies.

The doctrinal and other differences between the schools are not resolved by being reduced on their own level one to another or all to a conceptual common denominator, but transcended by referring them to a factor which, being supra-logical, can be the common denominator of contradictory assertions[17]

—that common denominator is, of course, the Buddha's Enlightenment.

However united all schools may be in their ultimate source and goal, their doctrines and methods, even their conceptions of what Enlightenment is, vary considerably. This immediately poses an enormous problem. How are we to decide which are genuinely Buddhist and which are not? What are the criteria for determining what the Dharma is? Sangharakshita looks to the Buddha's own words for a resolution of this problem. The Dharma, as we must more properly call Buddhism as the path to the goal of Enlightenment, is defined by the Buddha in the earliest scriptures in purely pragmatic terms. Sangharakshita quotes two important passages from the Pali Canon. In the first, the Buddha compares the Dharma to a raft that a man uses to cross from one shore, 'full of doubts and fears', to the further shore, 'safe and free from fears'. Once he has crossed to the further shore he has no more use for the raft.

Even so, brethren, using the figure of a raft have I shown you the Dharma, as something to leave behind, not to take with you. Thus, brethren, understanding the figure of the raft, you must [eventually] let go of right teachings, how much more so wrong ones.[18]

In other words, the Dharma is a means to an end, not an end in itself.

Sangharakshita further points out that

From the fact that the Dharma is, as the Buddha explicitly declares [in the parable of the raft], essentially that which conduces to the attainment of Enlightenment, it necessarily follows that whatever conduces to the attainment of Enlightenment is the Dharma.[19]

In the second passage, the Buddha confirms this point when he is asked how his teachings can be recognised. He affirms that they are

Whatever teachings conduce to dispassion not to passion, to detachment not to bondage, to decrease of worldly gains not to increase of them, to frugality not to covetousness, to contentment not to discontent, to solitude not to company, to energy not to sluggishness, to delight in good not delight in evil.... This is the Dharma. This is the Vinaya. This is the Master's Message.[20]

What determines whether a school or teaching is truly Buddhist is not that it contains some particular set of words, practices, customs, or institutions, but that it helps individuals to move towards Enlightenment.

To sum up, the transcendental unity of Buddhism lies in the fact that all schools and traditions acknowledge that same transcendental goal attained by the historical Buddha. Each school or tradition has, however, different means of approaching Enlightenment. In so far as they do in fact lead to the attainment of that goal, those means all represent 'Dharma, Vinaya, and the Master's Message', despite apparent contradictions between them. In this, then, lies the *methodological unity* of Buddhism. Unity in this sense

> consists in the fact that, through differences and divergencies of doctrine innumerable, all schools of Buddhism aim at Enlightenment, at reproducing the spiritual experience of the Buddha. The Dharma is therefore to be defined not so much in terms of this or that particular teaching, but rather as the sum total of the means whereby that experience may be attained.[21]

## THE HISTORICAL UNITY OF BUDDHISM

Although we may know the general criterion by which to test whether any particular teaching is truly Buddhist, it is not so easy in practice to untangle the immense and sometimes conflicting diversity of Buddhist schools. Modern Buddhists are faced with the whole range of Buddhist traditions. They are confronted not merely by those presently existing, but by those of the past as well, since scholars are revealing ever more about the history of the various schools. How are Buddhists today to understand this vast mass of teachings, practices, cultures, and institutions? How are they to evaluate it? How are they to use it?

In this respect they receive little help from Buddhists of the past. The more sectarian among both ancient Buddhists and their modern representatives have believed that all schools but their own are distortions of and deviations from the Buddha's teaching, themselves retaining the true, pure, and original Message of the Master. This attitude is now widespread among Theravadins—although by no means all are tainted with this sort of sectarianism, while not a few Buddhists of other schools are. Nichiren's followers in Japan have been the most extreme sectarians. They have largely seen theirs as a new dispensation that supersedes and thereby negates all other schools—although, from the point of view of other Buddhists, they themselves are questionably Buddhist.

The most sophisticated—and charitable—approach has been to see all known schools as deriving directly from the Buddha himself. Each school, according to these systems, is seen as enshrining either a particular phase in the Buddha's unfoldment of his teaching or else his response to people at a particular level of development. This approach is exemplified by early Chinese Buddhists, who were confronted with the problem of reconciling diverse teachings since they inherited the entire existing range of Indian Buddhism, all of which they accepted as authentic in spite of apparent discrepancies and contradictions. Chih-i, the most important of the Chinese systematisers and the founder of the Chinese T'ien-t'ai School, classified the stages of the Buddhist path according to the *order* in which he thought the Buddha had revealed the various scriptures.

The Tibetans too inherited the vast range of Indian Buddhist teachings. They regarded the Buddha as having taught the three great phases of Indian Buddhism—Hīnayāna, Mahāyāna, and Vajrayāna—to beings of inferior, middling, and superior capacity respectively. Tibetan Buddhists therefore say that the three *yānas* between them constitute the entire spiritual path, from beginning to end. Both the Chinese and the Tibetan perspectives really amount to the same: that the different traditions all embody different aspects and phases of the Buddha's actual, historical teaching. They then grade schools according to their depth and completeness: the higher teachings being those revealing the deepest truths to disciples at the highest stages of the spiritual path.

Tibetan Buddhism inherited this threefold classification into Hīnayāna, Mahāyāna, and Vajrayāna from India. As the Mahāyāna gradually emerged as a distinct tendency, its adherents had distinguished it from the Hīnayāna—they distinguished the 'Greater' from the 'Lesser' paths. Later, developments within the Mahāyāna traditions led to a further *yāna* being identified: the Vajrayāna—the 'Path of the Thunderbolt' or 'Diamond Path'. This classification was not, of course, used or accepted by all parties. The categorisation of the Buddhist tradition into three *yānas* has nonetheless become widely current in Western discussions of Buddhism and is, in a sense, now unavoidable. However, it is the source of a great deal of confusion.

The problem is that the language of the three *yānas* is used in three distinct ways. First, it is used in a quite neutral sense to classify the various schools of Indian Buddhism and their successors outside India. Secondly, it has been used as a polemical weapon: in itself, the term 'Hīnayāna', or 'Lesser Path', is derogatory. Thirdly, it is used to describe three different phases in the spiritual life of all individuals. These three usages are not usually distinguished and therefore lead to much confusion and controversy. As Sangharakshita says,

> There is a lot of sorting out that we have to do in this area. It isn't going
> to be easy because of the nature of the historical development of
> Buddhism.[22]

That historical development is extraordinarily complex. We shall see later some of the problems to which that complexity has given rise.

Sangharakshita uses the terminology of the three *yānas* quite freely in his writings and lectures. For much of his career he has broadly accepted the terms as applied within the Tibetan tradition. He has used them to classify Buddhist schools, at the same time identifying them with the three main stages in the spiritual career of the individual—as well, sometimes, as employing 'Hīnayāna' as a term of condemnation. However, he has more recently formed a very different view that supersedes, in a sense even criticises, his own earlier position. It is obviously important to remember this in reading his work.

> At that time [in the fifties and early sixties], I was still thinking things over and learning about the Vajrayāna. I was never in a hurry to come to conclusions, so when I learned these things I just tried to understand them as they were actually taught. I wasn't in a hurry to start interpreting in my own way. Since then I have had many years in which to think these things over and come to certain conclusions.[23]

We will now see the outcome of his patient reflection. We will examine, under the headings of the three usages of the *yānas*, his ideas on how the modern Buddhist should relate to the total Buddhist tradition.

## THE YĀNAS AS A HISTORICAL CLASSIFICATION

First, the *yānas* may be used to describe the three main trends in the historical unfoldment of Buddhism in India. Here there is an immediate and direct conflict between modern scholarship and the traditional perspectives of Chinese and Tibetan Buddhism. The modern representatives of the historical schools are inclined to maintain their customary ways of viewing the diversity of Buddhism: seeing the teachings of all schools as directly taught by the Buddha to beings of varying capacities. No doubt, in their familiar contexts these perspectives have their value. However, the development of a more intellectually rigorous approach to history and to the study of literary documents has made these positions untenable. Recent scholarly research has shown that there is little or no historical basis for deriving most Buddhist scriptures directly from the Buddha. Nor are there any grounds for grading scriptures according to stages in his teaching career.

Sangharakshita believes that Buddhists today must take advantage of modern scholarship. They must ensure that their statements about the facts of Buddhism as a historical phenomenon can be supported by evidence that has been critically evaluated. In the first place, they must do so for moral reasons: once facts are known, it becomes a lie to ignore them. More pragmatically, if Buddhists do ignore modern scholarship, they will alienate the sceptically-minded Westerner—as well as the growing numbers throughout the world who accept to some degree the scientific outlook. There is, moreover, no disadvantage to Buddhists in scholarly research into the origins of their religion. Buddhism, Sangharakshita says, unlike Christianity, has nothing to fear from the 'higher criticism', the scientific analysis of its texts and other records. The truth of Buddhism does not rest upon the historicity of certain events or upon the divine origins of certain texts. Sangharakshita himself has tried to take modern scholarship into consideration in coming to an understanding of the Buddhist tradition's development. However, as he is quick to point out, such scholarship is yet in its early stages and new facts are being discovered all the time. Indeed, Sangharakshita's own early work, particularly as represented by *A Survey of Buddhism*, is itself out of date in certain historical details, as he freely admits.[24]

Modern scholarship has led Sangharakshita to a new perspective on the Buddhist tradition. He accepts that many teachings attributed to the Buddha by various schools were probably not actually taught by him. As each school's doctrine developed over the centuries, new creations were fathered on the Buddha, to give them the authority of his name. Nonetheless, the fact that these doctrines were probably not taught by the Buddha does not lessen their possible value as means to Enlightenment. Whether taught directly by the Buddha or not, by the Buddha's own criterion, they may be 'the Master's Message'.

Though many Buddhist teachings may not actually have been directly taught by the Buddha, Sangharakshita has nonetheless drawn unfailing personal inspiration from the Buddha's life. That life, as recounted in the Pali Canon, is a source of example and guidance for him in his own life and work. He sees that ultimately Buddhism springs from the Buddha's experience of Enlightenment. The Buddha is therefore the basis of the *historical unity* of Buddhism, since all schools descend from him in unbroken historical continuity. The Buddha must therefore be the starting point for a consideration of the Buddhist tradition as a whole.

It is now almost impossible to say with any certainty exactly what words the Buddha spoke—we do not even know precisely which language he used. Nonetheless there is found in the scriptures of all schools, and therefore predating their division from each other, a core of common material about the Buddha's life and teaching. This common core contains what Sangharakshita calls, borrowing a phrase from Christmas

Humphreys, 'Basic Buddhism': all the classic formulae of Buddhist doctrine such as conditioned co-production, the Four Noble Truths, the Eightfold Path, and the Three Characteristics. These are the basic teachings of Buddhism, contained in the oldest texts of all schools and accepted by all Buddhists. On them

> rest, as on an unshakeable foundation, the loftiest superstructures and
> dizziest pinnacles of later Buddhist Doctrine and Method.[25]

They are the necessary starting point for any serious study of Buddhism, for

> without a previous knowledge of the earlier formulations of the
> Buddha's Teaching as preserved in either the Hīnayāna or the Mahāyāna
> collections of canonical literature, understanding of the later and often
> more elaborate formulations is impossible.[26]

Basic Buddhism then provides the *doctrinal unity* of Buddhism.

Basic Buddhism, as recognised by all schools, is as near as we can get to the original teaching of the Buddha. However, even within the earliest scriptures some evolution can be discerned. Textual analysis reveals that some portions are earlier than others, and behind them we can sense what Sangharakshita has called 'pre-Buddhist Buddhism': Buddhism, in the period immediately following the Buddha's Enlightenment, before he had developed the doctrines and institutions later identified as Buddhism. Behind the formalisms of the texts we catch a glimpse of the Buddha himself, struggling to communicate his experience to others, without the framework of language and thought that became Basic Buddhism. Sangharakshita regards this glimpse as very important. It reveals a picture of the Buddha that, no doubt, strikes a resonance in one who himself is trying to communicate those same truths in a new context. However, its importance is more general. It ensures that we do not see the Buddha as a polished churchman, giving scholarly talks and issuing administrative orders. We see him, Sangharakshita says, more like a wild shaman in the vast and lonely jungle, as yet with few words to convey his new and vital message. This glimpse of the unselfconscious origins of Buddhism helps us to see that spiritual life is something natural and immediate, not necessarily involving sophisticated superstructures of doctrine or organisation.

However, gradually the Buddha did develop the teachings of Basic Buddhism and the institutions of his new movement. After his Enlightenment, the Buddha gradually evolved a body of teachings and a spiritual community that directly expressed his own Enlightened experience. This is Buddhism at its most unified and harmonious.

> The equilibrium between its various aspects and elements was
> necessarily absolute, for it was the product of an Enlightened and hence
> perfectly balanced mind.[27]

The authority of the Buddha's person and the comprehensiveness of his teaching harmonised all the latent divergencies of a growing and disparate movement. Whatever their temperaments or personal inclinations, under his influence all his disciples felt themselves to be members of a single spiritual community, following a single path to a single goal. Sangharakshita calls this period of harmony 'Archaic Buddhism'.

> I think one could regard Archaic Buddhism as lasting roughly one
> hundred years. That is to say, during the Buddha's teaching life and the
> lifetime of at least the third generation of disciples after him.[28]

Within this era of the Buddha's immediate personal influence, elements of all the later developments in Buddhism are discernible. Out of tendencies present in the Buddha's own teachings gradually emerged new teachings and practices. This is, argues Sangharakshita, a natural and healthy phenomenon. Spiritual life is rich and multifaceted and it is impossible to exhaust every dimension and aspect of it. Comprehensive and profound as was his teaching, the Buddha touched on many themes whose implications he never worked out in detail. Different disciples and groups of disciples developed these tendencies latent in the original teaching, elaborating them more fully and working out those implications.

Another factor in the growing diversity of schools was the necessity of responding to the spiritual needs of different people. Although, in a sense, there is but one spiritual path, no two people follow it in precisely the same way. As general teachings are applied to more and more specific cases, ever more of the Dharma's riches are revealed. Again, Buddhism was spreading into new geographical areas all the time and conditions were constantly changing in those areas where it was already established. The Dharma had to be communicated appropriately in new cultural and historical circumstances, for it is not a static set of words, fixed for all time; it is a living communication between the Enlightened and the unenlightened that must constantly be renewed and related to the people to whom it is directed, as the Buddha himself clearly recognised.

In elaborating particular aspects of the Dharma, a sense of the integrity of the teachings would often be lost and a one-sidedness would develop. Those following the different trends of the original teachings began to diverge more and more from one another, gradually hardening into distinct schools. As time went on, there were increasing debates and controversies between the different schools, and they often formed their doctrines in dialectical relationship with each other. However, we must be careful not to think of this process as analogous to the historical evolution of Christianity. The successive *yānas* did not arise in the same way as the Protestant Reformation.

> Luther for the early part of his life was a Catholic, for there was nothing but Catholicism in Western Europe. He broke away from Catholicism to form something relatively new, which became Lutheranism. He did not belong to or revive a separate independent tradition already existing alongside Catholicism.
>
> But in the case of the Mahāyāna, there was already a living tradition, existing alongside the Hīnayāna, to which [the great figures of the Mahāyāna] already belonged and which they brought into greater prominence through their expositions and so on.[29]

The Hīnayāna, Mahāyāna, and Vajrayāna then were the three main trends in the unfoldment of these latent tendencies within Archaic Buddhism, each of which successively enjoyed a period of roughly 500 years of overall dominance. Sangharakshita has given comprehensive characterisations of these trends—although inevitably such general descriptions give rise to many exceptions. The Hīnayāna unfolded the ethical dimension of the Buddha's teaching through its emphasis on monastic life. It also elaborated his psychological teachings by systematically classifying mental states in the *Abhidharma* literature. The Mahāyāna, building on traditions going back to the Buddha, brought out the devotional side of spiritual life, through its worship of the stupas or reliquaries of the Buddha and through the cults of the archetypal Buddhas and Bodhisattvas. On the doctrinal side, it elaborated the metaphysical implications of the Dharma. Finally, the Vajrayāna took the imaginative and mythic aspects of the original teaching and, based on Mahāyāna metaphysics, developed a language of ritual and symbol. Thus Sangharakshita sees each *yāna* as unfolding elements germinal in the original teaching.

The process of unfoldment was not, of course, as tidy and self-conscious as this description suggests. All the tendencies were present from the beginning.

> One can't separate the *yānas* completely. Even though one was dominant, the other was quite effectively present nonetheless. While the Hīnayāna was *formulated* before the Mahāyāna, during the 500-year period when the Hīnayāna was mainly dominant the Mahāyāna was present as a purely spiritual transmission.[30]

The spirit of those latent tendencies within the original teaching was kept alive among certain groups of disciples and their successors. Under particular circumstances, the tendencies were gradually made explicit in texts, doctrines, and practices, to which later the generic terms 'Mahāyāna' or 'Vajrayāna' would be applied. But these were not, in the early stages of their evolution, seen as completely separate and isolated from the more highly formulated Hīnayāna teachings and practices. As each successive trend became explicit, it did so alongside and in relation to the trend or trends that had emerged before it. Chinese pilgrims to India reported

> that Mahāyāna and Hīnayāna monks lived side by side in the same *vihāra*. The only difference between them was that the Mahāyāna monks studied the Mahāyāna *sūtras* and worshipped the Bodhisattvas in addition to all the other things that the Hīnayāna *bhikkhus* were doing.[31]

Vajrayāna was also practised in the great monastic universities and its devotees were often, perhaps usually, monks ordained in the Hīnayāna ordination lineages and studying the Mahāyāna *sūtras*.

Buddhism had died out in India by the fourteenth century. However, it had, by then, been dispersed throughout Asia. The forms of Buddhism that have survived to the present are each based on one or more aspects of Indian Buddhism, further developed within their new setting. There are three major geographical groupings of these surviving historical forms of Buddhism:

> These are South-east Asian Buddhism, which is found in Sri Lanka, Burma, and Thailand, as well as in Cambodia and Laos; Sino-Japanese Buddhism, which exists not only in China and Japan but also in Korea and Vietnam; and Tibetan Buddhism, which from the Land of Snows spreads into Mongolia, Sikkim, Bhutan, and Ladakh. In terms of the three *yānas* South-east Asian Buddhism belongs to the Hīnayāna. Sino-Japanese Buddhism to the combined Hīnayāna and Mahāyāna, with the latter predominating, especially in Japan, while Tibetan Buddhism belongs equally to the Hīnayāna, the Mahāyāna, and the Vajrayāna, with each succeeding yāna providing the orientation for the preceding one.[32]

## THE YĀNAS AS POLEMICAL TERMS

The historical usage of the term *yāna* is quite value-neutral. It merely identifies three broad trends unfolding in Buddhist history. However, Mahayanists originally evolved the terms 'Hīnayāna' and 'Mahāyāna' with a definite evaluative significance. The 'Great Path' was certainly better than the 'Lesser' one. Sangharakshita considers that this polemical usage of the *yānas* must be carefully separated from the historical.

It must not, of course, be forgotten that the Theravadins do not accept
the label Hīnayāna at all. To be fair, it might be more accurate to call the
Hīnayāna a purely literary phenomenon, because the likelihood of
meeting an actual Hinayanist [in the polemical sense] in the flesh is
slight indeed. The term Hīnayāna is simply useful for the purpose of
referring to the early schools, and even later schools like the
Sarvāstivādin and Sautrantika, from which the Mahāyāna schools
evidently differed. Used in this way, it should not be understood in any
pejorative sense whatsoever.[33]

It is not, however, that Sangharakshita does not think that there was
some considerable truth in the historical Mahāyāna's criticisms of the
historical Hīnayāna. In *A Survey of Buddhism* he argues, perhaps a little
sweepingly, that, at the time that the Mahāyāna was arising, the
Hīnayāna schools had become conservative and literal-minded,
scholastic, one-sidedly negative in their conception of *nirvāna* and the
Way, over-attached to the merely formal aspects of monasticism, and
spiritually individualistic in the sense of being unconcerned with the
spiritual welfare of others.[34] However, these are not characteristics of the
Hīnayāna as such but of Hīnayāna schools at a particular stage of
development—or perhaps decay. The same criticisms can also be levelled
at various Mahayanists or Vajrayanists in certain periods of their history.
For instance,

It isn't only the Hīnayāna that developed a scholasticism. The Mahāyāna
developed a scholasticism. The Vajrayāna, too, strange and paradoxical
though it may seem, developed a scholasticism of its own. For instance,
some at least of the books on the Vajrayāna that emanate from Tibetan
sources today are highly scholastic. They don't, therefore, give a very
adequate feeling for the spirit of the Vajrayāna.[35]

The fact that all three historical *yānas* can be seen to degenerate, in
certain respects at certain periods, reveals an important dynamic within
the historical phenomenon, Buddhism. What commences as genuine and
creative spiritual vision gradually ossifies during its transmission
through the ages. Sangharakshita distinguishes, in this connection,
between 'the Dharma' and 'Buddhism'.

What tends to happen is that the Dharma as a purely spiritual
phenomenon crystallizes, with the appearance in the world of a Buddha,
into a system of methods and teachings which we call 'Buddhism'.[36]

This crystallisation is, of course, essential if the Dharma is to be communicated to others. The process of crystallisation can be seen in three distinct
phases in the evolution of each Buddhist school. First there is the direct
and spontaneous affirmation of the Dharma. Then there is a phase of

'tidying up' through philosophical systematisation. Finally, scholasticism ensues.

> Each stage, while in one sense a development of the preceding stage, is
> in another sense a descent from it. While in the first stage the standpoint
> is intuitive and transcendental, in the second it is philosophic, and in the
> third merely rational and logical.[37]

The process of crystallisation extends beyond this evolution of the conceptual expressions of the Dharma. Around the teachings there gradually accumulate patterns of behaviour, institutions, artistic expressions— eventually, a whole culture, influencing perhaps large numbers of people. However necessary and helpful this crystallisation is, in the end it will probably become a limitation.

> The fact that Buddhism has crystallized in one way—adequate for a
> certain time and for certain people—tends to prevent a different kind of
> crystallization in the future. It is as though the options are limited by the
> original crystallization....
>
> In this way Buddhism itself, as a culture, may sometimes obstruct the
> attempts of an Enlightened being to spread the Dharma. Buddhism
> eventually gets so weighed down by its different cultural forms that
> even the most heroic attempts of the most gifted teachers cannot make
> headway on behalf of the Dharma against what passes as Buddhism.[38]

Eventually the existing crystallisation must be shattered and a new and more spiritually dynamic pattern established. Sangharakshita sees that the preservation of the basic forms of the original teaching, even after their spirit has been lost, plays its part in helping to revitalise Buddhism. Spiritually gifted individuals, trying to function within Buddhist schools and cultures in their decay, can reconnect with the original spiritual impetus through the words of the Buddha and his Enlightened successors. This is, of course, a point of great relevance to those, like Sangharakshita, trying to rediscover the spark of the Dharma in what are largely the dead embers of oriental Buddhism.

For the purposes of the present discussion, the Mahāyāna's criticisms of the Hīnayāna can just as easily be levelled at the Mahāyāna itself in certain aspects and phases of its history—as well as at the Vajrayāna. The Mahāyāna's main criticism of the Hīnayāna was that it was spiritually individualistic. Hinayanists were supposed to be solely concerned with gaining personal freedom from suffering rather than helping others to liberation. This accusation provides the main polemical usage of the term 'Hīnayāna'. Hinayanists allegedly followed the 'Arahant Ideal', aiming at personal liberation alone. Mahayanists, on the other hand, pursued the 'Bodhisattva Ideal', aiming at the Enlightenment of all sentient beings.

But again, this characterisation has no basis in history. We should be very careful to distinguish the *yānas* used to represent the attitudes of certain individuals from the *yānas* as historical phenomena.

> I have met *bhikkhus* who are technically Hinayanists [in the historical sense] but who are spending their whole lives in propagating the Dharma just as though they were Bodhisattvas. I've met Tibetan Buddhist monks who didn't care at all about propagating the Dharma. Though technically they were following the three *yānas*, their attitude was 'Hinayanistic' [in the polemical sense].[39]

Sangharakshita has pointed out that, until forced out of their country by the Chinese invasion, the 'Mahayanists' of Tibet showed little concern for those in the West who had not heard the Dharma. Meanwhile, several 'Hinayanists' of South-east Asia began to establish missionary activities in some European and American cities, from quite early in the twentieth century.

## THE YĀNAS AS STAGES OF THE SPIRITUAL PATH

The third usage of the *yāna* model is the one that presents most problems for readers of Sangharakshita's writings. His later thought here is definitely at odds with his earlier. Once he had encountered Tibetan *triyāna* Buddhism he adopted its perspective. It was, after all, far more inclusive than the common Theravadin perception of all other teachings and schools as degenerate. Tibetan Buddhism generally sees the three *yānas* as representing the three principal stages of the spiritual path. All three phases of the historical development of Indian Buddhism were transplanted into Tibet and were made sense of in these terms. The scriptures of the Hīnayāna and Mahāyāna, and many of those of the Vajrayāna, were all seen as preserving the actual words of the historical Buddha. Each set of scriptures was said to embody his teachings to beings at a different level of spiritual experience or capacity. The Hīnayāna teaches the path of individual salvation to those of limited capacity. Average disciples learn the path of the Bodhisattva from the Mahāyāna. By means of the Vajrayāna superior beings may gain liberation in a single lifetime. Sangharakshita characterises the *yānas* from this perspective rather succinctly:

> If one wanted to summarize those three *yānas* seen as the three great main stages of the spiritual path, one could say that the keynote of the Hīnayāna is renunciation, of the Mahāyāna is altruism, and of the Vajrayāna is transformation. Renunciation in the sense of Going Forth: going forth from the world, going forth from the group. And altruism

because for oneself the distinction between self and others has lost at
least something of its significance. And then transformation because one
sees that spiritual life doesn't involve disowning anything or separating
oneself from anything, but simply of transforming one's natural energies
of body, speech, and mind into more and more refined forms. This is
really the essence of it.[40]

During any individual's spiritual career, taking place over many
lifetimes, all three stages must be traversed. Since these stages in spiritual
life were identified with the historical phases of Buddhist development,
as Sangharakshita puts it in an early work,

Just as the intra-uterine development of the individual recapitulates the
development of the race, so before he can issue from the womb of
ignorance, and be born into the World of Enlightenment, the student of
the Dharma must recapitulate in his spiritual life the history of
Buddhism.[41]

As we see in this passage just quoted, Sangharakshita has incorporated
a modified version of this Tibetan *triyāna* view into much of his work. In
particular, *A Survey of Buddhism* (1957) and his lecture series on 'Aspects
of the Bodhisattva Ideal' (1969) and 'Creative Symbols of the Tantric Path
to Enlightenment' (1972) speak this language. However, he has since
come to the conclusion that the three *yānas* cannot be seen as a spiritual
sequence.

Clearly there are deeper and deeper levels of the spiritual path.
However, we can't really equate them with the Hīnayāna, Mahāyāna,
and Vajrayāna in the traditional Tibetan sense.[42]

Sangharakshita values all three historical *yānas* equally. Each is largely
the elaboration of an aspect or aspects of the original teaching and
represents a particular emphasis. Teachings that relate to the deepest
levels of the path can be found in all three *yānas*.

The Tibetan schematisation, inherited from the late Pala dynasty
Buddhism of north-eastern India, enshrines the way in which Indian
Buddhists had coped with the evolution of doctrine. Sangharakshita
points out that in ancient India, as in the European Dark and Middle
Ages, there was little idea of historical development. The past was largely
seen as exactly like the present. Buddhists at any period would have
thought of themselves as living the same life and following the same
teachings as disciples had done in the time of the Buddha himself. This
determined the way in which they coped with the Buddhism they
inherited.

We have already seen that there is a tendency for original spiritual
vitality to be lost as its crystallisations harden around it. But to the Indian

Buddhists of the time those crystallisations actually *were* the teachings of the Buddha. Having no idea of historical development, they could not reject them nor could they correct them, so they created what amounts to a myth. They saw the Buddha as having taught everything that had come down to them—but for the sake of beings of lesser capacity. The more spiritually vital message they considered missing from what they inherited they then presented as the Buddha's further revelation for beings of superior spiritual attainment.

Sangharakshita sees an example of this process in the *White Lotus Sūtra*, an important Mahāyāna text. In the *Sūtra*, the Buddha is presented as teaching that the three paths of early Buddhism (not here the three *yānas* we have been dealing with) were really one. Here we must briefly recount a little doctrinal history, since it illustrates an important general historical dynamic. Originally, the Buddha's attainment of Enlightenment was considered exactly the same as that of his Enlightened disciples, who were known as *arahants*. They only differed in that the Buddha had gained Enlightenment without any help from a teacher, while the *arahants* had done so in his footsteps. The content of their Enlightened experience was, however, exactly the same as his. Over the centuries this view was lost. The idea gradually arose that the Buddha was much more developed than the *arahants*. So there came to be a choice. One could aim to become either a Buddha or an *arahant*. A third, intermediate, category was added, the *pratyekabuddha*. The paths to becoming a Buddha, an *arahant*, and a *pratyekabuddha* were considered real alternatives leading to real alternative spiritual goals. Actually, they simply represented scholastic misreadings of the original teachings.

> By the time the *White Lotus Sūtra* had emerged, the original teaching of the Buddha, as one may call it, had shrunk at the hands of some people and arahantship had become a rather individualistic sort of goal. Whoever composed the *White Lotus Sūtra* wanted to correct that development, but didn't understand that there had been some sort of historical development. They couldn't say, 'Look, this is not what the Buddha taught historically,' so they created a myth to explain the matter. They presented the Buddha as giving this *further* teaching that all the paths coalesced and that in reality there was only one path for all.[43]

In this way there came to be a 'stack' of teachings, each one correcting the degeneracy of the preceding by means of the myth of the Buddha giving further and higher teachings.

In Tibetan Buddhist schools the path of the three *yānas* is even further subdivided, in different ways by different schools. Some Chinese and Japanese masters similarly arranged the teachings in complex sequences.

Sangharakshita uses the term 'ultra-ism' to describe the phenomenon of continuously adding further stages.

> A certain name is applied to the ultimate stage. But, after a while, this term comes to be taken rather literally and therefore comes to mean something less than it meant originally. So you now have to go beyond it with another term that indicates what the first term meant before its meaning became debased. You see this with the word *arahant*. In the Pali texts [belonging to the earliest, Hīnayāna phase] *arahant* refers to one who has realized the highest truth by following the teaching of the Buddha. But in the Mahāyāna *sūtras*, because the whole notion of the *arahant* had become rather debased, you needed something that went beyond that. In this way there arose the Mahāyāna conception of the Bodhisattva and the supreme Buddha.[44]

Sangharakshita considers that Western Buddhists cannot accept these traditional schematisations of the teachings. For a start, they have no basis in history since we know that the Buddha did not literally teach many of the later doctrines attributed to him. We can also see that the different schools do not fit neatly into the classificatory schema. For instance, there are teachings in the Pali Canon, supposedly belonging to the Hīnayāna, that are clearly directed to individuals at a very high level of attainment. At the same time, some teachings found in the 'higher' *yānas* of the Tibetan systems are actually quite elementary: for instance, Sangharakshita considers that some of the practices in the *anuyoga-tantra* of the Nyingmapa are probably merely Indian hatha yoga exercises. Again, he says of *Dzogchen*, which is for the Nyingmapa the very highest stage of spiritual practice,

> If one looks at the actual material it seems to boil down to a quite simple practice of mindfulness.[45]

Indeed, he says of some teachings in the *anuttarayoga-tantra*, the summit of some Tibetan systems, that they are not really Buddhist at all, but rather unassimilated Hinduism. Finally, these schema present another difficulty. They were meant to comprehend all aspects of the Buddhist tradition. However, they only account for what schools and teachings were known to the systematisers—which was limited to what had at that time been transmitted to their country from India. Modern Buddhists are faced with the entire range of Buddhist schools, ancient and modern. Since several schools have their own classificatory systems, not only in Tibetan Buddhism but in Chinese and Japanese Buddhism too, there is a problem of reconciling the different systems. This would prove extremely complex, perhaps impossible, and would be of doubtful spiritual value were it achieved.

It is better, Sangharakshita says, to set all these systems aside and go back to the original teachings, on top of which the later teachings have been stacked. Since we cannot, with modern historical knowledge, accept the traditional mythic systems, many of the later teachings will be embedded in complex frameworks of ideas in which we can no longer believe. For instance, since we can no longer believe that the *arahant* represents a real alternative goal, we cannot accept the path of the Bodhisattva as a higher path.

> I think it is important to get back to basic principles—back to the simpler, the more easily understandable, more easy to handle. I think the stack has got so high we have just got to go back. Otherwise we have stack upon stack of practices which have superseded one another. So you might as well just drop all the later developments and go back to the original one, which is closer to the Buddha's own times and to the Buddha himself. We can do that on account of our historical perspective, whereas formerly Buddhists couldn't.[46]

One important reason for a return to basics is the avoidance of certain dangers inherent in the hierarchical arrangement of teachings. Inevitably people want to move on to the highest stage, missing out the initial levels. Sangharakshita calls this 'spiritual snobbism' and says that it was as common among Tibetans in India as it now is among Westerners in Europe and America.

> In Tibetan Buddhism you are supposed to go through all the *yānas*—the Nyingmapas have nine! Actually, people go through the first few *yānas* very quickly and really only 'practise' the last one![47]

Taking the *triyāna* system literally leads to a serious distortion of spiritual life.

> If you are not careful, you end up trying to practise some teaching which is really way beyond you and barely intelligible, not to say even fantastic in the literal sense.[48]

For instance, if one thought that there was a real *arahant* path, one would conceive of the Bodhisattva path as a really higher alternative. One would then tend to neglect the Hīnayāna teachings associated with the *arahant* path and start trying to practise the Mahāyāna. This means trying to be a Bodhisattva, aspiring to Enlightenment for the sake of all sentient beings. For most ordinary practitioners this cannot but be a kind of fantasy. They cannot really think of themselves personally as Bodhisattvas saving all sentient beings. At best this leads to a 'spiritual life' that is nothing but a harmless dream: at worst it leads to inflation and arrogance.

The language of the Bodhisattva Ideal arose, we have seen, as a corrective to a degeneration in the historical tradition. Lacking a historical perspective that would have enabled them to acknowledge that there had been a degeneration, the Mahayanists had to create a myth. They had to accept the shrunken ideal they had inherited, with its individualistic conception of the goal, and present the Buddha as teaching something further. The Bodhisattva Ideal, lofty and inspiring as it is, is not to be taken literally. It is simply meant to reintroduce the altruistic dimension to the Buddhist ideal. If it is taken literally it becomes a trap. Sangharakshita considers it safer and more spiritually efficacious to return to the essential principles of spiritual life embodied in the basic teachings. One needs no higher teachings beyond these. One simply needs to understand them ever more deeply and apply them ever more fully in one's own life.

This return to basic principles does not mean ignoring or discarding later developments. It simply means seeing them in the context of the earlier teachings. Sangharakshita views the entire later Buddhist tradition as having grown out of the Buddha's own teaching—as filling it out, amplifying and elaborating it, but not as superseding it or adding newer and higher stages. Not only does this greatly simplify the task of finding teachings to apply within our own spiritual practice, but it brings us closer to the Buddha. Those Buddhists, notably of Tibet and Japan, who are practising teachings that come from the later stages of the historical evolution of Buddhism are far removed from its origins. In their own cultural context this has not mattered since they have seldom been confronted with the original teachings. The modern practitioner, however, increasingly faces the entire Buddhist tradition and cannot ignore the Buddha and his original teachings. It must be possible to refer one's own practice back to the origins of Buddhism otherwise one will find oneself in a strange position.

> It might be rather disconcerting then to read the Pali Canon, and
> recognize absolutely nothing that you yourself are practising! It is
> difficult to see your connection, then, with the founder of your religion.
> So we don't want to be in that position. We have to be familiar with the
> earlier forms and base ourselves on them, and appreciate the later
> developments as growing out of those earlier forms.[49]

A common history and doctrine are practical exemplifications of the underlying unity of Buddhism. The most spiritually perspicacious alone will be able to discern the transcendental unity lying behind the extraordinary diversity of historical Buddhism and its present-day representatives. Most will only recognise their identity with other Buddhists because they perform the same practices, follow the same doctrines, and honour the same historical founder.

## TESTING THE TEACHINGS

While the entire Buddhist tradition can be seen in principle as an elaboration or rounding out of aspects of the basic teachings of the Buddha, evaluation is still required. Buddhism went through many twists and turns in its 2,500-year history. As well as many brilliant and spiritually efficacious new elaborations, there were also many degenerations and distortions. We must test individual teachings to see whether they do indeed conduce to the attainment of Enlightenment. This criterion has, however, its limitations: in the end, only the Enlightened can know what conduces to Enlightenment. Indeed, that pragmatic criterion can be used to justify mere heterodoxy and indulgence. Some trends in Buddhist history have tended to emphasise adaptability more than faithfulness to the letter of tradition, and this had led to degeneration and distortion. The Mahāyāna and Vajrayāna have particularly suffered from this tendency.

> Eventually, after having flourished in the land of its birth for more than fifteen hundred years, the Mahāyāna carried liberalism to extremes and exalted the spirit above the letter of the teaching to such an extent that the latter was almost lost sight of and the Dharma deprived, at least on the mundane plane, of its distinctive individuality.[50]

The Buddhism of Nepal and the last Buddhist remnants in Indonesia are, for instance, now indistinguishable from Hinduism except in name alone. The need to constantly find new ways of communicating the Dharma in new contexts must be balanced by a concern to keep alive what the Dharma really is. Teachings and practices must be evaluated in the light of the experience of the Enlightened.

Some guidance is to be found in the scriptures, which provide an important safeguard against excessive liberalism. Although most Buddhists do not blindly rely on the authoritative word of a sacred book, as so many Protestant Christians have done on the Bible, nonetheless the scriptures are an outstanding source of guidance and insight for most Buddhists. Sangharakshita's view of the Buddhist tradition as a whole can equally be applied to the scriptures. These form a vast body of material, for each school has its own canon, in parts overlapping with others and in parts special to it. Collectively, it is an extraordinary spiritual treasury, which by its sheer diversity testifies to the spiritual vitality of the Buddhist tradition. Set down over a period of some thousand years from the time of the Buddha's *parinirvāṇa* or death, much of it cannot be taken as recording the Buddha's actual words. There is however a common core of material found in all the canons, presumably therefore predating the schools' separation from each other. In that core is what we have called 'Basic Buddhism', the nearest we can get to the actual teaching of the Buddha. Even those parts that are later, and therefore less likely to have come directly from the Buddha, are nonetheless for the most part entirely in the spirit of that earlier teaching. They are genuine elaborations of it, exploring themes opened up in the original teaching, unfolding ever more fully each aspect of the Dharma in the way we have already examined above.

Sangharakshita considers that some knowledge of at least some few canonical texts is indispensable to a serious Buddhist practitioner. That study must be firmly based on a thorough acquaintance with the basic teachings as presented in the oldest texts—of which the most accessible to Western students are those found in the Pali Canon. In his teaching, Sangharakshita has strongly emphasised several important scriptures from various traditional sources. He has given lectures and conducted seminars on many major works and has written a comprehensive account of the canonical literature of Buddhism, *The Eternal Legacy*, again giving expression to his vision of the unity of Buddhism.

The scriptures act as a touchstone by which the validity of new developments can be tested. They are after all, to some extent, records of what the Buddha taught, particularly those portions that deal with Basic Buddhism. They therefore provide some contact with the mind of Enlightenment. If some new teaching evolves or an old teaching is elaborated, it should be possible to see whether it is in the spirit of the basic teachings of Buddhism as expressed in the scriptures. In his important essay, *The Meaning of Orthodoxy in Buddhism*, Sangharakshita gives as one definition of Buddhist orthodoxy:

> According to, or congruous with, the scriptures common to all schools of Buddhism, especially as expressed in the stereotype formulae such as the Four Noble Truths and the Three Characteristics (*tri-lakshaṇa*), which are found in both the Scriptures which are and the Scriptures which are not common to all schools.[51]

Another criterion is that the teaching should be

> of Right Views (*sammādiṭṭhika*); hence, adhering to the Dharma of the Buddha as formulated in the formulae such as the Four Noble Truths and the Three Characteristics (*tilakkhana*) without inclining either to the

extreme of Eternalism (*sassatavāda*) or the extreme of Nihilism
(*ucchedavāda*).[52]

These criteria ensure that the pragmatic definition of the Dharma as
whatever conduces to Enlightenment is not used to give licence to
self-indulgence and whim. In order to apply that definition effectively
one must know to some extent what Enlightenment is; only then will one
be able to tell whether a practice is actually leading towards it. The
scriptures and the basic doctrinal formulae, emanating from the Enlightened mind, offer some means of ascertaining whether the new
teaching is genuinely 'the Master's Message'—or *Buddha-sāsana*, as it was
traditionally termed.

## THE PRINCIPLES OF A NEW BUDDHIST MOVEMENT

Sangharakshita's understanding of the unity of Buddhism and his
perspective on the Buddhist tradition found practical application when
he came to found the FWBO in 1967. The principles on which it should be
formed were by then very clear to him. The first and most basic was that
the new movement should help the individuals it consisted of to grow
towards Enlightenment. Teachings and practices were taken up because
they worked. There was no question of simply continuing unthinkingly
any one school or tradition in its existing form. Using the Buddha's
pragmatic criteria for recognising the 'Master's Message', Sangharakshita built a body of teachings and practices—still growing and
changing—which met the spiritual needs of his disciples. Since he
viewed the entire Buddhist tradition as likely to contain valid means to
Enlightenment, he could draw from any part of it whatever was appropriate to the present. This was no mere eclecticism, in the sense of a
selection according to a preconceived system, rationally deduced. No
more was it simply a matter of personal whim or preference. Teachings
and practices were incorporated because they answered his disciples'
definite spiritual needs.

Clearly it was not possible to take up every teaching of every school of
Buddhism. Even within a single school there is far more material available than any individual could ever usefully take advantage of. There
had to be a selection—a selection based upon real spiritual needs. Indeed,
as Sangharakshita points out,

> In selecting doctrinal and practical elements from one or more Eastern
> Buddhist tradition the FWBO is doing no more, in principle, than
> individual Eastern Buddhists, or groups of Eastern Buddhists, do in the
> case of their own particular tradition. A Sinhalese Theravāda monk, for

example, while in principle accepting the Theravāda tradition *in toto*, will not familiarize himself with *all* the doctrines ... nor will he practise *all* the forty methods of meditation (*kammaṭṭhāna*) described in the *Visuddhimagga*.[53]

There was however a clear starting point. Sangharakshita saw the Buddhist tradition as consisting of elaborations and explications of the essential principles contained in the Buddha's original teaching. He therefore drew his main corpus of material from that core of doctrine he called 'Basic Buddhism'. Indeed, he considered that most of his disciples' spiritual needs could be met by their simply practising more and more deeply these fundamental teachings. He enjoined on his disciples the maxim, 'More and more of less and less': that is,

our principle of trying to go more and more deeply into the so-called basic teachings of Buddhism rather than trying to hurry on to teachings which are allegedly more advanced.[54]

The emphasis on the basic teachings also ensured the 'orthodoxy' of the new movement. Any innovations or importations from other sources could be tested against these teachings that embody the Buddha's own expression of the Dharma. Thus, although the FWBO did not adhere to any traditional school of Buddhism, Sangharakshita ensured that it was entirely traditional. It was based upon the Buddha's own Enlightened experience and followed as fully as it could the spirit of his teaching.

The movement he created was a living testimony to the unity of Buddhism. He took inspiration from most Buddhist sources.

As regards meditation, for instance, we teach the 'mindfulness of breathing' and the *mettā-bhāvanā*, the 'development of loving kindness', which are taken from the Theravāda tradition. We recite the Sevenfold Puja—which comes from the Indian Mahāyāna tradition. We chant mantras which come from the Tibetan tradition. And then of course there is our emphasis on the importance of work in the spiritual life, which is a characteristically Zen emphasis.[55]

He was not confined, however, to already existing teachings and practices. The spiritual needs of his disciples drew out aspects of spiritual life not fully explored before.

Naturally, we also have certain emphases which are not to be found in any extant form of Buddhism: for example, our emphasis on Right Livelihood, on Going for Refuge, and on 'more and more of less and less'.[56]

Besides these specifically Buddhist emphases, he took up various non-Buddhist teachings and practices. For instance, he has led study on an Islamic text, *The Duties of Brotherhood in Islam* by Al-Ghazālī,[57] which has been a source of great inspiration on the theme of friendship. He has encouraged the practice of T'ai chi ch'uan, hatha yoga, and karate and other martial arts as 'indirect' means of development—'indirect' in that they work indirectly on the mind to raise the level of consciousness as distinct from meditation, which works directly. Nor have Western art and literature been neglected. Sangharakshita has strongly advocated their appreciation, partly to heighten awareness through aesthetic experience and partly to provide exemplification of Dharmic principles from within Western culture.

While Sangharakshita is determinedly nonsectarian, he is not uncritical of aspects of the Buddhist tradition and its modern representatives. He asserts that a nonsectarian approach that acknowledges the unity of Buddhism does not imply an unquestioning acceptance of every teaching, practice, and institution called, or calling itself, Buddhist.

> It should never be forgotten that, for a preacher of the Dharma, to reveal truth and to dispel falsehood are the positive and negative aspects of one process, and the history of Buddhist thought bears testimony not only to the energy with which the Message of the Master was propagated but also to the vigour with which contradictory doctrines were opposed.[58]

From his early days in India, he has spoken out against what he considered the narrow-minded literalism of the Theravāda. Later he saw and pointed out various weaknesses within Tibetan and other forms of Buddhism. He casts a discriminating eye over the modern Buddhist scene, openly drawing attention to what he sees as failings—as well as giving praise where it is due. Sangharakshita considers there to be quite a bit of confusion, and even distortion of the Dharma, in many modern Buddhist groups. He sees it as his duty to point this out, hoping to awaken the confused to their condition and to alert others before they too fall victim.

Naturally, Sangharakshita does not think that the FWBO exhausts the possible forms the Dharma could take in the modern age. The FWBO itself is constantly changing and broadening and other groups will also be exploring other modes of expressing the Dharma. This means that Sangharakshita is open to friendship with any Buddhists who are sincerely trying to live the Buddhist life—although he insists that contact should not be of a merely 'official' kind between representatives of organisations.

> As regards the relation of the Order to the rest of the Buddhist world let me simply observe that it is a relation that subsists, essentially, with individuals, and that ... we are happy to extend the hand of spiritual fellowship to all those Buddhists for whom commitment is primary,

life-style secondary and who, like us, go for Refuge to the Buddha, the Dharma, and the Sangha.[59]

## THE REFUGE TREE

Sangharakshita's relationship to the Buddhist tradition and his commitment to the unity of Buddhism is embodied in an image central to the Order he has founded. In each of the Tibetan Buddhist schools there is a 'Refuge Tree', on which are arranged all the figures that, for that school, embody the principal 'Refuges' or ideals. Sangharakshita has created such a Refuge Tree for the Order, in this way making clear its distinctive emphases and its main influences. This Refuge Tree is incorporated in the 'Going for Refuge and Prostration Practice' undertaken by some members and prospective members of the Western Buddhist Order.

Seated in meditation, one visualises a vast tree, growing up from a rainbow-coloured cloud in the midst of an infinite blue sky. The tree has four branches arranged around a central stem, the branches and central stem each being surmounted by an enormous white lotus blossom. Seated on the central lotus is the Buddha Śākyamuni, the founder of Buddhism, from whose transcendental realisation all the various schools have unfolded. He is flanked by two smaller figures, Dīpankara and Maitreya, the Buddhas of the past and the future respectively. The three figures together represent the principle of Enlightenment, in which is found the transcendental unity of Buddhism, as transcending time.

On the lotus which branches towards the meditator sits Sangharakshita himself, the founder of the Order, this new expression of the Buddhist tradition. His place here in the tree implies no 'personality cult', but a recognition that he is the link between Order members and the wider tradition. The visualisation of one's own teacher in such settings is quite common in the Tibetan tradition. One sees Sangharakshita surrounded by his own eight teachers who are, in their turn, his links to the tradition: Hermit Chen and Bhikkhu Jagdish Kashyap, Chetul Sangye Dorje, Khachu Rimpoche, Dhardo Rimpoche, Dudjom Rimpoche, Jamyang Khyentse Rimpoche, and Dilgo Khyentse Rimpoche.[60] On the lotus to the left are the principal Bodhisattvas: Avalokiteśvara, Mañjuśrī, Vajrapāṇi, Tārā, and Kshitigarbha.[61] The inclusion of these figures demonstrates the Order's acceptance of the Bodhisattva Ideal in all its aspects and its drawing upon the highest resources of the Imagination. To the right are some of the Buddha's immediate disciples, embodying the basic teachings of Buddhism and the source of their transmission to the present time:

Śāriputra and Maudgalyāyana, the Buddha's two chief disciples, Ānanda, his friend and attendant for much of his life, Māhākaśyapa, who came to lead the Order after his death, and Dhammadinna, a nun of brilliant spiritual gifts whose insight into the 'cyclic' and 'spiral' nature of conditionality has had an important effect on Sangharakshita's thinking. On the lotus behind the central figure are piled high the scriptures of all the schools of Buddhism.

Above the head of Śākyamuni sit rows of teachers from all the main Buddhist schools. At the top are Nāgārjuna and Asanga, the founders of the Mādhyamaka and Yogācāra respectively, the two main philosophical currents in Buddhism outside the Hīnayāna. Below them are the Indian teachers: Śāntideva, the author of the *Bodhicaryāvatāra*, a text much studied in the Order and the source of its principal devotional ceremony, Buddhaghosha, the great teacher of the Theravāda School, and Vasubandhu, brother of Asanga and co-founder of the Yogācāra. Next come the Tibetans: Milarepa, the 'poet-saint' from whom derives the Kagyüpa, Atīśa, an Indian teacher who effectively reintroduced the Dharma to Tibet, Padmasambhava, the Indian guru who is said to have first established Buddhism there and is thus revered as the founder of the Nyingmapa School, and Tsongkhapa, the founder of the Gelugpa School. Then appear the Chinese teachers: Chih-i, the founder of the T'ien-t'ai, Hui-neng, the Sixth Patriarch of the Ch'an School, and Hsüan-tsang, the translator, scholar, and pilgrim, who travelled extensively in India in search of texts. Finally come the Japanese teachers: Dogen, the founder of the Sōtō Zen School, Hakuin, one of the principal figures in Rinzai Zen, Kukai, the founder of the Shingon Esoteric School, and Shinran, the founder of the True Pure Land School in Japan.

Above these teachers of the past are the five Jinas—the archetypal Buddhas of the five directions, embodying the principal aspects of transcendental Wisdom. The whole array of figures is surmounted by Vajrasattva, the embodiment of the Dharma in its complete and wordless purity, the transcendental unity of Buddhism.

Having visualised this image, one rises and, keeping the Tree before one in one's mind's eye, prostrates full-length before it again and again, saying 'To the Buddha for Refuge I go; to the Dharma for Refuge I go; to the Sangha for Refuge I go,' committing oneself fully to the ideal of Enlightenment through the Buddhist tradition as re-expressed by Sangharakshita for this modern age.

*Chapter Three*

# THE TRUE NATURE OF REALITY

*Hour after hour, day*
*After day we try*
*To grasp the Ungraspable, pinpoint*
*The Unpredictable. Flowers*
*Wither when touched, ice*
*Suddenly cracks beneath our feet. Vainly*
*We try to track birdflight through the sky trace*
*Dumb fish through deep water, try*
*To anticipate the earned smile the soft*
*Reward, even*
*Try to grasp our own lives. But Life*
*Slips through our fingers*
*Like snow. Life*
*Cannot belong to us. We*
*Belong to Life. Life*
*Is King.*[62]

ALL BUDDHIST SCHOOLS ultimately derive from the Buddha's experience of Enlightenment and all see Enlightenment as the final goal of their endeavour. In this lies Buddhism's transcendental unity. This sharing of a common source and goal cannot, however, disguise considerable mundane diversity among Buddhist schools about that experience. Enlightenment is the plenitude of wisdom. With the eye of Enlightenment, the Buddha saw things as they really are. He saw the true nature of reality. But what does this mean? What did he see? In the course of Buddhist history, complex and sophisticated metaphysical systems have been elaborated to convey that sublime truth—about which finally nothing can be said. Different schools have interpreted the Buddha's experience in very different ways. Pluralistic Realism, Absolutism, and Idealism have successively been advanced as the correct philosophical interpretation of the Buddha's understanding of reality.

How are modern Buddhists to make sense of this diversity and complexity? Even though the content of Enlightenment can never be adequately put into words, we surely need some understanding of it. Since we do not yet know the true nature of reality by direct experience, we need a way of at least thinking about it that will help us to gain it for ourselves. We need some philosophical perspective that gives conceptual expression to the Buddha's wordless understanding. From that perspective, we may recognise and test ethical and psychological teachings. But which of the many philosophical perspectives of historical Buddhism is the modern Buddhist to adopt? Should we, with the Sarvāstivādins, hold to the reality of the *dharmas*, the ultimate 'atomic' units out of which the entire universe is constructed? Should we, with the Mādhyamikas, consider those *dharmas* to be *śūnya* or 'void'? Is the 'mutual interpenetration' of all phenomena, of the Chinese Hua-yen School, the ultimate Buddhist perspective? How are these positions to be related to each other and what bearing do they have on the practice of the Dharma today?

From his first encounter with the Dharma, Sangharakshita wrestled with these problems, reading and reflecting on the metaphysical and philosophical implications of the Buddha's teaching. Indeed, just a year or so after discovering that he was a Buddhist, he submitted an article on the subject to *Buddhism in England*. The article was too long for publication and has now been lost. While he was wandering in South India he read more widely and contemplated more deeply yet. The first fruits of his thinking appear in an important article, 'Philosophy and Religion in Original and Developed Buddhism'.[63] He wrote this in 1949 at the age of twenty-four, while he was staying with his teacher, Jagdish Kashyap. The understanding expressed in this paper has provided the foundation for all his further thinking and teaching. He has seen no reason to modify what he then wrote, his later writings merely explaining more fully and expressing more elegantly the substance of that earlier interpretation.

His starting point was the realisation that the doctrine of *pratītya-samut-pāda* (Pali, *paṭicca-samuppāda*) or 'conditioned co-production' (sometimes translated as 'dependent arising' or 'universal conditionality') is the primary conceptual expression of the Buddha's Enlightenment.

> That this doctrine is nothing but the conceptualized formulation of the Buddha's supreme spiritual experience and that it may therefore be

regarded as His view of existence as a whole becomes clear when we consider that it was just this doctrine that He debated within Himself whether to make known to the world or not immediately after His Enlightenment.[64]

A text in what is considered one of the oldest strata of the Pali Canon shows the Buddha, at this moment, reflecting to himself:

> I have penetrated this deep truth, which is difficult to perceive, difficult to understand, peace-giving, sublime, which transcends all thought, deeply significant, which only the wise can grasp. Man moves in an earthly sphere, in an earthly sphere he has his place and finds his enjoyment. For man, who moves in an earthly sphere, and has his place and finds his enjoyment in an earthly sphere, it will be very difficult to grasp this matter, the law of causality [i.e. *pratītya-samutpāda*], the chain of causes and effects.[65]

Put briefly, the doctrine of conditioned co-production teaches that all phenomena arise in dependence on conditions. Each aspect of our experience has arisen out of a complex of conditions and will pass away when they cease to be. Meanwhile, it will itself be among the conditions out of which some future phenomena will arise. Thus a plant arises from a seed and itself provides the seeds from which new plants grow. There is nothing fixed and unchanging in our experience. The seed is just a stage on the way to the plant: the plant is but a step towards a new seed. There is simply a flow of dependently arising conditions. Nothing escapes this law: the whole of reality is one vast web of conditions, one process of becoming. The principle of conditioned co-production is summed up in the classic formula found throughout the Pali Canon and venerated in one form or another by Buddhists of all schools:

> This being, that becomes, from the arising of this, that arises; this not becoming, that does not become; from the ceasing of this, that ceases.[66]

While this formula may appear at first sight to be a quasi-scientific theorem, rationally deduced, it must be emphasised that it is the conceptual expression of *transcendental* insight.

> We must clearly understand that this insight is a purely spiritual attainment, and that it has nothing to do with any kind of conceptual construction. Though described by the Buddha in terms comprehensible to the intellect, it would be a mistake of the most disastrous kind to imagine that it was even remotely akin to the intellectual understanding of phenomena possessed, for example, by students of physical science. Such descriptions [i.e. the Buddha's doctrinal formulae] are symbolical merely, reflecting, as though through darkness well-nigh impenetrable, only a faint glimmer of the infinite light of his realization.[67]

The teaching of conditioned co-production is the Buddha's attempt to put into words his direct experience of the nature of things. We thus have a kind of descent. First, there is the Buddha's purely transcendental, supra-conceptual insight. Then there is the general formula, quoted above, which 'was an attempt to formulate that insight in intellectual terms'.[68] It takes the form of a universal law, applicable equally to all phenomena. Finally, that general formula is applied to various concrete situations. The Buddha particularly applies it to those experiences in human life which strike us most forcibly, for he knew that 'only by bringing his doctrine home to men's business and bosoms in this way could he make it comprehensible to them.'[69] The Four Noble Truths, one of the best-known basic teachings of Buddhism, is for instance the application of the general formula to human suffering. Indeed, it is precisely because suffering is such a universal and problematic experience that the Four Noble Truths have become so well known. In some cases, this *application* of conditioned co-production has become better known than the general formula itself, unfortunately even supplanting it sometimes. The purpose of this threefold descent is that we may

> pass from a knowledge of the conditioned nature of particular groups of
> phenomena to an understanding of conditionedness as a universal law,
> and from an understanding of this law to a realization of the
> supra-logical Truth which it represents.[70]

According to Sangharakshita, the full significance of this supremely important principle was gradually lost in the Hīnayāna schools. The loss came about because, in the first place, formulations of the principle came to be mistaken for the transcendental reality they attempted to convey: the letter came to be taken for the spirit. Intellectual formulations came to be regarded

> as constituting a fully adequate description of Reality.... Having
> identified the Truth with its conceptual formulations, it was not long
> before the Hīnayānists took the next step of equating the conceptual
> formulations of Truth with their verbal expressions and, after the oral
> tradition had been committed to writing,... with the very letters of the
> written text.[71]

In this way they mistook 'rational comprehension of the Doctrine for its actual realization'.[72]

But, more seriously, conditioned co-production gradually became identified exclusively with but one side of reality—with everything that spiritual life was lived to escape. It therefore ceased to be an adequate expression of the Buddha's insight into the nature of existence since it did not comprehend the other side of reality—everything that spiritual life was lived to attain. This had important methodological implications. It led to the Buddhist path being seen in predominantly negative terms. Spiritual life was increasingly thought of as getting rid of greed, hatred, and delusion, rather than as developing contentment, love, and wisdom. To understand this better, we must explore a little basic doctrine.

Buddhism makes a crucial distinction between *saṁsāra*, the 'faring on' in an endless succession of rebirths, and *nirvāṇa*, the 'blowing out' of the fires of greed, hatred, and delusion that consume the human heart. *Saṁsāra* is the futile and painful life of the worldling. *Nirvāṇa* is the peace and bliss experienced by the Buddha. The spiritual life is lived to escape from *saṁsāra* and to attain *nirvāṇa*. Gradually, conditioned co-production came to be identified exclusively with *saṁsāra*; *nirvāṇa* was therefore equated merely with its cessation. Spiritual life itself was simply seen as the ending of conditioned co-production. This came about because of the way in which some of the best-known applications of the principle of conditioned co-production had been handed down in tradition.

One of the most important and well-known of such formulae, the twelve *nidānas* or links, shows us how ignorance and craving drive the human being round and round the wheel of birth and death.[73] We see a sequence of twelve conditions, each arising in dependence on the preceding, each a link in the endless chain of *saṁsāra*. We see how, in dependence on ignorance, arise our *saṁskāras*, our *karmic* activity or habitual tendencies. Those tendencies lead us to be reborn in accordance with our past deeds: they shape for us a psychophysical organism, in contact with the external world. Contact brings feelings, pleasurable or painful. We start to crave the pleasurable or to hate the painful and so are led into a new cycle of birth and death. In the canonical sources, the twelve links are enumerated first in the order of their arising:

> In dependence on ignorance arise the *karmic* impulses, in dependence on the *karmic* impulses arises consciousness, in dependence on consciousness arises the psychophysical organism, in dependence on the psychophysical organism arise the six sense spheres, in dependence on the six sense spheres arises sense contact, in dependence on contact arises feeling, in dependence on feeling arises craving, in dependence on craving arises grasping, in dependence on grasping arises becoming, in dependence on becoming arises birth, and in dependence on birth arise old age and death, pain and suffering, grief, lamentation, and despair.[74]

The Buddha then enumerates the *nidānas* in the opposite order, in the sequence of their ceasing: with the ceasing of birth follows the ceasing of old age and death, with the ceasing of becoming follows the ceasing of birth, and so on down to, with the ceasing of ignorance follows the ceasing of the karmic impulses.

Ordering the links by the sequence in which they arise demonstrates the way *saṁsāra* works. It shows how, through spiritual blindness and escapist longing, we entangle ourselves in the endless cycles of rebirth, with their inevitable accompaniment of frustration and suffering. Escape from *saṁsāra*, in other words the movement to *nirvāṇa*, is shown by ordering the links according to the sequence in which they cease. We gradually undo the conditions by which we have created that frustration and suffering. In this way, conditioned co-production appears only to apply within *saṁsāra*. *Nirvāṇa* is not shown as also being governed by the principle of conditioned co-production; *nirvāṇa* appears merely to be the cessation of conditioned co-production. *Nirvāṇa* thus came to be spoken of in purely negative terms as a mere absence or cessation of the *saṁsāra*. This not only distorted the original symmetry of the Buddha's teaching, as we shall see, but also presented the end towards which all Buddhists are supposed to be working as a mere negation—an image hardly attractive to any healthy mind.

Sangharakshita resolved the problem with the help of the works of two modern Buddhist scholars: Mrs Caroline Rhys-Davids and Dr Beni Madhab Barua. Mrs Rhys-Davids, the wife of the distinguished founder of the Pali Text Society Dr T.W. Rhys-Davids, was a noted Pali scholar in her own right, but she brought somewhat greater feeling and imagination to her studies than did her more famous husband. In fact, some might say she sometimes brought rather too much imagination to her work, for she arrived at some very eccentric readings. Nonetheless she had some interesting and useful insights, one in particular having an important effect on Sangharakshita. She sensed in the Pali Canon, behind what she called the 'monkishness' of some of the texts, a vital spiritual message that was supremely positive, calling mankind to '"become" in a More towards a Most'.[75] She particularly believed that the preponderance of descriptions of the path and goal in negative terms did not represent the Buddha's personal teaching. She drew attention to an important passage in the Canon whose significance had previously been overlooked. The Buddha speaks, in this text, of a sequence of positive *nidānas*, leading up towards Enlightenment, balancing the sequence we have already examined.[76]

The Buddha enumerates this positive series of *nidānas* as arising directly out of the previous series of links. The former series is given in exactly the same order, except that the last *nidāna*, 'old age and death', is referred to by the compendious term 'suffering'. In the new series, in dependence on suffering, as the last *nidāna* of the old series, arises faith; in dependence on faith arises joy; then arise, each in dependence on the preceding, rapture, serenity, bliss, concentration, knowledge and vision of things as they really are, withdrawal, passionlessness, liberation, and knowledge of the destruction of the poisons—this being equivalent to Enlightenment or *nirvāṇa*. Sangharakshita has termed this latter sequence the 'twelve positive *nidānas*', while the former he refers to as the 'twelve cyclic *nidānas*'. The cyclic *nidānas* here show the way in which we become enmeshed in *saṃsāra*. The twelve positive *nidānas* demonstrate the way we move towards *nirvāṇa*. *Nirvāṇa* is thus not a mere eradication of *saṃsāra*, but has a definite positive character of its own. The important outcome of the rediscovery of this teaching is that the full significance of conditioned co-production is restored. *Nirvāṇa* too arises in dependence on a sequence of conditions.

Dr Barua came to the same conclusions, albeit from a somewhat different, more philosophical, point of view.[77] He too noted that in the modern Theravāda tradition, the last remnant of the historical Hīnayāna schools, conditioned co-production was confined to *saṃsāra*. He rightly insisted that, if the principle of conditioned co-production is the Buddha's all-inclusive formulation of reality, it must comprehend both *saṃsāra* and *nirvāṇa*, since by definition reality must include everything. Dr Barua demonstrated that the formulation is indeed inclusive of both. He referred to a passage in the Pali Canon in which the *bhikkhunī* Dhammadinna gives examples of two different kinds of conditioned relationship.[78]

In the first, the conditioning factor and what it conditions are both on the same level. There is simply an oscillation backward and forward between them: pleasure gives way to pain, which gives way to pleasure again. In the other, what is conditioned is at a higher level than the factor from which it arises. Here there is movement in progressive order, each condition giving rise to a higher kind: ignorance gives rise to knowledge, which gives rise to freedom, which gives rise to *nirvāṇa*. There is, in other words, a positive or progressive series of conditions, similar to the twelve positive *nidānas*. When Dhammadinna's words are reported to the Buddha, he fully endorses her exposition, saying that he would have spoken just as she had done. With some light from Buddhaghosha, the great fifth century CE Theravāda commentator on the Pali Canon, Dr Barua showed that Dhammadinna was illustrating two trends within conditioned co-production. The trend that consists in an oscillation between two conditions on the same level pertains to the 'world' or *saṃsāra*. The trend in which there is a progression from a lower condition to a higher pertains to *nirvāṇa*. Conditioned co-production is therefore an all-inclusive formulation of reality since both the *saṃsāric* and the *nirvāṇic* trends are contained within the one principle of dependent arising.

Thus, Sangharakshita arrived at 'a fairly complete account of the conceptual content of the Buddha's realization according to the oldest records available'. So important is this account for his later teaching that it is worth quoting one rendition of it in full.

> Reality being ineffable, positive and negative definitions are equally out of place. By following a Middle Path between affirmation and negation the Buddha's insight may, however, be formulated as the principle of universal conditionality, *pratītya-samutpāda*, or conditioned co-production. This doctrine is an all-inclusive Reality, or formulation of Reality, within which are included two trends or orders of things, one cyclic between opposites, the other progressive between factors which mutually complement and augment each other. The second trend is not merely the negative counterpart of the first, but possesses a positive character of its own. Upon this second trend the spiritual life is based. In relation to the first trend Nirvāṇa may be described only negatively, in terms of cessation; from the viewpoint of the world it will inevitably appear as a purely transcendental and, as it were, 'static' state. In relation to the second trend Nirvāṇa may be described as the farthest discernible point of the increasingly positive and progressive series of reactions away from the Saṃsāra; here it appears as 'dynamic' rather than static, the archetype of time rather than space. The advantages of this binocular view of Reality are enormous. Instead of being a mere defecation of things evil the spiritual life becomes an enriching assimilation of ever greater and greater goods. The *via affirmativa* is no less valid an approach to the goal than the *via negativa*.[79]

To sum up: reality is *pratītya-samutpāda*, a dependent arising. It is one vast process of becoming, in which there are no fixed or stable entities. Everything is constantly changing, giving rise to new things. Within this process of becoming we can see two different ways in which one thing arises from another. One factor arises from the other either on the same level or on a new and higher level. In nature we see the procession of the seasons, which follow one on the other in never-ending cycles. Most of our experience is of this kind: an oscillation between factors on one level. Spiritual life, however, consists in the development of ever higher states, one above the other. Through this positive sequence we climb towards *nirvāṇa*.

With the help of Mrs Rhys-Davids and Dr Barua, Sangharakshita rediscovered for himself the all-inclusive nature of conditioned co-production as the Buddha's formulation of reality. Conditioned co-production is, he realised, the unifying metaphysical teaching of Buddhism. It is 'the historical and logical basis of all later developments in Buddhist philosophy'.[80] The Mahāyāna, inheriting the Hīnayāna's restricted understanding of *pratītya samutpāda*, made up for the loss of a complete vision of reality in different, more metaphysically elaborate ways. New metaphysical doctrines were developed not only to counteract previous degenerations, but also 'as a result of the inherent urge of the Dharma towards perfect unfoldment'.[81] We will briefly examine one such unfoldment from its 'historical and logical basis', as an example of the process Sangharakshita saw underlying the development of Buddhist metaphysics in general.

The Mahāyāna developed the key concept of *śūnyatā*, literally 'emptiness', as a comprehensive expression for the nature of reality. *Saṃsāra* can be described as *śūnya* or empty:

> Phenomena are dependent for their existence upon causes and
> conditions. Being thus dependent they are devoid of independent
> selfhood. Consequently they are said to be *śūnya* or empty.[82]

So can *nirvāṇa*:

> This *śūnyatā* or emptiness of phenomena coincides with the reality
> indicated by the term Nirvāṇa; for the attainment of Nirvāṇa depends
> upon the realization of the conditionality of all phenomena.[83]

This can also be seen from another point of view:

> Nirvāṇa, being transcendent to all the categories of thought, is also
> *śūnya*, or rather it is *śūnyatā* or emptiness itself.[84]

The *śūnyatā* or emptiness of both *saṃsāra* and *nirvāṇa* are insights integral to the original teachings of Buddhism. The Mahāyāna, however, put the emptiness of *saṃsāra* and of *nirvāṇa* together, saying

> The emptiness of phenomena must coincide with the emptiness of
> Nirvāṇa, so that in reality the universe [is] not different from the
> Absolute.[85]

Thus, from the basic metaphysical principle of conditioned co-production, the Mahāyāna arrived at a new term, *śūnyatā*, expressing the meaning of that principle in a new way. In particular, this concept overcame the dualistic perspective that developed into the Hīnayāna, comprehending *saṃsāra* and *nirvāṇa* in one reality. Naturally, terms like *śūnyatā* or 'emptiness' or 'the Absolute' should not be reified. Such concepts can also be deconstructed: they themselves are *śūnya* and must not be taken as referring to a literally existing entity.

Over the centuries, other schools further elaborated this same basic principle. They talked of the all-inclusive reality, described by the Buddha as *pratītya-samutpāda*, in several new ways. All these metaphysical elaborations can, however, be traced back to that original principle of conditioned co-production.

> This testifies to the continuity and fundamental unity of all schools of Buddhist philosophy. The differences between them are to a large extent differences of method and approach rather than differences of belief. Only in the light of this conviction is it possible to regard the development of Buddhist philosophy as an intelligible process of organic growth instead of as a bewildering succession of conflicting doctrines and mutually exclusive creeds.[86]

Buddhists today are the legatees of the entire Buddhist tradition. They must make sense of the twists and turns of Buddhist metaphysics if they are to use the riches of that tradition. The key to that understanding, according to Sangharakshita, lies in viewing all later developments as unfolding from the original teaching of conditioned co-production. Modern Buddhists are facing very new cultural circumstances which require a new response from the Buddhist tradition. Sangharakshita believes they must start their thinking about the nature of reality where Buddhist philosophy began, with conditioned co-production, rather than with any of the developments that historically and logically derive from it. Otherwise, they will close themselves off from other aspects of the tradition and they may overlook the Buddha's simple, clear message in the complexities of dialectically unfolded ideas. Based on that simple message, they can then elaborate their own metaphysics, according to their own spiritual needs and in relation to the culture that surrounds them. No doubt, they will also draw on later developments for further inspiration.

Perhaps one of the most important aspects of Sangharakshita's reassertion of the all-inclusive nature of the principle of conditioned co-production is that it presents the spiritual path in positive terms. Spiritual life can be seen as a series of progressive steps rather than as a sequence of ever greater negations. This positive presentation has very great methodological significance. Sangharakshita has often pointed out that

> For most of us the central problem of spiritual life is to find emotional equivalents for our intellectual understanding.[87]

If our emotions are not engaged in our spiritual life, we will not make progress. A presentation in terms of the desirable end towards which we are moving is far more psychologically appealing for most people than one dwelling only on what we must leave behind. We will be much more likely to try to achieve the 'Great Bliss' or the 'Supreme Joy' than to 'extinguish the ego' or 'eradicate craving'.

This point became very clear to Sangharakshita on his return to Britain in 1964. He found that a negative presentation of the path and goal was common among British Buddhists. The emotional atmosphere was correspondingly dull, lifeless, and unwholesome. The Dharma was approached almost entirely in intellectual terms and little attention was given to the cultivation of the emotions. In his own teaching, he has recognised the need to bring the Dharma to life so that people can respond to it emotionally. He has recognised that the most important spiritual work lies in engaging the untamed depths of the mind. He has tried to find ways of presenting the Dharma that will inspire and enthuse people as well as make the path clear for them. In particular he has striven to find presentations of the teachings in terms that people can easily relate to.

### MIND—REACTIVE AND CREATIVE

Sangharakshita introduced some seminal new terms in a lecture, 'Mind—Reactive and Creative', which he gave at Reading University Buddhist Society in 1967, shortly after founding the FWBO. He used the new expressions 'reactive mind' and 'creative mind', to communicate the principle of conditioned co-production as presented by the Buddha and Dhammadinna in the texts cited above. These terms bring home the significance of the basic metaphysical teaching of Buddhism for the moment by moment living of the Buddhist life. They are now an important element in Sangharakshita's teaching. As he points out,

> Whilst these [reactive and creative] are not traditional Buddhist
> expressions, neither of them rendering any one technical term in any of
> the canonical languages, they seem to express very well the import of the
> Buddha's teaching.'[88]

In the teaching of 'Mind—Reactive and Creative', Sangharakshita applies the principle of conditioned co-production to the mind, because the mind is the methodological starting point. According to the Buddha, our actions stem from our minds and lead us either to suffering or to happiness. In the end it is our minds that we must transform through spiritual practice. Sangharakshita teaches that the mind can function in either a 'reactive' or a 'creative' way. The mind is functioning reactively when it is merely reactive to external stimuli, usually derived from the five senses. It is conditioned by external objects, automatic, mechanical and predictable, repetitive, programmed, and unaware. The creative mind, by contrast, is spontaneous, creating out of its own inner fullness and abundance. Even when there is an initial external stimulus it 'quickly transcends its original point of departure and starts functioning independently'.[89] It is responsive rather than reactive, melioristic, 'optimistic' in the deepest sense:

> The optimism of the creative mind persists despite unpleasant stimuli.…
> [It] loves where there is no reason to love, is happy where there is no
> reason for happiness, creates where there is no possibility of creativity,
> and in this way 'builds a heaven in hell's despair'.[90]

It is non-conditioned and free, ultimately being identical with the Enlightened mind itself. It is aware and therefore 'intensely and radiantly alive'.[91] The creative, it should be pointed out, is not here identified solely with the production of works of art. While the greatest art is the outpouring of the creative mind, the creative mind also manifests in human relationships, in meditation, and in any act that expresses an inner abundance rather than a mere reaction to external stimuli.

These two ways in which the mind functions, of course, are equivalent to the two trends within conditioned co-production. As we have seen, reality is nothing but becoming, a flow of conditions. Within that vast web of becoming there is a movement from one condition to the next, either by way of a reaction between opposites or by a progression from one factor to another that complements and augments it. The reactive mind exemplifies the reaction between opposites and the creative the progression.

Better to bring home these teachings to the imagination as well as to the reason, Sangharakshita has expressed them in two images. The reactive trend is cyclic, like a fixed wheel, turning and turning upon itself, without travelling in any direction. The creative is like a spiral, which rises higher and higher, each stage acting as the basis for a yet further one. The cyclic trend is particularly exemplified by the Tibetan Wheel of Life. This composite image starkly illustrates the rising and falling of beings, caught up in the reactive mode of conditionality, under the impulsion of their own greed, hatred, and delusion.

So far we have spoken mainly in terms of metaphysical theory, but that theory has immediate practical implications. Metaphysics must become spiritual practice. The task of spiritual life is to move from the wheel to the spiral. To begin with, both trends are present in our minds. Though the cyclic usually predominates at the outset, some creative impulses arise within us, at least from time to time. Developing mindfulness by means of the whole range of spiritual exercises, we gradually become more aware of what is happening in our minds. We become more aware of these two trends and begin to discriminate the reactive from the creative, the cyclic from the spiral. We gradually shift ourselves from the wheel to the spiral, from the reactive to the creative. We encourage the spiral trend to become ever more dominant within us. Enlightenment is the point at which the spiral trend has become completely triumphant. There is simply pure creativity, without any trace of reaction.

Even if Enlightenment is the point on the spiral at which all reactivity falls away, it is not the end of conditioned co-production. If conditioned co-production applies as much to *nirvāṇa* as to *saṁsāra*, then *nirvāṇa* itself must be conceived of in dynamic terms. *Nirvāṇa* too is a progression, albeit one we cannot possibly understand since it passes beyond the reach of our thinking and knowing. The twelve positive *nidānas* end with Knowledge of the Destruction of the Poisons only because we must stop somewhere. If we did not stop, we would have to enumerate an infinite progress of ever higher states. Enlightenment is, according to an image of Sangharakshita's, but the farthest point on our horizon, over which the Buddhas appear. As we approach nearer to that horizon, however, it recedes from us and the Buddhas appear over it in ever more subtle and glorious forms.

With this dynamic perspective, there is no danger of our seeing Enlightenment as a place we arrive at and settle down in—a kind of spiritual retirement home. We conceive of it as a way of being which, though immeasurably beyond our present experience, is connected to how we now are by a chain of ever more subtle states that imperceptibly merge into it. We also avoid the tendencies to ontological dualism in Hīnayāna metaphysics, which the Mahāyāna philosophers were very concerned to counteract. There are no really existent and independent states, *saṁsāra* and *nirvāṇa*. There is one process of becoming within which there are two trends, the *saṁsāric* and the *nirvāṇic*. Sangharakshita has even said that we should perhaps talk, not of achieving *nirvāṇa*, but of *nirvāṇising*— *nirvāṇising*, one might say, rather than *saṁsārising*.

Sangharakshita considers this dynamic conception of the path and goal far more spiritually efficacious than a static model. If spiritual life is a becoming at higher and higher levels, then we are confronted with the necessity of transforming ourselves now. *Nirvāṇa*, so to speak, may begin in our very next action, in so far as we act creatively rather than reactively. If, on the other hand, we speak of *nirvāṇa* as a place or possession, we are led to think of ourselves getting to it or possessing it without having changed at all; *nirvāṇa* becomes something we are going to add on to ourselves as we now are. Sangharakshita's sensitivity to the effects of these basic models of spiritual life is very characteristic. In his treatment of metaphysical issues, indeed of all subjects, he shows a vivid awareness of the nature of language and its effects upon us. In this respect, Sangharakshita follows in the best Buddhist traditions, for instance of Nāgārjuna and the great Ch'an masters. He recognises that our words and thoughts are different from the things they refer to. Such an awareness is an important aspect of spiritual life.

> Effectively to distinguish between thoughts and things, between the concepts which merely indicate realities and those realities themselves, is an art belonging to a highly advanced stage of philosophical discipline and spiritual culture.[92]

He is constantly pointing out the confusion that arises if we do not understand what we are doing with our words and concepts. In many discussions and seminars he has pointed out the literalism in most people's thinking and their failure really to look at what they mean.

> Most of the time we are actually misled by words. We use words in a quite satisfactory way for ordinary practical purposes: for instance, when I say 'Please pass the salt.' But when we start applying that same language to questions of what we call reality, then we come up against all sorts of difficulties. So we have to be aware of the limitations of language and of what we are trying to do with language when we discuss philosophical questions. Some, at least, of those questions can be reduced simply to semantic difficulties.[93]

The language we use to discuss spiritual life and experience ultimately derives from our sense experience. We have to appreciate that we are primarily using metaphors.

> All the words and expressions that we use are derived from our experience through our senses within space and time. But we apply that empirically derived language to non-empirical matters. For instance, we talk of one idea 'depending on' another. 'Depending' means 'hanging from'. How can an idea hang from another idea? Clearly you can't take the expression 'depending' literally. You don't mean the same as when you speak of one link of a chain depending on another. You can only take it poetically, and try to grasp, in a sense, intuitively what is meant when one speaks of one idea depending on another idea.[94]

When we speak of things beyond the senses where space and time do not apply, we use metaphors drawn from our sensuous experience within space and time. Thus we speak of 'attaining *nirvāṇa*' or 'gaining Enlightenment' as if *nirvāṇa* and Enlightenment were things we could possess. Unless we are aware of the metaphorical nature of language, we

start to take our metaphors literally and fall into intellectual confusion—
and intellectual confusion may lead us spiritually astray. For instance, if
we think of Enlightenment as something we acquire, adding it on to
ourselves as we now are, we will probably fail to change ourselves in the
radical way necessary for Enlightenment to come about.

Sangharakshita considers that we must appreciate that when we talk
of spiritual, philosophical, or metaphysical issues we are really using
language poetically, not 'scientifically'.

> I plead for a greater, more vivid realization of the poetic nature of
> speech. I think this ought to be our approach to language all the time,
> because language, as applied to non-material realities, is essentially
> metaphorical, poetry rather than prose.[95]

He himself is a very precise and careful thinker, who understands well
the implications of what he is saying. It is a standing joke among his
disciples that it can be very hard to ask him a question, because he first
analyses the question itself, exposing all the assumptions buried in it.
This is no idle pedantry but the expression of his strong awareness of the
perils of sloppy thinking and careless talking. While he has spent considerable energy in setting out a clear rational basis for spiritual life, he
recognises the limitations of the merely rational. He considers poetry a
far more adequate medium for the communication of spiritual truth,
having even threatened at one time to speak only in verse!

## THE HIGHER EVOLUTION

All the metaphysical systems known in Buddhism are attempts to use
metaphors to communicate, poetically, something of the nature of reality.
They do so in the context of the unfolding tradition. As we have already
examined, previous degenerations are corrected and more of the implications of the Dharma are gradually revealed. At each stage, Buddhist
thinkers must use the language, ideas, and images of their times. Though
they use the language of their contemporaries, they are trying to give that
language new meaning to express their new and distinctive understanding. This is no easy task. On the one hand they must use terms that
others can relate to; on the other they must give those terms a quite new
meaning. Sangharakshita sees the Buddha himself as having engaged in
this process: for instance, he tried to give the term *brāhman*, meaning one
born into the priestly caste, the new meaning of one who had developed
spiritually by his own efforts—in this case the attempt did not work.[96]

We have already seen, in his teaching of 'Mind—Reactive and Creative', Sangharakshita himself trying to find ways of communicating conditioned co-production to his contemporaries. Shortly after his return to England, Sangharakshita began to use one of the most influential concepts of modern thought as a medium for the exposition of the Dharma.

> In 1964,… having spent twenty years in the East, I returned to England, and soon felt the need, purely as a 'skilful means' (*upāya-kauśalya*), of a principle sufficiently familiar to the modern mind not to require much explanation and capable, at the same time, of being generalized in such a way as to provide a medium for the exposition of Buddhism. One day, while preparing a lecture, it flashed on me that the concept of Evolution was such a principle. At once everything fell into place.[97]

Actually, he recently discovered in some old lecture notes that he first applied the concept of evolution to Buddhism in talks given in Kalimpong in 1950. However, it was not until 1966 that he began to develop the theme, in a talk, 'Evolution, Lower and Higher', given at the Hampstead Buddhist Vihara, as part of his series 'Introducing Buddhism'. In another series of talks given in 1969, entitled 'The Higher Evolution of Man', he elaborated on the idea in greater detail.

Sangharakshita points out that, though there is no precise equivalent to this modern concept of 'evolution' among the technical terms of any Buddhist canonical language, words meaning 'growth' and 'increase' are common: for instance, the term *bhāvanā*, literally 'making to become', is used throughout the Pali texts in the sense of 'cultivation' or 'development'. *Images* of growth are also often found in the scriptures of all schools. In one of the best-known passages in the Pali Canon, the Buddha is shown using such an image, shortly after his Enlightenment. Considering the truth he has penetrated too difficult for others to comprehend, his 'mind inclined to little effort and not to teaching', he sees as in a vision all beings in their different conditions:

> Just as in a pond of blue, red, or white lotuses, some lotuses are born in the water, grow in the water, and do not rise above the water but thrive while completely immersed; some others are born and grow in the water, but reach the surface of the water; others again are born and grow in the water, and stand up, rising out of the water, undefiled by it.
>
> Even so, the Blessed One, surveying the world with the eye of an awakened one, saw beings with little dust in their eyes, with much dust in their eyes, with acute faculties, with dull faculties, of good dispositions, and of bad dispositions.[98]

Essentially, he realises that beings can grow and that some are mature enough to hear his message. This same theme of growth also appears in the famous 'Parable of the Rain Cloud', in the fifth chapter of the *White*

*Lotus Sūtra.* Just as a great rain cloud pours down its rain impartially on all the many kinds of vegetation, so, we are told, the Buddha preaches the Dharma to all beings equally, so that they all grow and flourish, each according to its own nature. We also see this principle of evolution in that progressive series to which Mrs Rhys-Davids drew attention. In many other formulations in all traditions of Buddhism, the path is clearly shown as an evolution or development.

Sangharakshita therefore considers his use of the concept of evolution to be completely in keeping with the spirit of the Dharma. He believes that the concept of evolution in many ways expresses the spiral mode of conditioned co-production better than any of the traditional words. The Buddha himself was not able to use such a term.

> We have, as the Buddha did not have, that evolutionary background, derived from scientific thinking in the last century, that gives us a very helpful vocabulary and terminology for talking about the spiritual life. The idea or concept of evolution, however loosely understood, is very much in the air. People know what you're talking about, or at least they have a rough idea. If that language of evolution had been around in the Buddha's day, the Buddha would probably have seized upon it most gratefully.[99]

We have already seen that there are two trends within the total process of becoming that is reality: one cyclic or reactive and the other spiral or creative. Growth is discernible in both these trends. In the cyclic kind of conditionality, growth is balanced by decay, as when a plant grows from a seed to a flower and then dies. The cyclic trend is exemplified on a much vaster scale by the entire grand sweep of the organic evolution of species, from the tiniest single-celled organism through to the higher primates and man. There is a movement from lower to higher life-forms, higher in the sense that they are more complex organisms, capable of supporting a more sophisticated sensory awareness. That evolution is itself part of a cycle: sooner or later a species will decay and disappear when it can no longer adapt to a changing environment. In the spiral kind of conditionality, however, there is continuous development from the first stirrings of spiritual commitment through to Enlightenment itself and beyond. Although downward movement on the spiral is possible, it happens not inevitably as in the cyclic process, but only when the requisite efforts are not sustained.

We can, then, speak of evolution running through both processes: from the humblest amoeba up to the self-conscious human being, and from that human to the superhumanity of the Buddha. However, it is a very different kind of evolution in each case. Sangharakshita refers to the cyclic kind as the Lower Evolution and to the Spiral as the Higher. The Lower is evolution as charted by the physical and life sciences. It is not a self-conscious process: no organism decides to evolve. It is not an evolution of individuals, for the individual organism simply lives a cycle of growth and decay. Through small mutations taking place amongst vast numbers of organisms over enormous periods of time, whole species evolve. The organisms of which the species consists become more complex, with more sophisticated sensory awareness.

The Lower Evolution, as we know it on this planet, culminates in the individual human being who stands on the threshold of the Higher Evolution. Indeed, human beings are the culmination of the Lower Evolution precisely because they are capable of undertaking the Higher Evolution. However, unlike the Lower Evolution, the Higher does not just occur. The whole human race will not automatically evolve to higher levels, generation by generation, as some seem to think. What is the latest and most modern is certainly not necessarily the best and most evolved. The Higher Evolution has to be consciously undertaken by the individual and requires personal commitment and sustained effort. It is the individual who is the 'unit' of the Higher Evolution, the equivalent of the species in the Lower Evolution. Indeed, Sangharakshita has described the individual who has embarked upon the Higher Evolution as a species in himself. However, whereas it has taken hundreds of millions of years for the Lower Evolution to achieve humanity, Buddhism teaches that it is possible for the individual human to traverse the whole Higher Evolution within the course of a single lifetime. The Higher Evolution is the Spiral; it is the unfoldment of the Creative Mind; it is the Buddhist path. Indeed, as Sangharakshita has said, Buddhism is the path of the Higher Evolution—'Buddhism, more than any other religion, [is] the leading historical embodiment of the principle of spiritual evolution'.[100]

The two halves of the total evolutionary process are not merely linked by humanity, which stands at the apex of the one and the threshold of the other. They are both essentially concerned with the same material. Both the Higher and the Lower Evolutions are at basis evolutions of consciousness. The Lower Evolution is an evolution within simple sense-consciousness. Sense-consciousness becomes more and more sophisticated until it is able to identify itself, to become self-conscious. This is the characteristic consciousness of the human state. The human being can identify himself, can acknowledge personal responsibility for his own future, and can form an aspiration to develop further as an individual. Self-awareness is, literally, crucial in the evolutionary process since it is at this point that the Higher Evolution begins. The self-aware individual can evolve his or her consciousness through many stages to transcendental consciousness and, finally, Enlightened consciousness itself—those steps and stages of evolving consciousness being charted in various ways in the Buddhist tradition. The great majority of human beings, however, never complete the promise of their own self-awareness, never, indeed, become fully self-aware.

In his lectures on this subject, Sangharakshita has examined many phenomena of human culture and history in the light of this evolutionary model. One of the key terms in his discussion of these matters is the 'group'—a term we shall be returning to in later chapters. Briefly, the group is the human social unit of the Lower Evolution. Sangharakshita uses the term 'the group' for the phenomenon in general, although the group as a whole is made up of many smaller groups: tribe and nation, class and caste, and especially the family, which is the most basic unit of the group. Most human beings immerse themselves in the group in one or more of its forms, living for its sake and its Lower Evolutionary ends: the survival and propagation of the species. Group members have no really independent life of their own, distinct from the group: their thoughts and views, their values and goals, are those of the group to which they belong. If the individual is to undertake the Higher Evolution, he must differentiate himself from the group in deepening self-awareness. Once individuals have begun to tread the path of the Higher Evolution they will eventually become what Sangharakshita has called 'true individuals', those within whom a higher or transcendental consciousness has arisen.

Sangharakshita offers principles for classifying religions and artistic endeavour according to whether they serve the Lower or the Higher Evolution. 'Ethnic religion' and 'folk art' are the productions of human beings who are still dominated by the Lower Evolution, and they serve the group within which they appear. Folk art, for instance, might extol the nation or tribe and incite enmity towards some other group. Ethnic religion similarly supports the group's values: blessing the family and its reproduction, even blessing troops before they go to war. 'Universal religion' and 'true art' are the creations of true individuals. In Sangharakshita's usage, 'universal religion' is not universal in the sense that it is the only true creed, which everyone should accept, as Christianity and Islam have so often presented themselves. A universal religion is one that all individuals can respond to because it is not limited to any particular group. It offers the individual the possibility of ascending the Higher Evolutionary path. Similarly, true art reflects the values of the true individual and of the Higher Evolution.

Though the Higher Evolution is undertaken by the individual and not by the group, it is not simply an egocentric individualism. It is not a wilful and egoistic assertion of independence from others or even indifference to them. Sangharakshita's conception of the true individual differs significantly in this respect from notions of individuality deriving from the Western Liberal and Romantic traditions. The Higher Evolution is a process of self-transcendence. The higher one mounts on the path, the less one looks at things from a selfish point of view and the more one enters into the sorrows and joys of others. Indeed a point comes when one ceases to make any distinction between one's own sorrows and joys and those of others. One simply responds to sorrow and joy, in whomever one finds them, with a heartfelt desire to alleviate the former and to promote the latter. The goal of the Higher Evolution is that transcendental consciousness in which all egoistic distinctions are dissolved and one recognises one's essential identity with all things.

The lone individual, treading the path of the Higher Evolution, feels an increasing solidarity with all life, but especially feels a strong affinity with others who tread the path. Thus the social context for the individual on the path of the Higher Evolution, replacing the Lower Evolutionary species or group, is the spiritual community, made up of those individuals who have dedicated themselves to the path. They join in a harmony and fellowship that become deeper and ever deeper as they move upwards on the spiral of evolution.

Sangharakshita's use of the concept of evolution provides a link between the most basic metaphysical formulation of the Buddha's insight and modern ideas. He has been able to use concepts new to Buddhism because he has rediscovered the full significance of conditioned co-production as the Buddha's earliest expression of his Enlightened understanding. Because he has seen what the essence of the Buddha's understanding is in the Buddha's own terms, he has been able to translate it into other, more current concepts.

His rediscovery of the comprehensiveness of conditioned co-production has also enabled him to see the *metaphysical unity* of Buddhism. Conditioned co-production is, he has seen, the historical and logical basis for all later developments in Buddhist metaphysics and therefore provides their principle of unity. In a sense, that understanding is the historical and logical starting point for the development of

Sangharakshita's own teaching. Understanding of the true meaning of conditioned co-production came early to Sangharakshita, for since writing in 1949 his article 'Philosophy and Religion in Original and Developed Buddhism', he has not changed his views on the matter. He has merely refined and elaborated its expression. Other aspects of his present teaching have taken longer to fall into place—and have done so essentially on the basis of his understanding of conditioned co-production.

*Chapter Four*

# GOING FOR REFUGE

*We cry that we are weak although*
*We will not stir our secret wings;*
*The world is dark—because we are*
*Blind to the starriness of things.*

*We pluck our rainbow-tinted plumes*
*And with their heaven-born beauty try*
*To fledge nocturnal shafts, and then*
*Complain 'Alas! we cannot fly!'*

*We mutter 'All is dust' or else*
*With mocking words accost the wise:*
*'Show us the sun which shines beyond*
*The Veil'—and then we close our eyes.*

*To powers above and powers beneath*
*In quest of Truth men sue for aid,*
*Who stand athwart the Light and fear*
*The shadow that themselves have made.*

*Oh cry no more that you are weak*
*But stir and spread your secret wings,*
*And say 'The world is bright, because*
*We glimpse the starriness of things.'*

*Soar with your rainbow plumes and reach*
*That near-far land where all are one,*
*Where Beauty's face is aye unveiled*
*And every star shall be a sun.*[101]

IN THE PREVIOUS CHAPTERS, we have examined Sangharakshita's views on the unity of Buddhism. Its transcendental unity is to be found in Enlightenment, the spiritual experience of the Buddha, which all sincere Buddhists are striving to recapitulate for themselves. All the varied Buddhist practices, teachings, and institutions are united methodologically in aiding the individual in his or her quest for Enlightenment. Historically, all the different schools are united in that they emanate from a common source, the Enlightened experience of the Buddha, Gautama Śākyamuni. They are further united in the acceptance of a body of doctrine—what Sangharakshita calls 'Basic Buddhism'—of which all later teachings, however divergent, are further explorations and elaborations. Finally, we have seen that the various interpretations of reality, arrived at in the long and complex history of Buddhist philosophy, are all derived, historically and logically, from the Buddha's principle of conditioned co-production. This provides the metaphysical unity of Buddhism.

We have thus sketched in the broad outlines of Sangharakshita's integral vision of Buddhism. We have also seen the Buddhist path in terms of evolution, offering another unifying perspective, this time from outside traditional terminology, using a key concept in modern thought. But in examining Sangharakshita's ideas on the unity of Buddhism we have left one area of enquiry yet unattempted: what does being a Buddhist actually consist in?

As we have seen, the spiritual life is an active one, a struggle to move upwards as an individual on the path of the Higher Evolution. One is not a Buddhist simply because one passively accepts the label 'Buddhist'. So, what is it to be a Buddhist? What does a Buddhist do that makes him or her a Buddhist? Here Sangharakshita discovered the cornerstone of his entire thought. He saw that it is in the characteristic act of a Buddhist that all other principles of unity find their expression—even, one might say, find their unity. We must finally embody what we believe and how we understand the world *in what we actually do*. Vision must eventually be transformed into living practice. As he gradually came to realise, it is Going for Refuge to the Buddha, Dharma, and Sangha that is 'the central and definitive Act of the Buddhist life' and 'the unifying principle, therefore, of Buddhism itself'.[102]

So central to Sangharakshita's thought is this single idea that in 1988 he wrote an extensive paper on the subject: *The History of My Going for Refuge*. In this work he charted his progress to the full realisation of its significance, weaving together innumerable threads of Buddhist doctrine

and tradition with his own unfolding spiritual experience. He had, from
the beginning, appreciated that the act of Going for Refuge signified
formal conversion to Buddhism. However, it took him many years to see
that act in its full breadth and depth.

> I did not appreciate how absolutely central the act of Going for Refuge
> really was, its centrality having been obscured for me by the Theravāda's
> one-sided emphasis on the monastic life, as well as by the blindly
> mechanical way in which the lay followers of the Theravāda habitually
> repeated the Refuge-going formula on ceremonial occasions.[103]

It is not only in the Theravāda that the full significance of Going for
Refuge has been lost. All Buddhist traditions have increasingly devalued
it. Each school has, for its own distinctive historical and doctrinal reasons,
begun to speak of the fundamental Buddhist act in other terms. Most
attach therefore little more than ceremonial significance to Going for
Refuge.

> So far as I can remember, in the course of my whole stay in India no one
> ever stressed to me the importance of Going for Refuge. Some people
> were very particular about the correct pronunciation of the Pali Refuge
> formula, but they paid no attention to what the words actually meant.
> Therefore I had to discover the significance of the Going for Refuge for
> myself.[104]

Gradually, Sangharakshita came to see how fundamental the act of Going
for Refuge is to Buddhism. It is Going for Refuge to the Three Jewels that
constitutes one's membership of the spiritual community.

> This, I realized, is how one could know who was a Buddhist. This was
> the criterion. A Buddhist is one who goes for Refuge in response to the
> Buddha and his teaching. A Buddhist is one who commits himself. He
> gives himself to the Three Jewels. This was the criterion in the Buddha's
> day and remains the criterion today.[105]

We will not now trace Sangharakshita's growing awareness of the full
implications of Going for Refuge, since we have his own account of it.
We will simply examine his mature idea of the primacy of Going for
Refuge to the Three Jewels of the Buddha, Dharma, and Sangha. When
reading his earlier works, the student of his writings should, however,
remember his later assertion of the axial position of Going for Refuge.

Going for refuge to something implies that one has confidence in it and
that one considers it a source of security and protection. It also implies
that one is seeking refuge from something that makes one feel insecure
and in need of protection. The insecurity felt here is not, of course, either
material or psychological—or rather, is not only material or psychological: it is existential. From all the deep uncertainties that surround our

lives, we fly for protection, we go for refuge, to whatever we think will keep us safe, whether it be material wealth, family and sex, or religion and philosophy. Most of what we cling to cannot give us real protection. Either it is insubstantial and delusive or else it is as subject to the variability of fortune as we are. As the Buddha says in the *Dhammapada*:

> Many people, out of fear, flee for refuge to [sacred] hills, woods, groves, trees, and shrines. In reality this is not a safe refuge. In reality this is not the best refuge. Fleeing to such a refuge one is not released from all suffering.[106]

The Buddha, Dharma, and Sangha, being transcendental ideals beyond all vicissitudes and yet attainable by each and every individual, are genuine sources of security. They bring us security not by hiding us from reality but by helping us to face up to it fully. Relying on them, we will achieve a state of consciousness in which none of the difficulties and dangers of life, on whatever level, can touch us any more. We will not need protection. We will be our own source of security, our own refuge.

> He who goes for refuge to the Enlightened One, to the Truth, and to the Spiritual Community,... [for him] this is a safe refuge, [for him] this is the best refuge. Going to such a refuge one is released from all suffering.[107]

The Buddha, Dharma, and Sangha, known collectively as the Three Jewels, are pivotal to Buddhism—'Indeed, the Three Jewels are Buddhism'.[108] The Buddha is not only the teacher from whom the Buddhist tradition stems, but also represents Enlightenment as a universal ideal and as ultimate reality. He is thus the goal of spiritual life, as well as the exemplar who has achieved that goal.

> When we Go for Refuge to the Buddha, we Go for Refuge to him as the living embodiment of a spiritual Ideal which is *a spiritual Ideal for us*, i.e. a spiritual Ideal that we can actually realize. When we Go for Refuge to the Buddha it is as though we say, '*That* is what I want to be. *That* is what I want to attain'.[109]

The Dharma is both all those teachings that lead to Enlightenment, and the principle of Truth itself, beyond all words, to which the doctrines of Buddhism point. It is both the communication of the Buddha's experience and the content of it. The Dharma can also be considered as the path or way, leading from our own present ignorance and suffering to the sublime wisdom and unalloyed bliss of Enlightenment. The Dharma is therefore the Higher Evolution of the individual.

> In Going for Refuge to the Dharma, we commit ourselves to the Path of the Higher Evolution. We commit ourselves to whatever helps us

develop spiritually—to whatever helps us to grow into Enlightenment, into Buddhahood.[110]

The sangha or spiritual community is, at its highest level, the *ārya-saṅgha*, the fellowship of all those who have attained direct realisation of the Dharma.

> In the case of the *Āryasaṅgha*, Going for Refuge to the Sangha means opening ourselves to the spiritual influence of the sublime beings of whom it consists. It means learning from them, being inspired by them, reverencing them.[111]

More broadly, the sangha consists of everyone who goes for Refuge to the Three Jewels.

> In the case of the Sangha in the more ordinary sense, that of the community of all Buddhists, [Going for Refuge] means enjoying spiritual fellowship with one another and helping one another on the Path.[112]

The expression 'Going for Refuge' is commonly found in that core of scriptural material accepted by all schools, describing the life and teachings of the Buddha himself. The Buddha, as he wandered from place to place, would meet and get into conversation with many people.

> As the conversation deepens, the Buddha begins to speak from the depths of his spiritual experience. In other words, the Buddha expounds the Dharma: the Dharma emerges....
>
> The person to whom he was speaking would be absolutely astounded and overwhelmed. In some cases he might not be able to speak or do more than stammer a few incoherent words. Something had been revealed to him. Something had burst upon him that was above and beyond his ordinary understanding. For an instant, at least, he had glimpsed the Truth, and the experience had staggered him.[113]

The impact of the Buddha's words and presence would awaken the hearer to the true meaning of his life. He would give expression to his conviction that the Buddha was indeed the Enlightened One, that he did teach the way to Enlightenment, and that his community was a true spiritual fellowship. Initially this would be expressed in a spontaneous outpouring. But gradually it took a standard form, now known throughout the Buddhist world in various languages and here given in its Pali form:

> *Buddhaṁ Saraṇaṁ Gacchāmi*; To the Buddha for Refuge I go;
> *Dhammaṁ Saraṇaṁ Gacchāmi*; To the Dharma for Refuge I go;
> *Saṅghaṁ Saraṇaṁ Gacchāmi*; To the Sangha for Refuge I go.

For all that these glimpses of conversion in the early Buddhist community are recounted in stock phrases and formulae, one can yet sense the heartfelt urgency with which people uttered these words that marked the complete reorientation of their lives.

> The Going for Refuge represents your positive emotional reaction—in
> fact your total reaction and your total response—to the spiritual Ideal
> when that Ideal is revealed to your spiritual vision. Such is its appeal
> that you cannot but give yourself to it.[114]

Thus, Sangharakshita argues, in the Buddha's own time, one became
his follower by reciting the formula of Going for Refuge. Even to this day,
probably all Buddhists would acknowledge that formal conversion to
Buddhism consists in this recitation. Once one has accepted that the
Buddha, Dharma, and Sangha are one's true sources of refuge before all
others, then one is a Buddhist. However, in all extant Buddhist schools
the full significance of this act has been lost, and it has now become more
or less of a formality. In some 'Buddhist countries' virtually the entire
population will recite the formula when they go to temples, but few will
do so with much consciousness of what the words really mean.

> I had plenty of experience of this in India. I found, for instance,
> Sinhalese, and Thai, and Burmese, and Indian Buddhists reciting the
> Refuges and Precepts on all sorts of occasions: at big public meetings; at
> weddings; at funerals; when performing name-giving ceremonies for
> children. People recited the Refuges and Precepts, but nobody bothered
> about their significance. They recited the Refuges and Precepts just to
> show that they were 'good Buddhists', or respectable citizens. There was
> no question of the Refuge formula being regarded as an expression of
> commitment to the ideals of Buddhism. That is why I say that the Going
> for Refuge has been devalued—not to say degraded and debased.[115]

Since 'Going for Refuge' lost its significance as a way of expressing the
essential act of a Buddhist, some other way of speaking of it had to be
found. Various ways of talking about that central act therefore developed,
in the dialectical pattern we have already seen at work in other spheres.

> 'Going for Refuge' apparently had degenerated. So something new took
> its place: the 'arising of the *bodhicitta*'. Then on top of that there was
> 'initiation into the lower Tantras', then 'initiation into the higher Tantras'
> on top of that.[116]

In the Hīnayāna schools, in fact if not in theory, becoming a Buddhist was
increasingly identified with being a monk and following the monastic
code. Thus monastic ordination came to be seen as the principal act of a
Buddhist, as it still is in the Theravāda today. For the Mahāyāna, being a
Buddhist meant being a Bodhisattva, so the fundamental act was identified with taking the Bodhisattva vows. Tantric initiation was seen as the
central act in the Vajrayāna. Within these three broad movements there
were many particular emphases and approaches. For instance, in the
Mahāyāna Pure Land schools, spiritual life came to consist entirely in

reliance on the original vow of Amitābha. The central act was, therefore, identified with the recitation of Amitābha's name. Thus came about an alarming diversity of ways of referring to the most basic Buddhist act.

The Tibetan tradition accepts all three *yānas*, not as mutually exclusive alternatives but as successive phases of a single path. Going for Refuge, Bodhisattva ordination, and Tantric initiation are conceived of as successive acts. What being a Buddhist consists in therefore depends on the level one has reached on the path. While this has the merit of retaining some awareness of the meaning of Going for Refuge, it relegates it to a limited, preliminary stage and therefore fails to acknowledge its full depth. As we saw in the previous chapter, the *triyāna* structure also preserves the myth of the Buddha having given further teachings to more highly developed individuals. This has little historical validity, being simply the way that later Buddhists corrected the degeneracy of the doctrines they inherited.

There is a further complication in the attempt to make sense of the various views on the fundamental Buddhist act. Sangharakshita considers that in each case there has been a tendency to formalism. Any act can be viewed in terms of its external expression or of the inner experience from which it flows. Inner and outer are but dimensions of a single whole yet, where the fundamental Buddhist act is concerned, there has been a constant tendency to detach the one from the other. The outer expression has become ever more of a formality and fails to be accompanied by the spiritual experience it originally expressed. We have already seen this process in the case of Going for Refuge. In the Buddha's own time, Going for Refuge represented a decisive inner reorientation in the direction of the Three Jewels. Increasingly, it simply came to signify that one was a member of the 'Buddhist' social group.

Sangharakshita sees similar formalism in all traditions. Becoming a monk or nun originally gave expression to one's renunciation of all worldly ties and aspirations. However, it has increasingly come to mean, in large areas of the Buddhist world, merely the taking up of a new and venerated social status, with its own perks and privileges. Genuine inner renunciation has become detached from the outer act of becoming a monk—since the *bhikkhunī* or nun's ordination tradition has long since died out in most parts of the Buddhist world, this degeneration is not open to women! The Bodhisattva ordination originally gave expression to the welling up of an overwhelming feeling of identity with all beings. This arising of the *bodhicitta* or 'Will to Enlightenment' leads one to dedicate one's life to the ultimate welfare of all. However, it has become more and more of a formality that people undertake simply as part of their general religious activities. In other words, Bodhisattva ordination has become detached from the actual 'arising of the *bodhicitta*'. Tantric initiation supposedly takes place at the highest reaches of the path and brings about a decisive imaginative connection with ultimate reality. But Tantric initiations have now become freely available and again are part of the ordinary religious life of the average Tibetan. Tantric initiation and the actual meeting with the *yidam* have become detached.

As we have seen in a previous chapter, an unwieldy edifice has been erected over the millennia, each new superstructure being raised on the decayed remnants of the preceding one. The Buddhist world is thus left with a multiplicity of ceremonies and formulae that give expression to the outward dimension of the essential Buddhist act. It also has many different ways of talking about its inner dimension of spiritual experience. The problem is further compounded by the fact that outer and inner dimensions have become progressively detached from each other. This has left us with that complicated 'stack' of teachings and practices. Sangharakshita believes that stack has got so high that there has to be a radical re-evaluation of the whole tradition. This means going back to the earliest way of speaking about the fundamental Buddhist act.

> Here we are, confronted by the Buddhist tradition. We find Going for Refuge mentioned in the Pali Canon and the arising of the *bodhicitta* mentioned in the Mahāyāna. We have got to reconcile them, we have got to bring them together. We can't really genuinely see Going for Refuge as an aspect of the arising of the *bodhicitta*, because the Going for Refuge came first. If we are to connect them we have to see the arising of the *bodhicitta* as an aspect of Going for Refuge. We reduce the arising of the *bodhicitta* to Going for Refuge, not the other way round, because of the historical priority of the Going for Refuge. Otherwise we can only leave them separate.
>
> So we have got to go back to the original Going for Refuge, and see these later developments as contained potentially within it. Otherwise we have stack upon stack of practices which have superseded one another.[117]

Going for Refuge was the term used at the time of the Buddha for the basic act of a Buddhist. The expression is still current, albeit used in a debased way, in all Buddhist schools. Sangharakshita has therefore come to consider Going for Refuge 'the central and definitive Act of the Buddhist life' and 'the unifying principle, therefore, of Buddhism itself'.[118] This does not mean that other ways of talking about that central act are incorrect. It is simply that, without being related to Going for Refuge, their true relationship to one another cannot be seen and their meaning is therefore distorted. Recognising Going for Refuge as the central principle unifies them and reveals their true significance. Sangharakshita sees Going for Refuge as taking place on different levels and within different aspects of life. All the various ways of talking about and ritually enacting that basic Buddhist act give expression to the different aspects of Going for Refuge. We must now examine in more detail Sangharakshita's idea of the depth and breadth of Going for Refuge.

Going for Refuge consists essentially in turning from the mundane to the transcendental. One first acknowledges that there is a higher reality, embodied in the Three Jewels. Recognising that one can actually realise that reality oneself, one feels an overwhelming and intuitive response to it. One reorientates one's whole being in its direction, gradually disentangling oneself from the motivations and interests that had previously driven one.

> One goes for Refuge to the Buddha, the Dharma, and the Sangha,—or, in more contemporary idiom, commits oneself to them,—when one decides that to attain Enlightenment is the most important thing in human life, and when one acts—or does one's best to act—in accordance with that decision. This means organizing one's entire life, in all its different aspects, in such a way as to subserve the attainment of Enlightenment.[119]

Although we have spoken of a single act, it is not an act that is performed but once in an individual's lifetime. At every stage of spiritual life one must turn more and more radically from the mundane to the transcendental. Thus Going for Refuge

> takes place on different levels, passage from one to another of which constitutes one's spiritual life as a Buddhist.[120]

Furthermore, that act does not take place simply in one department of life. It is a total act involving every nerve and fibre of one's being, having repercussions in all aspects of one's experience and activity. That single act can then be seen from many different points of view, corresponding to the many different categories into which human life can be divided. Thus, there are different aspects or dimensions of Going for Refuge. The recognition that Going for Refuge has levels and dimensions allows us to see more of its real nature. Going for Refuge is dynamic in that it is repeated more and more wholeheartedly at every level of the path. It is comprehensive, in that it eventually must transform every aspect of human experience.

## LEVELS OF GOING FOR REFUGE

Sangharakshita has distinguished five levels of Going for Refuge: Cultural, Provisional, Effective, Real, and Absolute.[121] Although this classification is his own, it has traditional precedent, for the Pali texts distinguish the mundane from the transcendental Going for Refuge.

In Sangharakshita's system, the lowest level is 'Cultural' Going for Refuge, which he sometimes also calls Ethnic or Formal. Here being a Buddhist is more or less nominal. It is not a matter of personal spiritual conviction but of group membership, and the formula of Going for Refuge is recited with little consciousness of its real significance.

> [This is] the Going for Refuge of those Eastern Buddhists who [do] not actually follow Buddhism as a spiritual teaching (though they might be positively influenced by it on the social level), and who [make] no effort to evolve spiritually, but who [are] nonetheless very proud of Buddhism as part of their cultural heritage and who definitely [consider] themselves (ethnic) Buddhists. Such people [recite] the Refuges as an affirmation of their cultural and national identity and even [go] so far as to claim that they [are] 'born Buddhists', though in truth one could no more be born a Buddhist than one could (according to the Buddha) be born a brahmin.[122]

In the West, this level consists of those who participate in a Buddhist group for predominantly social reasons. Spiritually limited as is this Cultural Going for Refuge, it is not without value. Such nominal Buddhists are at least influenced by the Dharma on the social and ethical level. Moreover, the Dharma is available to them as a positive ideal. Given sufficient opportunity and encouragement, they may move on to higher levels of Going for Refuge.

At the next level, 'Provisional' Going for Refuge, there is some definite response to the Three Jewels and some awareness of their true significance. One who goes for Refuge provisionally will experience strong feelings of devotion and reverence towards the ideal. He or she will acknowledge the worth of those who are fully committed to the spiritual path.

> [He or she has] started taking Buddhism seriously to some extent, even started practising it to some extent, but [does] not really commit himself (or herself) either to Buddhism or to his (or her) own spiritual development. He (or she) might, however, be aware of the possibility, even the desirability, of committing oneself, and might be thinking of doing so later on.[123]

Such a person might be the member of a traditional Buddhist culture who has begun to have some real understanding of what Going for Refuge means. In the Western context, they would be among those associated with a Buddhist movement, regularly attending classes in meditation and Dharma study. However, despite devotion to the Three Jewels and some understanding of the Dharma, they still have many other competing interests and ambitions. These do not, at this stage, allow effective dedication to the spiritual path.

By contrast, one who goes for Refuge *effectively* can put enough energy behind Going for Refuge to make it an effective act. Despite other competing interests and ambitions, they are sufficiently drawn to the Three Jewels to be able to commit themselves to making systematic steps towards them. It is really at this point of 'Effective' Going for Refuge that the spiritual life begins in earnest. Here, the decisive reorientation from the mundane towards the transcendental is made. However, success is not yet assured, even on reaching this stage. Although one has turned towards the transcendental, one has not yet made the transition to it: one has no direct experience of the Dharma. If one ceases in one's efforts one will be inexorably drawn away from the path. Indeed, Going for Refuge can only remain effective at this stage if the individual is surrounded by conditions that support his or her efforts. Such conditions include genuine spiritual friendship, real Dharmic guidance, even living and working situations that enhance rather than detract from the following of the spiritual path.

It is only with 'Real' Going for Refuge that one gains that transforming insight that brings one on to the transcendental path. So important is this transition that we must briefly explore its significance. In the Buddha's original teaching, the spiritual path is divided into two great halves: mundane and transcendental. When one first sets out on the path, one's essential view of things is still worldly. There is intellectual under-standing of the Dharma and emotional attraction to it, but one's deeper psyche is untransformed. One's Going for Refuge may be effective enough to keep one moving forward, but it is not yet real, so that one may still fall back if one relaxes one's efforts. This is the mundane path. In the course of Going for Refuge more and more effectively, one's intellectual understanding of the Dharma and emotional attraction to it are trans-formed into *prajñā* or Wisdom. Seeing things now as they really are, one cannot fall back into a mundane way of looking at things. From then on, one sees things from the point of view of Enlightenment, not of the world. One has gained the transcendental path. This is the point where the creative mind predominates over the reactive—although the reactive is not yet exhausted. It is the point on the path of the Higher Evolution where transcendental consciousness arises and one becomes a true individual. We will be exploring further Sangharakshita's views on this transition in later chapters.

Real Going for Refuge is the 'point of no-return' at which one cannot fall back from the path. One's whole outlook has been utterly transformed by a glimpse of the true nature of reality. So penetrating is this glimpse that one can no longer be drawn from a wholehearted quest for complete and full Enlightenment. One is now, indeed, assured of gaining Enlightenment because one cannot, so to speak, help making the effort that will bring one to it. This crucial transition is the first goal of spiritual life. Different Buddhist traditions speak of this transition in different ways: Stream Entry, Irreversibility from Full and Perfect Enlightenment, attaining the path of Vision, the seeing of the *jñānasattva*, the Opening of the Dharma Eye, etc. Since these different ways of speaking of this transition belong within different doctrinal systems, most are seen within their own systems as different experiences. However, Sangharakshita reconciles all these various ways of viewing the fundamental Buddhist act by referring them back to Going for Refuge. All refer to Real Going for Refuge.

'Absolute' or 'Ultimate' Going for Refuge is the point of full Enlightenment. Here, the cyclic trend of conditionality is completely exhausted and there is only a spontaneous unfolding of the spiral trend in unending creativity. Here even Going for Refuge is transcended, since one has oneself become the refuge. In fact, in so far as all dualistic thought has been left behind, there is no refuge to go to and no one to go to it. Once again, Sangharakshita is keen to guard against thinking of Absolute Going for Refuge as a fixed place, in which the Enlightened settle down. He points out that even the Buddha seemed to feel the need of some higher principle.

> After his Enlightenment, the Buddha looked around the cosmos and saw that there was no being whom he could live worshipping and reverencing. It is as though the Buddha himself, even after his Enlightenment, felt this need to look up to something beyond. He eventually realised that there was the Dharma, there was that transcendental law in accordance with which he had realised the Truth and become the Buddha. So he resolved to live worshipping and revering that.
>
> [This makes it clear that] we shouldn't think of Enlightenment as a sort of fixed, final, terminal state, lying literally at the end of a path. That is, up to a point, a helpful way of thinking, but you also need to think of Enlightenment as always, as it were, being there. You have to have both ideas at the same time, which is not a very easy thing to conceive of.[124]

## ASPECTS OF GOING FOR REFUGE

In this way Sangharakshita identifies Going for Refuge as the act that characterises every stage of the path. Indeed, the following of the path consists in deepening and ever deepening one's Going for Refuge to the Three Jewels. He reconciles, in this single concept that all schools acknowledge, all the different conceptual maps employed by the various schools to chart the stages of the path. Not only are they reconciled in it but they each make their distinctive contribution to drawing out its full meaning and significance. Each approaches that fundamental act from a particular point of view, throwing into relief one or another aspect of it.

> These are the conclusions I have come to in the course of the last twenty-five years or so. I have more and more seen everything as contained within the Going for Refuge. I don't see the arising of the *bodhicitta* or Tantric initiation, for instance, as going beyond the Going for Refuge, but only as revealing different aspects of it more fully and more clearly. At the very beginning, there were just the bare fundamentals, which were sufficient. As time went on, as so many people went for Refuge, people with so many different needs and so many different approaches, there was more and more elaboration, and that elaboration enriched the concept of Going for Refuge. But the different approaches ended up smothering and concealing the Going for Refuge, rather than revealing it.[125]

Sangharakshita's idea of those approaches as dimensions of Going for Refuge once more reveals the true meaning of that act. His perspective does not negate later elaborations but shows them as enrichments of the central concept.

The language of the Bodhisattva Ideal is perhaps the best-known alternative to that of Going for Refuge. This speaks of the basic act in terms of the arising of the *bodhicitta*, the 'will to Enlightenment', which is a deep urge to go forward on the path for the benefit of all beings. Clearly it draws out what Sangharakshita calls the altruistic dimension of Going for Refuge. There cannot really be two separate paths, one individualistic and one altruistic, between which one can choose, as the popularised Mahāyāna may seem to suggest. The spiritual path is of its very nature altruistic, a growth in harmony, friendship, and compassion. Ultimately it completely transcends even the distinction between self and other. Going for Refuge means becoming more and more altruistic.

The arising of the *bodhicitta* became detached from Going for Refuge for the reasons we have already explored. There was a degeneration and narrowing of the original ideal. Since the Mahayanists did not have an idea of historical development, they could not identify that narrowed ideal they inherited as a degeneration. They had to accept it as the direct teaching of the Buddha. They could only correct what they saw as the Hīnayāna's one-sided individualism by erecting a new and higher path on top of the old and narrowed one, recasting the spiritual path and its definitive act in terms of altruism. Modern Buddhists need not accept this stacking up of teachings. They must surely find a different way of relating the language of the Bodhisattva Ideal to the basic teachings of Buddhism. This can only be done by relating the Bodhisattva Ideal back to Going for Refuge and seeing it as an exploration of but one of its aspects. The arising of the *bodhicitta* and the Bodhisattva Ideal reveal the altruistic dimension of Going for Refuge.

Sangharakshita considers that the Bodhisattva Ideal in particular needs putting into perspective for urgent methodological reasons.

> You can't even consider the description of the Bodhisattva [as working for inconceivable lifetimes to save all sentient beings] as applying to the ordinary practising Buddhist. It is absolutely inconceivable. It has got out of all proportion as far as you personally and almost any other human being are concerned. Therefore, I see the Bodhisattva Ideal and the *bodhicitta*, presented in that way on that scale, as representing the archetype. We participate in that to the extent that we can, but we do not take it upon ourselves in its entirety. We, as ordinary human beings, can't possibly do that. In a way, the Bodhisattva Ideal and the arising of the *bodhicitta* in the Mahāyāna tradition have lost all connection with the individual practice of the individual Buddhist. Therefore I think it is all the more necessary to fall back on the Going for Refuge as the basic Buddhist act, not on the arising of the *bodhicitta* and becoming a Bodhisattva—which represent the archetype of Going for Refuge, on a cosmic scale.[126]

Although Sangharakshita draws on and is greatly inspired by the Mahāyāna Bodhisattva Ideal, he thinks it should be taken as myth rather than as a practicable spiritual ideal for the individual. Although it should quickly be noted that to say it should be taken as myth, in Sangharakshita's thinking, does not mean that it should be dismissed or treated as a mere allegory. As we shall see later, he places great importance on archetype and myth. However, he thinks that one should be careful not to take myth literally. He does not think, for instance, that it is appropriate for individuals to take the vow of the Bodhisattva to save all sentient beings, as is commonly done in the Mahāyāna and as he did himself in 1964. He now considers that the Bodhisattva vow, dedicating oneself to the Enlightenment of all beings, can only be thought of in collective terms.

> I see less and less the taking of Bodhisattva vows as an individual thing in the ordinary sense. The Bodhisattva vow goes beyond the framework

of subject and object. It goes beyond the distinction between one's own individual development and helping other people to develop. So the vow cannot be taken by individuals. If you take some of these Bodhisattva vows seriously, you cannot, if you've got the least scrap of imagination, imagine yourself as an individual ever carrying them out. Something different is clearly involved: a process in which you may participate but which is not anything that you as an individual can ever do. I have, therefore, tended to think that the Bodhisattva vow should be 'taken' by the Order as a whole. The Bodhisattva spirit, the *bodhicitta*, should pervade the Order as a whole and all its activities. This is why, from quite early on, I spoke of the Order as embodying the figure of the thousand-armed, eleven-headed Avalokiteśvara, with each Order member being one of those thousand arms or thousand hands, each bearing its particular implement or emblem.[127]

Sangharakshita considers Tantric initiation too as an aspect of Going for Refuge.

I don't regard the Going for Refuge to be introductory to the arising of the *bodhicitta*, and the arising of the *bodhicitta* to be introductory to *abhisheka* or Tantric initiation. In the same way as the arising of the *bodhicitta*, I regard the *abhisheka* as an aspect of Going for Refuge. Going for Refuge is the fundamental, basic, definitive Buddhist act. It is all contained there. It has all grown out of that or been elaborated from that. You could say that the *abhisheka* represents the release of the tremendous energy inherent in the act of Going for Refuge itself. Your own Going for Refuge releases energy. *Abhisheka* is not something that you get given to you as an extra sort of goody, after you have Gone for Refuge.[128]

Another aspect of Going for Refuge is drawn out by the language of 'Going Forth' into homelessness—the act of leaving behind all worldly ties and of renouncing the group. This act is represented in most Buddhist monastic traditions by the 'lower' or *śrāmaṇera* ordination. However, it has a much broader significance than this ceremony suggests. At every stage of the path one must leave behind the lower to move on to the higher. If one is to go for Refuge to the Three Jewels, one must Go Forth from mundane refuges. This is not merely an inward process of changing attitudes but has direct practical consequences. Going Forth, Sangharakshita notes,

Draws attention to the extent of the reorganization which, regardless of whether or not one becomes a monk in the formal sense, the experience [of Going for Refuge] inevitably brings about in the pattern of one's daily life'.[129]

Another term, Stream Entry, draws attention to the 'permanent and far-reaching effects' of the fundamental Buddhist act. Going for Refuge itself, while it is the primary term for that basic act, 'draws attention to the emotional and volitional aspect of this experience'.[130]

Sangharakshita considers that the language of Going for Refuge provides the most helpful model of spiritual life. Even though ultimately all duality is transcended in Enlightenment, our conception of spiritual life cannot but be dualistic. We must think that there is a state we are now in and a state that we wish to attain. How we think about the relationship between those two states has major repercussions on our spiritual life. One can think of the state one wishes to attain either as something outside one that one is opening oneself up to or as a potential one has within one that one is trying to reveal. Going for Refuge speaks the language of opening oneself to the higher. Some Buddhist, and some non-Buddhist, traditions speak the language of revealing one's potential. In so far as you are the Buddha potentially, then the Buddha is, it is said, already within you. The best-known example of this is the Zen saying that you are the Buddha already. While this has some metaphysical validity, Sangharakshita considers it methodologically unhelpful.

> This language of potentiality is very, very dangerous—not in the sense that it's untrue, but that it can be misunderstood and misapplied. The danger is that you start thinking of these higher levels as potentialities of you [as you now are] as though you can attain them, achieve them, appropriate them, while remaining yourself unchanged. But you can't. The accent is so heavily on you that you can't really become that higher potential. For you to achieve that higher level, paradoxically you have to cease to exist: you have to die so it can take your place. It's much better to put it all the other way round, and to speak not of this higher potentiality belonging to you, but of yourself as belonging to that higher potentiality. It's not that you've got to appropriate it: you've got to surrender to it. You've got to go for Refuge to it. Otherwise the egotistical attitude remains unchanged and you just go on appropriating and appropriating.[131]

The language of potentiality is quite common in Western Buddhist circles and Sangharakshita thinks it is often used for populist reasons: it flatters people to think that they are potential Buddhas—even more that they are the Buddha already. However, they do not then make the kind of radical change necessary really to become Buddhas. They do not go for Refuge to the Buddha. Thus, Going for Refuge is fundamental to Buddhism in another sense: there is no spiritual development without dying to what one now is so that one can be reborn as what one goes for Refuge to.

### THE CONTEXT OF GOING FOR REFUGE

Thus Sangharakshita reveals the true significance of Going for Refuge as the fundamental Buddhist act, repeated at every stage of spiritual life and including every aspect of experience. However, one should not think of Going for Refuge as an isolated act: it belongs in a wider context.[132] In *The History of My Going for Refuge*, Sangharakshita shows first the social context of Going for Refuge. Although it is the act of an individual, many individuals may make it. By doing so, they come into a new and significant relationship with one another. Sharing as they do commitment to the spiritual path, there is a very deep connection between them. Those who genuinely and effectively go for Refuge share a harmony and empathy that amount to a new kind of consciousness. The nature of this new kind of consciousness is quite hard to understand and communicate, since it is neither of the group nor of the individual, but above and beyond them both. It combines the complete autonomy of the individual with complete harmony with others who share the same commitment to the path. It is

> a special kind of consciousness common to, in a sense even shared by, a
> number of truly human individuals who follow the same spiritual
> disciplines and have the same spiritual ideals, or who are engaged in the
> same creative activities.[133]

This new kind of consciousness characterises the sangha or spiritual community. Thus, the social context of Going for Refuge is the sangha.

Going for Refuge belongs also within the context of the Higher Evolution. As we have seen, the Higher Evolution is that series of ever higher states of awareness through which, with conscious commitment and personal effort, the individual gradually ascends. Effective Going for Refuge is the act of commitment that the self-aware individual makes at the outset of his spiritual career, dedicating himself to the path. This is clearly illustrated in the teaching of the twelve positive *nidānas*. These are the links in the progressive order of conditionality that form the path, whether we talk of it as the creative Spiral or the Higher Evolution. The first *nidāna* or link is *duḥkha* or 'suffering': the inevitable experience of pain, frustration, and imperfection that comes from being bound up with the wheel of cyclic conditionality. As Sangharakshita says, what *duḥkha* really means is,

> in positive terms, that Nirvāṇa alone is peace, and negatively that
> conditioned things are painful because we seek in them for that absolute
> bliss which only the Unconditioned can bestow and have, therefore,
> inevitably to experience disappointment and frustration.[134]

Once one becomes aware that cyclic existence, the reactive mind, or the Lower Evolution are inherently unsatisfactory, then one can be open to the mind's deeper creative potential. And so, in dependence on *duḥkha*, arises *śraddhā*. *Śraddhā* is often translated as 'faith', but this has, for many people in the post-Christian West, quite the wrong connotations.

> *Śraddhā* is not faith in the sense of belief, or in the sense of believing to be true something which cannot be rationally demonstrated. If we want a definition of faith we may say that it is 'the emotional response of what is ultimate in us to what is ultimate in the universe'. Faith is an intuitive, emotional, even mystical response to what is of ultimate value. For Buddhism, faith means specifically faith in the Three Jewels.[135]

That response, when felt sufficiently deeply and strongly, will result in one's committing oneself to the Three Jewels. That act of commitment is Effective Going for Refuge. Going for Refuge is therefore the active dimension of *śraddhā* or faith.

Although Going for Refuge first appears in a decisive form at the *nidāna* of *śraddhā*, it is present in every stage of the path. No step in the Spiral Path of the positive *nidānas* is really left behind. Each is taken up and transcended in the succeeding, higher stage. Thus the highest link in the positive chain includes all the other links, although it also passes beyond them. Going for Refuge is present at each stage as that ever more radical turning towards the Three Jewels. It is Going for Refuge that drives one to leave behind what one has presently achieved and to seek yet greater heights. Going for Refuge therefore takes place within the context of the Higher Evolution, of which it is the vital fuel and spark.

While Sangharakshita identifies Going for Refuge as the dynamic of the Higher Evolution, he stresses that Going for Refuge is the expression within the context of Buddhism of a general principle: the principle of moving from the mundane to the transcendental, from the Conditioned to the Unconditioned. That principle is also expressed in non-Buddhist traditions, albeit often obscurely and distortedly.

> At least for some people operating within some other religions, there is some movement from what we would call the Conditioned to the Unconditioned, buried underneath them. They don't have to be organised religions. One can even see some such movement in the works of great artists and writers—there is a movement from the mundane to the transcendental, at least for some of them. The general principle is the same. But often it is mixed with other things, and even if there is some faint reflection of the principle it is often so obscured by these other factors as to be virtually valueless. For instance, you might think that you go from the Conditioned to the Unconditioned by believing in a

personal God who is going to save you and transport you there. That
would not be Going for Refuge in our sense.[136]

This principle is not 'Buddhist' in the limited sense. It is part of the
universe itself and simply finds particularly clear and powerful expression in the Buddhist concept of Going for Refuge. The Higher Evolutionary context is therefore universal.

The Higher Evolution itself, however, takes place within the context of
the wider evolutionary process. Although the two halves of the total
process are quite distinct with very different characteristics, nonetheless
there is a single thread running through them. There is an 'upward
movement of life and consciousness'[137] that can be seen in both the Lower
Evolution of species and the Higher Evolution of the individual, although
in the Lower Evolution that upward movement is not the expression of
a conscious intention, as it is in the Higher. Thus, there is

> a parallel, or even a partial coincidence, between the process of spiritual
> development as depicted in traditional Buddhist teaching and the course
> of human [Lower] evolution as described by modern science.[138]

That parallel or partial coincidence is not without basis in Buddhist
tradition. The Bodhisattva, the Buddha-to-be, is often represented as
having been born even as an animal in some of his previous lives. The
term 'Bodhisattva' was originally applied to the Buddha from the time
of his birth to the time of his Enlightenment when he became the Buddha.
However, his struggle for Enlightenment came to be seen as spanning not
merely one life but myriads of lives. There is a large class of literature, the
*Jātakas*, which tells of the previous lives of the Buddha, showing him
perfecting the path over countless ages. Some of the *Jātakas* are contained
in the canons of various schools; others are noncanonical, although they
are among the best known and best loved literature of Buddhism. In the
canonical *Jātakas*, the Bodhisattva appears as a famous seer or teacher or
king. As Sangharakshita says, he is seen

> *taking the lead*, whether in the sphere of ethical and religious life or in the
> sphere of political activity.[139]

In the noncanonical stories he is depicted rather more broadly, and it is
in these tales that he sometimes appears as an animal. In whatever form
he appears, he is always the outstanding figure in the group in which he
is found; he is always *taking the lead*, thus representing 'the growing point
of evolution within each class or group of beings'.[140] At the same time, he
is the Bodhisattva, the being who is totally dedicated to the pursuit of
Enlightenment. In this way the noncanonical *Jātakas* signify that the
Lower and Higher Evolutions are aspects of a single 'upward movement

of life and consciousness'.[141] So Sangharakshita speaks of a single principle manifesting at every level of evolution, whether Lower or Higher.
This principle is, for the Mahāyāna, the *bodhicitta* or 'Will to
Enlightenment'. Sangharakshita calls it the 'Bodhisattva principle' or the
'principle of perpetual self-transcendence'. It is this principle of self-
transcendence that we have seen as the upward movement of life and
consciousness, underlying both the Lower and Higher Evolutions. Always, at every stage and phase of the evolutionary process, the principle
of perpetual self-transcendence manifests itself.

That upward surge of life and consciousness is, of course, within the
context of the Higher Evolution, Going for Refuge. Going for Refuge can,
however, be seen to be present not just in the Higher Evolution but at
every stage of the evolutionary process because

> Looking at the process, what one in fact saw was a Going for Refuge.
> Each form of life aspired to develop into a higher form or, so to speak,
> went for Refuge to that higher form. This might sound impossibly
> poetic, but it was what one in fact saw.[142]

In the Higher Evolution that aspiration to develop into a higher form
becomes conscious of itself in and through the committed individual.
When it does so it is Effective Going for Refuge. But Going for Refuge is
present at every level and stage and is identical with the principle of
self-transcendence, with the Bodhisattva principle, and with the *bodhicitta*. The language of the Bodhisattva principle and of the *bodhicitta*
simply draws out its altruistic dimension. Considered as the universal
principle that underlies the entire evolutionary process, Sangharakshita
calls this the 'Cosmic Going for Refuge'.

> I have spoken of a Cosmic Going for Refuge. I have identified in Going
> for Refuge the whole principle of evolution. It is not just a little Buddhist
> practice. It is a reflection, within the context of Buddhism, of a principle
> that governs the whole of life and attains greater and greater clarity of
> expression until it gains its greatest clarity of expression in Going for
> Refuge. Going for Refuge is at the centre of Buddhism because evolution
> is at the centre of life.[143]

Sangharakshita has advanced his idea of the Cosmic Going for Refuge
rather tentatively, and has never written systematically on the subject.
Clearly there is a great deal of room for misunderstanding and for taking
literally what is meant as a poetic metaphor.

> When I spoke of the Cosmic Going for Refuge, which I did in a rash
> moment, I wasn't thinking in terms of a sort of collective Going for
> Refuge on the part of the whole cosmos. I was thinking that every
> individual thing in the cosmos might be said to have an inbuilt tendency

to transcend itself. At least it has the possibility of transcending itself, given the right circumstances and conditions. I wasn't making an objectively, scientifically verifiable statement so much as speaking in more poetic and metaphorical terms.[144]

The point of this metaphor, Sangharakshita says, is to communicate that ultimately the cosmos has meaning and purpose. The universe is not simply a mechanism that has evolved human consciousness by a random process. Spiritual life, as we have already seen, necessarily involves us thinking dualistically: what we now are is different from what we are trying to become. It is the spiral path that connects the one to the other, and we ascend that path by Going for Refuge to what we are trying to become. The Higher Evolution is thus purposive, because we are consciously working towards a goal. But how are we to understand the Lower Evolution? How are we to resolve the gap between what we once were and what we now are? What has brought us to the point of Going for Refuge? We can either see that process as fortuitous or as itself having a purpose. Taken literally, both are equally untrue, since they are applying limited concepts drawn from our ordinary sense experience to the universe as a whole. However, from a spiritual point of view, the metaphor of the entire universe as having a purpose is far nearer the truth and far more helpful. It comes nearer to expressing the Buddha's insight into the essential interconnectedness of all things.

The individual's spiritual efforts are not merely the efforts of an individual entirely isolated from everything else: they take place within a vast context. The individual's efforts and the upward movement of life and consciousness that is their context are both manifestations of the single principle of the Cosmic Going for Refuge. They are therefore organically connected. The individual can reveal ever more of the significance of his or her own efforts because those efforts are interconnected with the entire context. Through those efforts, because of that interconnectedness, he or she reveals 'something of the nature and significance of the wider context itself'.[145] Going for Refuge is then the key to evolution itself—a key in the sense of

a concept, or an image, in the light of which the whole process can not only be rendered more intelligible but brought within a wider, more 'cosmic' context.[146]

Through our Going for Refuge we are united, as it were, with all living beings, who in their own way, and on their own level, in a sense also [go] for Refuge. Thus Going for Refuge [is] not simply a particular devotional practice or even a threefold act of commitment, but the key to the mystery of existence.[147]

## Chapter Five

# THE SPIRITUAL COMMUNITY

*He wanted that His followers should be flames*
*And burn up to the Zenith. Now they are*
*Faint embers underneath a mound of ash,*
*Afraid of claiming kinship with a star.*[148]

SANGHA OR SPIRITUAL COMMUNITY is integral to Buddhism. It is the third of those Three Jewels that, according to Sangharakshita, *'are* Buddhism'. However, Buddhists do not agree about precisely what the sangha is. Sangharakshita's recognition that the fundamental act of Buddhism is Going for Refuge also reveals what a Buddhist is, and therefore who are the members of the sangha or Buddhist spiritual community. A Buddhist is one who goes for Refuge. The sangha is, therefore, made up of all those who go for Refuge. Going for Refuge is the unifying principle of the Buddhist sangha. It resolves the deep divisions between the Buddhist schools, sects, and communities, with their various ways of under-standing the spiritual community and its membership.

Since Going for Refuge takes place on different levels, clearly there are also different levels of sangha. At the highest level, the sangha is tradi-tionally said to consist of all those who have attained the transcendental path (*lokottara-mārga*). This transcendental sangha consists of those who

> have certain transcendental attainments and experiences in common.
> These people may or may not be in physical contact, but are united on a
> spiritual plane, because of the spiritual experiences they have in
> common. The Sangha on this level is a purely spiritual body: a number
> of people living at distant places, at different times, but sharing, above
> space and time, the same spiritual attainments and experiences.[149]

Since different Buddhist systems view the path in different ways, there are a variety of terms for the members of this supreme sangha. From the point of view of the Hīnayāna, it is made up of the *āryas*, those who have attained Stream Entry and beyond; while the Mahāyāna sees it as comprising the Bodhisattvas in whom the *bodhicitta* has arisen. Both *āryas* and Bodhisattvas are, in Sangharakshita's understanding, those who 'Really' go for Refuge, simply viewed from different perspectives. All those who Really go for Refuge make up the *ārya-saṅgha*, the Real or transcendental sangha. This *ārya-saṅgha* exemplifies the ideal of spiritual community in its fullest sense, since there is between its members a degree of harmony and understanding that cannot be shaken or destroyed. The members of the transcendental sangha collectively constitute a true refuge: since they cannot fall back into the mundane, they represent an ideal in which one can have full confidence.

The resolution of conflicting viewpoints on the transcendental sangha is relatively easy, but when it comes to the mundane spiritual community the situation is much more complex. Most people in the West, many Buddhists included, are unaware of the large number and diversity of independent ecclesiastical corporations that exist in the Buddhist world today. Many think, for instance, that the Dalai Lama is 'head of Tibetan Buddhism' or that the yellow-robed Theravadin monks belong to a highly centralised and disciplined body, like some Catholic monastic orders. This, however, is not so.

> There is no great unitary sangha in the East, to which all *bhikkhus* belong. There is a large number of sanghas, some affiliated to the Hīnayāna and some to the Mahāyāna, and some even, in a sense, to the Vajrayāna. And there is no technical mutual recognition between them.[150]

Within Tibetan Buddhism, for instance, there are several mutually exclusive orders, among which, as Sangharakshita found, there is quite a bit of rivalry and even hostility: he had, for instance, considerable difficulty persuading monks of different Tibetan schools even to celebrate major Buddhist festivals together. Again, the different Tibetan orders do not all acknowledge the spiritual authority of the Dalai Lama. Although he is widely respected, he is, strictly speaking, not even the head of the Gelugpa order to which he belongs, and is certainly not the 'Pope of Buddhism'. Theravāda monks, too, are divided into several different *nikāyas*—'groups' or 'sects'. These *nikāyas* do not accept each other's ordinations and will not participate together in *saṅgha-karma* or formal acts of the sangha, such as the acceptance of new monks into the order. In China and Japan too there are similar divisions. Technically, the Buddhist world is in multiple schism, as defined by the *Vinaya*, the collection of canonical texts that set out the way in which the monastic order should function. The *Vinaya* defines schism as the refusal by one body or branch to recognise the *sangha-karma* of another.

In some cases the differences between these independent bodies are quite small: a matter of how the robe should be worn or of other minor points of procedure. However, the great diversity of doctrine and practice, as well as of cultures within which Buddhism has spread, has also led to substantial differences. It is no longer easy to perceive them all as parts of a single spiritual whole. So complex and tangled has the issue become, and so degenerate are some Buddhist communal bodies, that Sangharakshita has felt it necessary to go back to first principles. He has, in effect, started again, founding a new order that is unencumbered by Buddhist ecclesiastical history, although firmly traditional in its basis. Just as he has a distinctive perspective on the development of Buddhist doctrine, he has a comprehensive interpretation of the Buddhist sangha's history. This interpretation helps to make clear what he considers the spiritual community to be and thus clarifies the principles on which the sangha must be based in the present era. We will therefore briefly examine his understanding of the history of the Buddhist spiritual community.

## THE DEVELOPMENT OF THE BUDDHIST SANGHA

In the earliest phase of Buddhism, there was not an organised community of the kind to which we are now accustomed. There was simply the Buddha, the Enlightened teacher, surrounded by his followers, who went for Refuge to him. It seems that to begin with there was no set or established formula for entry into that band of followers: there was no 'ordination ceremony'. In one way or another, the new disciple would give expression to his or her commitment to the Buddha, his teaching, and the community of his disciples. After a while, the formula of Going for Refuge became established as the means by which individuals would express that commitment. There were few rules, the community being guided mainly by principles laid down by the Buddha in the course of his teaching. Slowly a pattern of life emerged that supported the spiritual efforts of his disciples. Although, to begin with, there was little formal organisation of this community of disciples, it naturally formed itself into four parts, according to two basic divisions then current in Indian society.

Firstly, as in most traditional societies, men and women customarily associated principally with members of their own sex. They therefore formed separate communities within the overall community of the Buddha's disciples. Secondly, Indian society consisted at that time, on the one hand, of 'householders', who formed the great majority and who lived with their families and participated fully in civic life, and, on the other, of *śramaṇas* (Pali, *samaṇas*), 'wanderers', 'recluses', or 'ascetics' who had renounced all worldly responsibility and simply wandered from place to place, begging for their sustenance. This class of wanderers encompassed vagabonds and social misfits as well as spiritual seekers and yogins. Nonetheless, it was widely believed that feeding such wanderers brought 'merit', worldly good fortune, and they were accorded an honourable place in society. The Buddha himself was a wanderer. He had left wife and family in quest of truth some years before his Enlightenment. For the remainder of his life he lived without a settled abode and entirely dependent on alms. Although many of his disciples were drawn from this class of wanderer, many were householders. There were thus four divisions within the Buddha's community: male householders, female householders, male wanderers, and female wanderers.

Most of the Buddha's leading disciples were wanderers, either having left the household life before encountering his teaching or 'Going Forth' as wanderers under his inspiration. Clearly, those without family and civic responsibilities were in a far better position to study and practise his teaching. The wandering life was therefore very much recommended by the Buddha. Nonetheless, the earliest texts say that considerable numbers of his householder disciples, both men and women, did gain the transcendental path while still living a lay life, and were therefore members of the transcendental sangha. Though divided by manner of life and social custom, all four branches of the total community of the Buddha's followers were united by their common devotion to the Buddha and their efforts on the path. They were united most fundamentally in their common Going for Refuge to the Buddha, Dharma, and Sangha.

Not all Buddhists today accept Sangharakshita's view that the early sangha included all four communities. The Theravāda largely defines the sangha as the community of *bhikkhus*, as distinct from the male and female lay followers (there being no longer a community of nuns in the full technical sense, the *bhikkhunīs* or nuns do not enter the consideration). Sangharakshita substantiates his point by referring to the Buddha's own position, as recorded in the Pali Canon.

His impatience with the formalistic element in religion, and His uncompromising insistence on the necessity of personal realization of Nirvāṇa, moreover ensured that they would be distinguished, if at all, according to their intrinsic merits rather than their socio-eclesiastical status.[151]

He quotes a saying from the *Dhammapada*, in which the Buddha asserts that it is not the wearing the yellow robe of a mendicant that makes one a wanderer or a *bhikkhu*, but the development of genuine spiritual qualities.

> Even though a man be richly attired, if he develops tranquillity, is quiet, subdued, and restrained, leading a holy life and abstaining from injury to all living beings—he is a *brāhmaṇa*, he is a *samaṇa*, he is a *bhikkhu*.[152]

In this saying, the Buddha was not implying that the wandering life did not provide the best spiritual opportunities for most people.

> That the wandering monk, totally free from all worldly concerns, had a far better chance of reaching the Goal, was admitted, even emphasized; but that a householder, if sufficiently resolved, might sometimes reach it too, and that in the last resort it was transcendental attainment that mattered, not the wearing of yellow robes, more than one such saying of the Buddha testifies.[153]

In another passage from the Pali Canon, the Buddha identifies the sangha as consisting of all four divisions even more explicitly.

> Brethren, these four persons, who are full of wisdom and insight, are well-disciplined, learned [in the Dharma] and have reached complete righteousness, shed lustre upon the Sangha. Which are the four? Brethren, the bhikkhu, the bhikkhunī, the upāsaka [male lay devotee], the upāsikā [female lay devotee], who are full of wisdom and insight, well-disciplined, and learned, and have reached complete righteousness, shed lustre upon the Sangha. Brethren, these four beings do indeed shed lustre upon the Sangha.[154]

Finally, the fact that lay devotees, male and female, attained the transcendental path means that they must be included in the sangha.

> The Pali scriptures contain a number of references to householders who were Stream Entrants. Dozens and dozens of names of householder Stream Entrants are given. So they were certainly, by definition, members of the *ārya-saṅgha* [i.e. the transcendental sangha]. So if they were members of the *ārya-saṅgha*, surely they must be considered members of the sangha in the ordinary sense.[155]

It seems that, in the Buddha's time, there were very close relations between the different communities within the sangha.

> There were *bhikkhus* and *upāsakas* or lay-devotees from the beginning, but only in the sense that some people took refuge in the Buddha and continued to live as householders, while others continued to wander or left household life and started wandering. The wanderers found it easier to bond themselves together into a sangha. But even so there was not that degree of distinction as obtained at a later period between what came to be called *upāsaka* and what came to be called *bhikkhu*.[156]

From that time onwards, the histories of the four divisions of the total community are unequal. The wanderers, both male and female, over the years after the Buddha's death, gave up the wandering life and became cenobitical. They increasingly developed into formalised ecclesiastical bodies with procedures for ordination, discipline and expulsion, and rules governing all aspects of their life. These rules were based on the *Vinaya*, texts that had their origin in the Buddha's own pronouncements on the proper conduct of his wanderer disciples in various situations. These two bodies, known as the *bhikkhu* and *bhikkhunī* sanghas, then gradually separated into several independent communities, each with their own *Vinaya* and somewhat different rules and procedures. Exactly why they separated is not clear: perhaps it was mainly because they became geographically isolated from each other, but disputes over doctrine and practice may also have played their part. The *bhikkhunī* sangha, after surviving for a millennium, eventually died out in all but one such branch, the Dharmagupta, which is maintained to this day only in China and Korea. There are 'nuns' in other parts of the Buddhist world, but they are not *bhikkhunīs*, in the full technical sense of being ordained according to the rules laid down in the *Bhikkhunī-Vinaya* and following the way of life it prescribes. The *bhikkhu* sangha has fared far more successfully and is found in most parts of the Buddhist world, in various divisions and subdivisions that are often mutually exclusive.

The communities of male and female 'lay' or householder followers appear never to have achieved any degree of institutional identity in India. Indeed, we know very little about them and their early history.

> There seems to be no record of lay people meeting regularly. We can't however attach too much importance to that, because there are no actual accounts of the *bhikkhunīs* meeting—although we know they must have had meetings since their *Vinaya* was parallel to that of the *bhikkhus* [and required regular meetings]. So it is quite possible that the lay people did meet, but that the *bhikkhus*, who after all compiled the *Tipiṭaka* [i.e. the Pali and other canons], didn't take very much notice of it. We know that lay followers, to use that term, observed the full moon and the new moon days, and they observed extra precepts on those occasions, including fasting. This whole subject needs proper investigation.[157]

Although some of the Buddha's advice and guidance to his lay followers have survived in the early texts, no formal rule appears ever to have been drawn up for them. As we have seen, the act of Going for Refuge gradually degenerated, leaving no formal act of entry into the lay divisions of the total sangha. Although some texts have been called a 'layman's *Vinaya*', they are far from equivalent to the monastic codes. This lack of identity, Sangharakshita believes, was both part cause and part consequence of a growing distortion of the Buddha's message. Increasingly, being a Buddhist was identified with being a monk.

> In the course of time, the *bhikkhu* members of the sangha seem to have developed in one direction and *upāsaka* [i.e. lay devotee] members of the sangha in another. It does seem that quite early on those who had gone for Refuge but stayed at home considered themselves as supporting the sangha rather than as being really a part of it.[158]

This is the general state of affairs to this day in countries where the Theravāda is dominant. Often the term 'sangha' is used simply to denote the monks. It is widely held in Theravāda countries that only monks can gain the transcendental path—if anyone can, for it is also widely held that transcendental attainments are no longer possible at all. Paradoxically, while the monks are thought of as the real Buddhists in the sense that they are actually on the path to Enlightenment, the term Buddhist is also identified 'with the entire population of a Buddhist country. Thieves, prostitutes, drunkards, and policemen—all [are] Buddhists'.[159] All consider themselves 'born Buddhists'. Being a Buddhist is thus conceived of in purely formal terms. It is a matter either of living a particular life-style or else of being a member of a particular group.

Sangharakshita considers that this formalism has led to severe degeneration in the Theravāda tradition. While he did meet good and sincere Theravāda monks, his experience has led him to conclude that many *bhikkhus* believe it enough simply to have become a monk. They consider themselves genuine followers of the Buddha without making any spiritual effort and sometimes not even following the letter of the *Vinaya*, let alone its spirit. Since they are the recipients of great reverence from the lay population, which also provides them with their material needs, there are great temptations to hypocrisy and to arrogance—temptations to which, as Sangharakshita saw, all too many *bhikkhus* fall prey.

> The kind of veneration shown by the Theravadin laity to bhikkhus, by prostrating before them, seating them on a higher level, serving them on bended knees, and giving even the juniormost of them precedence over the highest lay dignitaries, has a negative rather than a positive psychological effect on them.... In the case of the majority the effect is very negative indeed, serving as it does to reinforce their sense of the superiority of the bhikkhu to the layman and giving them, in some instances, a quite inflated idea of their own importance and even of their own spiritual attainments.[160]

Again, Sangharakshita did meet Theravāda laymen who sincerely practised the Dharma, but he found that most considered that their main
religious duty was feeding and reverencing the monks. They often did
this not so much out of genuine respect for spiritual life but on the
quasi-magical grounds that it would bring them material benefits by way
of merit, as well as a favourable rebirth.

In the world of Mahāyāna Buddhism a somewhat different state of
affairs exists. We have already seen that the Mahāyāna arose partly as a
corrective to the narrowed ideal of the later Hīnayāna. One of the
degeneracies it sought to counteract was the excessive emphasis on
monasticism, and particularly the tendency to see it as the only vehicle
for spiritual life. The Mahāyāna could not accept that being a Buddhist
simply meant being a monk.

> The Mahāyāna tried to bridge the gap [between monastic and lay] in
> various ways. For instance a favourite way in Mahāyāna *sūtras* is to have
> the most unlikely sort of person, that is to say lay, young, and even
> female, rebuking elderly *bhikkhus* for their lack of spiritual development
> and understanding. The point being made is that one must not attach too
> much importance to these formal distinctions of monk and lay, old and
> young, even male and female.[161]

In particular, the Mahāyāna restated the ideal in terms of the Bodhisattva
path, which could be followed by monk and lay alike. Thus, though the
Mahāyāna world preserves the monastic community with its ceremony
of ordination, it allows to all, whether householder or monastic, the
possibility of taking the Bodhisattva ordination with its own sets of vows
and rules. In this way, it restores something of the balance of the Buddha's
original community of followers. Later developments took this process
further. In Tantric Buddhism, the emphasis came to be placed on initiation as the basic rite which is open to monk and lay. Not being a monk
was, in certain cases, a definite advantage because one could then practise
'sexo-yogic' rituals. In Japanese Buddhism, the *bhikkhu* sangha has not
survived at all, Bodhisattva ordination having entirely replaced it in most
schools.

While the Mahāyāna has restored the original balance of the Buddha's
community, Sangharakshita considers that it has done so in a way that
introduces problems of its own—without resolving all the abuses of the
Hīnayāna. As we have already seen, the Mahayanists had no understanding of the nature of historical change, nor did they have a critical
approach to the texts they had inherited. They could only renew the
spiritual vitality of Buddhism by accepting the broad Hīnayāna position
as a preliminary and inferior goal, to which they added the fuller

revelation of the Bodhisattva Ideal. Bodhisattva ordination, the act of the Mahāyāna that unifies both monk and lay, took place, theoretically speaking, in succession to the Hīnayāna path. First one completed the Hīnayāna phase, which was supposed to consist in ethical purification and renunciation of worldly interests in pursuit of personal liberation. Then one undertook the vow of the Bodhisattva, to save all sentient beings from suffering.

Lofty and inspiring as is this aspiration, most practitioners cannot undertake it authentically since it is impossibly beyond them. The vow is actually the expression of a transcendental experience. Without that experience one cannot understand what the vow truly signifies, let alone really mean it when one utters it: it 'becomes a little bit theatrical'.[162] Thus, while Bodhisattva ordination has the merit of unifying the Buddhist community, it does so by means of a sort of hypocrisy—which can perhaps, in its own way, be as damaging as the identification of spiritual commitment with being a monk or nun. To establish the spiritual life of all Buddhists on an aspiration that belongs properly to the transcendental path reduces it to fantasy: the repetition of high undertakings that one cannot possibly fulfil. It quickly leads to a formalism of its own kind.

The Mahāyāna lacked the historical perspective to question the Hīnayāna position in terms of basic principles laid down by the Buddha. It therefore in no way attacked its monastic formalism. Indeed it became heir to it, albeit tempered by the more ample Bodhisattva ordination in which monk and lay could both participate. That monastic formalism is present in its most extreme form in the one extant Hīnayāna school, the Theravāda. To a greater or lesser extent, however, it also taints the Mahāyāna. Thus, even in *triyāna* Tibet, the term *dge 'dun* or sangha is popularly used only to mean 'monks'. The formalism consists in the fact that being a monk has become increasingly identified with being proper-ly ordained, in the manner prescribed by the *Vinaya*, rather than with living a certain kind of life-style according to certain moral principles. In the Theravāda this formalism is compounded, since being a true or serious Buddhist is largely identified with being a monk. Therefore being a Buddhist is identified with being validly ordained according to the *Vinaya*.

As he has revealed in his book, *Forty-Three Years Ago,* Sangharakshita was forced to confront monastic formalism early in his own career as a monk. Six years after being ordained as a *bhikkhu*

> I discovered ... that one of the bhikkhus taking part in my ordination
> had rendered himself [liable to expulsion], as at least some members of

the ordaining chapter were aware. He had been guilty of a breach of the training rule prohibiting intentional sexual intercourse, and in fact had a 'wife' and son living with him at his temple, the former being officially his cook.[163]

This 'monk' was actually technically no longer a monk, since the breaking of this rule entails automatic expulsion, according to the *Vinaya*. The *Vinaya* further states that the ceremony of ordination is not valid if there is present within the *sīmā* or 'ordination boundary' a monk who is 'not pure' through breach of this and other basic rules. Thus Sangharakshita came to discover that his own ordination was technically invalid. He was not actually a *bhikkhu* as for six years he had thought himself to be. Over the following years, he came to know that several of the monks who had participated in his ordination were also technically not *bhikkhus*. They too were in breach of one or other of the rules meriting automatic expulsion or suspension—as some of the others must have been aware.

Should he seek re-ordination? That would have been difficult because, in the first place, it was clearly not 'the done thing' in the Theravāda to discuss such matters.

> Seeking re-ordination (or rather, again seeking to be ordained) would mean having to explain why I considered this to be necessary, and I already knew that questioning a bhikkhu's 'complete purity' was something rather frowned on in Theravadin monastic circles.[164]

But more significantly, how could he ever guarantee that any new ordination was valid? Even if all the monks in the *sīmā* were 'pure', what about all the monks who had ordained *them*? It would take only one of them having been 'impure' to invalidate his new ordination. Since at least five monks must be present at an ordination (ten in the 'Middle Country' of north-eastern India), the validity of each ordination rests upon the validity of hundreds of thousands of ordinations stretching back to the time of the Buddha. Each of those ordinations had to be valid for every subsequent one to be so. It is almost unthinkable that this could have been the case—especially as Sangharakshita's own experience in the modern Theravāda showed that very little real attention was given to ensuring the 'purity' of all monks present.

> In the event I did nothing about my discovery. I continued to meditate and study, continued to work for the good of Buddhism, and observed the Vinaya or Monastic Code to the best of my ability, just as though I had been validly ordained and *was* technically a bhikkhu. My confidence in the Theravadin branch of the Monastic Order may have been undermined, but my faith in the Dharma and the spiritual life, and in the monastic life-style, remained unshaken.[165]

Despite the technical invalidity of his own ordination and the doubt it cast on the validity of the ordination of every other *bhikkhu*, Sangharakshita knew that the ceremony had been deeply significant for him. He says of his *bhikkhu* ordination,

Whilst the ceremony was in progress I experienced an extraordinary sense of peace, satisfaction, fulfilment, acceptance, and belonging. It was a feeling such as I had not experienced before, and in subsequent years I was never surprised when an elderly monk told me that receiving monastic ordination had been the greatest experience of his whole life.[166]

His discovery of the invalidity of his own ordination led him to think about ordination in general. It helped him to disentangle himself from monastic formalism and to reveal what the significance of the ceremony really was. He gradually came to understand that what the ceremony had truly signified for him was acceptance into the total spiritual community, rather than merely into the monastic order.

This acceptance into the wider Buddhist community was symbolised for him by the fact that in his 'ordination chapter' were monks from four different nationalities, who unusually came from different Theravāda *nikāyas* (it not being possible, then, to assemble in India the requisite quorum of monks from a single *nikāya*). Furthermore, outside the *sīmā* sat a Ladakhi incarnate lama of the Tibetan tradition and behind him were gathered white-robed lay followers. It seemed to him as if his own ordination crossed the boundaries of Hīnayāna and Mahāyāna and of monk and lay. Although some of those who had participated in his 'ordination' were 'impure' as monks, their acceptance of him into the Buddhist community still had great meaning for him.

Though most of the bhikkhus who had taken part in my ordination were, like the bhikkhu with a wife and son, bad monks, they were, like him, good Buddhists. They looked after pilgrims, edited Buddhist magazines, published books on Buddhism, ran schools and dispensaries, organized Buddhist festivals, gave lectures, and received new converts into the sangha or Buddhist spiritual community, besides observing the basic ethical precepts and practising a little meditation. In the case of some of them, at least, these activities were the expression of a deep and genuine devotion to the Dharma, for whose sake they had, despite their sexual peccadilloes, made many sacrifices. I am therefore glad I was ordained by them, and in the case of two or three of them cherish fond memories of our subsequent association.[167]

Sangharakshita saw that there was a single cause both for the monastic formalism of the Theravāda, and to an extent of the Mahāyāna as well, and for the Mahāyāna's unrealistic resolution of the monk–lay divide by means of Bodhisattva ordination. The significance of Going for Refuge had been lost as the basic act by which one became a Buddhist and thereby a member of the spiritual community. If those who are leading a lay life and those leading a more monastic one all go for Refuge, there is then no spiritual divide between them and therefore no need to reconcile them in the Bodhisattva ordination. This does not, however, mean that the Bodhisattva Ideal itself must be dispensed with; it simply finds its correct place as the altruistic dimension of Going for Refuge. Similarly, monastic ordination assumes its proper place as the taking up of a particular way of life in furtherance of one's Going for Refuge. In Sangharakshita's phrase, 'Going for Refuge is primary, life-style secondary.'[168]— although he is at pains to point out that 'secondary does not mean "unimportant"', as we shall see later. The technical correctness of the ceremony by which one becomes a monk is not of crucial significance. This does not mean that, if there is such a ceremony, it should not be done as correctly as possible. The point is that one's being a monk depends ultimately on what one does and how one lives rather than on the way the ceremony is performed and by whom.

## ORDINATION AS THE EXPRESSION OF EFFECTIVE GOING FOR REFUGE

For Sangharakshita, 'ordination' is the formal expression of Effective Going for Refuge. Until Going for Refuge has become Effective, there can be no ordination because there is, as yet, no effective commitment. One is not yet able to dedicate one's life to the Three Jewels. There is no need for further ordinations after Effective Going for Refuge because the act of Going for Refuge contains within it all aspects of the spiritual path. There is no need for the Bodhisattva ordination because Going for Refuge has an altruistic dimension implicit within it. If one is actually Going for Refuge there must be a deepening element of concern for others. There is no need for Tantric initiation because Effective Going for Refuge is the activation of one's spiritual energies. If one puts one's Going for Refuge into effect, then, in time, all its different aspects and levels will be revealed.

In deepening one's Going for Refuge, one may wish to study and practise particular aspects of the path, take up new meditation practices, or observe a particular life-style, such as a monastic one. However, these do not require new ordinations. In Effectively Going for Refuge one has already made the effective commitment to spiritual life that is now being worked out in detail. To undertake the visualisation of a particular Buddha or Bodhisattva does not need a new initiation. One has already made the crucial connection with all the Buddhas and Bodhisattvas in Effectively Going for Refuge. A ceremony might mark becoming a monk but that ceremony would consist in taking certain vows, not a new ordination.

Ordination has two principal aspects: expression of Going for Refuge and acceptance into the spiritual community of those already Effectively Going for Refuge. The explicit expression of Going for Refuge is integral to spiritual growth. One needs to bring it into the public arena, to make it known, so that it can become part of one's own identity. It is not enough to 'know it in one's heart', it must be expressed to become effective. Ordination provides the opportunity for this expression. Sangharakshita is very critical of modern attitudes that devalue formal expression, since they reinforce an idea of the individual as isolated from all context. He upholds the basic psychological truth that, for the most part, until an inner change has been *expressed* it has not really taken place.

Ordination also marks one's acceptance into the effective spiritual community. One expresses one's commitment before a senior member of the sangha. He or she witnesses one's Going for Refuge and confirms that it coincides with his or her own Going for Refuge. In publicly witnessing one's Effective Going for Refuge, that senior member of the sangha acknowledges that one is now a member of the sangha too. Because he or she accepts that one is Going for Refuge effectively and sincerely, the sangha as a whole can do so too. From that point on, one enters into an entirely new relationship with all other members of the spiritual community.

According to Sangharakshita, entry into the spiritual community involves participation in a new mode of awareness,

> a special kind of consciousness common to, in a sense even shared by, a number of truly human individuals who follow the same spiritual disciplines and the same spiritual ideals, or who are engaged in the same creative activities.[169]

This 'collective' consciousness is very difficult to define, there being

> no suitable term in the English language, or indeed in any other European language, unless the Russian *sobornost* comes near it to some extent.[170]

It is, however, very different from the collective consciousness of the group and from individual consciousness, being a 'third order' of consciousness above and beyond them both. Since this is one of Sangharakshita's most important teachings that has considerable practical consequence, we must explore it in more detail.

## THE INDIVIDUAL AND THE GROUP

We have already seen that Sangharakshita sees the total evolutionary process as consisting of two great phases: a Higher and a Lower. The fulcrum of evolution is the self-aware individual who stands at the summit of the Lower Evolution, as its final product, and at the threshold of the Higher, as its future subject. The subject of the Lower Evolution is the species, for individual organisms do not themselves evolve but simply participate in the evolution of the species to which they belong. The individual however 'is a whole species in himself'[171] and may traverse the entire Higher Evolution by his own efforts. The human race as a whole straddles the Lower and Higher Evolutions. The great majority of its members are most of the time preoccupied with the concerns of the Lower Evolution; only a few seriously dedicate themselves to the task of further development as individuals. Although all human beings are capable of self-consciousness, most never develop it to any extent. Those who do not develop greater self-consciousness remain immersed in the human equivalent of the Lower Evolutionary species: the group. Sangharakshita has coined the terms 'statistical individuals' or 'social units' for individual human beings still immersed in the group, to distinguish them from the individual, in his special use of the term.[172]

In Sangharakshita's usage, the term 'group' acquires the specific meaning of the human Lower Evolutionary collectivity, bonded by ties that are 'usually more or less material'.[173] The group in the widest sense is made up of numerous greater or smaller groups, sometimes overlapping and sometimes antagonistic. Each of these groups is bound together by the ties of blood and kinship, of soil and culture, or of economic and political interest. They are united by mutual need, the need for security being an especially powerful and basic bonding agent.

> We can define the group as a collectivity organized for its own survival, in which the interests of the individual are subordinated to those of the collectivity. The group, or collectivity, is also a power-structure in which the ultimate sanction is force. The group did not just make survival possible for its members; in the case of humans, it made it possible for them to enjoy higher and higher levels of material prosperity and culture. It made possible the emergence of folk art and ethnic religion; it made possible the emergence of civilization. But there was a price to be paid by the proto-individual, and that price was conformity with the group. The individual was regarded as being essentially a member of the group. The individual had no existence separate from the group, or apart from the group.[174]

Groups tend to be conservative and conformist, granting their members little latitude for deviation from their norms, since deviation threatens their survival. The 'statistical individuals' who make up a group do not, even dare not, think for themselves. They derive their values and their outlook on life from the groups to which they belong. If one is to evolve as an individual one must separate oneself from the group. One must learn to think and feel for oneself, accepting full responsibility for one's own life and future.

The Higher Evolution commences when the individual emerges from the group. The primary characteristic of the individual is self-awareness.

> When one is aware of being aware, one is conscious of oneself as an individual, conscious of oneself as separate from the group. One is conscious of one's ability to think and feel and act differently from the group, even against the group. An individual of this type is a true individual. Such a person is not only self-aware but is emotionally positive, full of good will towards all living beings. He is also spontaneous and creative because he is not determined in his thinking, feeling, or acting, by previously existing mental, emotional, and psychological patterns—whether his own or those of other people. The true individual is also responsible, aware of his own needs, aware of others' needs, and prepared and willing to act accordingly.[175]

Elsewhere Sangharakshita speaks of the individual as characterised by

> emotional positivity, responsibility, intelligence, creativity, spontaneity, imagination, and insight.[176]

Sangharakshita's use of the expression 'individual' has sometimes been misunderstood. One critic accused Sangharakshita and his new Buddhist movement of using 'modernist narratives' and of appearing to 'embrace enthusiastically the personalist understanding of religious significance which developed in liberal Protestantism'.[177] Sangharakshita deals extensively with the assumptions underlying this interpretation in his *The FWBO and 'Protestant Buddhism': An Affirmation and a Protest*. He makes it quite clear that he does not agree with 'modernist narratives of the self' or with 'the personalist understanding of religious significance':

> To me the idea that there exists a self which is pure, that this self is enslaved by socially imposed beliefs and customs, and that all one has to do in order to 'be oneself' and realize one's potentiality is to break free of them, is simply false.[178]

The notion of 'the individual' must be seen within the overall context of his teaching and not interpreted in terms of modern individualism.

To make this point clear, Sangharakshita carefully distinguishes the individual from the individual*ist*.

> The individualist still 'shares' the consciousness of the group.... The
> individualist has, we could say, a larger 'share' of this group
> consciousness than other members of the group, and therefore asserts his
> or her own interests at the expense of others in the group. The individual
> is therefore alienated from the group in what we may call a vertical
> direction, while the individualist is alienated from the group
> horizontally. The individualist is a sort of broken-off fragment of the
> group, reacting, even rebelling, against the group; he is the group writ
> small, a sort of one-man group—which is really a contradiction in terms,
> like a one-man band. The individual, on the other hand, has passed, or
> begun to pass, beyond the group, beyond group consciousness; he is no
> longer limited by group consciousness.[179]

To be an individual does not simply mean being free of the group: it
involves the attainment of definite qualities, among which are friendliness and goodwill towards others. Indeed, growth in individuality is far
from growth in individualism—it is growth in selflessness. Moreover, the
individual recognises the evolutionary necessity of the group. Without
it, human beings would not survive to become individuals. Indeed, so
long as the group allows those of its members who wish to become
individuals to do so, the individual supports the group. Sangharakshita
terms a group that does encourage transition to individuality, a 'positive
group'.

In using this language of the group and the individual, Sangharakshita
is once again employing terms without precise equivalents in the canonical texts to communicate the essential meaning of terms that are certainly
found in them. For instance, the basic teachings distinguish two kinds of
self-conscious being.

> Intelligent sentient beings are either *āryas* or *anāryas*. In the Scriptures the
> latter are generally referred to as *prithagjanas* (Pali, *puthujjanas*) or
> average men. As they outnumber the *āryas* by many millions to one the
> term *bahujana* or 'many-folk' may also be applied to them. An average
> man is one who, dominated by the delusion of 'I' and 'mine' identifies
> himself with, or imagines he possesses, form, feeling, conception,
> volition, and consciousness. He is the fool (*bāla*) described in the
> *Dhammapada* verse 62: '"Sons are mine, wealth is mine", thus the fool
> torments [himself]. Indeed he does not belong to himself. Whence sons?
> Whence wealth?' Not knowing the true Dharma, he develops
> attachments to things which should be avoided.[180]

Clearly the *prithagjana* is the group member and the *ārya* corresponds to
the true individual of Sangharakshita's terminology. The term
'individual' itself in particular suggests a taking of personal responsibility for one's own life, and especially for one's own further development. The Buddha repeatedly stressed this quality and particularly

refused to be seen as a personal saviour. He insisted that he 'only showed the way' and that the path could be followed by individual effort alone.

## THE THIRD ORDER OF CONSCIOUSNESS

To become conscious of oneself as independent of the group is to become an individual. In Sangharakshita's language, it is to move from the first to the second order of consciousness: from group consciousness to individual consciousness. However, that is not the end of the matter. The individual experiences himself in relation to other individuals, and this experience brings into being the third order of consciousness: the 'collective' consciousness of the spiritual community. In participating in this order of consciousness there is no loss of individuality: 'It has no collective identity in which you lose your own, or in which you become submerged.'[181] Each member is fully and completely aware of himself and there is no giving up of individual thoughts and feelings to the collective. Rather individual thoughts and feelings coincide, freely and spontaneously. Sharing a common commitment to the Three Jewels, members of the spiritual community base their lives upon the same ideals and values. They look at the world from the same perspective—although some, so to speak, view that same perspective from a greater altitude. The third order of consciousness is only 'collective' in this sense. There is, as Sangharakshita has it, a 'coincidence of wills'.

In so far as there is a coincidence of wills within the spiritual community, there is very great harmony and fellowship between its members. Each member finds others who understand and share his or her own most cherished aspirations. This is obviously deeply satisfying and inspiring. The more fully each goes for Refuge, the more profoundly he or she will share in this 'collective' consciousness. Ultimately, participation in the consciousness of the sangha is identical with the experience of the transcendental path. So close can one member of the spiritual community come to others that the notion of a separate self, isolated from all others, is dissolved. This 'third' kind of consciousness is so unfamiliar to us that we all too easily misunderstand it as loss of individuality and renewed immersion in the group. Sangharakshita has suggested the analogy of the orchestra, which 'is a spiritual community—at least while it is playing'.[182] Each instrument in an orchestra has its own part to play but all are harmonised in the music they are together creating.

On a yet more lofty and imaginative plane, Sangharakshita has invoked the image of the archetypal Bodhisattva Avalokiteśvara, in his thousand-armed form, as embodying this third kind of consciousness. Avalokiteśvara symbolises transcendental compassion, a state that completely transcends all egoism. To draw out the active dimension of compassion, he is sometimes depicted with a thousand arms reaching out from his body in a great halo of compassionate activity, and eleven heads seeking out suffering in all the directions of space.

> The Order, and especially the unity of the Order, is symbolised by the figure of the eleven-headed and thousand-armed Avalokiteśvara. Each Order member represents one of those thousand arms and hands, joined on to the body of Avalokiteśvara. Each hand holds a single implement: a flower, wheel, vase, bow and arrow, and so on. Each instrument represents the particular activity of each individual Order member. They represent the particular talent or gift that each individual Order member makes to the Order, to the movement, to the world, as a whole. But all those symbols, all those implements, all those hands, all those arms, all those heads, are integrated into this one figure, the body of Avalokiteśvara, which is the Order.[183]

Each is separate and unique, yet each is joined to the one body of the Bodhisattva. Each is animated by the same Going for Refuge, of which the Bodhisattva Avalokiteśvara represents the altruistic dimension.

The 'collective consciousness' of the spiritual community naturally arises when individuals who go for Refuge are drawn together. It is a profound spiritual experience and therefore requires no practical justification. However, Sangharakshita points out that the sangha has important practical implications for the developing individual. In the first place, the spiritual community is likely to consist of individuals from many different backgrounds and of many different temperaments. Inevitably one will be thrust together with people with whom, in worldly terms, one might find it difficult to get on. Yet they are members of the same spiritual community: they too have Effectively Gone for Refuge. One cannot ignore them and one must learn to overcome the biases and prejudices of culture and character that divide one from them:

> In this way, members of the spiritual community ... help one another to overcome purely subjective, purely personal limitations and learn how to relate on the basis of what is higher.[184]

The spiritual community also provides a network of support and guidance to those struggling to become individuals and to follow the path of the Higher Evolution. That support is, in most cases, decisive: without it, few could complete the path. To understand this more clearly, we must look a little more closely at some of Sangharakshita's ideas on the nature of the path. Until the point of Real Going for Refuge, spiritual life is always a struggle between the two fundamental tendencies of reality: the *saṁsāric*/cyclic/reactive and the *nirvāṇic*/spiral/creative. These tendencies are within one's own heart and mind and are constantly battling for supremacy. Sangharakshita has spoken of these two trends as two 'gravitational pulls' that play upon the emerging individual.[185] The gravitational pull of the Unconditioned draws us on to Enlightenment. It is that powerful attraction that leads us to go for Refuge. However, the Conditioned also exerts its gravitational pull.

Initially, one is almost entirely dominated by the very powerful attractions of the world and the group, which draw nascent individuality back into the undifferentiated darkness of the Lower Evolution. Though the Unconditioned does exert its influence at this stage, the pull of the Conditioned is much stronger. As one goes for Refuge more and more deeply, one gradually overcomes the pull of the Conditioned. At the point of Real Going for Refuge or Stream Entry, the pull of the Unconditioned, for the first time, outweighs the pull of the Conditioned. Attraction towards the Lower Evolution is still felt but the pull of the Higher is now dominant. In a sense, at this stage there is no longer any struggle between them—the struggle has been won.

The most difficult period of spiritual life, therefore, lies between Effective and Real Going for Refuge. Having effectively committed oneself, one must traverse the mundane path against the strong current sweeping one back towards the Conditioned. It is only a very rare few, the Buddha himself being the outstanding and perhaps only example, who can swim against that tide, alone and unaided. Not only is that pull within one's own breast: its presence there is reinforced by its omnipresence in the world around one. The world is dominated by the group and the group is dominated by the gravitational pull of the Conditioned. One needs the help and support of others on the path: one needs the sangha. Members of the spiritual community 'support one another, encourage one another, inspire one another'[186] in those times of crisis and despondency that inevitably come as they battle against the gravitational pull of the Conditioned. Since the spiritual community consists of individuals at different levels of development there is usually someone more developed than oneself, at least to some extent, who can help one forward on the path. At the very least, there are individuals on one's own level who can give one the sympathy and support that one needs. The help that members of the spiritual community give to one another enables them to continue Going for Refuge against the pull of the Conditioned.

When Sangharakshita started the Western Buddhist Order, he had had little personal experience of sangha throughout his years as a Buddhist. Not that he had been isolated or lonely in an ordinary sense: he had many friends and was clearly well liked by most people who met him. However, though he was in friendly contact with *bhikkhus* from many schools, he found no spiritual fellowship with them. On occasions of real spiritual need, in his early days in Kalimpong, he was alone. Later, he did experience deeper communication with one or two of his Tibetan teachers and in Lama Govinda he found a 'kindred spirit'.[187] However, he never participated in a broader spiritual community. Indeed, in 1978 he told a small group of disciples with whom he was on retreat that, for the first time, he felt himself to be a full participant in sangha. Before that, he had accepted that, though he might initiate a sangha for others, he would probably never experience himself, so to speak, as its beneficiary.

Although he had no real experience of sangha, Sangharakshita had plenty of experience of Buddhist organisations. Indeed, he had seen many problems and deficiencies in those organisations while he was in India—and he saw more when he came back to London. We have already explored his criticisms of the modern monastic sangha, but he found severe limitations in all the Buddhist groups with which he worked. A significant proportion of the governing body of the Maha Bodhi Society, the leading Buddhist organisation in India, was made up not of Buddhists but of Hindus, one member being notoriously anti-Buddhist. For this reason, Sangharakshita, while aiding the Society in its more constructive work, never became a member and made sure he was not identified with it. He found a similar situation in England, on his return in 1964.

The leading English Buddhist organisations were not run principally by Buddhists. They were societies, established on the model of learned societies, like the Pali Text Society, that had pioneered exploration of the wisdom of the East. Anyone could join who was prepared to pay a subscription, thereby acquiring the right to vote in the election of the governing body. Most members took little active interest in the organisation of these societies. However, some of those who did were people who enjoyed the modicum of power and prestige that went with being on the governing body. In India, in fact, the prestige could be quite considerable. Inevitably, under the control of such people, little could be achieved for Buddhism—although sometimes they managed to do some harm.

> One thing was clear to me: Buddhist organizations could not be run by
> non-Buddhists. They could not be run simply by people who were good
> at running organizations, however efficient those people might be. They

certainly could not be run by people who were after mere power or influence. Neither could they be run by those who had only an intellectual interest in Buddhism. It was clear that a Buddhist spiritual movement could be run only by those who were committed to Buddhism: those who were committed to the Dharma and actually practised the Buddha's teachings. (Strange as it may seem, at the time this did not seem to be generally realized.)[188]

It was with this experience very much in mind that, in April 1968, he founded the Western Buddhist Order.* Its purpose was, he declared in a lecture given on the day of the first ordinations, to enable people to commit themselves more fully to the Buddhist way of life, to provide opportunities for spiritual fellowship, and to provide an 'organizational' base for the propagation of Buddhism.[189]

In many respects it represented a radical departure from Eastern Buddhism, although it was based firmly upon principles established by the Buddha himself. It was to be a genuine spiritual community, and not a society. One entered it by Effectively Going for Refuge. Initially Sangharakshita had planned that there should be four grades of ordination: the *upāsaka/upāsikā*, *mahā-upāsaka/upāsikā*, Bodhisattva, and *bhikkhu/bhikkhunī* ordinations. However, as the Order unfolded, so did his thinking. He saw that further ordinations were neither necessary nor appropriate. There was really only one ordination in Buddhism and that consisted in the formal act of Going for Refuge to the Three Jewels and thereby acceptance into the spiritual community. The spiritual community comprised all those who Effectively went for Refuge, whatever their life-style and whatever the level of Going for Refuge they had attained beyond the Effective.

The first members of the Order were ordained as *upāsakas* (m.) and *upāsikās* (f.), the terms used in traditional Buddhism for lay Buddhists. However, Sangharakshita saw more and more clearly that Order members could not properly be classified as either lay or monastic, though some members of the Order lived at home with their families and some were leading what amounted to monastic lives. Before all else, members of the Order simply went for Refuge to the Buddha, Dharma, and Sangha.

---

* In India the Order is known as the 'Trailokya Bauddha Mahasangha'—the 'Buddhist Order of the Three Worlds'.

The categories of lay and monastic were entirely secondary to that essential spiritual act. In 1982, Sangharakshita therefore suggested that the style of the ordination should be changed to 'Dharmacari' (m.) and 'Dharmacarini' (f.), which means 'Dharma-farer' or 'practitioner of the Dharma'.* The term goes back to the Buddha himself, being found in the *Dhammapada*:

> The *Dhammacari* lives happily, (both) in this world and in the world beyond.[190]

This title or 'style' thus emphasises both the Order's discontinuity with the categories of modern oriental Buddhism and its continuity with the essential Buddhist tradition.

Transcending the distinction between monks and laity, a distinction having its roots in ancient Indian society, allows members of the Western Buddhist Order a much broader range of life-styles. The greater flexibility of modern Western society permits a complete spectrum of social arrangements. Every way of life is possible, between the extremes of complete immersion in family life and immurement in a monastery. Thus, for instance, some men or women, while fully completing their family responsibilities, might spend some time in 'semi-monastic' residential communities. Others, while living most of the time a monastic life-style, might remain sexually active outside their residential community—that sexual activity, of course, being subjected always to ethical considerations. Many different life-styles are, even at this early stage, now represented within the Western Buddhist Order.

Unlike most traditional orders, the Western Buddhist Order consists of both men and women equally—although, as we shall see, men and women in the Order carry out many activities separately. Men and women

> receive the same ordination, engage in the same spiritual practices, and undertake the same organizational responsibilities.[191]

The Order also transcends the divisions of the modern Buddhist world and is not sectarian,

> in that it does not identify itself with any one form of Buddhism. Instead it rejoices in the riches of the whole Buddhist tradition and seeks to draw from those riches whatever is of value for its own practice of the Dharma.[192]

---

* In India, because the Sanskrit word *Dharma* carries the connotation of Hindu caste duty, Order members are referred to by the Pali, Dhammacari and Dhammacarini.

It crosses many national and cultural barriers, already having members from twenty-five or more nationalities. There are members from all over the developed world, as well as from India—where, at the time of writing, one quarter of the Order is to be found. This transcendence of so many of the divisions prevailing in the world, as well as those afflicting the world of Buddhism, is made possible by Sangharakshita's insistence on the primacy of Going for Refuge.

> Let us do away with our divisions. Let us do away with the divisions
> between monastic and lay Buddhists, between men and women
> Buddhists, and between the followers of different sects and schools of
> Buddhism. Let us have an integrated Buddhism and an integrated
> Buddhist community. Let us base ourselves firmly and unmistakably
> upon our common Going for Refuge to the Buddha, the Dharma, and the
> Sangha.[193]

The Order founded by Sangharakshita does not fall in with the categories of oriental Buddhism, any more than it does with the religious categories of the West. It is therefore not easy to express what an Order member is. Order members are not *bhikkhus* and *bhikkhunīs*, no more are they *upāsakas* and *upaṣikās*. Members of the Order are not priests and have no sacerdotal role as intermediaries between the transcendental and the world. They are not clergy in the sense of automatically having professional responsibility for the running of a Buddhist movement. They are simply individuals who are united in their common Effective Going for Refuge. Indeed, the Order has no official organisational existence, being a purely spiritual body. Nonetheless, many, if not most, Order members do help with the running of the Friends of the Western Buddhist Order or FWBO, often referred to as 'the Friends'.*

The FWBO is the organisational framework through which Order members teach the Dharma and provide the conditions for themselves and others to practise it. It is the bridge between the world and the Order, by means of which those who wish to may go for Refuge themselves. Groups of Order members in different locations establish various institutions, like public centres for the teaching of Buddhism, residential communities, and co-operative business ventures. These together form the basic matrix of the movement. Though most Order members choose to engage in this work, and many do so full-time, some have no formal or regular links with the institutions of the FWBO. They might, for instance,

---

* In India, 'Trailokya Bauddha Mahasangha Sahayak Gana' or TBMSG.

be engaging in scholarly research or in artistic activities. There is no obligation on Order members to work for the Buddhist movement in any direct way. However, Effective Going for Refuge has an altruistic dimension integral to it. The activity of all Order members should, therefore, by definition be of benefit to others in some way.

Sangharakshita's vision of the sangha as the expression of a third order of consciousness, arising out of the shared Going for Refuge of its members, is an important theme within the Western Buddhist Order. As we shall see, Sangharakshita has greatly stressed spiritual friendship and he has constantly emphasised the need for deeper and more effective communication between Order members. He has established the Order on very clear spiritual principles and has done what he can, through exhortation and example, to ensure they are expressed in practice. Sangharakshita has done everything he can to ensure that the Western Buddhist Order is not just an organisation but truly a sangha, the embodiment of a new kind of consciousness. That new kind of consciousness, when it is fully realised, is transcendental. Indeed, Sangharakshita identifies it with the *bodhicitta*, that 'will to Enlightenment' that, in the Mahāyāna tradition, animates the Bodhisattva to work for the good of all beings.

> It seems that the *bodhicitta* is something more likely to arise within a community, within an order of people who are working to allow it to manifest.... It's much more like, in a way, the whole Order getting it—how, one just doesn't know at present, but it is certainly much more like that. It might be focused, as it were, in certain individuals, but it really concerns the Order, even the movement as a whole.... [The *bodhicitta*] is more likely to arise in the case of a number of people working hard together, and stimulating and sparking one another off, rather than in the solitary individual, in whose case it may tend to be more like an individual experience in the narrower sense. At the same time it's not a 'collective' thing in the sense of a product of mass psychology. We don't really have a word for it. It's more a matter of fellowship, or a manifestation of spiritual communion.[194]

This is the aspiration that Sangharakshita has for the Order he has founded.

## Chapter Six

# THE FUNDAMENTAL CODE OF ETHICS

*Think not, my friends, that piling stone on stone,*
*Or laying brick on brick, as now we must*
*In this degenerate age, shall from the dust*
*Raise up those glories which were overthrown*
*When, like autumnal floods, from icy zone*
*Islam rolled down. Oh do not too much trust*
*Arches that ruinate and gates that rust*
*To guard the Buddha's treasure for His own!*

*Within our minds must Nalanda arise*
*Before we draw up plans, or measure ground:*
*If the foundation on our thoughts we lay,*
*Calm meditation, contemplation wise,*
*Above mundane vicissitudes shall found*
*A Nalanda that cannot pass away.*[195]

THE BUDDHIST WORLD IS AS DIVIDED on ethical matters as it is on most others.
For instance, the different sects into which the original united monastic
community broke up each had its own set of monastic rules and precepts.
Thus the Theravadin *bhikkhus* observe 227 rules, while the *bhikkhus* of the
Mahāyāna, following the traditions of other early schools, observe 258,
218, or 263. However, the most significant divisions are not between the
different sects and schools but within them. Different sets of rules apply
to those within each socio-religious category. The *bhikkhus* and *bhikkhunīs*,
where these latter still survive, both observe different ethical codes, as do
*śrāmaṇeras* or novice monks and *śrāmaṇerikās* or novice nuns. There are
various codes for the benefit of *upāsakas*, and *upāsikās*. Another set of vows
is usually undertaken at the time of Bodhisattva ordination: sixty-four is

common, but there is no universal pattern. Tantric initiates also often make vows at the time of *abhisheka* or initiation.

Not only is there a bewildering diversity that contributes to lack of unity, but there is also degeneration. In some parts of the Buddhist world, as we have seen, ordination as a *bhikkhu* has been viewed as the real point of entry into the Buddhist community, and *bhikkhu* ordination has itself mainly been understood as the taking on of the code of 200 or more rules, rather than as the act of Going for Refuge to the Three Jewels. But, as Sangharakshita argues,

> Some of the precepts observed only by the monks are of no real ethical
> significance, being in some cases concerned with matters of a quite
> trivial nature and demonstrably the product of social conditions
> prevailing at the time of the Buddha or shortly after.[196]

Typically, in Sangharakshita's experience, the observance of these quite trivial matters is emphasised more than basic ethical principles. Not eating after midday and the correct way of wearing of robes are valued more than temperance and lack of vanity. The importance given to such customs only serves to heighten the divisions between the monks and the laity. Because they do not observe these rules of monastic custom and etiquette, non-*bhikkhus* seem even more like 'second-class Buddhists'.

> If the spiritual unity of the Buddhist community is to be preserved from
> disruption, therefore, what is needed is (a) an uncompromising assertion
> of the primacy of Going for Refuge as the fundamental Buddhist act, and
> (b) a drastic reduction of the rules comprising the seven different [ethical
> codes observed by the different socio-religious classes: *bhikkhus*,
> *bhikkhunīs*, *śrāmaṇeras*, *śrāmaṇerikās*, *śikshamānās* or 'female probationers',
> *upāsakas* and *upāsikās*] to those precepts of genuinely ethical significance
> which they have in common, together with a firm insistence on the
> necessity of one's actually observing those precepts.[197]

In founding the Western Buddhist Order, Sangharakshita gave all his disciples, whatever their different ways of life, the same set of ten precepts to observe. This set is quite traditional, being found in both earlier and later scriptures. Sangharakshita considers that it offers what he calls a *mūla-prātimoksha* or fundamental code of ethical conduct. It could be, he believes, that 'drastic reduction of the rules to those precepts of genuinely ethical significance' that the spiritual community so urgently needs. Before we can examine this list, however, we must look more closely at Sangharakshita's understanding of Buddhist ethics.

## CHRISTIAN MORALITY

When Sangharakshita came to teach Buddhism in the West, he soon encountered a major problem. Whether or not they had been brought up as Christians, many of the people he met seemed to have been negatively affected by Christianity. This was especially true in the field of morality. He found that most people seemed unable to think of morality except in Christian categories and were either reacting to conventional Christian moral teaching or unconsciously still under its sway. Buddhist morality has a quite different basis and structure, and Sangharakshita has been at pains to differentiate the ethical teachings of the Dharma from those of the Abrahamic religions. Whatever the subtleties of modern theology, the reality of general Christian, Jewish, and Muslim morality, as it affects the average believer, is that it is

> conceived of very much in terms of Law. A moral obligation or moral rule is something laid upon man by God.[198]

Though many people no longer believe in God, and certainly would not consciously subscribe to the view of him as Cosmic Judge and Lawgiver, nonetheless the influence of this kind of prescriptive morality is still dominant in Western culture. Many still consider morality 'as an obligation laid on them from without, a command which they are obliged to obey', whether they believe in God or not. Sangharakshita rather playfully suggests that traditional Western morality today amounts to:

> not doing what we want to do, and doing what we do not want to do, because—for reasons we do not understand—we have been told to by someone in whose existence we no longer believe![199]

Sangharakshita found that many of his own disciples, although nominally Buddhist, were still struggling with the effects of Christianity in this respect. They were still subject to feelings of neurotic obligation and guilt. That Cosmic Judge still exercised a mental tyranny of which they were but semiconscious. Sangharakshita argued that one must stop being an unconscious Christian before one could fully be a Buddhist. One must get rid of the lingering and oppressive sense of neurotic guilt that can arise from Christian conditioning. It was in this context that he entered public debate on the future of the blasphemy law in England, after there had been a successful prosecution for blasphemy in 1977. The common law offence of blasphemy, which to that date had not been invoked for more than fifty years, consists in saying or publishing anything offensive to any one Christian. Sangharakshita strongly advocated the abolition of the law. One of his arguments was that blaspheming

against God and other aspects of Christianity may be a therapeutic
necessity for some people:

> In order to abandon Christianity completely—in order to liberate himself
> from its oppressive and stultifying influence—it may be necessary for
> the ex-Christian not only to repudiate Christianity intellectually in the
> privacy of his own mental consciousness but also to give public
> expression in words, writing, or signs to his *emotional* rejection of
> Christianity and the God of Christianity, i.e. it may be necessary for him
> to commit blasphemy. Such blasphemy is therapeutic blasphemy.[200]

## BUDDHIST MORALITY

Buddhism itself, Sangharakshita insists, requires no protection from
blasphemy, since its morality is not structured on the external commands
of an all-powerful God-as-Lawgiver. It could even be said that it is
impossible to blaspheme against Buddhism. Christians might feel the
need for such protection because they see God as the supreme monarch
of the universe, blasphemy against whom is cosmic high treason. But,
Sangharakshita shows, for Buddhists to feel offended by insults to the
Three Jewels would, in the Buddha's own words, 'stand in the way of
their own self-conquest'. Furthermore, their reactions would prevent
them from judging the truth or falsehood of the accusation.[201]

> Buddhism is concerned primarily with the emotional and
> intellectual—with the 'spiritual'—development of the individual human
> being, and … the Buddhist's reaction to 'speaking in dispraise' of the
> Three Jewels must, like his reaction to everything else, be such as to help
> rather than to hinder this process. In other words the centre of reference
> for Buddhism is man, that is to say, man as a being who, if he makes the
> effort, is capable of raising himself from the state of unenlightened to
> that of enlightened—spiritually enlightened—humanity or
> Buddhahood.[202]

For Buddhism, 'the criterion of ethics is not theological but
psychological', and is to be found in the quality of the mental states
underlying an individual's actions.[203] The primary terms of ethical
evaluation are not 'good' and 'bad' but 'skilful' and 'unskilful' (Sanskrit,
*kauśalya* and *akauśalya*; Pali, *kusala* and *akusala*)—'skilful' in the moral
context signifying that which is associated with the mental states of
generosity, friendliness, and wisdom, and 'unskilful' with greed, hatred,
and delusion. *Śīla* or moral action is thus action that gives expression to
and is accompanied by disinterestedness, friendliness, and wisdom,
while immoral action emerges from greed, hatred, and delusion. Morality

is, however, not a matter of mere good intentions. The word 'skilful' suggests intelligence and competence, not just wanting to act well but having the understanding and experience to be able to do so. *Śīla* is also not just 'the occasional good deed', it is good behaviour or habitual good action. Sangharakshita gives a comprehensive definition:

> Buddhist morality can therefore be said to consist in the habitual performance of bodily, vocal, and mental actions expressive of volitions associated with disinterestedness, friendliness, and wisdom.[204]

While this definition gives a working basis for examining Buddhist ethics, *śīla* cannot be fully appreciated without understanding the wider context within which it is to be found. Ethics is only Buddhist if it is placed in the context of the path to Buddhahood. This is made clear in the teaching of the Threefold Way, one of the most important formulations of the path, constantly reiterated by the Buddha in the last weeks before his death.[205] According to the Threefold Way, spiritual life begins with *śīla* or morality, then proceeds to *samādhi* or meditation, and concludes with *prajñā* or Wisdom. Ethics is only *śīla* in the Buddhist sense if it is a step on the path. Since the path leads towards the goal of Buddhahood, moral action is not merely the expression of skilful states of mind but has Buddhahood as its ultimate object.

> It is, in fact, only those actions of body, speech, and mind which are expressive of skilful volitions that have the Buddha, as Spiritual Ideal, as their object, which can properly be said to constitute Buddhist morality.[206]

Treading the path with the Buddha as one's object is, of course, Going for Refuge to the Three Jewels. Buddhist morality, therefore, has Going for Refuge as its context.

## THE MIDDLE WAY

*Śīla* is not mere goodness. Its full application depends on comprehension of Buddhism's most profound psychological and metaphysical teachings, since it is the enactment of those teachings in everyday life. Sangharakshita makes this clear in a particularly brilliant rediscovery of the essential meaning of the Middle Way, an important traditional doctrine.[207] This teaching is found most notably in what is claimed to be the Buddha's first discourse, the *Dhammacakkappavattana Sutta*.[208] The Buddha declares that there are two ethical extremes to be avoided by one who goes forth in quest of truth: the extreme of self-indulgence and the extreme of self-torture. The Middle Way between them, he says, is the Noble Eightfold Path, by means of which he gained Enlightenment. Here the

Buddha presents the Middle Way as lying between ethical extremes. Taking a narrow interpretation of this exposition, most commentators do not realise the full significance of the Middle Way.

> Few modern exponents of the Dharma, particularly those who take their stand on Theravadin texts alone, fail to commit the mistake of commenting upon this aspect of the Fourth Truth [i.e. the Eightfold Path as the Middle Way] from an exclusively ethical point of view. And the result? One of the profoundest teachings of Buddhism is degraded to the practice of an undistinguished mediocrity.[209]

In fact, Sangharakshita argues, the Middle Way is coextensive with the Dharma itself. The triadic principle of two extremes with a middle path between them is to be found in every aspect of human experience. In particular it can be seen on three levels: metaphysical, psychological, and ethical. On the metaphysical plane, the Middle Way lies between the extremes of Eternalism and Nihilism. Eternalism is the belief that there is, behind the appearances that make up our experience, Absolute Being: eternal, unchanging, and perfect. Nihilism, on the other hand, argues that ultimately nothing really exists. All erroneous philosophical and metaphysical positions are species of these two extreme views. The various theistic religions are all varieties of Eternalism. The materialist, who believes that consciousness is simply a side-effect of matter, is in Buddhist terms a Nihilist.

Conditioned co-production, the Buddha's basic expression of his insight, is the Middle Way on the metaphysical plane. It carries us between the extremes of Eternalism and Nihilism. Phenomena have no fixed and unchanging existence, yet are not thereby nonexistent. They simply arise in dependence on conditions and, without those conditions, pass away. All things are ultimately *śūnya*, empty of a fixed substance. This means that we cannot define or grasp them either as existent or nonexistent. We cannot therefore characterise reality either in terms of Being or Nothingness. Both are extreme views. Both are just mental constructs that cannot capture the true nature of things. Only if we try to understand conditioned co-production will we avoid these extremes.

These extremes manifest also on the psychological plane. Eternalism has its psychological counterpart in the belief that, behind the human personality, there is a fixed, unchanging, and eternal soul that will survive after the death of the body. Nihilists, on the other hand, believe that no element of personality survives death. The Middle Way manifests on the psychological plane as the principle of *anātman* (Pali, *anattā*). *Anātman* is the application of conditioned co-production to the phenomena of personality. There is no fixed, unchanging soul or *ātman*, but this does not mean that consciousness is merely an epiphenomenon of the body, extinguished with its death. There is simply a continuum of psychic and psychophysical events, each giving rise to succeeding events. The phenomena of personality cannot be grasped as either existent nor non-existent.

The holding of one-sided views about the ultimate nature of things and about the nature of the person has repercussions on ethical practice. Belief that life ultimately has no meaning leads to the view that personality is simply a by-product of the body. This, in its turn, leads to the ethical extreme of self-indulgence:

> Pleasure will be set up as the sole object of human endeavour,
> self-indulgence lauded to the skies, abstinence contemned, and the
> voluptuary honoured as the best and wisest of mankind.[210]

The contrary metaphysical belief that the universe is grounded upon Absolute Being has its correlative on the psychological plane. This is the view that behind and beyond the phenomena of personality is a soul. That soul is seen as ultimately identical with Absolute Being as completely different from the body. The holding of this view in its turn leads to the view that spiritual life consists in

> effecting a complete disassociation between spirit and matter, the real
> and the unreal, God and the world, the temporal and the eternal; whence
> follows self-mortification in its extremest and most repulsive forms.[211]

Thus if we do not understand Buddhism's metaphysical and psychological insights, if only at the intellectual level, we are unlikely to live ethically, in the full Buddhist sense.

## THE TEN PRECEPTS

So far we have dealt with Sangharakshita's views on Buddhist morality in very general terms, but action is, by its nature, specific. The Buddhist tradition, therefore, offers definite guidance on what kind of behaviour is likely to be morally skilful and what is not. This guidance comes in the form of those many lists of precepts, rules, vows, and customs observed among the various sects and the different socio-religious groups within them. These 'patterns of ethical behaviour' contain items of very different kinds, which Sangharakshita analyses in three categories.

Firstly, there are items that apply to people living a particular kind of life. Here, general ethical principles are adapted to specific circumstances, like those of a householder or, more commonly, a monk or nun. The monastic life, in Buddhism, is lived to help spiritual development. Living a simple, communal life, it will probably be easier to cultivate the basic spiritual and ethical qualities, for instance, of unselfishness and detachment from material possessions. People living together for that purpose will develop a routine consisting of definite customs and patterns of behaviour. Their way of life can be described in terms of a set of rules. Inevitably, any such list of rules will, to a large extent, be determined by the historical and cultural setting at the time it was laid down. Some Buddhist traditions have preserved ancient lists of rules but have tacitly set them to one side and adapted to new conditions. Others have been extraordinarily literalistic and conservative; their rules have been handed down unchanged for hundreds of years, without any attempt being made to modify them in changing circumstances. This has resulted, for instance, in Western men and women trying to live in the modern European or American suburbs a way of life established in the jungles of ancient India.

Secondly, some lists of vows, precepts, and rules apply basic ethical principles to particular aspects of the path. For instance, those following the Bodhisattva path will take special vows, such as undertaking to save all beings from difficulties. The Bodhisattva vows and precepts work out basic ethical principles in terms of the altruistic dimension of spiritual life. Those taking Tantric initiations often vow to perform regularly the *sādhana* or meditational-cum-devotional practice into which they have been initiated. They also often undertake a vow of secrecy concerning the initiation. Here, basic ethical principles are worked out in terms of the particular practice undertaken.

The third kind of list is the most general. It simply consists of fundamental ethical principles in a form applicable to all, regardless of their socio-religious status or of which aspect of the path they are practising. These precepts constitute a description of the behaviour of one whose mind is completely skilful and whose actions, therefore, cannot but be moral. They are the 'spontaneous outward expression of an emancipated mind'.[212]

> One who is Enlightened, or who has attained Buddhahood, thereby
> realizing the plenitude of wisdom and the fullness of compassion, will
> inevitably behave in a certain way, because it is the nature of an
> Enlightened being to behave in that way. Furthermore, to the extent that
> *you* are Enlightened, to that extent you *also* will behave in that way. If
> you are *not* Enlightened, or to the extent that you are not Enlightened,
> then the observance of the *śīlas* or precepts will help you to experience
> for yourself the state of mind of which they are, normally, the
> expression.[213]

According to Sangharakshita, the total spiritual community is made up of individuals following a wide range of life-styles and at all levels of the path. They can only experience their ethical unity in those precepts that describe a pattern of ethical behaviour applying to them all. There must, as we have already seen, be that 'drastic reduction of the rules [contained in all the various lists] to those precepts of genuinely ethical significance which they have in common'.[214] Those precepts are, Sangharakshita concludes, the Ten Precepts. It is for this reason that they are observed by all members of the Western Buddhist Order, whatever their way of life. The Ten Precepts constitute that *mūla-prātimoksha* or fundamental code so necessary to the unity of the sangha. It must be noted that the Ten Precepts referred to here are not the well-known ten *śrāmaṇera* precepts. The *daśa-śīla* or Ten Precepts of what Sangharakshita calls the *mūla-prātimoksha* are, however, equally old and probably more widely distributed throughout the canons of all schools. They are also far more comprehensive, as we shall see.

The Ten Precepts are found in the scriptures both as lists of behaviour to be refrained from and as positive qualities to be developed. Traditionally, the negative formulation is used for recitation, but Sangharakshita considers it necessary to bring out the positive aspirations as well. He has therefore composed lines expressive of the positive aspect of each precept. In the Western Buddhist Order the list of negative formulations is usually recited first in Pali and then the positive verses are repeated in the local language. Here we will list the precepts in English in both negative and positive forms:

1. I undertake the training principle of abstaining from killing living beings.
With deeds of loving-kindness, I purify my body.
2. I undertake the training principle of abstaining from taking the not-given.
With open-handed generosity, I purify my body.
3. I undertake the training principle of abstaining from sexual misconduct.
With stillness, simplicity, and contentment, I purify my body.
4. I undertake the training principle of abstaining from false speech.
With truthful communication, I purify my speech.
5. I undertake the training principle of abstaining from harsh speech.
With words kindly and gracious, I purify my speech.
6. I undertake the training principle of abstaining from frivolous speech.
With utterance helpful and harmonious, I purify my speech.
7. I undertake the training principle of abstaining from slanderous speech.
(The positive counterpart of this precept is included in the previous stanza.)
8. I undertake the training principle of abstaining from covetousness.
Abandoning covetousness for tranquillity, I purify my mind.
9. I undertake the training principle of abstaining from hatred.

Changing hatred into compassion, I purify my mind.
10. I undertake the training principle of abstaining from false views.
Transforming ignorance into wisdom, I purify my mind.

The following of these fundamental precepts is the direct and natural expression of Going for Refuge to the Three Jewels. Going for Refuge

> means organizing one's whole life, in all its different aspects, in such a way as to subserve the attainment of Enlightenment.[215]

The precepts are the means by which that organisation is carried out, extending Going for Refuge into every aspect of one's life.

> By its very nature the Going for Refuge must find expression in the observance of the Precepts. If it does not find such expression this means that as a Buddhist one is virtually dead and that the Going for Refuge itself, becoming more and more mechanical, will soon cease to be effectively such.[216]

One can only go for Refuge if one observes the precepts—and one can only really observe the precepts to the extent that one goes for Refuge. The connection between them is organic, Going for Refuge being like one's life-blood as a Buddhist and the observance of the precepts like the circulation of that blood through one's entire being.

The Ten Precepts are not to be regarded as rules 'in the narrow, pettifogging sense of the term', but rather as both 'principles of ethics' or *kauśalya-dharmas* and as 'items of training'—*śikshāpadas*. The 'principles of ethics' embodied in the precepts are inherent in the act of Going for Refuge. As one tries to transform every aspect of one's life in accordance with one's Going for Refuge, quite naturally,

> one's behaviour comes to be increasingly governed by ten great ethical principles, the principles of non-violence or love, of non-appropriation or generosity, and so on.[217]

They are thus not imposed from without, but emerge from the Going for Refuge itself. They are certainly not simply rules one obeys to avoid 'getting into trouble'.

As 'items of training' the precepts are the essential elements in spiritual education. The more one learns to put them into effect, the deeper one will go for Refuge. One learns them from others more experienced than oneself—and this is why one 'takes' the precepts at ordination from one's preceptor. Learning the precepts involves, according to Sangharakshita, first imbibing their spirit rather than their letter. Then, one must learn how to apply them in daily life, perhaps even by making rules and taking vows. Finally, one must learn how to confess and make good any breaches of the precepts. The sangha as a whole can be considered as a moral training ground since, simply by one's receptive presence within it, one will imbibe the essential spirit of the precepts and will learn how to apply them by watching others do so.

The Ten Precepts form the only list found in traditional sources that can be common to all within the sangha, no matter what their life-style. Although the list of Five Precepts is well known and widely used in Buddhism, Sangharakshita believes that it is not sufficiently comprehensive or far-reaching. Unlike other Buddhist codes, including the Five Precepts, the Ten Precepts consist only of ethical principles and not of rules or of applications of morality within specific ways of life. That the Ten Precepts can be applied to all within the sangha is demonstrated by the Buddha himself. In various *suttas* of the Pali Canon he is shown teaching the Ten Precepts to people from different socio-religious categories. For instance, on separate occasions he teaches them to *bhikkhus* and to a 'female lay devotee'. He specifically recommends their application to all classes of humanity. He even recommends them to all kinds of nonhuman self-conscious beings, thus emphasising that the Ten Precepts consist of ethical principles applicable throughout the entire universe.[218]

Moreover, the Ten Precepts form the only traditional list of ethical principles that clearly reveals how Going for Refuge is to be extended into every aspect of life. Buddhism commonly analyses the total human being into three major categories: body, speech, and mind. As one goes for Refuge, one's body, speech, and mind must be progressively transformed in accordance with the ethical principles inherent in Going for Refuge. For a list of those ethical principles to be comprehensive it must therefore cover all three aspects. In the case of the Ten Precepts, the first three are concerned with the body, the next four with speech, and the last three with the mind. This list therefore exemplifies very fully

> The total transformation of the individual as the consequence of his Going for Refuge.[219]

In *The Ten Pillars of Buddhism*, Sangharakshita collects some of the chief canonical sources for the Ten Precepts.[220] In the Theravadin Pali Canon the list is frequently mentioned, appearing for instance in the *Kūṭadanta Sutta* of the *Dīgha-Nikāya*, the *Sevitabba-asevitabba Sutta* of the *Majjhima-Nikāya*, and some fifty or so short *suttas* of the *Aṅguttara-Nikāya*. The list is also found in the *Mahāvastu*, a work of another early school. The list is also well known in the Mahāyāna, appearing in the *Aṣṭāhasrikā-prajñāpāramitā Sūtra*, the *Vimalakīrti-nirdeśa*, and the *Suvarnaprabhāśa Sūtra* or *Sūtra of Golden Light*. The Ten Precepts, then, are perhaps uniquely qualified to form the *mūla-prātimoksha* that can be a basis of ethical unity for the entire Buddhist sangha.

In his exploration of the ethical principles set forth in the Ten Precepts, Sangharakshita demonstrates that they are very profound indeed. None is more profound than the principle of nonviolence expressed in the first precept. This principle runs 'very deep in life, both social and spiritual'. It is

> the most direct and important manifestation of the spiritual and existential act of Going for Refuge.[221]

As such it finds expression not only in the first precept but in all the others as well. Though the first precept is cast negatively simply as abstention from killing living beings, it implies much more than that:

> To kill a living being means to inflict upon him the greatest of all sufferings or evils, for inasmuch as life itself is the greatest good, so the greatest suffering, or greatest evil, that can befall one, is to be deprived of life.[222]

One can only be deprived of what one considers good by means of force or violence—whether physical or emotional or in the form of deceit. The precept is really therefore about nonviolence, killing being simply the most extreme form of violence. Moreover, since we ourselves do not wish to be deprived of life, killing is

> the absolute negation of the solidarity of one living being *qua* living being with another.[223]

The deeper significance of the first precept consists therefore

> in the fact that killing is wrong because it represents the extremest form that the negation of one ego by another, or the assertion of one ego at the expense of another, can possibly take.[224]

It is thus the rejection of the 'Golden Rule': 'Whatsoever ye would that men should do to you, do ye even so to them,'[225] or 'Do as you would be done by.' Without the Golden Rule there can be no human society or culture and no spiritual life.

The positive counterpart of the first precept speaks not simply of refraining from violence but of acting with loving-kindness. The positive dimension of the ethical principle of nonviolence is therefore the principle of love. Love is

> no mere flabby sentiment but the vigorous expression of an imaginative identification with other living beings.[226]

Abstaining from violence and living by love goes beyond merely personal concerns. Sangharakshita argues that the principle of love is indispensable to the survival of humanity now that there are nuclear weapons capable of obliterating human life on this earth.

> Ever since the dawn of history ... two great principles have been at work in the world: the principle of violence and the principle of non-violence or, as we may also call it, the principle of love.... The principle of

violence is a principle of Darkness, the principle of non-violence is a
principle of Light. Whereas to live in accordance with the principle of
violence is to be either an animal or a devil or a combination of the two,
to live in accordance with the principle of non-violence is to be a human
being, in the fullest sense of the term, or even an angel.[227]

With the invention of weapons of mass destruction, the principle of
violence has a terrible potential that can only be averted by humanity
learning to live in accordance with the principle of nonviolence—the
principle of love.

The principle of violence is found only in the group, for the principle
of love underlies the spiritual community. In effectively Going for
Refuge, and therefore taking on the Ten Precepts, one is making a transition from operating by the principle of violence, what Sangharakshita
calls the 'power mode', to operating by the principle of nonviolence or
the 'love mode'. That transition does not, of course, take place all at once.
However, when one effectively goes for Refuge one dedicates oneself to
living by the love mode as much as one possibly can. Power is the
capacity to use force, violence being 'the actual use of that capacity to
negate the being of another person'.[228] Every human being has some
degree of power. Operating in the love mode means that, because of our
imaginative identification with others, we refrain from using that power
to negate the being of others. Indeed, we try to help them. The power
mode by definition cannot be used within the spiritual community, since
it is the absolute denial of sangha. Outside the spiritual community, its
members may at times use power to defend themselves. If they do find
themselves in that position, power 'must always be subordinated to the
love mode'.[229]

Each of the succeeding nine precepts reveals different facets of that
fundamental principle of nonviolence or love. For instance, taking the
'not-given', against which the second precept is an injunction, is violence
against the person by taking their property. However, the precept really
embodies the principle of non-exploitation, and exploitation goes far
beyond the merely economic field. One can also take the not-given by
abusing others' time or energy, for example. Generosity, the positive
counterpart of this precept, is related to love. Love is

a self-giving of person to person or, if you like, a surrender of person to
person ('surrender' here meaning the complete abandonment of any
advantage derived from the power mode).[230]

Generosity is a giving of property to a person as an expression of love.
Where love exists in its fullness even a sense of property is transcended,
so that there can be no question of generosity but only of sharing or

common 'ownership'. It is towards this transcendence of property or sharing that the spiritual community should tend. Sangharakshita points out, quoting from the Perfection of Wisdom *sūtras*, that the profoundest level of generosity is 'where the giver, the gift, and the recipient of the gift, cease to be distinguishable'.[231] This level of generosity is equivalent to the transcendental path.

The violence in sexual misconduct such as rape and adultery is obvious. However, contentment, the positive counterpart of the third precept, implies more than curbing such violence and the absence of sexual craving. It means overcoming sexual polarisation and progressing

> From an absolute identification with one psycho-physical sex to a
> relative and provisional identification with it, and from a relative and
> provisional identification with it to no identification at all.[232]

This has very far-reaching implications, to which we must return later.

The fact that there are four speech precepts emphasises the importance of speech as an intermediary between thought and action—and also the difficulty of transforming it. Sangharakshita stresses that unless there is truthful speech there can be no civilisation and culture, for 'whoever is guilty of false speech in fact undermines the foundations of society'.[233] Certainly no spiritual community can exist without truthful speech, since it is the basis of real communication. Harsh speech 'poisons the atmosphere' and kindly speech 'purifies and invigorates it'.[234] Our speech can only be meaningful when our lives have a definite purpose and goal. Meaningful speech is

> a means to Enlightenment inasmuch as it is a communication in depth
> between two or more people who are committed to the Ideal of
> Enlightenment, or who have gone for Refuge.[235]

Slanderous speech disrupts the spiritual community, whereas harmonious speech heals disputes and draws people together.

The Ten Precepts represent progressively more refined and subtle applications of the principle of love or nonviolence. Indeed they can be seen as being distributed over the stages of the Threefold Way of morality, meditation, and wisdom. This vertical inclusiveness again demonstrates the fittingness of the Ten Precepts as a *mūla-prātimoksha*. The first three precepts, pertaining to the body, and the next four, which concern speech, together constitute the stage of morality. Morality here applies to external behaviour—all ten precepts obviously also represent Buddhist morality in the wider sense of 'the art or science of human conduct and character as possessing value in relation to a standard or ideal'.[236] Of the last three, the mind precepts, the first two belong to the stage of meditation and the last to wisdom.

The seventh precept enjoins abstention from covetousness. Covetousness is a state of mind in which

> the self or ego reaches out towards the non-self or non-ego with a view
> to appropriating and even incorporating it, thus filling the yawning pit
> of its own inner poverty and emptiness.[237]

It is also a state of 'perpetual frustration' and of 'existential polarization between coveting subject and coveted object'.[238] The positive counterpart of this state is thus one of inner wealth and fullness, of depolarisation, of detachment, contentment, and tranquillity. All the practices and institutions of spiritual life will help one to practise this precept. However, the roots of covetousness go as deep as the ego itself. It will usually be necessary to practise those meditation techniques that deal with it directly, such as the 'Recollection of Death' or the 'Contemplation of the Six Elements'.

Hatred is the state that arises when the reaching out of self for non-self that is covetousness is checked or hindered. It is

> the murderous wish to do the utmost harm and damage to whatever
> interposes itself between coveting subject and coveted object.[239]

The positive counterpart of abstention from hatred is compassion, since 'hatred and compassion are mutually exclusive'.[240] Hatred involves the complete rejection of other beings and therefore negation of the altruistic dimension of Going for Refuge. Again there are specific meditation practices that work against hatred and cultivate compassion, such as the *karuṇā-bhāvanā*. Sangharakshita also recommends devotional practices, specifically the Sevenfold Puja, of which we shall hear more later, and the practice of 'Rejoicing in Merits'—actively singing the praises of others.

The final precept, which represents the stage of wisdom, is concerned with the eradication of *mithyā-dṛishṭis* (Pali, *micchā-diṭṭhis*) or false views. A false view is, in the first place,

> a wrong or false way of seeing things, and in the second place a wrong
> or false view as expressed more or less systematically in intellectual
> terms in the form of a doctrine.[241]

What makes such views wrong is the fact that they give expression to the mental states of covetousness, hatred, or delusion. Right view is twofold. In its transcendental aspect it is simply the way the Enlightened see things. In its mundane aspect it is those ideas and beliefs that accord with the teachings by means of which the Enlightened have communicated their experience. By undertaking this precept, one is committing oneself to eradicating confused and emotionally clouded ideas and to trying to gain an intellectual comprehension of the Dharma. However, this does not simply mean that one learns to parrot the doctrines of Buddhism. By taking up right view, one is trying to gain for oneself the insight that right view expresses. Right view is ultimately non-view: though the Enlightened One sees things as they really are, 'he has a "critical" awareness of the impossibility of giving full and final expression to his vision in fixed conceptual terms.'[242] One therefore cannot cling to any particular formulation in a rigid and dogmatic manner.

Wrong views are destructive of spiritual life in so far as they distort what it actually is and what it entails. They may even completely undermine its possibility. Indeed, wrong views may destroy the possibility even of a truly human life if they deny the bases of civilisation and culture. There are various canonical lists of wrong views and Sangharakshita has found himself forced to address their many modern varieties that so strongly affect the people he is teaching. He has commented that widespread literacy and more effective media of communication, while they have considerable advantages, also foster and spread wrong views more rapidly than ever before in human history. Most people today are strongly influenced, albeit usually quite unconsciously, by a mass of views that actually bring them only confusion, conflict, and unhappiness.

One of Sangharakshita's most constant activities since the foundation of the Order has been the isolation of each strain of wrong view as it comes into fashion, analysing and exposing it so that it does not infect the movement. Such views include an unquestioning belief in 'progress', a shallow egalitarianism, and an automatic rejection of organisations and institutions. Clear thought is obviously an important antidote to many of these views, and Sangharakshita has constantly urged his disciples to greater clarity. Besides the study of the Dharma, he recommends the study of logic and encourages discussion and debate as a means of stimulating clear thinking. Some of his own more polemical writing, such as *The FWBO and 'Protestant Buddhism'*, has as much the function of educating his followers in the task of tackling wrong views as of answering the perpetrators of those views themselves.

The circumstances of the contemporary world make it very difficult to observe the tenth precept, since false views are so widespread. If we want even to begin to practise it we must do three things:

(a) We must become more acutely aware of the extent to which our thinking, and the expression we give our thinking, is influenced by the false views by which we have been surrounded since birth. (b) We must realize not only that false views are the product of unskilful mental states but that, so long as they are not definitely abandoned, they actually reinforce the unskilful mental states which produce them, thus double obstructing the path to Enlightenment. (c) We must resolve that whenever we discuss personal spiritual difficulties, or issues concerning the Order and the Movement as a whole, and above all when we discuss the Dharma itself, we should do so in terms of Right Views,—if possible in terms of Wisdom,—and *not* in terms of any of the false views which are currently fashionable in the outside world.[243]

However, removing wrong views as formulated in specific ideas, although essential, is not enough. One must also attack wrong views at their roots in covetousness and hatred, both of which have their ultimate roots in delusion. Once more, it is primarily through meditation that this attack is carried out.

The far-reaching nature of the Ten Precepts is perhaps displayed nowhere more clearly than in the tenth, for its positive counterpart is Wisdom itself, the content of Enlightenment. When understood sufficiently profoundly, the Ten Precepts, together with Going for Refuge to the Three Jewels, comprise the whole of spiritual life. It is in Going for Refuge to the Three Jewels and practising the Ten Precepts that the life of a member of the spiritual community consists. In establishing a system of 'chapters' for the Western Buddhist Order, groupings of between four and ten members that are the basic 'working unit' of the Order, Sangharakshita stressed that communication in chapter meetings should be based upon the observance of the Ten Precepts. They should encourage members to go for Refuge more deeply and to practise the precepts, being of a confessional nature.[244] The core of the ceremony of ordination into the Western Buddhist Order consists simply in the recitation of the Refuges and the Ten Precepts. Once this is concluded, the preceptor exhorts the new Order member, 'Having well observed the Three Refuges together with the Dharmacari/Dharmacarini ordination precepts, with mindfulness strive on'—the latter phrase being the last words of the Buddha to his disciples before he died.

## THE MONASTIC LIFE-STYLE

So far we have been examining Sangharakshita's idea of the *mūla-prātimoksha*. He suggests that the Ten Precepts can act as a point of unity for all Buddhists since they embody the essential ethical principles by which Going for Refuge is extended into every aspect of life. Going for Refuge, and the activation of the essential ethical principles, will manifest in particular ways of life. But, Sangharakshita insists, Buddhists are united in the act of Going for Refuge before they are divided by different ways of life. In a key maxim, he says 'Commitment is primary, life-style secondary.' Here, commitment means Going for Refuge to the Buddha, Dharma, and Sangha. 'Life-style' is the particular way of life led by the individual who goes for Refuge, whether that life-style is more or less monastic or more or less 'lay'. Sangharakshita is careful to point out that 'secondary' does not mean 'unimportant'. One's way of life as a Buddhist should be the expression of one's commitment in Going for Refuge to the Three Jewels and of the ethical principles embodied in the Ten Precepts. For instance, one could not be a slaughterman or a mercenary and effectively go for Refuge.

Nonetheless, there is a range of life-styles that can be genuine expressions of Going for Refuge and that may conform to the Ten Precepts. Sangharakshita does not consider that taking up any one of these life-styles requires a new ordination or the adoption of new precepts. It is open to any member or group of members of the spiritual community to take upon themselves additional vows or rules. Doing so may help them to go for Refuge more deeply and put the Ten Precepts into practice more effectively. Thus an individual might make a vow to do a certain amount of study each week or else to give up some bad habit like smoking cigarettes. Those living in a community might decide collectively to meditate together every day. Some might even decide to undertake the rules of a traditional *bhikshu-prātimoksha*. Any additional vows or rules taken on would not, strictly speaking, be new precepts. They would simply be a more thoroughgoing application of the ethical principles embodied in the Ten Precepts or a more detailed working out of them within the particular circumstances of a certain life-style.

Traditionally, most Buddhists have greatly honoured the monastic life-style above all others. What then is the place of monasticism in modern Buddhism? Neither Sangharakshita's exposure of the modern *bhikkhu*-sangha's failings nor his concern to put commitment before life-style should be taken as implying that he is against monasticism as an expression of the spiritual life. He himself lives as a monk, as he has done for most of his adult life. What he rejects is

> the identification of the spiritual life with the monastic life and the monastic life itself with pseudo-monastic formalism, an identification that has the effect of displacing the Act of Going for Refuge from its central and definitive place in the Buddhist life, creating a division between the Monastic Order and the laity, and relegating the latter to the position of second-class Buddhists, besides seriously undermining the whole structure of Buddhism, both theoretical and practical.[245]

Indeed, he says he would 'like to see a revival of Sūtra-style monasticism throughout the Buddhist world', and hopes to see many more 'monks' and 'nuns' within the Western Buddhist Order.[246]

Sangharakshita defines a monk or nun as one who is vowed to chastity, fewness of possessions, simplicity of life-style, careerlessness, and community living—although chastity is really the basic vow. However, the Sanskrit word *brahmacarya*, normally translated as chastity, implies far more than mere abstention from sexual activity. Sangharakshita takes *brahmacarya* as deriving etymologically directly from *brahmā*, meaning a particular kind of god. This etymology is disputed, but true or false it does illustrate the real meaning of the word. The *brahmās* in classical Buddhist cosmic taxonomy are a class of sublime spiritual being, perhaps equivalent to the higher angels in Western systems. They live in a range of heavenly realms corresponding to the *dhyānas* or states of superconsciousness. Indeed, those who enter such states are said to be able to perceive the *brahmās* and enter into communication with them. The *brahmās* have entirely transcended the world of gross sensuous matter, as one does when one enters the *dhyānas*. They abide in a visionary dimension of pure or 'archetypal' form (*rūpa-loka*).

Most significantly for the present discussion, the *brahmās* have also transcended sexual dimorphism. They are neither male nor female but androgynous. They therefore experience no sexual polarisation and none of the craving that accompanies it—again paralleling experience of the *dhyānas*. However, the fact that there is no gross matter in their dimension and that they experience no sexual polarisation does not mean that their world is weak, attenuated, or dull. It is, in fact, exceptionally beautiful, although its beauty is of a very refined kind. They experience the same uninterrupted bliss and delight as accompanies *dhyāna*.

*Brahmacarya*, according to Sangharakshita, therefore means living the life of a *brahmā*, living in that state of refined wholeness in which there is no sexual polarisation. To be a *brahmacari* is not to give up sex in the sense of painfully and forcibly pushing it to one side: it is to transcend sex—or to try to transcend it—in order to enjoy a far more deeply satisfying experience of wholeness and refined pleasure. And of course it is not merely to go beyond sex, it is to live less and less bound by the senses and by the ordinary world with its possessions and securities. One who observes *brahmacarya* increasingly finds a deeper source of happiness and fulfilment. This is really what it is to be a monk or nun.

As a consequence of observing *brahmacarya*, the monk or nun will naturally tend to limit possessions, making do with what is strictly necessary and not hoarding money or belongings. Monks and nuns will live a simple life-style—not easy to achieve in the modern consumer society. Sangharakshita stresses that it will not be a 'sordid simplicity' but a refined one, reflecting aesthetic as well as ethical and spiritual values, if indeed these can be separated. It will be a simplicity like that of a Greek vase painting or a Japanese 'Zen garden' of rocks and raked sand.[247] It is not possible to lay down exactly what can and cannot be a component of that simple life-style. Monks and nuns will have to work that out for themselves within their own particular settings. The monk or nun will not have a worldly career in the sense of

> gainful employment that acts as the focal point of one's worldly
> ambitions and is the means by which one supports oneself and one's
> family.[248]

This does not necessarily mean that he or she will not work, but that any work done will not be incompatible with *brahmacarya* nor will it be a focus for worldly ambition. Finally, those leading a monastic life need spiritual friends. Of course, everyone following the path needs spiritual friends, but monks and nuns will probably feel the need more acutely than others. Most people fulfil their need for emotional warmth and intimacy through their sexual relationships. Since monastics are not engaging in sexual activity, they will experience a stronger need for spiritual friendship, partly as a means of fulfilling those emotional needs. Ideally therefore monks and nuns will belong to monasteries, living with other monastics of the same sex. At least they will try to live in a 'closed residential spiritual community, that is, one that does not admit visitors of the opposite sex'.[249]

Though monks and nuns observe these vows, they do so in the context of Going for Refuge and the Ten Precepts. The monastic vows do not involve new ethical principles. They are simply

> a more thoroughgoing application of the principles underlying certain of
> the rules of training observed by the laity, i.e. observed by monks and
> laity in common. A Buddhist monk, it must be emphasized, is not a
> monk who happens to be a Buddhist but a Buddhist who happens to be
> a monk, and as such he has infinitely more in common with a Buddhist
> who is not a monk than he has with a monk who is not a Buddhist.[250]

In the Western Buddhist Order there is no monastic ordination. Some Order members do undertake a vow of chastity, observing

> the Third Precept not in the form of abstention from sexual misconduct
> (Pali, *kāmesu-micchācārā*) but in the form of abstention from unchastity
> (Pali, *abrahmacariya*).[251]

Those who take such vows for extended periods are then called *anagārikas* (m.) or *anagārikās* (f.). This traditional term literally means 'homeless one', and has been brought into prominence by such well-known twentieth century Buddhists as Anagarika Dharmapala. The 'status' of *anagārikas* within the Order is, however, the same as that of every other Order member—

> which is to say, they have no status, the concept of status being one that is meaningless from the spiritual point of view.[252]

The taking of the vow is not a career move—as Sangharakshita has seen it to be for many who become *bhikkhus*. It is taken

> in order to deepen [one's] experience of Going for Refuge and to help shift the locus of [one's] being from the kāmaloka or world of (sensuous) desire to the rūpaloka or world of (archetypal) form, that is, to the Brahmā-realms.[253]

*Anagārikas/ās* do not take vows of fewness of possessions, simplicity of life-style, careerlessness, or community living and are thus not necessarily monks or nuns by Sangharakshita's definition. However, since they take vows of chastity they will have a natural tendency to live more and more as monks or nuns in the full sense.

> When I say that I would like to see more monks in the Western Buddhist Order it is the fact that anagārikahood has this tendency that I have in mind, rather than the formal taking, by the individual anagārika, of (monastic) vows other than that of chastity.[254]

Sangharakshita's rediscovery of the primacy of Going for Refuge provides the basis of unity for the entire Buddhist sangha. The Ten Precepts offer a further unifying factor. All Buddhists could see themselves primarily as extending Going for Refuge into every aspect of their lives according to the ten great ethical principles inherent in the Ten Precepts. While the Ten Precepts provide a clear basis for ethical unity, they do not deny the great variety of life-styles within which it is possible to go for Refuge. Unity is not incompatible with diversity. In particular, ethical unity based on the Ten Precepts does not deny the very great value of monastic life as a means of deepening Going for Refuge and shifting the locus of one's being from the *kāma-loka* to the *brahmā-loka*. Sangharakshita's vision of the unity of Buddhism is now complete and we must pass on to consider his ideas on the more practical application of Buddhist principles.

*Chapter Seven*

# SPIRITUAL FRIENDSHIP

*Forgive me if I have stained*
*Your beauty with my desire,*
*Or troubled your clear serene*
*Light with my fury of fire.*
*Forgive me; let us be friends.*

*Forgive me, if I have looked*
*For response that you could not give,*
*Or raised in the deeps of my heart*
*This red rose too sickly to live.*
*Forgive me; let us be friends.*[255]

ALTHOUGH WE HAVE ALREADY EXAMINED Sangharakshita's ideas on sangha, we have done so only in very general terms. We must now consider his views on the nature of the human relationships of which the sangha consists. Here we find him exploring in depth a theme on which the Buddhist tradition to this point has little explicit teaching. There is no systematised body of ideas on the subject and little theoretical underpinning of its importance. This does not mean that the Buddha and his followers down the ages have not valued friendship. There are numerous references to the theme scattered throughout the Buddhist scriptures, and friendship is clearly a living force within the tradition from its earliest times. Perhaps, in those cohesive societies in which Buddhism has till now been transmitted, friendship was simply taken for granted and needed no theoretical support. In our own socially fragmented times, human relationships are under much conscious scrutiny. There is therefore a pressing need to understand the nature of friendship and its bearing on spiritual life. In fact, Sangharakshita believes that friendship is one of the keys to human development. He has therefore placed a distinctive emphasis upon it, making it one of the particular marks of the Order and movement he has founded, as well as exemplifying it in his own relationships.

As perhaps befits the subject, he has written little about friendship, communicating his views mainly through study seminars, lectures, and personal discussion. He has lectured on several incidents in the life of the Buddha that illustrate the theme and he has conducted seminars on various texts that treat of this virtue, notably an Islamic text, *The Duties of Brotherhood in Islam* by Al-Ghazālī, and two poems by Dr Johnson, 'An Ode on Friendship' and 'On the Death of Dr Robert Levet'. He has frequently drawn his disciples' attention to the vigorous Western classical tradition on friendship, stretching back to Plato and Aristotle. At one time he planned to lead a series of seminars covering the principal texts of that tradition.

Sangharakshita believes that personal relationships are necessary to spiritual development.[256] Very few people, if any, are able to make spiritual progress on their own. Most will need the stimulation and encouragement, support, and example of friends on the path. Without that friendship they will easily lose inspiration and become discouraged and confused. This does not necessarily mean that one must be with others all the time—indeed, periods of complete solitude are also needed. Nor does it inevitably follow that one must live in a residential spiritual community—although that would probably, for most, be best. It means that personal relationships with others who go for Refuge are an essential part of spiritual life. If one wants to move forward on the path, one must take friendships seriously and work upon them.

While there is no developed and systematised body of doctrine on friendship within the Buddhist tradition, there is certainly evidence of its importance. Sangharakshita uses as his primary reference a well-known incident in the Pali Canon in which Ānanda, the Buddha's close friend and attendant, says to him that half the spiritual life (Sanskrit, *brahmacarya*; Pali, *brahmacariya*) consists in spiritual friendship (Sanskrit, *kalyāṇa mitratā*; Pali, *kalyāṇa mittatā*). The Buddha replies, 'Say not so, Ānanda! Say not so, Ānanda! It is the whole, not the half of the spiritual life.' He adds that one who enjoys such a friendship will develop all the different limbs of the Eightfold Path until Enlightenment itself is reached. *Kalyāṇa mitratā* is thus the means to liberation from all suffering.[257] Some modern scholars translate *kalyāṇa mitratā* as 'friendship with what is lovely' rather than 'lovely or spiritual friendship', but this is to overlook common Buddhist usage. A *kalyāṇa mitra* is generally understood to be a spiritual friend, meaning a person more experienced on the path than oneself, who gives instruction, guidance, and support. *Kalyāṇa mitratā* is the abstract form of this term. *Mitra* means simply 'friend', while *mitratā* is 'friendship'. *Kalyāṇa* is a word rich in meaning, connoting both moral and aesthetic qualities: 'beautiful, charming, auspicious, helpful, morally good'.[258] It is thus 'spiritual', in the sense of pertaining to the higher human and trans-human virtues.

Sangharakshita understands this revealing comment of the Buddha's as meaning that spiritual life consists essentially in connecting with what is *kalyāṇa*—in other words, with those higher virtues and qualities that characterise *dhyāna* or deep states of meditation and are ultimately inter-fused with transcendental Insight. He identifies three principal modes through which those higher qualities may be experienced: through meditation, aesthetic experience, and human communication. Whatever the medium of *kalyāṇa mitratā*, the effect is to draw one beyond oneself towards the *kalyāṇa*. *Kalyāṇa mitratā* gives one access to those higher spiritual experiences that provide a basis of inspiration and confidence to move forward on the path. Without that contact, one has no foretaste of where one is going. One has no inspiration to make the efforts necessary for spiritual progress. Through meditation one gains access to the *dhyānas*. One makes contact with far higher dimensions of consciousness than one normally dwells in, dimensions characterised by great positivity and happiness, as well as great delicacy and refinement of feeling. The experience of beauty, whether through the medium of the genuine arts or of nature, also transports one beyond oneself into a state of mind that can be similar to meditative states. However, for most people, the most powerful and effective way of making that connection with the *kalyāṇa* is through friendship with another human being. Deep communication may bring one to that higher dimension of the *kalyāṇa*.

## THE GURU

Traditionally Buddhists have understood the *kalyāṇa mitra* to be the spiritual teacher. In so far as relationships within the sangha have been explored at all, it is those of what Sangharakshita calls a 'vertical' kind that have received attention: between the more and the less developed— between the guru and the disciple. Sangharakshita acknowledges the importance of such vertical relationships. In his lecture, 'Is a Guru Necessary?', he stresses that human evolution is extremely difficult without contact with someone more evolved than oneself—for most people, he says, there is no other way.[259] At the same time, he points out that such a relationship is a human one and should be based on genuine communication and mutual affection and regard. It is quite hard for modern Westerners to comprehend such a positive relationship with a spiritual teacher, Sangharakshita considers. There has been a reaction against all forms of hierarchy, which has almost destroyed what tradition of discipleship there has been. This does not mean that the East necessarily provides good models. He is critical of Eastern attitudes to guru–disciple relationships, which are seldom based on real human communication. Indeed, the disciple frequently has, and is encouraged to have, very exaggerated ideas about the guru's spiritual attainments and even human abilities.

Sangharakshita distinguishes between the guru as the 'bearer of the archetype' and as the 'exemplar of the ideal'. The bearer of the archetype is a human being who has become, for some people, a living symbol for a higher dimension of reality. For instance, the Pope is not seen as just a religious leader, but as Christ's Vicar on Earth, the holder of the Keys of St Peter. The exemplar of the Ideal is a human being whom one sees as a human being—but a human being who embodies spiritual ideals more fully than one does oneself. Something of this can be seen even in ordinary friendship, when a friend has qualities one admires and tries to emulate, although the friendship remains very much a human relationship. In Eastern traditions, the guru is often seen as the bearer of the archetype, a kind of living icon. For instance, in Tibetan Buddhism one is encouraged to see one's guru as a Buddha. Again, the Dalai Lama is considered to be the manifestation of the archetypal Bodhisattva, Avalokiteśvara.

In its traditional context this idealisation may have some value, surrounded as it is by many cultural conventions—although it is nonetheless open to abuse. In the West, without a supportive cultural environment, such an approach very often leads to confusion and even damage. This danger is already evident in the cases of a number of popular gurus who claim, or have had claimed on their behalf, complete Enlightenment, etc. Curiously, some Westerners seem especially susceptible to this sort of exaggerated claim, projecting upon gurus from the East quite superhuman attainments and thereby opening themselves to delusion and exploitation. Buddhism in the West has also been tainted with this phenomenon, Tibetan teachers particularly being often presented in this way.

Sangharakshita recognises that the idealisation of human teachers may fulfil a necessary and healthy function. By making a human being a symbol for some trans-human ideal, one may gain access to deeper levels of meaning. This is a spontaneous mechanism of the mind. One often makes contact with one's higher ideals by projecting them on to others, seeing them as having qualities one wishes to develop oneself. However, he considers it best that those who bear the archetype are figures from the past, like the Buddha himself and other great Buddhist teachers. One's own guru or *kalyāṇa mitra* should be an exemplar of the ideal for whom one feels real affection as well as respect, admiration, and receptivity, and with whom there is mutual awareness and understanding. If there is too much idealisation and projection there can be no genuine communication and therefore no drawing up of the disciple to the *kalyāṇa mitra's* level.

## COMMUNICATION: HORIZONTAL AND VERTICAL

'Communication' is a key term in Sangharakshita's understanding of sangha and friendship. By 'communication' he means not merely the exchange of information or ideas but a 'vital mutual responsiveness',[260] an 'existential contact' that is an 'action and interaction of being'.[261] That existential contact or vital mutual responsiveness can only take place to the extent that there is a shared vision and a shared commitment on which that vision is based. There is only communication to the extent that there is a Going for Refuge to the Three Jewels in common.

> Communication ... is a common exploration of the spiritual world by
> people who are completely honest and in full harmony with one
> another.... In fact, the communication is the exploration and the
> exploration is the communication.[262]

Communication involves the complete opening of two people to one another. It begins with self-disclosure, what Sangharakshita calls

> the great benefit and blessing of being able to share our thoughts and
> feelings with another human being.[263]

—which is perhaps even a psychological necessity. In the context of Going for Refuge to the Three Jewels, at least part of what is shared will be experience of the Dharma—

> We share our enthusiasm, our inspiration, and our understanding. We
> even share our mistakes. Here communication takes the form of
> Confession.[264]

Communication is, of course, not merely verbal. It can take place in silence. Where people are particularly attuned to one another, it can even flash directly from mind to mind.

The consequences of such true communication are far reaching indeed. In opening up to each other on the basis of a common Going for Refuge, sharing their experience of the Dharma, and exploring together the spiritual world, the parties to genuine communication will be 'sparked off'. They will experience an intensification of that common element of Going for Refuge and will be precipitated into a deeper experience of the *kalyāṇa*. Where one party to the communication is Going for Refuge more deeply than the other and has a greater familiarity with the spiritual dimension, communication will be 'vertical'. The *kalyāṇa mitra* or 'guru' will have a powerful impact on the being of the disciple who will thereby be raised up towards his or her level. Although the disciple is the one who most obviously grows as a consequence of the communication, the *kalyāṇa mitra* too is affected. The *kalyāṇa mitra* needs the disciple as much as the disciple needs the *kalyāṇa mitra*, if for somewhat different reasons. Sangharakshita illustrates this point in discussing why the Buddha was, for most of his life after his Enlightenment, accompanied by what is usually referred to as a 'personal attendant'—Ānanda being the most famous of these constant companions and close friends to the Buddha. The fact that Ānanda was 'in attendance' on the Buddha for the last twenty years of his life was not because the Buddha needed a 'spiritual valet-cum-private-secretary' but because

> The Enlightenment experience is not self-contained in a one-sided way.
> The Enlightenment experience contains an element of 'communication',
> and contains, therefore, an element of spiritual friendship, even
> 'transcendental friendship' or friendship on the highest conceivable
> level.[265]

While vertical communication draws the disciple up to the level of the guru, 'horizontal' communication works in a different way. Where both parties are more or less on the same spiritual level, there is an enhancement in each of the Going for Refuge that they hold in common. Because the Three Jewels are at the centre of both their lives, they will meet on that basis, intensifying their experience of the spiritual dimension. There will also be between them a transference of spiritual qualities and of aspects of the Dharma that each will have developed to different degrees. One friend may, for instance, have a clear grasp of the Dharma as conceptually expressed, while the other may have strong feelings of faith and devotion. Through their communication each will tend to absorb the qualities of the other.

It is this horizontal aspect of *kalyāṇa mitratā* in particular for which there is no developed teaching in Buddhist tradition—although many canonical stories attest to the value placed by the Buddha on close harmony with those who share one's spiritual aspirations. In Sangharakshita's estimation, placing the emphasis almost entirely on guru–disciple relationships at the expense of those between disciple and disciple has had serious consequences. Not only has it led to a lack of appreciation of an important dimension of spiritual experience, it has contributed to the devaluation of the principle of *kalyāṇa mitratā* itself. In *kalyāṇa mitratā* what is important is not so much whether the person one is communicating with is more developed than oneself; what is important is that one is genuinely *communicating*. When communication is really taking place there is no self-conscious awareness that one party is more or less developed than the other. There is simply that vital mutual responsiveness that transforms all who participate in it, no matter what their relationships with each other. Since the disciple may equal or overtake the guru at any time, relationships cannot be seen in too fixed or rigid a manner. They certainly cannot be transformed into the set ecclesiastical hierarchies that are common even in the Buddhist world.

Although spiritual friendship is an important tool of spiritual development, it should not be thought of too much in utilitarian terms. *Kalyāṇa mitratā* needs no justification—it is its own justification. Sangharakshita makes this clear when he speaks of two factors being of the essence of spiritual friendship: communication and 'taking delight'.

> The aspect of 'taking delight' means that we not only see a person as a person, but also *like* what we see, enjoy and take delight in what we see, just as we do with a beautiful painting or poem—except that here the painting or poem is alive: the painting can speak to you, and the beautiful poem can answer back! This makes it very exciting and stimulating indeed. Here we see, we like, we love and appreciate a person entirely for their own sake, and not for the sake of anything useful that we can get out of them. This also happens in ordinary friendship to some extent, but it happens to a far greater extent in spiritual friendship—*kalyāṇa mitratā*. The primary meaning of *kalyāṇa* is 'beautiful'. In spiritual friendship we take delight in the *spiritual* beauty of our friend: we rejoice in his or her merits.[266]

Spiritual friendship is not simply one of the spiritual life's essential props but one of its greatest joys and blessings.

Sangharakshita has, scattered through his lectures and seminars, and to some extent his writings, much advice about the practice of friendship. For instance he has important things to say about the need for members of the spiritual community to care for each other:

> The responsibility for the care of each member rests on the entire spiritual community. Ultimately all are responsible for each, and each is responsible for all to the extent of his strength. Otherwise, there is no spiritual community.[267]

He considers that friendship involves fidelity and that this has major spiritual implications, suggesting the ability to live 'on the "mental" level'—by remaining faithful to one's friends and behaving in the same way towards them in their absence as one would if they were present.[268] Thus fidelity is a mark of maturity and of individuality. Perhaps the deepest dimension of friendship is the tendency to self-sacrifice. This too has profound spiritual implications:

> One could say that friendship itself is a spiritual ideal, in the sense that it sometimes involves self-sacrifice, therefore a negation of self. And negation of self [in this sense of going beyond self] is surely in itself, so to speak, a spiritual thing?[269]

Passing beyond identification with self is the goal of Buddhism. To the extent that one is able to give up self-interest to the interest of one's friend, even to the point of self-sacrifice, one is moving forward on the path. Indeed, the effort to be a friend is commensurate with the spiritual path since to be a real friend one must be entirely dependable—and one can only be entirely dependable, a true Refuge, if one is a Stream Entrant. Only at that point does one cease to be so much at the mercy of one's emotional states that one cannot be entirely relied upon.

> If you make an effort to be a real, absolutely dependable friend, in fact you're trying to approach the point of Stream Entry. The desire not to let your friend down can be a very, very powerful motivation. And that can therefore be a spiritual practice, even a means of achieving Stream Entry. You really very much want to help your friend, to be a refuge for him. So you have to *make* yourself a refuge for him. You are willing to do for him what you're not willing to do for yourself. So the demands of friendship really stretch you on occasion. By being stretched in this way you can really grow and develop as a human being, even spiritually. Perhaps you can even enter the Stream in that way. People have sacrificed their lives for their friends. And the state of mind of a person who is willing to sacrifice his life for a friend—is very difficult to imagine. There is something more than human about it.[270]

## SPIRITUAL FRIENDSHIP AND WESTERN SOCIETY

As we have seen, Sangharakshita's own experience of Buddhist groups in India gave him little opportunity to appreciate the full significance of sangha. For instance, the Maha Bodhi Society's Headquarters in Calcutta was technically a monastery yet there was no *kalyāṇa mitratā* among the monks who lived or visited there. He knew that he should have been receiving something more from his brother-monks, many of whom were his seniors in the Order by many years, but at that stage he was not fully aware of what it was that he was missing. When he returned to England in 1964, although there were several *bhikkhus* resident at the Hampstead Buddhist Vihara when he arrived, there was no spiritual community among them—nor even any desire for it or feeling that anything was lacking.

In India, he did have very positive relations with a few people who could be said to have been his *kalyāṇa mitras*. He developed a warm friendship with his first teacher, Ven. Jagdish Kashyap—who clearly esteemed Sangharakshita's friendship very highly. Dhardo Rimpoche, being a rather reserved Gelugpa lama, took longer to get to know, but after they had travelled together on pilgrimage they became firm friends, collaborating on several Buddhist projects in Kalimpong. Dhardo Rimpoche more recently said that he had learnt from his contact with Sangharakshita that one could teach the Dharma in the context of friendship. He had been accustomed to functioning as a guru in the Tibetan style: sitting on his brocade-covered throne and wearing his pandit's hat, he would lecture for many hours to a silent audience. When Sangharakshita visited him, they would sit together and discuss the Dharma quite informally. Khachu Rimpoche, the very friendly abbot of the Royal Monastery of Sikkim, was one of the very few people who took the initiative in approaching Sangharakshita, going out of his way to befriend him and to help him in his practice of Vajrayāna meditation.

Sangharakshita saw that there was quite a strong feeling of solidarity among the monks he knew, as well as quite a bit of warmth and friendliness. However he considered that their common social position in relation to the laity gave them a clear identity as a group. Their solidarity was, for the most part, nothing more than group cohesion and had little of genuine sangha or *kalyāṇa mitratā* about it. Thus, though he had experienced genuine spiritual friendship with a few people, the survival of the degenerate forms of sangha largely without its substance for many years obscured from him the real state of affairs. It was not until he was completely free of the traditional Buddhist world, after leaving the Hampstead Vihara, that he began to see that world in full clarity. And it was only as he began to create a new Buddhist movement that the principles of sangha and of *kalyāṇa mitratā* became more and more plain to him. However, from the start, he knew that his new Buddhist movement must have *kalyāṇa mitratā* at its heart. One of his principal reasons for establishing the Western Buddhist Order was, as he declared on the day of the first ordinations, to 'provide opportunities for spiritual fellowship'[271] of both a horizontal and a vertical kind.

Before he came to establish the FWBO, Sangharakshita experienced a lack of *kalyāṇa mitratā* among British Buddhists. He had found the atmosphere at the Hampstead Vihara stiff and cold and had tried hard to introduce a more emotionally positive atmosphere. On an early FWBO retreat, noticing that there was little real communication between participants, he experimented with a set of simple exercises, learned from an educationalist in India, that helped people to understand what communication was and to begin to explore its depths. The 'communication exercises' are done in pairs, each set of two sitting facing one another. In the first exercise, 'just looking', the participants learn to be silently aware of each other—and to become conscious of the communication, the 'mutual responsiveness', that begins to develop between them. Two further exercises involve the exchange of predetermined sentences whose content is irrelevant, thus exploring the non-conceptual content of speech. The exercises are very effective, particularly helping people to overcome social inhibitions to communication, and they became a common feature of FWBO programmes.

More generally he found that problems in human relationships were among the most persistent and intractable for many of his disciples. Many difficulties stemmed from the inevitable tensions that arise when one party to a relationship begins to take an interest in spiritual life and the other does not. This problem is inherent and universal. Whether parents or children, husbands or wives, or friends and companions, one will find one has less and less in common with those who do not go for Refuge as one begins to do so oneself, and will inevitably find other relationships in their stead. One will begin to form deeper and deeper friendships with others on the path. Some people, of course, are very fortunate in that the shift from the group to the spiritual community takes place quite smoothly and naturally, but for many this will not be the case. The disruptive effects of this shift may well give rise to almost intolerable conflicts for some people—and many will give up spiritual life rather than face the problems that arise.

While this shift in the major relationships of one's life is inherent in one's deepening spiritual commitment, conditions in the West make it more difficult to undergo it smoothly. In modern Western society there is very little appreciation of the value of the spiritual path. Most people will therefore find that the group members who surround them are at best indifferent to and uncomprehending of their efforts, and at worst hostile to them. There is, in Sangharakshita's phrase, no 'positive group' that, while being a group in the full sense of the term, appreciates and supports the spiritual life.

Besides providing little support or sympathy for spiritual life, the culture of the modern West creates other barriers to the development of true friendship. Sangharakshita's general analysis of Western culture is that it undervalues genuine social relationships and therefore offers little basis for the development of spiritual friendship. Inevitably Sangharakshita has viewed Western culture from within a particular context, although his wide reading and careful attention to current affairs have given him a much broader perspective. His closest experience of modern Western society has, since his return from India, been in England. While the social patterns found among the English are certainly not universal, they typify a trend already manifest, to a greater or lesser degree, in most parts of Western Europe and North America and increasingly becoming worldwide. The mobility of society means that few people have stayed in one place long enough to form the strong connections that come from constant proximity. There is therefore a lack of facility for making such connections. Modern urban life is often impersonal and allows very little sense of belonging to a greater whole. This leads to an accent on self as an isolated unit, merely consuming personal relationships like any other product on the market. The traditional extended family has decayed into the nuclear family. Sangharakshita considers that form of family-unit, in the main, to provide an unwholesome environment for its members, on whom it places what are often intolerable strains. The isolated nuclear family is frequently a breeding-ground for neurosis and worse since its members expect to find all their social needs within its restricted circle.

In the fragmented modern society, most of the traditional relationships outside the family have become increasingly impersonal and superficial: instead of a relationship between master or mistress and someone personally serving them there is simply a contract between employer and employee; teachers and pupils very seldom have any personal connection with each other; even well-known features of social life a few years ago, such as the family doctor or the village policeman, are now a rarity. Marriage and parenthood are the only remaining binding social obligations recognised by most people. However, marriage and parenthood too are being reduced simply to the sexual relationship. Friends have become less and less significant and the sexual relationship is expected to be the central and all-sustaining one. Since ordinary friendship has become more rare there is no basis for genuine spiritual friendship—for one must be capable of being an ordinary friend before one can become a spiritual friend.

## THE SINGLE-SEX IDEA

The crisis in Western society is particularly obvious in relations between the sexes, and Sangharakshita soon began to recognise that this was one of the chief issues confronting Buddhists in the West. When he left England in 1944, men and women still had different and well-defined social roles. They would naturally spend quite a bit of time apart and usually had a wide range of friends and companions of their own sex. In India this was even more the case, men and women being seldom seen together in public and even having different spaces within the home. He fell in with prevailing Indian social custom and thought little about it, especially as he was a monk and was therefore expected to be circumspect in his dealings with women. Returning to England, he found that customs had changed and that men and women now did not occupy such distinct social spheres—this was, after all, the era when the term 'unisex' was devised and when the bastions of single-sex education began to fall even at Oxford and Cambridge Universities. Again, he followed the practice of the times and all the Buddhist activities he organised were for both men and women together.

After some time, he began to see that the constant proximity of the sexes was not necessarily advantageous to spiritual life, even perhaps to ordinary human life. For a start, an element of sexual attraction was present in the mixed situations he organised, especially since many of his disciples were quite young. This introduced a tension into the atmosphere that was inimical to the cultivation of meditation—at times even to the simple study of the Dharma. Then he saw that the sexes' broadly different approaches to life in general applied also to spiritual life. He encouraged experiments with retreats and other activities for men or women separately. By chance, a residential community was formed that consisted only of men, proving particularly successful and being ancestral to the many current single-sex communities within the movement. Within a few years of the founding of the FWBO, many of its activities, beyond the beginners', were for men and women separately, and the 'single-sex idea' became, not without much debate and some conflict, an established part of Sangharakshita's teaching and of the practice of the movement he founded.

> For those individuals who go for Refuge, or who seek to go for Refuge, the best life-style—circumstances permitting—is one that contains a strong single-sex element, either by virtue of the fact that one lives in a single-sex spiritual community and/or works in a single-sex co-operative or by virtue of the fact that one is a regular participant in single-sex retreats, study groups, etc.[272]

Probably no other idea of Sangharakshita's requires more cool and careful reflection. Western society as a whole is in a vast transition from traditional structures. Where that transition is leading us is, as yet, far from apparent. Much attention has been given to the most basic issues of gender, sexuality, and parenthood, since these are the principal determinants of society's future shape. It is now widely assumed that men and women should have the same opportunities and that therefore all facilities should be open to both equally. Sangharakshita's 'single-sex idea' appears to swim against these popular attitudes.

What he actually proposes is far more radical than the simple equality of the sexes—and, at the same time, far more realistic than the mere abolition of the separate spheres within which men and women have traditionally moved. He is perhaps one of the few modern Buddhist teachers to offer a sophisticated rationale of a practice that Buddhist tradition has taken for granted since its inception. Having developed for 2,500 years in cultures in which the sexes' separate spheres were taken for granted, the tradition has no explicit set of ideas to make clear why having separate activities for men and women can be beneficial. Since Sangharakshita's thinking on this matter is complex, containing several separate strands, we will follow them one by one.

Perhaps the first point to be made is that Sangharakshita considers that there are broad and basic differences between men and women in respect of their psychological make-up, arising out of their biological specialisation. Their different functions in sex and procreation give them different interests and different approaches to life. Clearly, they also have much in common, otherwise they could not communicate at all. Again there are frequent exceptions to any general characterisation of either sex, since human beings are so various—in so far as they are self-conscious, they can mould their characters in many ways, both neurotic and healthy. Nonetheless, the differences between men and women are significant and must be taken into account when considering social questions as well as the forms and institutions of the spiritual community.

These differences of approach and outlook at the 'psycho-biological' level are, to a large extent and much of the time, opposing. This is even the case with those who are homosexual, whether male or female, the essential differences being deeper than sexual orientation. Where there is no conscious effort to develop as individuals, the natural condition is therefore the 'war of the sexes'. If there is no effective spiritual commit- ment 'I think you can probably get at best an armed truce'! This being the case, Sangharakshita considers it wisest to acknowledge the conflict and to deal with it openly, rather than try to cover it up. Only then can it be prevented from causing too much disruption and finally be transcended.

> The indiscriminate way in which we mix up men and women on all possible occasions is flying in the face of biological and psychological facts. Most of the separation that has occurred within the FWBO is therefore quite healthy. Clearly, you can't separate men and women completely in all cases, on all occasions. However I think we could do with a lot more separation even in general society in Britain than usually is the case. It makes for a more healthy relationship between men and women if they don't see quite so much of each other, and aren't together on all possible occasions.[273]

A common commitment to the Three Jewels goes beyond gender and therefore beyond the underlying tension between the sexes. However, until that commitment is strong and mature it will be easily overpowered by more basic conditioning. For men and women to meet on all occasions as more than just men with women and women with men requires a high degree of spiritual maturity. Sangharakshita considers that spiritual maturity is most likely to come about if one's spiritual life has a 'strong single-sex element'.

The basic tension between the sexes has consequences for their com- munication. Sangharakshita does believe that deep and genuine friendship between a man and a woman is possible. However he con- siders it to be very rare indeed, maturing for example when a husband and wife have been together for many years, have got well beyond being in love and mere sexual attraction, and have come to know each other very thoroughly and deeply, while having quite independent lives. The deepest and most significant friendships therefore, in the very great majority of cases, are likely to be between a man and a man or between a woman and a woman. This does not mean that men and women within the movement he has founded never meet or that there is not good and positive communication between them. Indeed, friendly and considerate relations between men and women are very much encouraged. Nonetheless it is generally acknowledged that one's deeper friendships are likely to be with members of one's own sex.

The underlying tension between men and women is not only experienced as an opposition but also as an intense attraction. The sheer otherness of each sex from its counterpart leads easily to the psychological phenomenon of projection: seeing in a member of the other sex qualities that are unrealised in oneself. Thus, classically, the male sees in the female all the softness, compliance, and concern for others that he does not show in his own life; the woman sees in the man the strength, initiative, and independence that she herself fails to express. Human beings are, of course, so variable that these stereotypical examples are by no means universal—although actually they are very common. Most men and women will find themselves somewhere on the 'masculine' or 'feminine' end of the spectrum respectively, although in some cases it might even be that the two sets of qualities are completely reversed: the man having the conventionally 'feminine' qualities and the woman the 'masculine'. Whatever their dominant characteristics, the difference between the sexes leads them to look at each other with a mysterious longing, at the same time as they are repelled by a deep and natural incompatibility of aims and interests. Such projection, since it leads to a distortion in perception, stands in the way of friendship and often leads to reaction and disillusionment.

The decay of traditional society with its broad network of social relationships surrounding each individual has left the sexual relationship as the primary one. People often expect to satisfy all their social needs within that one relationship. Sex itself carries a greater and greater load, becoming not merely a biological function or a source of pleasure but the chief means of emotional expression. This has left friendship between members of the same sex with scarcely any real significance. This is a very recent phenomenon—indeed, in many other eras or societies one's relationship with friends would have been far more important than one's relationship with one's spouse. Sangharakshita believes that there must be a revival of ordinary friendship before there can be spiritual friendship.

One of the barriers to such a revival is the fear of homosexuality, which Sangharakshita has observed particularly among men. In the post-

Freudian world, it is realised that there is a tinge of eroticism to most relationships, and many men are afraid of that element of sexual attraction frequently present, at least on the periphery, in their relations with male friends. Since homosexuality is often identified with effeminacy, the fear of homosexuality is tied up with lack of confidence that one is really a man. This itself is connected with the loss of an identifiable 'man's world' within which men can feel themselves accepted as men, regardless of sexual orientation. It is common for men never to develop any satisfactory male identity, moving straight from dependence on their mothers to dependence on girlfriends and wives—the lack of genuine confidence in masculinity being sometimes compensated for by a swaggering machismo. Sangharakshita believes that men must break down their fear of homosexuality by facing the fact that there may be some element of sexual attraction towards their friends.

> This is not necessarily to say that they should have sexual contact with men, but at least they should not be afraid of the idea. They have to realize that physical, even sexual, contact between men is *just* physical or sexual contact between men. It is a quite ordinary thing, and one's fear of that should not be allowed to get in the way of one's friendships.[274]

Ordinary friendship between women has perhaps fared rather better in modern society than that between men, although compared with the past it is probably much decayed. The single-sex situations that Sangharakshita has encouraged within the FWBO give both men and women a greater opportunity for developing friendship with members of their own sex.

We have already seen, when speaking of *brahmacarya*, that spiritual life leads in the direction of androgyny. This is a state in which there is no self-identification either as a man or as a woman. Gender is part of the way in which most of us think about ourselves: we identify ourselves as either male or female. This identification substantially determines our behaviour, particularly in relation to members of the opposite sex. Most frequently, when with members of the opposite sex, men and women experience even more strongly that identification as a man or as a woman—they become psycho-sexually polarised. This is a limitation and a denial of what one is most truly and deeply. Every human being has both the masculine and the feminine within them. To put it another way, every human being can be a human being before they are a man or a woman. Therefore,

> one should not think of oneself as being either a man or a woman in any absolute or exclusive sense.[275]

To go beyond sexual polarisation is no easy task, demanding consider-able and sustained effort.

> For those who wish to develop as individuals, and to progress on the
> path to Enlightenment, meditation and all kinds of single-sex situations
> are, in the absence of transcendental insight, absolutely indispensable.[276]

Both meditation and single-sex situations provide

> an opportunity of transcending, for a few moments, the state of sexual
> polarization and being simply a human being and—to some extent—a
> true individual.[277]

Paradoxically therefore, the purpose of single-sex activities within spiritual practice is to overcome identification with one or other sex so that one no longer needs to be separate from the opposite sex. By spending much of one's time with members of one's own sex one will be less and less drawn into sexual polarisation. One will come increasingly to experience oneself beyond exclusive identification with one's biologi-cal sex. The first objective of Sangharakshita's 'single-sex idea' is the creation of a more healthy and tension-free human environment, in which the 'battle of the sexes' is contained—and perhaps a truce is called. But the higher purpose of single-sex activities is to enable individuals to develop to a point where they have ceased to identify primarily with their biological sex and therefore no longer become sexually polarised in the presence of members of the opposite sex. Once this point has been reached, it no longer matters whether one is with men *qua* men or with women *qua* women: one will simply experience oneself as a human being with other human beings. Here, at the level of the transcendental sangha, there is no need for separate activities for men and women. But this, as Sangharakshita is quick to point out, is a level achieved by very few.

### WOMEN AND SPIRITUAL LIFE

In examining Sangharakshita's ideas about basic social relationships we must look at an issue that is currently in the foreground of public debate: the status of women—and, in this context, their place in the spiritual life and community. His views here are complex and are all too susceptible of misreading, since they do not altogether chime with popular opinion.

It should first be understood that Sangharakshita believes women to have the same spiritual potential as men and that they, as much as men, should be actively encouraged to realise that potential. This view is enshrined in action. The Order he has founded consists of men and women equally, sharing one ordination and having exactly the same 'status'—that status being a 'no-status', since status has no place in the spiritual community. He has given as much care and attention to the spiritual welfare of women in the movement as he has to that of men.

However Sangharakshita has given considerable thought to the relative aptitude for spiritual life of men and women in general. He believes that this issue needs to be explored and not dismissed on the assumption that men and women are the same in all respects. In the first place, Buddhist tradition, going back to the Buddha himself, speaks of the disadvantages of being born a woman. Some modern Buddhist apologists are quick to point out that the Buddha was simply talking of the disadvantages of being born a woman in a repressive patriarchal society. Others dismiss these traditions on the grounds that the Buddha and later teachers who espoused them were all men and shared masculine prejudice towards women.

Sangharakshita does not believe that the point can be so easily brushed aside, especially since he does not accept the assumptions on which the dismissals are based. He does not accept that history reveals the consistent oppression and enslavement of women by men. As we have seen, he views the 'natural' relationship between the sexes as fundamentally one of tension—and he does not consider men, by any means, to have always had the upper hand in that struggle. The 'fortunes of war' have gone now one way and now another, any advantage gained in a single battle being lost in the next—although the war is on the whole really a series of small skirmishes between individuals.

> the feminist reading of history as the story of Woman's oppression and exploitation by Man belongs not to history but to mythology, and can be compared with the anti-Semitic reading of history as the story of the world-wide conspiracy on the part of the Jews to concentrate wealth and power in their own hands so as to be able to enslave the Gentiles (cf. the spurious 'Protocols of the Elders of Zion'). Men have of course sometimes oppressed women (and women, men), just as Jews have sometimes enslaved Gentiles (and Gentiles, Jews!), but in neither case are the facts sufficient to justify a reading of history either in feminist, or in anti-Semitic, terms: such interpretations are not history but myth.[278]

Secondly, Sangharakshita considers that this topic needs to be explored because it will help both women and men to work constructively with their basic biological conditioning. That conditioning has a powerful influence upon us and he has given much thought to its relationship with spiritual life. As we have seen, he views spiritual life as a path of Higher Evolution which requires one to transcend, without denying, one's biological nature. Men and women have different functions in the reproductive process and therefore different biological drives and impulses. Since their basic psychological make-up is strongly influenced by those drives and impulses, men and women have broadly different basic psychologies as well. Naturally, human nature being so various, no generalisation about these matters will invariably include all men and women. Nonetheless, most women's psychological make-up is strongly conditioned by their physiological capacity to bear children, a capacity of which they are constantly reminded by their own bodies. This often leads them to invest themselves heavily in biological imperatives that find expression in a complex web of social conditioning. They frequently become keenly interested in sexual relationships, the getting of husbands, childbirth, child-rearing, and all that surrounds these matters.

A man's role in procreation is much more brief, and though his interest in sex is often very powerful indeed, it seldom leads to a comparable emotional investment in the details of family life. Of course, most men in the world are involved in families. However, their motivation is not so much biological in basis but psychological. A major component in their involvement, besides a desire for regular sex, is often a need for security and comfort. Women who have a desire to commit themselves to spiritual life usually experience a sharper conflict between their interests in a domestic life and in a spiritual one than would most men. For men, the conflict is likely to be more focused on whether or not to pursue a career. Because men are not so strongly bound by these biological imperatives, their energy can more easily be free for other matters, both good and evil. Indeed, the psychological make-up that men derive from their biological role often more readily provides the drive and initiative required to translate an attraction to spiritual life into an effective commitment to following a spiritual path. Unfortunately they often squander that freedom and drive on worldly ambition.

Men and women need to face up to the basic facts of their biological natures and to see that those natures are not, in themselves, part of spiritual life. Biological urges—to have sex, to have children, and so on—should be seen as biological urges, not spiritual ones. It is also important to acknowledge the greater role that these urges play in most women's experience and that women are therefore likely to have a stronger investment in that biological dimension than are men. Again, it is important to recognise that many men, because of their aggressive drive, which seems usually to be a much stronger aspect of their basic psychological make-up, often find it easier to mobilise their energies to make their Going for Refuge effective than do many women. A clear and open acknowledgement that men and women often want different things and function in different ways makes it easier to find social arrangements that fulfil the needs and aspirations of all. It can provide the basis for a truce between the sexes and, indeed, ultimately a transcendence of gender-based differences altogether.

To sum up, Sangharakshita affirms that women can go for Refuge to the Buddha, Dharma, and Sangha, just as much as can men. This affirmation is witnessed by the fact that he has ordained women into the Western Buddhist Order, some of them with young children too. One must take each individual, woman or man, as one finds them, acknowledging and encouraging whatever spiritual aspiration they may have. Nonetheless, based on his experience with his female disciples and friends, he follows Buddhist tradition in regarding women generally as at somewhat of a disadvantage, at least at the commencement of spiritual life. He has however also said that, once men and women have actually committed themselves to the path, differences in this respect become less and less.

Sangharakshita has given great encouragement to women in the movement to be self-reliant and independent of men. Indeed, he has told male Order members that the best thing they can do for women is to 'get out of their way', so that they have the opportunity and necessity to exercise the initiative that men so often take on their behalf. Within the context of the single-sex idea, the wisdom of this policy has already been amply demonstrated.

> the FWBO and WBO offer the individual woman incomparably more
> freedom and scope for personal development than the Women's
> Movement (i.e. Feminism, Women's Lib. etc.) can possibly do. The FWBO
> and WBO in fact make the Women's Movement unnecessary.[279]

Women in the FWBO have developed, on their own initiative, a full range of facilities that provide for their spiritual needs, and the movement now enjoys two well-developed 'wings': a men's and a women's. In these wings, men and women can both find all the support and opportunity they need for spiritual growth. Naturally, for men and women to have separate spheres within which to live out their spiritual aspirations is not in itself enough. There are still many difficulties to be worked with. Men have especially to overcome a tendency to negative competitiveness and rivalry among themselves, as do women a certain lack of enterprise.

It must also be borne in mind that, although men and women have separate spheres within the movement, they belong to the same spiritual community. One purpose of that spiritual community is to transcend sexual polarisation and to enable men and women to meet each other simply as human beings who go for Refuge. There are therefore frequent occasions on which men and women in the Order and movement meet and work together. Some Order chapters are mixed and there are regular conventions and other events attended by both Dharmacaris and Dharmacarinis. Men and women Order members participate fully and equally in the running of public Dharma centres. Indeed, although most people acknowledge that their closest and deepest friends are likely to be members of their own sex, there are good friendships between some Dharmacaris and Dharmacarinis. In general, relations between men and women in the movement are very positive indeed.

## Sex and Spiritual Life

A particularly tangled strand running through this discussion is the powerful fact of sexual desire. We must therefore look briefly at Sangharakshita's ideas on the subject. In the first place, he has no sympathy with views of sex as sacred or as a means to spiritual growth or of teaching the Dharma. He sees that sexual desire is to be transcended and that considerable effort must go into bringing that transcendence about. Behind sexual desire is that irreducibly unskilful element of polarisation between coveting subject and coveted object that the spiritual life is lived to go beyond. But to be beyond sexuality is not to deny it:

> A castrate is not an angel, certain representations of angels in Christian
> art notwithstanding. Here as elsewhere in the spiritual life what is
> needed is not negation but transformation.[280]

Brahmacarya, usually translated as 'chastity', is, when it is fully accomplished, not a grey and colourless state in which all pleasure and enjoyment is pushed aside, but a fullness and overflowing of happiness and pleasure that goes far beyond the temporary thrill of physical sex. Thus one cannot move to brahmacarya by abruptly stopping engagement in sexual activity. One can, says Sangharakshita, only give up a lower pleasure when one has some experience of a higher. Brahmacarya is something one must work towards. One gradually learns to enjoy more and more refined pleasures, and to gain deeper emotional satisfaction in communication with friends, as one withdraws more and more energy from sexual activity. He speaks of brahmacarya as a principle that one can be trying to put into practice on ever deeper levels, although one may not yet have got to the point of transcending sex altogether.

Sangharakshita realistically acknowledges that most people trying to follow the path could not dispense with sexual activity in a positive and healthy way. However, if they do continue to be sexually active, they must make sure that they can satisfy their desires in as skilful a manner as possible and with minimum disruption to their spiritual lives. Here the important point is that sexual activity should not be too central to one's life.

> It is possible for a human being to develop spiritually while still engaging in a certain amount of sexual activity. But that is provided that not too much importance is attached to that activity, that our emotions are not invested in that sexual activity to a very great extent, and provided especially that there is a strong spiritual ideal seated right at the centre of the mandala.[281]

The *maṇḍala* or 'magic circle' is here used as a symbol for the total contents of one's life. Everything is arranged in order of importance around the central element, which is one's main theme and interest. Sex should certainly not be at the centre of one's mandala: 'For most people, sex has a legitimate place somewhere near the periphery of the personal mandala'.[282]

So long as there is no infringement of the ethical principles enshrined in the Ten Precepts, Sangharakshita does not think that the particular way an individual gains sexual satisfaction is necessarily a moral issue. Masturbation, homosexuality, whether male or female, and heterosexuality are all, in themselves, morally neutral. Sangharakshita has also said that he sees no moral issue in transvestism, even in 'bondage', excepting where this involves violence. Human sexuality is very varied and surprisingly malleable, and inevitably there will be a wide range of tastes and activities. Presuming that one is observing the precepts, the main issue for one's spiritual life is not what one's present sexual behaviour is: it is that one should be applying the principle of *brahmacarya* more and more deeply. One should be progressively overcoming psycho-sexual polarisation and experiencing more and more the intense pleasure of more refined and integrated states.

Sangharakshita has frequently insisted that the FWBO should be open to people whatever their sexual orientation, making it clear, for instance, that homosexuals are welcome at the movement's centres. At the same time he is critical of the tendency for 'sexual minorities' to define themselves simply in terms of their sexuality, labelling themselves as 'gay', 'transvestite', and so on—although he recognises that this is a reaction to centuries of persecution. Such identification puts sex at the centre of the mandala, rather than on the periphery where it belongs. In the context of the spiritual community, one is primarily a human being who goes for Refuge, and only secondarily one who is attracted sexually to one's own sex or who likes to wear clothes usually associated with the opposite sex.

## THE 'COUPLE'

Apart from the irreducible element of craving present in sexual activity, which will be overcome only gradually, the major danger sex presents to spiritual life is neurotic attachment.

> When one comes into close physical, or emotional, contact with another person within the context of a sexual relationship, usually all sorts of psychological projections take place, and sometimes a very complicated, even negative, situation develops.[283]

Sexual infatuation—being 'in love'—has some superficial resemblance to friendship because there is apparently very strong concern for the other person. However, the element of craving is predominant and the self-interestedness of the seeming concern is demonstrated by the speed with which 'love' can turn to jealousy and then to hatred. What often happens is that sexual infatuation leads on to mutual dependency in which each partner relies on the other for the fulfilment of various psychological needs. This is the 'couple'.

> By the couple, in this context, one means two people, usually of the opposite sex, who are neurotically dependent on each other and whose relationship, therefore, is one of mutual exploitation and mutual addiction. A couple consists, in fact, of two half-people, each of whom unconsciously invests part of his or her total being in the other: each is dependent on the other for the kind of psychological security that can be found, ultimately, only within oneself.[284]

Given the decay of the traditional pattern of relationships, the isolation of the nuclear family, and the glorification of sexuality in modern society, added to the natural tensions and attractions between the sexes, the 'couple' is a fragile and unwholesome unit. It offers little real stability and happiness and, by virtue of the clinging and delusion that it embodies, is antithetical to spiritual life.

> Two such half-people, uneasily conjoined as a couple, can no more be part of a spiritual community than Siamese twins can be part of a *corps de ballet*. Their 'presence' within the spiritual community can only have a disruptive effect. The couple is therefore the enemy of the spiritual community.[285]

The more space partners to a sexual relationship have between them, the less will it be loaded with psychological projection and emotional expectation—the less will it be a 'couple'.

> In the FWBO ... people who are having sexual relationships often live in
> separate communities, the man living in a men's community, the woman
> living in a women's community. I would say that this not only helps to
> ensure that the sexual relationship occupies only a peripheral place in
> those two people's mandalas, but also ensures a happier, more truly
> human relationship between them, because they allow themselves [and
> each other] space.[286]

An obvious problem arises in so far as a proportion of men and women
are sexually attracted to members of their own sex. A homosexual couple
however is no less the enemy of the spiritual community than a
heterosexual one. What then are homosexuals to do? How can they avoid,
in a single-sex situation, psycho-sexual polarisation with those members
of their own sex to whom they are attracted? Clearly there is no institutional way of resolving this problem. Sangharakshita recommends that
homosexual men and women participate fully in single-sex activities:

> Homosexuals are, after all, men or women. They have more in common
> with other members of their own sex, in most cases, than they have with
> members of the opposite sex. So, despite the fact that some of them may
> get distracted on a single-sex retreat, I think nonetheless it's the
> single-sex retreat they have to go on. The emphasis must however
> always be on the fact that one is there on retreat for the sake of the
> Dharma and not for other purposes.[287]

The single-sex idea should not be seen only in terms of avoiding
problems.

> One also needs to see another, positive aspect of the single-sex principle,
> which is the development of friendship. Gay people, too, still need to
> develop friendships of a non-sexual character with members of their
> own sex. Obviously, a [single-sex situation] is one in which they can do
> that. They can be given to understand that no one is frowning on their
> sexuality, but it isn't appropriate here. Here is an opportunity for them to
> develop friendships. And it's sometimes very difficult for gay people to
> develop friendships because of the sexual complication, but on a
> single-sex retreat they are almost forced into that situation.[288]

Sangharakshita's ideas on the spiritual benefits of single-sex situations
do not imply that those in more conventional marriages cannot develop
as individuals. However they will probably have difficulties to work with
which others do not have. Their relationships with their spouses will
often involve projection and dependency of which they may not be fully
aware. One partner may wish to commit themselves to the Buddhist path
while the other does not—or does not want to do so as deeply—and this
may well lead to tensions and conflict. Finally, children may be involved,
adding further complications of attachment, and more restrictions on

time and energy available for spiritual practice and for spiritual friendship. Once more it must be stressed that Sangharakshita does consider that those with families can go for Refuge—but they will have difficulties that their brothers and sisters who are not parents will not have.

## CHILDREN AND SPIRITUAL LIFE

However, he realises that, for many women, having a child is virtually a psychological necessity, in so far as they feel a strong impulsion to do so. Not all women feel such an urge to motherhood but, in Sangharakshita's experience, the majority do. This will inevitably lead to some inner conflict for many women who also feel drawn to spiritual life.

> From what I've seen of women who have had children and women who haven't had them, it's probably wiser for a woman who wants children to 'give in', so to speak, and have children, even though she is also quite genuinely concerned with her spiritual development. I'm pretty certain she doesn't speed up the process of spiritual development just by not having children. I'm not saying that if she has them that will definitely contribute to her growth. But probably in the long run it will be easier and more straightforward for her to evolve if she has children.[289]

Women don't necessarily evolve spiritually simply by bypassing that biological urge. The conflict engendered by suppressing it may be more detrimental to spiritual growth than actually having a child. Indeed, his experience has been that, after the first two years or so, during which the mother must give all her attention to the child, she is gradually able to put more and more time into spiritual practice and into her spiritual friendships. He does not think women are, in the end, held back by having children.

Men do not usually have the same sort of urge—this is one of the areas where the interests of the sexes do not always coincide. Some of course do want children and are happy to play a part in bringing them up. Sangharakshita considers that having children is a kind of vocation and that only those who really feel that calling should do so. He regards the way in which people often come to have children as irresponsible and not likely to be for the welfare of the offspring: sexual attraction and emotional infatuation lead to a couple forming, contraception goes wrong, and a child is born. He thinks that men and women should be much more aware that, usually, the heterosexual act has the possibility of resulting in a child—indeed, he has come to the conclusion that, in most cases, pregnancy is inevitable in any long term sexual relationship.

No contraception is infallible—'except chastity'—and abortion is not an option for a Buddhist, Sangharakshita stresses, since the Buddhist tradition considers it a form of taking life.

Sangharakshita thinks that a woman should decide whether she wants to be a mother—and then look for a suitable setting to have a child in. She must try to find a man who wants a child himself and is willing to play a part in its future. Rather than marriage being based simply on romance, he thinks it should be entered into more like a business partnership. He even suggests that one should consult widely before choosing a partner—perhaps even leaving it to others to arrange! We have already seen that Sangharakshita has considerable reservations about the nuclear family as a healthy environment, whether from a general human point of view or from that of the spiritual path. He therefore suggests that the growing 'positive group' that collects around each FWBO centre offers a new possibility. Those women who want children can have them, without necessarily expecting the father to live with them all the time.

> The woman [who is having a child], like the female of any species in that
> situation, is relatively helpless, so she wants a situation of security
> within which the child can be born and spend the first few years of its
> life. I don't see that as unreasonable at all. I think the problem starts if
> she expects that security necessarily from the 'seed provider', and all the
> more so if he himself is involved in the spiritual life. But I don't think
> that it's necessary, within the context of the FWBO, to expect the
> biological father to fulfil the function that he used to in the past, because
> there is the positive group, which should as it were take over at least
> some of those functions. I think we can develop a new pattern here.[290]

Naturally the child's needs must be carefully considered and this new pattern can only develop when the positive group can genuinely provide emotional and material support. There is some evidence of that new pattern already emerging within the FWBO, at least in its very early outline. Some mothers with children live together in small communities, husbands or lovers living in nearby men's communities and usually playing a large part in the lives of their children. Sangharakshita has suggested that eventually boys could go off to live with their fathers in their communities. In view of a child's needs for stability and emotional sustenance, the new pattern can only emerge very slowly—children's lives should not be toyed with in the way that the superficial sexual radicalism of the sixties often did. Nonetheless, the old patterns in society at large are rapidly breaking down, certainly in Britain. The number of mothers struggling to bring up children on their own is rising drastically all the time. The support of the positive group may permit the development of a new and healthier pattern, which especially allows for the needs of parents who want to develop as individuals, as well as for those of the growing child.

Sangharakshita's general policy is to acknowledge the basic human facts of gender, sex, and procreation. Having acknowledged them, he has encouraged the evolution of social structures that allow them to manifest healthily and to the best advantage of all concerned. Particularly, they should inhibit spiritual life as little as possible. In this context, that especially means permitting the development of strong friendships with members of one's own sex. Naturally, prevailing social custom has to be taken into account. There is unlikely to be much reaction from the public in Britain's big cities against the new social patterns that Sangharakshita encourages. After all, such unconventional phenomena as unmarried mothers, sexual 'deviance', and even sexual promiscuity have been generally accepted, if not necessarily approved of, with a typically British tolerant indifference. However, in other parts of the world there may not be the same tolerance—and that tolerance may not endure, even in Britain. Indian society is certainly not so flexible. Deviance is not at all tolerated and Buddhists are a minority in an explosive social and political situation. Fortunately, the survival of traditional social attitudes and of the extended family in India offers on the whole a more positive atmosphere and thus requires less radical measures.

We must not forget that this chapter began with a consideration of *kalyāṇa mitratā* or spiritual friendship. Although we have explored Sangharakshita's often radical views on wider social relationships, it is ultimately spiritual friendship that is important, not gender, sexuality, and procreation. Sangharakshita has encouraged the development of a social environment within the FWBO in which human relationships are positive and fulfilling. In that environment the factors of gender, sexuality, and procreation can be acknowledged without allowing them to become too dominant and therefore stand in the way of spiritual life. Within the social environment of the Order and the FWBO, friendship can flourish, and if it does truly flourish it may become spiritual friendship, *kalyāṇa mitratā*. Friends may begin to experience through their friendship more and more of the *kalyāṇa*, the beautiful. In doing so they may ultimately find the highest fruit of friendship, which is transcendental Insight itself.

*Chapter Eight*

# A SYSTEM OF SPIRITUAL DISCIPLINE

*Here perpetual incense burns;*
*The heart to meditation turns,*
*And all delights and passions spurns.*

*A thousand brilliant hues arise,*
*More lovely than the evening skies,*
*And pictures paint before our eyes.*

*All the spirit's storm and stress*
*Is stilled into a nothingness,*
*And healing powers descend and bless.*

*Refreshed, we rise and turn again*
*To mingle with this world of pain,*
*As on roses falls the rain.*[291]

JUST AS SANGHARAKSHITA HAS REFLECTED deeply on the Dharma since he first became a Buddhist, so he has applied himself conscientiously to spiritual discipline. He has had little personal guidance on the actual practice of the Dharma—he has had to find his own way through the maze of techniques offered by current Buddhist schools. It is probably his clear perception of the basic principles of the Dharma, which he seems to have had from the outset, that has enabled him to avoid the many pitfalls with which the way is strewn. That clarity has also enabled him to evolve a system of spiritual discipline suited to the modern practitioner.

From the start Sangharakshita seems to have understood the place of methods and techniques within Buddhism. We have already seen that he identifies the Dharma as 'the sum total of the means whereby the experience [of Enlightenment] may be attained.'[292] In this principle lies

Buddhism's methodological unity. All the various techniques of meditation, the vast range of colourful ceremonies and rituals, and the widely differing institutions of Buddhism, can be judged solely by this criterion. We must ask: do they assist the individual to move forward on the path towards the Goal?

This judgement is, of course, no simple one, for it requires some spiritual insight and experience to be able to recognise genuine progress. It is made yet more difficult by the fact that practices are often effective only in a relative sense: they suit certain people under certain circumstances at certain stages of their spiritual careers. Moreover, techniques cannot be judged outside their contexts: each is practised within a total system of spiritual discipline, with its supporting matrix of ideas. The nature of any particular system largely determines the usefulness of a technique placed within it. This has very important consequences for the translation of the Dharma from one culture to another. Practices cannot be simply ripped from their old settings and transplanted into new ones. Each technique must be carefully related to a complete system of spiritual discipline so that all the parts work together towards the same end of Enlightenment. A practice that is highly effective in one context may be valueless in another—or, worse, may even be damaging.

Sangharakshita has had some experience of the harmful effects of certain practices, applied inappropriately. Early in his own career, he tried *pranāyāma* or 'breath control' exercises from the Indian yogic tradition, following instructions he found in a book. These had 'a terribly disintegrating effect upon my whole being,'[293] and he soon gave them up. Later he saw a close friend taken to the verge of madness by these same exercises, which, he discovered, informed practitioners say should never be embarked upon without a highly experienced teacher. Although he was never again to experience so directly such obviously deleterious effects, he saw others severely damaged by practices taught inappropriately. On his return to England in 1964, he found that a particular form of practice, known as 'vipassanā', was very popular. During retreats, relative beginners would be asked to spend long periods each day meditating, often having had little sleep and very frugal meals. The meditation consisted of observing the body, whether sitting or walking, and carrying out a mental running commentary on one's experience: 'Breathing in, breathing out, etc.' or 'lifting left foot, placing it down, lifting right foot....'

> Shortly after my arrival in England, I was taken to a meditation centre where Thai *bhikkhus* and one or two of their English disciples were

teaching vipassanā. A retreat was in progress and I saw how people were being taught. They struck me at once as being just like zombies. It was really quite dreadful to see. Some twelve to fourteen people had been seriously mentally disturbed as a result of this practice, two or three even had to be confined to mental hospitals. Later on, someone who had become very depressed after going through this meditation centre even committed suicide.[294]

These practices are, in their appropriate contexts, venerable techniques of the Buddhist tradition. However, used in such a forced way with beginners, they could be highly damaging—more especially so since many British Buddhists of that era were rather over-rational at the outset. Sangharakshita banished this way of teaching meditation from the Hampstead Buddhist Vihara soon after his arrival—and this was, he suspects, partly responsible for his not being invited back there in 1967. Fortunately, most modern teachers of these and similar methods are well aware that they can induce a state of alienation, in which feelings are inhibited and even repressed. Many now ensure that there is at least some balancing element of emotional cultivation.

Other abuses of spiritual practice observed by Sangharakshita have not held such obvious dangers, but they equally play upon the weakness and credulity of some followers. Some teachers, for instance, make exaggerated claims for their chosen technique, boasting that it is uniquely beneficial, perhaps alone sufficient to lead to Enlightenment. Overemphasis on a particular technique leads to one-sided development or neglect of the broader aspects of spiritual discipline, such as ethics, without which no single technique can ever be effective. Some Zen teachers have emphasised that sitting in meditation is sufficient practice in itself, at the expense of Dharma-study and other fundamental ingredients of a successful spiritual life—ingredients that would be integrated into Zen practice in its home environment. Sometimes, important practices are devalued by being taught outside their traditional context of meaning. Some Tibetan teachers, for instance, have given practices involving the visualisation of Buddhas and Bodhisattvas to people who have no Buddhist commitment. For such people these practices cannot but be quasi-magical incantations. Many take them up because they think they will give them power or a short cut to spiritual attainment. There is probably no extant Buddhist tradition that has not lent itself to one or another abuse of this kind in the new spiritual supermarket of the West.

In Sangharakshita's view, many teachers coming from the East, as well as their Western disciples, have failed to realise the relationship of technique to context and culture. In this way the tradition's ancient treasury of practices has often been distorted and the effect of these techniques neutralised. Once taken from their traditional contexts, techniques of spiritual discipline that have developed in the East must be carefully fitted into a new pattern of practice that is balanced and coherent. The common failure to do this arises from a lack of clarity on the Dharma's basic principles and of perspective on the historical development of Buddhism.

By the time he came to found a new Buddhist movement in the West, Sangharakshita had a thorough grasp of Dharmic principle and a comprehensive understanding of Buddhist history. It is on this basis that he has built a system of practice that is clearly defined yet flexible, simple but effective. We must therefore see how spiritual practice fits into his basic understanding of the Dharma. The starting point must be his identification of the principle of *pratītya-samutpāda* or conditioned co-production as the Buddha's primary formulation of reality: all things arise in dependence on conditions and, in their absence, pass away. As we have earlier seen, within the all-embracing principle of universal conditionality can be perceived two trends: the *samsāric* and the *nirvāṇic* or, in Sangharakshita's terminology, the cyclic/reactive and the spiral/creative. The spiritual life consists in ascending the spiral trend of conditionality—or in allowing the creative mind to unfold more and more fully. It is therefore a growth or an evolution. Specifically, it is the Higher Evolution of the individual.

What evolves is consciousness: completing the emergence of self-consciousness from sense consciousness, and rising then to transcendental consciousness and ultimately to the consciousness of a Buddha. The Higher Evolution of consciousness is the bringing into individual awareness of a principle that underlies the whole evolutionary process, both Higher and Lower: the principle of Going for Refuge. Going for Refuge becomes effective when the individual commits himself to the evolution of his own consciousness and makes the systematic and sustained efforts needed to ascend towards the goal of Buddhahood. The Higher Evolution, in other words, requires personal commitment and effort. It cannot happen automatically or by the intervention of an outside agency. What we have referred to as 'practices' are the methods used by individuals to climb for themselves the Spiral Path of the Higher Evolution.

Sangharakshita distinguishes two different kinds of methods for evolving consciousness: those that work 'subjectively' or directly to raise the level of awareness, and those whose action is 'objective' or indirect.

> Meditation is the subjective or direct way of raising the level of consciousness. In meditation we raise the level of consciousness by working directly on the mind itself.[295]

Though meditation is of very great importance in Buddhist practice, it is certainly not the only method or group of methods. Indeed, in the early stages of spiritual life, when there is perhaps insufficient psychic integration for sustained meditation, indirect techniques may be more important than direct.

> It is true, of course, that the raising of the level of consciousness by direct methods is at least as important as raising it by indirect methods; we might even say that it is perhaps more important. But we should not forget that other methods do exist; if we did forget this, our approach would be too one-sided; and if we acted upon this, we would tend to make the spiritual life itself one-sided and even to exclude certain kinds of people—people of certain temperaments, for example—who were not, perhaps, particularly interested in meditation.[296]

Sangharakshita lists a range of indirect methods of raising the level of consciousness, including a positive change of environment, a regular and disciplined way of life, hatha yoga, the various *do* or 'ways' of Japanese culture from flower-arranging to the martial arts, appreciation of or participation in the arts, ceremony and ritual, association with *kalyāṇa mitras* and other members of the spiritual community, even

> simply helping other people. We might devote ourselves to helping the sick, the destitute, and the mentally disturbed, as well as to visiting those in prison. We might do these things very willingly and cheerfully, disregarding our own comfort and convenience—might do them without any personal, selfish motive. This is what in the Hindu tradition is called *nishkama karma yoga*, or the yoga of disinterested action. This too is an indirect means of raising our state of consciousness.[297]

He points out that this list is by no means exhaustive, and that the different methods can be combined in various ways. Indeed, spiritual life is made up of a broad range of methods, direct and indirect, which work together to raise the level of consciousness. The balance of direct and indirect methods, and the precise choice of techniques within each category, will depend upon the temperament and experience of the individuals practising and the particular circumstances they find themselves in. For instance, indirect techniques will not carry us up through all the levels of consciousness. The higher we ascend on the path, the more we will have to apply direct techniques in order to proceed further.

We will now examine some of the methods Sangharakshita recommends to his disciples and that thus form his system of spiritual discipline. We will do so using the traditional formula of the Five Spiritual Faculties as a framework, since Sangharakshita often uses it to emphasise the need for balance in spiritual life. Balance between the different techniques is one of the most important considerations in forming a system of spiritual discipline and this formula makes clear the essential elements in that balance. Unless the Five Spiritual Faculties of faith and wisdom, meditation and energy, and mindfulness are in balance with each other, spiritual practice will be one-sided and perhaps even distorted. We must make sure that we apply methods that cultivate emotion as much as reason, expression as much as introspection. Above all, we must cultivate mindfulness in all aspects of our lives, including our application of spiritual techniques, for mindfulness is the faculty that keeps the others in balance. We will begin our examination of Sangharakshita's system with mindfulness itself, since this faculty is of such decisive importance to spiritual life in general.

## MINDFULNESS

One of Sangharakshita's most impressive characteristics is his mindfulness. All his bodily movements are conducted with a self-possession and grace that combines deliberation with naturalness, giving him a kind of majesty. This physical dignity is very pleasing to observe, belying his rather unathletic physique; for, having been forbidden all exertion from an early age in the belief that it might overtax his heart and kill him, he has paid little attention to bodily cultivation—as he ruefully observes, his disciples should not be influenced by him in all respects, especially in this. His formidable mindfulness is also to be witnessed in his personal communication. He gives his whole attention to his interlocutor, clearly taking in not only what is being said but all the overtones and undertones of expression and gesture. In many ways and on many levels, he shows an exceptional sensitivity to the world around him, and he is scarcely ever caught unawares. However, the degree of mindfulness that Sangharakshita presently displays has been hard won and is the fruit of a lifetime of effort.

He considers that the foundations of his mindfulness were laid during the two childhood years he spent confined to bed. Even after he was released from his sickroom, at the age of ten, his parents were ever watchful that he did not strain his heart by over-excitement or sudden movement. In this way, he learnt a care and restraint in bodily action that he later turned to advantage as he strove for mindfulness. Speaking of his early years in India, he says:

> I was very concerned with the whole issue of mindfulness. I was very conscious of the fact that I was not always mindful in my behaviour—walking and speaking and so on. The situation in which I most easily lost my mindfulness was discussion. I would just get carried away, even if it was a discussion about Buddhism, and would realise afterwards that I had lost my mindfulness, getting sidetracked from my overall purpose in engaging in the discussion. I used to be quite regretful or disappointed that yet again I had got carried away. I found it quite difficult to bring this under control, but I eventually succeeded, although it took some years.
>
> For years together I was very concerned about general mindfulness: about speaking mindfully, sitting mindfully, walking mindfully, eating mindfully. However, I now think that I was probably not nearly mindful enough in ordinary, everyday matters.[298]

To begin with, that mindfulness might sometimes have been rather forced and one-sided, as he readily admits. Yet those early efforts have flowered into the effortless awareness which now invests his every action and word.

Mindfulness or *smṛti* (Pali, *sati*) is, of course, not itself a technique or method, but rather a quality which one tries to bring into being. Mindfulness is

> a state of recollection, of undistractedness, of concentration, of continuity and steadfastness of purpose, of continually developing individuality.[299]

It could be said that all the various techniques and methods of Buddhism aim to cultivate greater mindfulness. However, one must constantly make a specific effort to be mindful, just as Sangharakshita himself did. One does this, in the first place, by paying particular attention to all one's bodily movements and by trying to maintain a sense of one's basic purpose in life, no matter what one is doing. One must become aware of the situations and circumstances in which one's awareness slips and bring extra heedfulness to bear when they occur. Sangharakshita speaks of a common process in developing mindfulness: first, one simply acts without real awareness of what one is doing or why one is doing it; then one becomes aware, after the event, that one has acted without any sensitivity or sense of purpose and determines to be mindful in future; next one is aware, during the action itself, that one is not really mindful of what one is doing; finally one is fully aware of what one is doing while one is doing it.

Drawing together several traditional accounts, Sangharakshita distinguishes four main areas in which mindfulness is to be applied: one must be aware of 'things', of self, of others, and of reality.

Awareness of things is a nonutilitarian perception of the world of natural objects that surrounds us. This does not mean that it is a cold, mechanical way of viewing things. It is an aesthetic appreciation, akin to the experience of the artist, and, taken to its highest degree, leads us to experience our fundamental affinity with all things:

> This should be our attitude towards the whole of nature: ... towards the sun, the moon, the stars, and the earth; towards trees and flowers and human beings. We should learn to look, learn to see, learn to be aware, and in this way become supremely receptive. Because of our receptivity we shall become one with, or at least fused with, all things; and out of this oneness, this realization of affinity and deep unity, if we are of artistic temperament we shall create, and truly create.[300]

Awareness of self can be viewed under three subheadings: awareness of the body and its movements, awareness of feelings, and awareness of thoughts.

> These three kinds of awareness of oneself ... should be practised, we are told, all the time, whatever we are doing. All through the day and even, with practice, at night—even in the midst of dreams—we should continue to be aware. If we are aware in this way all the time: aware of how our body is disposed, how we put down our foot or raise our arm; aware of what we are saying; aware of our feelings, whether happy, sad, or neutral; and aware of what we are thinking, and whether that thinking is directed or undirected—if we are aware in this way all the time, even for the whole of our lives if possible, then we shall find that gradually and imperceptibly, but none the less surely, this awareness will transmute and transform our whole being, our whole character.[301]

Awareness of other people first involves simply looking at them and seeing them as they are—this is the mindfulness that the first of the communication exercises, mentioned in Chapter Seven, helps to cultivate. However, again mindfulness is not a cold and unfeeling stare. It is appreciative and sympathetic: being aware of others as persons not as objects. Being aware of them in this way leads to us communicating with them and enjoying our contact with them, taking delight in them. Awareness of others leads to *kalyāṇa mitratā*.

Awareness of reality is not simply a recollection of various doctrinal lists, as it is sometimes assumed to be. It is a 'direct non-discursive contemplation'[302] of the ultimate nature of things. This is, of course, the most difficult aspect of mindfulness to realise—and the most far reaching in its consequences. Even if, at first, one is not able to contemplate the true nature of reality directly, one can at least maintain a thread of connection with that highest truth throughout the day, for instance by simply recollecting the Buddha from time to time, or by repeating a mantra, or else by keeping in mind some pithy saying of the Buddha.

Western Buddhists' attempts to practise mindfulness have sometimes led to rather unfortunate results, as Sangharakshita witnessed on his first return from India. So prevalent was the zombie-like state of pseudo-mindfulness that he had to coin a special term for it, 'alienated awareness', and to give lectures distinguishing it from 'integrated awareness'.

> Briefly, we may say that alienated awareness is awareness of ourselves, without actually experiencing ourselves, especially without experiencing our feelings and emotions. In its extreme form alienated awareness is awareness of one's own non-experience of oneself, even awareness that one is 'not there', paradoxical as that may seem. Obviously this is a quite dangerous state to be in. Alienated awareness may be accompanied by various physical symptoms, especially by severe—even excruciating—pains in the head.
>
> Integrated awareness, on the other hand, is awareness of ourselves, while at the same time actually experiencing ourselves. Our experience of ourselves may be either positive or negative; we may be in either a positive or a negative mental state.
>
> Alienated awareness is therefore that awareness which is alienated from the experience of self, especially from the experience of the emotions; integrated awareness is that awareness which is integrated with the experience of self, especially with the experience of the emotions.[303]

The state of alienated awareness Sangharakshita witnessed at that meditation centre in 1964 was largely induced by the way mindfulness was taught to relative beginners: with prolonged periods of silence, food and sleep reduced to a minimum, no emphasis on emotional cultivation through chanting or other devotional ceremonies, and a very conceptual approach to observing one's movements. However, the tendency to alienation is common in Western culture as a whole. Sangharakshita considers that the present 'age of transition' to some extent accounts for the prevalence of alienation: the rapid and sweeping changes widespread in the modern world give rise to feelings of anxiety and loss of identity. Alienation from the experience of the body is often also the consequence of Christian conditioning. A conventional Christian upbringing frequently teaches that the body is shameful and particularly inculcates feelings of guilt about sex. Alienation from the emotions is learnt early in life.

When we find that certain feelings are unacceptable to our parents we suppress our real emotions, and assume we experience what we think others want us to feel. As to thoughts, we are not so much alienated from them as

> fail to have any thoughts at all. This is because nowadays so many
> agencies—parents, teachers, the various media, etc.—are telling us what
> to think.[304]

The state of alienation is then endemic. When coupled with a wrong understanding of Buddhism, it leads to the extreme zombie-like states witnessed by Sangharakshita. Sometimes, for instance, mindfulness itself is interpreted as standing aloof from experience, watching one's body, feelings, and thoughts as though from a distance—here the practice of mindfulness is the systematic cultivation of alienation! Sometimes the Buddhist categorisation of mental states into 'skilful' and 'unskilful' is simply assimilated to the old Christian notions of 'good' and 'bad'. The 'bad/unskilful' feelings and thoughts are then repressed through neurotic guilt. As a final element in the poisonous brew, the well-known Buddhist doctrine of *anattā* (Pali; Sanskrit, *anātman*) can easily be misunderstood. *Anattā*, literally 'not-self', is an important application of the principle of conditioned co-production. If reality consists in nothing but a flow of dependently arising conditions, there can be no fixed, unchanging substances—no souls, no 'self'. However, the self that the doctrine of *anattā* denies is a fixed, unchanging self—the *ātman* of the Upanishads, not the empirical self that we experience as a flow of mental and bodily events. From an ultimate, metaphysical point of view there is no self, but from the point of view of our immediate experience there is.

> The teaching is metaphysically true: in a metaphysical sense there is no
> individual self. We, however, don't take this metaphysically. We take it
> psychologically; in this way all the harm is done.[305]

The result of all these factors conspiring together is that some modern Western Buddhists, perhaps more commonly a decade or two ago, have suffered from an alienation that they mistake for spiritual development.

> A strange pseudo-spirituality develops in some Buddhist circles. The
> people there are on the whole quite mindful: they shut the door silently;
> if it's a rainy day they wipe their feet before they come into the house.
> They don't get angry—or at least they don't show it. They are very
> controlled and very quiet. But everything seems a bit dead; they don't
> seem really alive. They have repressed their life-principle and have
> developed a cold, alienated awareness.[306]

There are several Western groups that speak of Buddhism almost exclusively in terms of mindfulness. In a sense, this is perfectly valid, since the genuine cultivation of integrated awareness would include all other aspects of spiritual life—this is perhaps a general principle: the whole Dharma is contained in each of its parts, *so long as those parts are understood deeply and comprehensively enough.* However, more often than not, mindfulness is identified with particular techniques for cultivating mindfulness: walking slowly, watching each movement, etc.

> I think there is some danger of speaking of the spiritual life, or of
> Buddhism, exclusively—or almost exclusively—in terms of mindfulness
> and awareness. It does tend to become a bit dry, just a bit too one-sidedly
> sober.[307]

Sometimes this way of viewing the path seems to become an excuse for not making the kind of radical change in one's life necessary for spiritual development to occur. One just carries on as normal, 'being mindful in everyday affairs'.

The chief antidote to these phenomena, besides a clear understanding of the distinction between alienated and integrated awareness, is a balanced spiritual life, in which all the Spiritual Faculties are represented and held in equipoise. For the great majority, this balance can only be fully effected when they can immerse themselves in a way of life that supports their spiritual efforts from every point of view. Such a way of life will be a matrix of many methods of raising consciousness, direct and indirect, supporting spiritual efforts in every field. That matrix in the end is not so much a set of practices but a whole culture or civilisation, even a whole society. It is to answer this need for a developed context that supports individual effort that Sangharakshita has created his new Buddhist movement, the FWBO.

## MEDITATION

A figure seated in meditation is probably the most characteristic and well-known image of Buddhism. However, Sangharakshita is keen to guard against a common tendency amongst some Western Buddhists to identify spiritual life almost exclusively with sitting in meditation, considering 'practice' to refer only to time spent on the meditation cushion. Sangharakshita points out that one of the words used for meditation, both in Pali and Sanskrit, is *bhāvanā*, which literally means 'cultivation' or 'development'. But spiritual life as a whole is *bhāvanā*: it consists in the cultivation or development of higher states of consciousness in accordance with the progressive order of conditionality—with the steps and stages of the Higher Evolution. Meditation is therefore simply one aspect of *bhāvanā*: although no doubt in the end its most important and essential aspect.

> In practice, [meditation] needs to be supported quite strongly by indirect methods of development, except perhaps in the case of very exceptional people.

If this point is not understood, it leads to the kind of problem we have already examined.

> If people are just concentrating on meditation, changing the mind directly, it often means they neglect the whole of the external world, the whole of the physical side of life, so that they become alienated.[308]

In the end, meditation should be seen not so much as a set of techniques, but as 'an uninterrupted flow of skilful mental states'.

> This is what meditation essentially is, and this is quite a useful way of looking at it, since it makes it clear that meditation does not necessarily mean sitting in meditation. Meditation, essentially, is simply this flow of spiritual thoughts [i.e. skilful mental states]—whether we are sitting, walking, standing, or doing anything else.[309]

Nonetheless, that uninterrupted flow of skilful states has to be brought into existence. While indirect techniques will help us to a considerable extent, the mind must still be addressed directly if the flow of skilful states is to be at all lasting. For most of us that means, at least at some point in our lives, spending time each day applying techniques of meditation while sitting quietly in seclusion. The faculty of *samādhi* or meditation will have to be developed. We will probably have to continue to make a regular effort over many years, which may include periods exclusively devoted to meditation.

Sangharakshita has had extensive and consistent experience of sitting meditation throughout his time as a Buddhist. He made his first efforts at the age of nineteen, while serving with the army in India. In Delhi, he read of a meditation technique in a work by the great Hindu nondualist philosopher, Shankara. This he immediately began to apply, sitting under his mosquito net in the barracks, surrounded by his slumbering companions.

> As I practised, body-consciousness faded away and my whole being was permeated by a great peaceful joy.[310]

He made two more brief experiments with meditation while still in the army. He tried *pranāyāma* or breath-control exercises, with the disturbing results already noted. Later, while stationed in Singapore, he encountered a well-known Sinhalese monk, Bhikkhu Soma, who strongly recommended a basic Buddhist meditation technique: *ānāpāna-sati* or the 'mindfulness of breathing'. The *bhikkhu* had practised *ānāpāna-sati* himself, and affirmed that he had gained great benefit from it. Explaining that tradition held this to be the practice used by the Buddha on the eve of his Enlightenment, he gave Sangharakshita a copy of his own English translation of its principal canonical source. Once more, as the barrack-room slept around him, the young soldier sat under his mosquito net, carefully watching the flow of his breath.

> This time success was immediate. My mind became at first buoyant, then filled with peace and purity, and finally penetrated by a 'quintessential, keen, ethereal bliss' that was so intense I had to break off the practice. Obviously, the conditions under which I was then living were not ideal for meditation. I therefore resolved to continue the practice later, when they had become more favourable.[311]

Once he had quitted the army and taken up a wandering life, he began to practise the 'mindfulness of breathing' again. For almost ten years he dedicated himself to it daily, missing only occasionally when he was travelling and lacked the appropriate conditions.

> From the beginning I was very self-motivated in every respect. So once I had taken up a particular form of meditation—apart from the occasional feeling of laziness and reluctance to get up early in the morning—I found that I was able to persist with it. I can't recollect that I had any serious difficulties.
>
> Somewhat later I did have experiences of intense existential fear and things of that sort, but by that time I had a general understanding of the Dharma and had, at least to some extent, some spiritual friends, and I was able to carry on despite such experiences. I seem to have always had a very deep innate conviction that all would be well, I just had to carry on.[312]

Some years after he had started practising the mindfulness of breathing, he became aware that he needed to introduce another dimension into his meditation, an other-regarding, outward-reaching dimension. He had encountered many references to a practice known as the *mettā-bhāvanā* (Sanskrit, *maitrī-bhāvanā*) or 'development of loving-kindness', and this he now incorporated into his own regular discipline. In this case, he gained little guidance from those around him. Though the technique was often referred to in canonical and other sources, it was not taken very seriously in modern Buddhist circles. Those few people he knew who practised it at all, did so in a rather dilute and cursory fashion. He therefore had to make the *mettā-bhāvanā* into an effective practice for himself, intensifying it on the basis of hints and suggestions found in canon and commentary. Eventually he came to appreciate that the *mettā-bhāvanā* complemented the mindfulness of breathing. With this counter-balance, the effort to focus the mind was less likely to lead to excessive introversion and indifference to the surrounding world—and especially not to alienated awareness.

He came to explore a third area of meditation as the resolution of a fundamental spiritual dilemma, encountered early in his career: the problem of the ego—that idea of oneself as ultimately separate from everything else, delusive clinging to which is the source of all our trouble and pain. The goal of spiritual life is the transcendence of the ego. To overcome the ego requires one to go against the whole current of one's conditioning—and for this one must make a tremendous exertion of will. The problem is that the exertion of will, so essential if one is to overcome the ego, seems simply to reinforce the ego. How can one, by an effort of egoistic will, get beyond the ego? First light on this problem came from reading Thomas Merton's *Seeds of Contemplation*. Merton, an American Trappist monk who was subsequently to develop a strong interest in Buddhism, suggested that the way to subjugate the ego was to surrender one's will absolutely to one's spiritual superior. Though one would be making an effort of will in one's practice, it would be subordinated to a higher principle, embodied in one's master.

Sangharakshita was, at that time, travelling with his first teacher, Bhikkhu Jagdish Kashyap, and determined at once to put his new insight into practice. However, the unassuming Indian *bhikkhu* consulted Sangharakshita on every detail of their journey—indeed, he seemed more inclined to submit himself to his pupil's will than to make known his own! Nonetheless, it was in obedience to the injunction his teacher gave him a few weeks later, to 'Stay here and work for the good of Buddhism,' that Sangharakshita settled in Kalimpong. And there he remained for the next fourteen years.[313]

However, he was now on his own and the problem of the ego remained. He came to see a way forward in rather unusual circumstances: through a close friend who believed himself to be in contact with God! This friend received what he considered divine guidance, by means of automatic writing, and he urged Sangharakshita to take advantage of this for his own spiritual life. Sangharakshita could not take seriously the source of his friend's inspiration—especially as God seemed to have been listening to some of Sangharakshita's own lectures. Nonetheless, he took the point. If he could not find a human teacher to whom he could subordinate his will, then one had to be found on a purely spiritual plane, by means of the uplifted imagination. He had learnt something of the philosophical background to Tibetan Buddhist practice from another friend, the German scholar and artist, Lama Govinda, and he realised that here lay a way beyond the ego. In contemplating the visionary forms of Buddhas and Bodhisattvas, one was contacting a higher dimension of reality, transcending one's own ego, thus at last resolving the problem.

In the Tibetan system, one begins to meditate upon a Buddha or Bodhisattva after initiation by a qualified guru, who so to speak formally introduces one to the reality embodied in the visualised image. Sangharakshita decided that he would only take initiation from a teacher whom he felt to have some real connection with that visionary dimension, and thus the ability to introduce him to it. In 1956 he met Chetul Sangye Dorje, a very unconventional lama who came and went across the borders of Tibet in a rather mysterious way. Despite his rough appearance and strange manner, he was very highly regarded, even by members of the Tibetan hierarchy. Indeed, it was he who made such an impact on Thomas Merton, who also took initiation from him. The Chetul initiated Sangharakshita into the *sādhana* or visualisation practice of Green Tārā, a female Bodhisattva-figure, embodying transcendental compassion. Sangharakshita faithfully performed this practice for some six years. Later he received other initiations from various lamas and was thus able to explore different facets of the realm which had now opened up to him. He says that from the point of his initiation by Chetul Sangye Dorje 'my whole spiritual life was guided from that higher dimension'.[314]

Sangharakshita learnt a great deal about meditation from Mr Chen, a Chinese Buddhist who lived in Kalimpong. This somewhat eccentric hermit followed an intensive daily routine of meditation, never leaving his hermitage, which was situated, rather surprisingly, right on the edge of the Kalimpong bazaar. Mr Chen was not only an accomplished yogi but also a very learned man with a brilliant mind, having studied deeply both Chinese and Tibetan Buddhism. Mr Chen had practised Vajrayāna meditation extensively and also had first hand experience of Ch'an, the Chinese school ancestral to the Japanese Zen School. For several years, Sangharakshita was invited to visit Mr Chen once a week, a rare honour, and was able to benefit from his wide-ranging knowledge of the meditation traditions of many Buddhist schools. Although Mr Chen refused to be considered a teacher, Sangharakshita has said that he was the only person who ever gave him much practical guidance on meditation.

In his own teaching, Sangharakshita follows basic Buddhist tradition in dividing meditation into two broad types: *śamathā* (Pali, *samatha*) or 'tranquillity' and *vipaśyana* (Pali, *vipassanā*) or 'insight'. *Śamatha* prepares the mind by purifying, integrating, and refining it, while *vipaśyana* is the application of the mind, made subtle and concentrated by *śamatha*, to perceiving the true nature of reality. Thus, one's spiritual career commences with developing the basis for the penetration of truth. Once that penetration has taken place, one's task is to deepen and extend it, so that every corner of one's being is illumined by it.

*Śamatha* itself comprises two phases. First there is 'concentration'.

> Concentration is of a twofold nature, involving both a narrowing of the focus of attention and a unification of energy. As such, concentration can be spoken of as integration, which is of two kinds, the 'horizontal' and the 'vertical' as I shall call them. Horizontal integration means the integration of the ordinary waking consciousness within itself, or on its own level, while vertical integration means the integration of the conscious mind with the subconscious mind, a process which involves the freeing of blocked somatic energy as well as the tapping of deeper and ever deeper energies within the psyche.[315]

Horizontal integration corresponds to the creation of integrated self-awareness, and is mainly achieved by the exercise of mindfulness. Vertical integration has two aspects. First it includes the integration of subconscious energies into consciousness. Then higher potentialities of the mind are brought into experience—but this takes us beyond 'concentration' and into 'absorption'. Concentration is simply the struggle to bring all one's energies, conscious and unconscious, to bear on a single point, rather than have them divided and wandering beyond one's control. This is the earliest phase of meditation.

The second phase of *śamatha* Sangharakshita calls 'absorption'. Here vertical integration is carried yet further, as higher states of consciousness latent in the mind are incorporated into experience.

> Here the purified, integrated conscious mind is itself integrated with the *superconscious*. And the energies of the superconscious—energies, that is to say, which are purely spiritual—begin to be tapped. Absorption represents, therefore, the unification of the mind on higher and ever higher levels of consciousness and being.[316]

At this point, one makes a transition from the *kāma-loka* or 'realm of sensuous experience' to the *rūpa-loka* or 'realm of pure form'. This transition can only be made if what are known as the Five Hindrances are suppressed: desire for sensuous experience, ill will, restlessness and anxiety, sloth and torpor, and doubt. These basic tendencies hold the mind back from higher states of consciousness and keep it bound to the senses. The hindrances must therefore be suspended if one is to move from the *kāma-loka*, in which experience is mediated by the senses, to the *rūpa-loka*, in which the imagination, the higher faculty of the mind, is the organ of perception. However, in this phase the hindrances are merely temporarily suspended; their eradication takes place far on in the phase of *vipaśyana*.

The 'stage of absorption' encompasses many levels of progressively more subtle states of mind. Traditionally these are divided into two sets of four: the four *rūpa-dhyānas* and the four *arūpa-dhyānas*. The list of the four *rūpa-dhyānas* is the basic one and they are informally referred to as 'the *dhyānas*'. Sangharakshita has described the first *rūpa-dhyāna* as the 'stage of integration', in which one experiences the fruits of concentration. One enters this experience when one has achieved temporarily both horizontal integration of the conscious mind and vertical integration of the subconscious mind, and has succeeded in holding the hindrances at bay. It is a state of inner peace and freedom from conflict, very happy and restful. One's mind is not distracted and active, and one is not thinking about anything apart from the practice itself. Nonetheless, though it is a state of peace, it is not a blank, and is filled with a sense of satisfaction and pleasure. Absorption at this stage is not very intense and Sangharakshita considers that it is quite easily attainable within a few weeks or months of starting to meditate. He also calls this the 'human stage', since it provides a kind of benchmark of humanity. Most of us, he says, accept a far lower level of consciousness than is easily within our reach. Any human being can, under reasonably favourable circumstances, dwell constantly in this happy and integrated state, even when not actually sitting in meditation.

> *Dhyāna*, in the sense of the experience of superconscious states, is a natural thing. Ideally, as soon as one sits down to meditate, as soon as one closes one's eyes, one should go straight into *dhyāna*. It should be as simple and natural as that. If we led a truly human life, then this would happen. In our practice we have to strive, struggle, and sweat, not to meditate, not to get into the *dhyāna* states, but to remove the obstacles which prevent us assuming those states. If we could only remove these obstacles, we would go sailing into the first *dhyāna*.[317]

The second *dhyāna* is the 'stage of inspiration' or the 'stage of the artist'. Here one experiences energies bubbling up from a deeper level that influence and transform one's consciousness. These energies seem to come from outside one's conscious being. Sometimes they even appear in visionary form, as divine beings who, like the ancient muses, are heralds to new spiritual dimensions. Sangharakshita himself recollects having many such visions, in which he would hear 'teachings coming in the form of voices or communications'.[318] In the 'stage of permeation', the third *dhyāna*, one no longer feels as if inspired from an outside source but actually dwells immersed in the dimension from which the inspiration had previously appeared. This is the 'stage of the mystic'. Finally, one becomes so completely rapt in that higher state of consciousness that it begins to radiate out from one as an active 'force-field', influencing the world around one, even giving rise to various psychic phenomena. For meditation

> includes the development of such supernormal—though not 'super-
> natural'—powers of the mind as telepathy, clairvoyance, clairaudience,
> and the recollection of one's previous existences—powers which
> sometimes arise quite naturally and spontaneously in the course of
> meditation.[319]

In *The Thousand-Petalled Lotus*, his memoirs of his early years in India, Sangharakshita recounts having several experiences of clairaudience and the like, as he began to meditate. Such experiences can indeed arise at any stage of meditation—or even without meditation at all—however, they particularly characterise the fourth *dhyāna*, which is thus the 'stage of radiation' or the 'stage of the magician'.

The four *arūpa-dhyānas* are simply further refinements of the fourth *rūpa-dhyāna* and we need not explore them in detail here. In principle the process of refinement of consciousness can be extended indefinitely, and an infinite progress of ever more subtle states could be enumerated. However, Sangharakshita is keen to point out the artificiality of any schematisation of mental states. In particular, no mechanical description of psychological characteristics can ever do justice to states as delicate and refined as the *dhyānas*.

> Each *dhyāna* represents a whole range of psychic territory, as it were. It's
> not just one dead level. Looked at from a distance, in very broad, general
> terms, it's as though the *dhyāna* is one step; but looked at more closely
> that step is made of a number of little steps.[320]

In the end we must consult our own experience, not lists—even lists hallowed by tradition.

Lofty as the *dhyānas* may be, they still belong to the stage of *śamatha*, the first of the two great phases of meditation. For, however high one may fly in the realm of superconsciousness, one will always come back to earth: the *dhyānas* are not, by themselves, permanent achievements. As soon as one ceases to make the requisite efforts, or as soon as the conditions that support *dhyāna* are absent, one will fall back to lower states. *Dhyāna* alone is not enough: *dhyāna*, or more broadly *śamatha*, simply gives one the basis of integration, refinement, and purification in dependence on which *vipśyana*, Insight into the true nature of reality, may arise. In the phase of *vipaśyana*, one applies the full force of that pliable and concentrated mind to the examination of one's experience. With the weight and purity of *śamathā* behind one, one can then see life for what it truly is: *pratītya-samutpāda*—a process of ever flowing appearances, all arising in dependence on conditions, none permanent or substantial, all imperfect and unable to grant real satisfaction. Insight comes when, having soaked one's mind in *dhyāna*, one reflects upon the truth, usually by means of one or another of the most basic Dharmic formulae: such as conditioned co-production itself, the three *lakshanas* or characteristics of conditioned existence, or the four *viparyāsas* or 'mental perversities'. One will then be able not merely to understand them conceptually, but directly to know that they are true as a matter of one's own deep and immediate experience.

Although the terminology of *vipaśyana* is predominantly cognitive, Sangharakshita stresses that we should not think of 'Insight' as an intellectual attainment. As we shall see in a later chapter he suggests that the breakthrough from the mundane to the transcendental can be seen in terms of Imagination: the faculty whereby one perceives archetypal images. Insight takes place when reason and emotion are united and transcended in the uplifted Imagination, by which one perceives directly the archetypes of Enlightenment. This is the line of approach taken in the visualisation practices preserved particularly in the Tibetan tradition. Sangharakshita also points out that Chih-i, the principal figure in the Chinese T'ien-t'ai School, speaks of Insight, at one point, as receiving the praises of all the Buddhas and their prophecies of future Buddhahood.[321] This corrective to a one-sidedly cognitive language for entry into the transcendental is all the more necessary in the West, where an almost entirely intellectual approach to the Dharma is common.

The tendency to see Insight in a one-sidedly cognitive way perhaps also underlies a tendency among some modern Buddhists to regard *dhyāna* as dispensable. Exponents of the 'New Burman Satipatthana Method',[322] together with some followers of the 'vipassanā' schools and some Zen practitioners, argue that *dhyāna* is not needed as a basis for *vipaśyana*. One well-known teacher, Thich Nhat Hanh, even argues that the emphasis on *dhyāna* was interpolated into the Buddha's teaching after his death, 'probably due to the influence of the Vedic and other yogic meditation schools outside Buddhism'.[323] There is however little historical or textual basis for this assertion, the *dhyānas* being mentioned in all strata of Buddhist canonical texts. Sangharakshita regards *dhyānic* experience as essential for most people—although he does not exclude the possibility that some very exceptional individuals might enter the transcendental path without it. Only through *dhyāna* can one sufficiently integrate, purify, and refine one's mind to absorb the impact of *vipaśyana*. Without the integrating and purifying influence of *dhyāna* and *śamathā*, any review of doctrinal formulae will remain merely theoretical. The full weight of *dhyāna* is required to turn a conceptual formula into living experience.

> A lot of so called 'vipassanā' meditation appears to consist in just a discursive review of very complex doctrinal schemes and categories with minimal concentration, so that actually no insight is generated.[324]

As we have seen, not only is this procedure unlikely to succeed, it may result in a one-sidedness, even alienation.

> I think for the average practitioner it is safer to develop concentration, *śamathā*, to a point as far beyond neighbourhood concentration as you can [i.e. beyond the initial concentration that immediately precedes entry into *dhyāna*]. This has a very integrating effect on the whole psycho-physical organism. Then you 'return', in a manner of speaking, to a state in which you are able to be mentally active, and you try to develop insight from that state, with the help of the various doctrinal categories. This is the standard Buddhist, especially let's say 'Hīnayāna', procedure, which would seem to go back to the days of the Buddha himself.[325]

Sangharakshita bases himself here on a very important principle, which he sees as essential to the successful practice of the path: since the lower stages of the path provide the conditions for the arising of the higher, no higher stage can be perfected until the lower ones preceding it are completed. This is not to say that there cannot be *some* experience of the higher stages without the lower being completed. The conditions for a higher experience may be temporarily produced, usually by a forcible effort of will—but that effort will not be sustainable. For the full and permanent experience of the higher, the lower must be made firm. Sangharakshita expounded this principle in a lecture on 'The Path of Regular Steps and the Path of Irregular Steps', a teaching he derived from Chih-i, of the Chinese T'ien-tai School.[326] It is possible to make a certain amount of progress by dabbling in spiritual practice, even practice that is really appropriate to a level of experience way beyond one. This way of proceeding appeals particularly to the intellectually sophisticated Westerner who is used to a consumer society in which one expects to have whatever one wants whenever one wants it. We can however only make progress in this way up to a point.

As we follow the Path of Irregular Steps we find, sooner or later, that we are slowing down. We find, sooner or later, that we are up against an invisible obstacle.... If we want to overcome this invisible obstacle—if we want to make progress and continue to make progress—there must be a radical change, and that change consists in making the transition from the Path of Irregular Steps to the Path of Regular Steps.[327]

Although, in the early stages of their spiritual careers, most people will go some way along the Path of Irregular Steps, the transition to Regular Steps must eventually be made if their efforts are to bear any significant fruit. On the Path of Regular Steps, we systematically stabilise and perfect each step before we take the next. Thus, of the three great phases into which the path is commonly divided, we perfect *śīla* or morality before we move on to *samādhi* or meditation, and we perfect meditation before we move on to *prajñā* or Wisdom. When applied to meditation, the Path of Regular Steps means that we must first perfect *śamathā*, in the sense of having prolonged and deep experience of *dhyāna*, before we can gain any decisive experience of *vipaśyana*. Nonetheless, most people do begin on the Path of Irregular Steps and any system of spiritual discipline must take this into account. At the same time, it must provide for their eventual need to progress by Regular Steps. There must be a general trend within that system towards regularity.

The principle of Regular Steps not only implies that a preceding stage must be made secure before the succeeding one can be completed, but that once the succeeding has been established there is no need to continue to work on the preceding. Once *vipaśyana* has been established, there is no necessity to work on *śamathā*.

> If you develop any degree of *genuine vipaśyana* you cannot lose that. If you can be sure that you have got some definite Insight, you then simply have to deepen that. You don't need to sit and develop *śamathā*—unless, of course, you feel that your Insight is very weak, in which case you have to sit and develop *śamathā* in order to put more concentrated energy behind that *vipaśyana*.[328]

For some time, Sangharakshita himself has found it unnecessary to actually work at *śamathā*.

> For a few years now, I have felt that I was quite easily able to go on deepening my Insight without recourse to a deeper experience of *śamathā*. So this is what I now do. One can go back to *śamathā* from time to time if circumstances require, but it has ceased to be necessary as a support for the further deepening of *vipaśyana*. I can work on *vipaśyana* without having first been in that more deeply concentrated state represented by *śamathā*. For instance, if I wake up in the night I can work on *vipaśyana*, I don't need to sit up. Or if I am sitting in my chair I can

work on it—I sometimes do this in the early morning without actually getting into a meditation posture. It doesn't make any difference to the actual working on the *vipaśyana*.

I haven't said very much about this for obvious reasons—because I don't want to discourage from sitting [for meditation] those who need to sit![329]

Four or five years before the time of writing, Sangharakshita again began sitting regularly for meditation. He will not however reveal, even to his closest disciples, exactly what he is doing, on the grounds that others might start to imitate him inappropriately! He will only say that he is experimenting with different ways of meditating. No doubt the fruits of these experiments will eventually find their way into the system of spiritual practice followed within the Order and movement.

So far, Sangharakshita's personal exploration of meditation has shaped that system to a decisive degree. From the vast range of possible techniques within the Buddhist tradition, he has chosen a few practices that are simple to execute and universal in their application. He refuses to identify meditation with any one technique from any particular tradition. All techniques within all the different systems of spiritual discipline of the Buddhist tradition follow the same basic pattern: first *śamathā* is developed, then *vipaśyana*.

One has to understand that, when it comes down to actual methods and techniques, and actual practice, of meditation, the Mahāyāna and even the Vajrayāna still rely very heavily on the Hīnayāna. If one goes at all closely into so-called Mahāyāna and Vajrayāna meditation practices, one realises that basically there isn't very much that is really distinctive.[330]

In the Hīnayāna and the Mahāyāna, broadly speaking, *śamathā* is developed by means of concentration on an object, whether it be the breath or a disc of coloured clay. In Vajrayāna visualisation practice, the repetition of a mantra acts as a focus for concentration, leading to *śamathā*, as does absorption in the beautiful and inspiring visionary form of a Buddha or Bodhisattva. *Vipaśyana*, for the Hīnayāna, comes from reflecting on the three characteristics of conditioned existence—impermanence, insubstantiality, and suffering or imperfection; for the Mahāyāna, contemplation of *śūnyatā* is one of the routes to Insight; while in the Vajrayāna one might reflect on the real nature of the visualised image—that it has been produced and then dissolved, appeared yet was insubstantial. In essence, the procedure is the same in each system, although the emphases and actual methods may be different. The problem is that, because the Mahāyāna and Vajrayāna present themselves as 'higher' than the Hīnayāna, both their traditional followers and Western *aficionados* ignore the more thorough grounding in *śamatha* that the Hīnayāna encourages. Inevitably people want to rush on to contemplate *śūnyatā* or visualise complex mandalas, filled with demonic figures dancing in sexual union. They do not want to calm and concentrate their minds by watching their breath.

Sangharakshita sees all the various meditation techniques in the Buddhist tradition as based on the same underlying principles. He sees meditation fundamentally as direct work on the mind to produce a continuous flow of positive or skilful mental states. At first, the flow of skilful mental states will be of a temporary nature. It will still be possible to fall back into negative, unskilful states as soon as efforts cease and conditions are no longer favourable. Eventually, a permanent change will be effected and skilful states will flow continuously, without any possibility of regression. That permanent change is brought about by the deep, intuitive penetration of the true nature of reality, known as *vipaśyana* or Insight. Before there can be *vipaśyana*, the mind must be refined, purified, and integrated. There must be *śamatha* if one is to absorb the impact of truth as one reflects upon one or other of its formulations. This is what meditation really is.

On the basis of this understanding Sangharakshita has formulated a system of meditation that provides a structure for practice within the Order and the FWBO. He defines a sequence of four stages into which meditation practices can be grouped, starting with the 'stage of integration'. Integration is the foundation for the entire spiritual path. If there is no integration, there are effectively several personalities encompassed within a single body, and no one direction can prevail. Spiritual progress can only take place to the extent that there is a single individuality, constellating all the different forces of the psyche. The 'horizontal' integration of consciousness is thus the essential basis for that unwavering commitment necessary to ascend the Higher Evolutionary path. The 'vertical' integration of conscious and subconscious energies, which takes place as we move into the first *dhyāna*, is also indispensable for further growth. Without it, conscious commitment will be constantly negated by the undertow of unresolved craving. This twofold integration is brought about primarily by concentration upon an object, around which all the energies of the mind can accumulate.

In principle any object could act as a focus for concentration, and many have been meditated upon in the Buddhist tradition. However, the most commonly used object is the breath, and the mindfulness of breathing (Pali, *ānāpāna-sati*) is the key practice at this stage and is therefore the practice taught to beginners at all FWBO centres. As taught by Sangha-rakshita and now used throughout the FWBO, the mindfulness of breath-ing consists of four stages of progressively more intensive concentration upon the process of respiration. There are several reasons why the breath is so appropriate. First, it can be directly sensed and is therefore very easy to contact and settle upon. Furthermore, the experience of breathing can be a very pleasant one. The way in which one breathes is closely linked to one's mental state: when the mind is calm, the breath is calm, while mental agitation is accompanied by agitated breathing. Simply watching the breath as it comes and goes, very smoothly and regularly, brings about a sense of peace and harmony. That sense of peace and harmony is then mirrored in the breath itself, which becomes finer and more gentle, thus offering a progressively more subtle object of concentration. In this way, the mindfulness of breathing tranquillises the mind and deepens absorption.

Since the breath is a very intimate bodily sensation, it readily leads on to a broader awareness of self: of the body and its movements, of one's emotions, and of one's thoughts. It thus serves as a point of entry to the whole field of mindfulness, not only of self, but of the world around us, of others, and of reality. Another important reason for using the breath as a focus at this stage is that it requires no knowledge of Buddhism or commitment to it. It can be approached by the beginner purely as a 'psychological' exercise, without any overtly Buddhist content. One can proceed with meditation as a psychological exercise until one finds the need for the deeper, more sustaining context of the Dharma.

There is, however, a danger that the effort to concentrate may become one-sided, leading to alienated awareness, in which there is awareness without experience, especially of the emotions. It is therefore essential that, soon after commencing the 'stage of integration', one begins the 'stage of positive emotion'. Sangharakshita lists five basic positive emo-tions that underlie the spiritual life. First, there is *maitrī*—a Sanskrit word very difficult to translate into English, so Sangharakshita simply uses it in its Pali form, *mettā*, which he considers will have to be naturalised as 'Buddhist English'. He defines mettā as 'the sort of love one feels towards a friend, but carried to a very high pitch of intensity'. It is characterised by 'an ardent desire for the welfare or well-being of the person who is its object', by being disinterested, calm, and universal, and by its 'tendency to fulfil itself in action'.[31] Finally, it is ecstatic, in the sense of carrying one out of oneself, although without losing its deep tranquillity. *Karuṇā* is compassion, mettā directed towards someone who is suffering; while *muditā* is sympathetic joy, mettā directed towards one experiencing happiness and joy. *Upekṣā* is equanimity, a state of such emotional equipoise that one feels an equal mettā for all beings. The final 'spiritual' emotion is *śraddhā*, 'faith' or 'devotion', a natural and heartfelt response to whoever or whatever represents the spiritual ideal.

Sangharakshita has come to attach greater and greater importance to the positive emotions. This is especially so since he sees the predominant atmosphere of much of the developed world becoming ever more emotionally impoverished and even negative.

> As I come into contact with more and more Order members, mitras, and
> Friends, and even people outside the Movement, I see more and more
> clearly the importance of positive emotions in our lives—whether
> spiritual lives or worldly lives. I would say that the development of
> positive emotions ... is absolutely crucial for our development as
> individuals. It is, after all, our emotions which keep us going; we are not
> kept going by abstract ideas. It is our positive emotions which keep us
> going on the Path, giving us inspiration, enthusiasm, and so on, until
> such time as we can develop Perfect Vision [i.e. Insight or *vipaśyana*] and
> be motivated by that.

He goes on to say that

> Positive emotion, in the quite ordinary sense, is the lifeblood of the
> Order. If there is no positive emotion in the Order, there is no life in it at
> all, and no life, therefore, in the Movement.[332]

Mettā is the basic positive emotion and its cultivation is the starting point for all the others. The *mettā-bhāvanā*, the 'cultivation of mettā', is therefore the meditation practice that characterises this 'stage of positive emotion'—although the *karuṇā-bhāvanā*, *muditā-bhāvanā*, and *upekshā-bhāvanā* are also important, as are practices that cultivate faith and devotion. In the *mettā-bhāvanā*, as taught by Sangharakshita, one systematically develops mettā, first towards oneself—for a healthy self-love is the basis, at the mundane level, of goodwill to others. One then extends mettā, in turn, to a 'near and dear friend', a neutral person, and an enemy. Finally, having equalised the emotion towards all four persons, one radiates it out, from the spot where one is practising, towards all living beings throughout the entire universe.

These first two stages of Sangharakshita's system of meditation, the stages of integration and positive emotion, are *śamathā* practices, involving the development of a positive individuality—the cultivation of a happy and healthy, human personality. Sangharakshita attaches great importance to the establishment of such mundane sanity. The effect of spiritual practice should be to make one, on the whole, far more positive and self-confident and a much more balanced human being. Nonetheless, that mundane personality, however good in itself, at some point must be left behind. No matter how refined and positive one's idea of oneself may be, it is still essentially false, founded upon a convenient illusion. One must go beyond one's identification with the subjective pole of experience: 'the subject–object distinction itself must be transcended' and 'the happy, healthy individual which you now are—or were—must die'. The next step is therefore the 'stage of death', during which we undertake practices that help to 'break up our present, mundane individuality'.[333]

There are several practices that have this effect—the recollections of impermanence and of death, and various meditations on *śūnyatā*, as well as meditation on the *nidānas* or links in the chain of cyclic and spiral conditionality. However, it is the 'Six Element Practice' that 'is the most concrete and most practical way of practising at this stage'.[334] This meditation consists in examining the six elements of earth, water, fire, air, space, and consciousness as constituents of the psycho-physical organism. As one reviews each of them, one reflects that it is conditioned, impermanent, and not a stable source of self-identification. One learns that one's usual sense of oneself is limited and limiting, and one begins to let go of everything with which one's old self-image is bound up. At death one will be forced to give up all these elements, so one mentally gives them up now, returning them to the universe from which they originally came. One thus dies a spiritual death—dying, not to the physical body, but to the conditioned individuality, clinging to which keeps one from the experience of reality.

This facing up to the emptiness of mundane selfhood can be very frightening, but even the fear can be an essentially positive experience. Sangharakshita himself had to live with such 'existential' fear for a number of years while he was in Kalimpong.

> It would appear that, for some people at least, the experience of
> causeless, nameless fear, often prolonged, and of great intensity, is a
> necessary part of the process of spiritual development. But the function
> of the experience, however dreadful, is positive. Indeed one might say,
> the more dreadful, the more positive.[335]

Since the 'Six Element Practice' helps one to face up to the underlying insubstantiality of one's self-view, it is a *vipaśyana* or Insight meditation. Its fruit is therefore transition from the mundane path to the transcendental.

The phase of spiritual death reveals only one side of *vipaśyana*. There is not only a negation of the mundane personality but the dawning of a new and positive experience. The 'stage of death' is followed by that of 'rebirth': 'out of the experience of the death of the mundane self the transcendental self arises'.[336] As Sangharakshita is quick to point out, the greater part of Buddhist tradition would not consider this terminology to be orthodox. However, he uses it advisedly, with his usual keen awareness of the language he employs. In the first place, the common Buddhist tradition is that both the conditioned and the unconditioned are devoid of selfhood. There are however traces of another approach even in the Pali Canon, in which the term *mahāttā*, 'great self', is once or twice used.* That other approach is also quite explicit in the Mahāyāna *Mahā-Parinirvāṇa Sūtra*. Sangharakshita argues that we 'need not be afraid of using words like "true selfhood", just occasionally'.

> I think it's time we reminded ourselves that if the Unconditioned transcends all dualities then surely it should also transcend the duality between self and not-self. It ought therefore to be possible, at least occasionally, to speak of reality in terms of selfhood, just as it is possible to speak of it in terms of not-selfhood.
>
> … So perhaps there is some justification for introducing a sort of quasi-metaphysical notion of true selfhood, at least when we allow ourselves a sort of terminological holiday.[337]

The reason for using such terminology, 'just occasionally', is to guard against viewing the transcendental not merely as transcending selfhood but as completely impersonal. This is not only a gross error but one that makes Enlightenment seem decidedly unattractive.

> After realizing the Goal, the historical Śākyamuni Himself did not cease to function recognizably as a person. Personality and the Goal are not, it would therefore seem, incompatible. In any case, the inadequacy of all positive descriptions being fully admitted, it is not a question of defining the Goal as *being*, in the ultimate sense, personal, but of describing it as though it was such for practical purposes. After all, personality, even of the 'normal' human type, is the highest category available to ordinary consciousness and premature renunciation of the use of it might involve the risk of the Goal being conceived not as transcendent to personality so much as infra-personal.[338]

It therefore makes just as much sense to speak in terms of giving up a lesser, mundane self for a greater, transcendental one—and it is certainly more methodologically efficacious.

---

* *Aṅguttara-Nikāya* i, 249, also *Itivuttaka* 28a and 29. *Itivuttaka 80* refers to *bhāvitattā*: 'cultivating the self' or 'developing the self'.

That transcendental self is represented by the figure of a Buddha or Bodhisattva that the meditator visualises in his mind's eye, seated before him in the midst of the radiant blue sky.

> The visualized figure before you,... sublime and glorious though it may be, is in fact the new you—you as you will be if only you allow yourself to die.[339]

By visualising that figure, entering into communication with it, Going for Refuge to it, one has direct contact with one's own highest Ideal. As one contemplates the Buddha or Bodhisattva, one reflects upon the meaning of the vision. One considers both the symbolism of the particular figure and the significance of the vision as a vision: it appeared and then its 'baseless fabric' was dissolved, just as all things will be. In this way one is led, by intense involvement with the visionary image, to an understanding of the true nature of reality. This is a very powerful and effective form of meditation. However, it requires strong faith in the figures as representing the Ideal, as well as a high degree of meditative absorption. It therefore only reveals its full meaning to those who have a definite spiritual commitment—to those who Effectively go for Refuge. Within the Western Buddhist Order such practices are therefore usually only given at the time of ordination, the point of Effective Going for Refuge.

Some fifteen Buddhas and Bodhisattvas, all of them widely known within the Mahāyāna tradition, are now meditated upon within the Western Buddhist Order—and more will be included as need and inspiration arise. All these practices derive immediately from Tibetan Buddhism, of which Sangharakshita had extensive experience over many years, having received initiation and instruction from a number of prominent lamas. More recently, however, he has distanced himself from the theoretical and ecclesiastical framework of Tibetan Buddhism.

When the Order was first started, he introduced his disciples only to those visualisation practices for which he had received the relevant initiations from Tibetan gurus. Later he came to consider that this restriction was unnecessary, since he no longer viewed initiation from the perspective of Triyāna Buddhism. Tantric Initiation is not a further step *beyond* Going for Refuge and the Bodhisattva vow. Rather it is itself, like the Bodhisattva vow, an expression of Going for Refuge, and thus requires no special ceremony separate from the ceremony of Effective Going for Refuge—that is, of ordination. Within the Western Buddhist Order, initiation is carried out during the private ordination ceremony, thus emphasising the coextensiveness of initiation with ordination—and, thereby, with Effective Going for Refuge. No additional initiation is required for those members of the Order who wish to take up further practices, since the ceremony of ordination, so to speak, includes all initiations.

Understanding visualisation practices in this way clarifies who is qualified to hand them on to others. In the Tibetan tradition, the initiator has to have received initiation himself into any practice he hands on, as well as authorisation to initiate others. Sangharakshita, however, does not consider this necessary. He sees all the different Buddhas and Bodhisattvas as representing a single transcendent reality viewed from different perspectives. One forms a decisive connection with that reality in the act of Effectively Going for Refuge to the Three Jewels. Those who perform initiations must genuinely and deeply go for Refuge themselves and be able to recognise Effective Going for Refuge in others. At the same time, they must be in contact with that transcendent reality through their own meditation practice so that they can help the person they are initiating to make a connection with the Buddha or Bodhisattva they are going to be meditating on. If the initiators have contemplated one Buddha or Bodhisattva they have, in principle, contemplated them all. In a sense, there is only one practice, with a number of different aspects.

The 'stage of rebirth' is the pinnacle of the system of meditation. However, even those who have received initiation into this final stage will still have to work at the lower ones. They will, for instance, still have to develop *samathā* if they do not have the weight of concentration to work on *vipaśyana* without it. This means that they must practise the mindfulness of breathing and the *mettā-bhāvanā* from time to time, perhaps even regularly. Visualisation practice, spiritual rebirth, only has meaning in the context of spiritual death—and therefore the 'Six Element Practice' must also be practised. Once one has a firm basis in integration, positive emotion, and spiritual death, then one's visualisation practice will be a real vehicle for spiritual rebirth.

Sangharakshita advocates another practice, but it is one that cannot be assigned to a single stage of the system. 'Just Sitting' is woven into one's practice of the other techniques, providing an antidote to an overly grasping and wilful approach. In all the other practices some conscious effort is required, and that effort can all too easily become rather forced. 'It is difficult to say much more about this [practice] than "when one just sits, one just sits".' In a sense one does not do anything at all. However, it is very difficult really to 'just sit'. One's mind all too easily grabs on to this or that object which takes one away from the immediate experience of simply being present. For most people, 'Just Sitting' will not be really just sitting. Nonetheless it will help them to counterbalance that tendency to force and strain that so easily creeps into meditation. Thus periods of the other practices should be balanced by periods of 'Just Sitting'.

> In this way we go on: activity—passivity—activity—passivity—and so on.... We can go on in this way all the time, having a perfect rhythm and balance in our meditation practice: there is taking hold of and letting go; there is grasping and opening up; there is action and non-action. Thus we achieve a perfectly balanced practice of meditation, and the whole system of meditation becomes complete.[340]

## ENERGY

Thus far we have examined Sangharakshita's system of spiritual discipline under the headings of mindfulness and meditation, two of the Five Spiritual Faculties. We must now touch, rather more briefly, on the remaining Faculties of energy, faith, and wisdom. Meditation must be balanced by *vīrya* or energy, otherwise introspection becomes dull and enervated. In fact, it ceases to be meditation at all and becomes mere lethargic self-absorption. Energy here is 'striving for the good and wholesome'.[341] It is the driving force essential if one is to move forward towards the Goal. All aspects of spiritual practice must be pursued with energy, otherwise no progress will be made at all. Here, however, we will examine energy especially as a balancing factor. Just as meditation must be balanced by energy, so energy, too, must be balanced by meditation, if it is not to become mere animal strength, ambitious impetuosity, or neurotic restlessness. Energy in this context represents the whole active, outwardgoing dimension of spiritual life.

Sangharakshita emphasises physical health as a basis for the vigour needed to pursue the spiritual path. A regular life, with a healthy, balanced and adequate diet and sufficient physical exercise, is an almost indispensable starting point for most people. Without it, they will not have the vitality to begin spiritual practice. While he does not encourage the body fetishism of the 'health culture', he certainly exhorts his disciples to look after themselves in a sensible way. For instance, he has endorsed the practice of hatha yoga, T'ai Chi Ch'uan, and the other martial arts as means to physical health, but more importantly as ways of stimulating and channelling energy. For the younger this is especially important: energy congeals or becomes destructive if it does not have some skilful outlet. He not only recommends physical exercise but also physical work. Especially when it is done in the context of the spiritual community and for the sake of the Dharma, physical work can be a spiritual practice, particularly in so far as it stirs up energy.

Sangharakshita has had to strive against a prevailing identification of the spiritual with the inactive, nonphysical, and delicate. Western Buddhists certainly inherit this assumption in part from their own culture, but it is reinforced by attitudes common in the East. Probably as a legacy of the Indian caste system, it is widely held in the Theravāda world that the monk should do no physical work. This is especially significant in that, for the Theravāda, the monk is considered the real Buddhist.

> The fact that the *bhikkhus* don't work, or even are not allowed to work, is most unfortunate. I've seen quite a few *bhikkhus* who love to work, but the lay people won't let them. This is a real pity, because they have got the energy and the willingness to work, but the laity think it is not right that they should do those practical things. A lot of monks have got their energy bottled up, which isn't very good for them.[342]

Speaking of the positive atmosphere in an FWBO community whose members were all working hard together on the construction of a Buddhist centre, he said,

> The work is very important, because if you're working, especially in that sort of context, you're putting energy into something, with the result that energy does not stagnate. If there is any sort of curse of monasticism in the East, and it is a real curse, it's simply stagnation and idleness.[343]

The outstanding exception to this general censure of Eastern monasticism is the Ch'an and Zen tradition, in which work is an integral part of monastery life. Sangharakshita often quotes the saying of one of the Zen masters, 'A day of no working is a day of no eating.'

Over the years, Sangharakshita has inspired groups of his disciples to work together. The need to convert and renovate buildings to be used as FWBO centres and communities was the occasion for the first significant taste of working together for the Dharma. That need has grown and there are usually three or four building projects in progress in the movement at any one time. Incidentally, this is an area where women in the movement have notably broken away from conventional gender roles, forming teams to convert their own buildings. Since the late seventies, several 'team-based Right Livelihood businesses' have been formed in various parts of the world—with varying degrees of success. Apart from enabling people to earn a living in an ethical way, these projects help them to activate and engage their energies so that they are available for their spiritual lives. However, Sangharakshita goes further than this. He sees work in these settings as potentially spiritual practice in a fuller and deeper sense. In an oft-quoted phrase, he has said that 'Work is the Tantric guru.'

In the Tantric tradition, the guru is often portrayed as very skilfully confronting the disciple both with his own shortcomings and with the true nature of things. He often uses very practical situations to force a realisation. Probably the most well-known example of the Tantric guru is Marpa. He made his disciple, Milarepa, build one tower after another, only to tell him each time to knock it down again. In this way Milarepa was purged of his previous evil actions. Work confronts us with ourselves and, if we are at all honest, forces us to change. More than that, work helps us to harmonise vision with practical reality.

> Work enables one to bring one's energies into harmony with one's awareness. In a way, it's quite easy to understand things, but to bring your energies practically into harmony with that understanding is quite another matter. But that is an important aspect of spiritual life: not only to see clearly but to function smoothly.[344]

A further dimension to work as spiritual practice is revealed when it helps other people—especially when it helps them spiritually. One's work and one's spiritual ideals are then fully aligned and one can throw oneself wholeheartedly into what one is doing. Those building or running a Buddhist centre, raising money to spread the Dharma, publishing Dharma books, and so forth will have no doubts about the value of their work. They will experience their work not as a mere job but as a vocation. Work that genuinely relieves people's physical or psychological sufferings will have similar effects. It is partly for this reason that Sangharakshita encouraged his disciples to establish a charity, the Karuna Trust, whose initial aim was to aid, both materially and Dharmically, ex-Untouchable Buddhists in India, but which now has worldwide objectives. Working for others is not only deeply satisfying, it has far-reaching spiritual consequences. If one is truly working for others, to any extent, one will be transcending oneself, breaking down that rigid self-identification that the spiritual life is lived to destroy. When work of this kind is part of a balanced pattern of spiritual life, it can be very effective indeed. With all the support of the spiritual community and of a wider spiritual commitment and practice, work may be a vital ingredient in one's gaining Insight.

Sangharakshita's distinctive acceptance of work as an integral aspect of spiritual practice has important implications: an artificial division cannot be made between the 'spiritual' and the 'organisational' aspects of the Buddhist movement. There is of course a sense in which the two could be very distinct: before he founded the FWBO he had noticed that

in each of the different Buddhist groups you usually had one or two quite high-powered people who kept things moving and did all the work. It was pretty obvious that their basic motivation was quite neurotic. Such people would get into an organization, even into a Buddhist group, and at once rise to a leading position just because of the force of their neurotic energy.[345]

He was determined that this would not be the case in the new Buddhist movement he had founded, and he made sure that those who held organisational responsibilities were members of the Order, therefore having a definite spiritual commitment. In fact, they were taking those responsibilities as an expression of their Going for Refuge, rather than of mere neurotic energy. The greater the responsibility taken within the movement, the greater the degree of understanding and commitment demanded: for even organisational responsibility within a spiritual movement implies a deep understanding of the principles upon which it is founded.

Most of the disciples in whom Sangharakshita places greatest spiritual trust are those who have worked hard for the movement in a practical way for many years. By their work they have demonstrated their commitment to the spiritual ideals that the movement embodies. This does not mean that they are 'career Order members' who have simply manoeuvred themselves up the hierarchy. They have applied themselves faithfully to meditation, study, and other forms of spiritual practice and are the leading teachers and *kalyāṇa mitras* to whom many people look for guidance and example. The point is that the spiritual life does not exclude organising. If one sees the full significance of the Dharma both for oneself and others, one will want to help to establish all the conditions necessary for it to flower. One of those conditions is an organisational framework.

Sangharakshita himself has toiled selflessly for the Dharma, from the moment in 1950 that his teacher, Jagdish Kashyap, left him in Kalimpong with the injunction to work for the good of Buddhism. Starting a new Buddhist movement has been no easy matter, demanding great energy, courage, and resourcefulness. He says of himself, in this connection,

One of the illusions about myself I do *not* cherish is that I was the most suitable person to be the founder of a new Buddhist movement in Britain—in the world, as it turned out. I possessed so few of the necessary qualifications; I laboured under so many disadvantages. When I look back on those early days, and think of the difficulties I had to experience (not that I always thought of them as difficulties), I cannot but feel that the coming into existence of the Western Buddhist Order was little short of a miracle.[346]

In a sense this labour of love was not natural to him.

Given a perfectly free choice, I would probably have preferred to spend the whole of my time in some solitary mountain retreat, quietly pursuing a regular programme of study, meditation, and literary work.[347]

Yet he has never wavered in his efforts or regretted that mountain retreat. His work has evidently led him beyond himself, opening him up to a reality that transcends his narrow individuality:

There are times when, far from feeling that it was I who took on the responsibility [for founding the Order], I feel that it was the responsibility that took on me. There are times when I am dimly aware of a vast, overshadowing Consciousness that has, through me, founded the Order and set in motion our whole Movement.[348]

## FAITH

To have energy to strive for what is good and wholesome, one must have a response to the good. That response is śraddhā or 'faith', the next of the Spiritual Faculties. Faith is, in the first place,

the capacity for being emotionally moved and stirred by something that transcends the senses and even the rational mind—at least for the time being.[349]

The Buddha is the primary object of faith, and faith is

the act (expressed by 'taking refuge') or state (condition of being established in the refuge) of acknowledging unquestioningly that the man Gautama, or what appears as the man Gautama, is in possession of Full Enlightenment.[350]

Sangharakshita points out that such faith is not 'blind', resting as it does on three grounds: intuition, reason, and experience. Faith as intuition is a 'harmonic resonance' between the 'element of Buddhahood' in us and the Buddha—between 'what is ultimate in us and what is ultimate in the universe'.[351] We naturally and spontaneously respond to anybody or anything that expresses or represents Buddhahood—'by reason of the affinity existing between his actual and our potential Buddhahood'.[352] Most essentially, faith is this intuitive response. The spiritually immature, however, are likely to confuse an intuitive response with all sorts of other desires. Faith must therefore be grounded on reasoned investigation of the object to which one is responding—and an investigation of one's response itself. In this way one avoids the extremes of blind faith enjoined in much of Christianity and in various modern brands of guru worship.

Finally, experience must test intuition and reason, revealing in time whether faith is well-founded. It is only when we ourselves attain the successive stage of the transcendental path that faith becomes direct knowledge.

Faith is a rather unfashionable faculty nowadays. The blind belief so often called for by Christianity has poisoned the notion of faith for many; technological success has created a new religion in which the only faith is in the inevitable advancement of science; and 'pseudo-liberal' ideas have made reverence and respect for what is higher seem pathological. Modern intellectual arrogance and emotional aridity mean that few are able to exercise this basic human capability, except upon the most trivial of objects: pop-stars and footballers. Sangharakshita himself seems however to have had a strong capacity to respond to high ideals from an early age. He has always enjoyed the Buddhist ceremonies and rituals in which faith finds both a means of expression and of development.

His first act of Buddhist worship was, at the age of eleven, burning 'sticks of very sweet incense', in a brass incense burner in the shape of the Buddha, which he had bought in an bric-a-brac shop![353] He did not discover an outlet for devotional feelings in his first contact with a Buddhist culture—the Buddha images in a Sri Lankan temple were 'too much like gigantic wax dolls to inspire me with devotion'.[354] The mindless emotionalism of much Hindu worship, as well as the slovenliness of Hindu temples, repelled him. Perhaps his first experience of real devotion in a specifically Buddhist context was when he saw the twenty-foot high figure of Maitreya, the Buddha-to-come, in the Tibetan temple at Ghoom, near Darjeeling in northern India: 'To me the great figure portended the dedication of my own life to the service of the Dharma.'[355]

Once he had dedicated himself to the service of the Dharma, devotional practices became a regular part of his life. At his own hermitage in Kalimpong he had a shrine-room which he cared for himself, keeping it clean and arranging flowers before the Buddha image. Not only did he thereby give expression to faith but to aesthetic feelings—in fact, he had come to realise that the two were very closely connected. Before his morning meditation in the shrine-room, he would chant the *Ti Ratana Vandanā*—verses in Pali in praise of the Three Jewels, deriving from the Pali Canon and commonly used in the Theravāda world. Each evening, after meditation, he would perform 'puja' or 'worship', a ceremony of recitation and chanting before the Buddha image. At first his puja came exclusively from Pali sources, but later he added verses and mantras from the Mahāyāna and Vajrayāna traditions.

Sangharakshita introduced the important Buddhist practice of puja into British Buddhism, shortly after his arrival in England in 1964. When he suggested that it might be appropriate to have a devotional ceremony or two during the annual summer school of the Buddhist Society, he was told that 'English Buddhists do not like that sort of thing'. In the event, most people did attend—and clearly liked it very much. Once he had founded the FWBO, puja was a regular feature of the movement's events. Following the traditional Mahāyāna form of the Sevenfold Puja, he compiled a ceremony for regular use within the movement, arranging verses from an English translation of the *Bodhicaryāvatāra*, a Mahāyāna text parts of which are often used for devotional purposes. He has compiled various other ceremonies, including one he composed himself in an Anglo-Saxon metre, known rather inelegantly as the 'Short Puja'. These ceremonies are usually performed every day on retreats, and often at meditation classes and in communities.

The cultivation of faith raises much deeper issues that we will explore in a later chapter, issues concerning the relationship of faith to culture and to the imagination. Briefly, Sangharakshita considers faith and imagination to be very closely connected, indeed from a certain point of view they are the same thing. With the collapse of the traditional culture of the West, there has been an impoverishment of the imagination at every level and in every sense. The worlds of vision and dream have been relegated to psychopathology, at best offering insights into our deeper desires and interests. For traditional Buddhism these worlds are real and alive, as existentially valid and significant as that of everyday consciousness. Those worlds must be brought back to life again if faith is to have the imaginative space within which it can spread its wings. The reinvigoration of the imagination is no easy task and the way forward is not clear. It will probably take many centuries for Western Buddhists to develop a culture within which imagination can play its full part. Sangharakshita is very aware both of the difficulties and of the necessity. He has worked steadily and prudently to stimulate the imaginations of his disciples: introducing them to the myths and symbols of the Mahāyāna and Vajrayāna, and pointing out the imaginative vitality of the Hīnayāna scriptures—as well as making links with the myths and symbols of Western culture. The modest devotional ceremonies used in the FWBO are stimulants both to faith and to imagination.

## Wisdom

We have seen that, until faith is mature, reason and experience are required to ensure that emotional response is not tainted and blind. Balancing the faculty of faith is that of *prajñā* or Wisdom—although, at this stage, it is not so much Wisdom as intellectual understanding, and it balances not mature faith but emotional response. Reason and emotion must be in harmony: emotion must be infused with clarity, and understanding and intellect with depth and power. Ultimately intellect and emotion are brought together and transcended in Insight, but till then attention must be given to both faculties to make sure they are in harmony. In many ways, Sangharakshita believes, Western man's emotions are so undeveloped in relation to his intellect that this is his primary area of work. However, he cannot therefore neglect the intellect since it is precisely ideas that often hold him back from emotional development.

Sangharakshita views the modern climate of ideas with a sad eye, seeing little that is supportive of spiritual life and much that is directly contrary to it. Egalitarianism destroys respect for teachers and leaders; the language of rights leads to a sense of deprivation, even among the most materially fortunate; scientism leads to nihilism and reductionism; gender politics obscure basic human facts and distracts from fundamental ethical issues; the idealisation of sex and sexual relationships squanders energy and brings little but suffering; materialism leads to the belief that satisfaction can only come from the senses; populism leads to mistrust of high culture; popular psychology breeds self-obsession; rationalism mistakes thinking for knowing; cynical scepticism destroys a sense of values and of ultimate purpose to human life: modern man is a confused and sorry specimen, distinguished only by the extent of his need for some new meaning in his spiritual darkness.

Inimical as Christianity is to Buddhism, Sangharakshita believes that this modern congeries of 'pseudo-liberal views', as he calls them, is a far greater enemy to the developing individual. Even worse than pseudo-liberalism is 'political correctness': for example, the censoring of language for any trace of what is deemed to be racism, sexism, ageism, etc.

> 'Political correctness' in general, I have come to believe, is one of the
> most pernicious tendencies of our time. It is far more pernicious than
> pseudo-liberalism, of which it is probably the extreme form.[356]

Careful study of the Dharma and clear thought is required to free oneself of pseudo-liberal views, for they not only infect the culture that surrounds the movement but still taint many of those within it, coming as they do from that culture. Study of the scriptures and of the works of reliable writers (although, as Sangharakshita has often shown, study of unreliable writers can be very illuminating too, when directed by one with a discerning mind), listening to lectures by those who genuinely know the Dharma, discussion, and reflection are all key practices in coming to a view of life that supports and encourages the following of the path.

Study of the Dharma with someone who truly understands it brings one into contact with the brilliant light of truth, which exposes one's wrong views. A seminar with Sangharakshita, for instance, can be both an illuminating experience and a disturbing one. As it proceeds, one sees ever more clearly how little one has really thought about the opinions one holds. So many of them are simply picked up, like viruses, from the pool of *micchā-diṭṭhis* or false views that infect our culture. Not only is there a need to open oneself up to the radiance of the Dharma but one must think clearly. Sangharakshita considers that most people do not really think very much, following blindly views and opinions they have received, without testing them even for simple logical coherence. He has encouraged his disciples to study logic and tries to foster careful evaluation of ideas and texts.

Sangharakshita believes that an education in the Dharma must be part of a broader cultural education. The steady demise of Christianity and the growing dominance of pseudo-liberal views has led to the gradual dismantling of traditional Western culture. There is much that is of value in that culture, particularly those aspects that belong to traditions stretching back beyond Christianity. Yet we are increasingly cut off from the classics of literature and art that have carried value and meaning over the generations. This culture, or perhaps civilisation, offers a basis for the Dharma, since it does, at its own level, preserve a moral perspective and a living imaginative landscape. As we shall see in a later chapter, Sangharakshita holds that when great literature or art is examined in its depths it touches on the Dharma: the Dharma providing the general principles, literature and art the specific exemplifications.

In surveying Sangharakshita's view of spiritual practice under the heading of the Five Spiritual Faculties, we have not attempted to be entirely comprehensive, although perhaps the principal issues have been touched upon. While we have been looking at a range of practices, we should not forget that spiritual life is very broad and cannot be summed up in any particular technique. Practices and techniques are part of the way in which we try to go for Refuge. They are the methods we use to ascend the Spiral Path. Furthermore, whatever techniques we use should be balanced: meditation must be balanced with energy, faith must be balanced with wisdom, and mindfulness must be the factor that ensures a balance between the others. However, other factors must also be borne in mind and kept in balance. We have already devoted a chapter each to spiritual community, friendship, and ethics. These are also key aspects of a total spiritual life, and thus in a sense practices. We shall, in the chapter that follows, be looking at broader social, political, economic, and institutional issues, for in the end the spiritual life depends upon a complete way of life in which the individual is able to make his effort in a harmonious way, supported and encouraged by his surroundings.

*Chapter Nine*

# THE NEW SOCIETY

*I come to you with four gifts.*
*The first gift is a lotus-flower.*
*Do you understand?*
*My second gift is a golden net.*
*Can you recognize it?*
*My third gift is a shepherds' round-dance.*
*Do your feet know how to dance?*
*My fourth gift is a garden planted in a wilderness.*
*Could you work there?*
*I come to you with four gifts.*
*Dare you accept them?*[357]

SANGHARAKSHITA HAS COME TO UNDERSTAND BUDDHISM as implying a radical
political programme, involving an almost unimaginable change in the
way society functions throughout the globe. He has not always seen these
broader implications of the Dharma. Although he imbibed something of
his father's socialist sympathies, his early interests were almost entirely
literary, artistic, and philosophical, and he approached Buddhism very
much from that point of view. He certainly did not, however, lack the
Bodhisattva spirit and he dedicated his life, from an early stage, to
communicating the Dharma to others. Nonetheless, he had not seen the
relevance to Buddhism of political issues. It was his contact with Dr
Ambedkar, the great leader of the ex-Untouchables, and the movement
of conversion he initiated, that opened Sangharakshita's eyes to the social
dimension of the Dharma. Most ex-Untouchables lived in extreme pover-
ty and ignorance, largely deprived of economic opportunity by their caste

status. However, it was not merely for their material advancement that a great social change was needed.

> I saw, as a result of my connection with them, the need to transform the whole of one's social life. It was not enough just to transform one's individual life. In fact, it was hardly possible, certainly for the majority of people, to transform their individual life without a corresponding transformation of the collective life of society itself.[358]

As a result of his contact with Dr Ambedkar and the ex-Untouchables he not only saw the need for social change, he saw its possibility. If he had not witnessed for himself what they achieved, he says he would have been sceptical that religious ideas could transform the lives of large numbers of people in this century. Sangharakshita's close involvement with that movement gave him first hand experience of what was possible, for, since the fifties, Buddhism has begun to work a social revolution in the lives of several million Indians.

> I regard what is happening in India as a very hopeful sign indeed—and not just a sign of the revival of Buddhism in a narrow sense. It presents an example of a tremendous positive upheaval brought about in society by almost purely spiritual means. There has been a radical change in the ex-Untouchables' whole way of life and position in society, from top to bottom. It's far more than just a change in religious belief.[359]

The phenomenon of mass change brought about by almost purely spiritual means is an example Sangharakshita offers to his disciples of what they can do, individually and collectively.

> If you were sufficiently alert, active, inspired, and dedicated, and if there were a number of you working together, perhaps you could exert a substantial influence on whole societies in different parts of the world—especially where those societies were in a state of flux and looking for some kind of general stability, and some kind of vision or blueprint for the future.[360]

That this profound change among the ex-Untouchables in India was brought about largely by one man, Dr Ambedkar, he cites as further inspiration.

When he returned to England and established the FWBO, Sangharakshita saw more evidence of the effect that environment could have on people's states of mind. From time to time he conducted residential retreats, some for a weekend and some for as long as two weeks, usually in a pleasant country location. It was obvious that the setting itself helped to make people more happy and relaxed. Added to that, there was a simple daily routine and a programme of innocent activities in the company of friendly and like-minded people. It was hardly surprising that, within a few hours of one of these retreats starting, most participants already began to experience a better state of mind—before they had really had time to do much direct spiritual practice. Many found returning from retreat extremely painful. They wanted to continue the happy and meaningful experience of the retreat and did not want to go back to situations that left them dull, tense, and unfulfilled.

In an attempt to preserve something of the retreat atmosphere, some of his disciples began to live together, with Sangharakshita's active encouragement. In these residential spiritual communities they were able to continue to deepen the friendships they had experienced on retreat. Some experimental retreats were for men and women separately and showed that it was much easier to engage in spiritual practice without the element of inter-sexual tension. Because of this experience, most of the communities gradually became single-sex—and again were found particularly positive. Slowly the principles and practice of successful community life were hammered out. In 1975 one large men's residential community was formed to convert a derelict building into a public centre, and a team of women similarly worked on a large community nearby. Many difficulties were encountered, for members had to discover how twenty or thirty people could live and work together in such intensive situations. Nonetheless, over the course of these projects, a strong sense of comradeship developed. People were living the greater part of their lives completely within the world of the community and, on the whole, this had a very beneficial effect indeed. Here was a glimpse of what was needed—and of what was possible.

Around this time Sangharakshita appropriated the term 'New Society' to indicate the ideal social setting for spiritual practice. He began very actively to encourage his disciples to form 'new societies in miniature': environments in which people could meet all their material and social needs, while also having the fullest possible support for spiritual development. 'Right Livelihood businesses' were started in which Buddhists could work together whilst also raising funds for the movement—although these, of their very nature, have been quite hard to sustain. The basic institutions of the movement were now clear. There were centres where one could encounter the spiritual community and the Dharma, and where one could learn to meditate and begin one's studies. Then there were residential communities. These could be of many different kinds, according to the level of involvement, activities, and inclinations of community members. Finally there were businesses. These were initially legally established as co-operatives, but that framework was found administratively inconvenient—thus losing the rather catchy alliteration of centres, communities, and co-operatives! Centres, communities, and Right Livelihood businesses together are the foundations on which the FWBO is erected. They are the heart of the radical social project in which the movement is engaged, under Sangharakshita's direct inspiration.

The social and political dimension of Sangharakshita's vision rests upon essential Buddhist principles. We will now briefly explore the theoretical background to his ideas in this field, using the terminology already established in earlier chapters.

The central act of the spiritual life is Going for Refuge to the Buddha, Dharma, and Sangha. As one goes for Refuge, one ascends the Spiral Path of the Higher Evolution. One moves through the series of positive mental states that arise in accordance with the progressive order of conditionality and exemplify the creative mind. Going for Refuge, at the Effective level, is the act of an individual. It is a personal act of commitment that no one else can make for one. To that extent, it is an act of free will.

However, the notion of free will should not lead us to forget that Going for Refuge is an act that arises in dependence on conditions. According to Buddhism's most fundamental insight, all phenomena are dependent on conditions and this must include the experiences and volitions that make up the spiritual life. The progressive order of conditionality is a sequence of positive mental states, each of which conditions the arising of the next. Each higher state comes into being when we have established the antecedent mental conditions.

Preceding states of mind are, however, not the only conditions in dependence on which Going for Refuge arises. It takes place within a context and that context also helps to shape it. Going for Refuge is thus dependent not only on internal factors but external ones as well. To understand this further, we must explore the relationship between the mind and the world within which it functions. In Buddhist terms, the world we experience and the mind that experiences it are related in accordance with a specialised form of conditioned co-production: the principle of *karma*.

Sangharakshita describes the principle of *karma* as stating the relationship between willed action and its experienced effect. *Karma* or volitional action leads to *karma-vipāka*, the 'ripening, maturity, effect, or result' of willed action. The states of mind with which we act shape the kind of experiences we will have: skilful actions based on healthy mental states will produce pleasurable experiences, and unskilful actions based on unwholesome states lead to suffering. However, though mind or consciousness determines experience, according to the law of *karma*, Sangharakshita points out that each fresh mental event arises out of a context of past and present experience. Our minds may determine what kind of experience of the world we are to have, but those experiences of the world provide the conditions within which our minds then operate.

The relationship between mind and world is well exemplified in the twelve cyclic *nidānas*, demonstrating the *samsāric* trend of conditionality, or in Sangharakshita's terms, the cyclic or reactive trend. This traditional teaching, illustrated at the rim of the Tibetan Wheel of Life, traces the chain of conditions that lead from spiritual ignorance through repeated birth, death, and rebirth. In dependence on our fundamental ignorance in past lives, the complete psychophysical organism in contact with the external world unfolds in this life. The human being in his or her environment is thus the *vipāka* or ripening of past *karma* performed in a state of spiritual blindness. From our blindness comes our experience: our mind forms our experience of the world.

The cycle then continues. That contact between organism and world produces feelings: pleasurable, painful, or neutral. We then react to the feelings with various forms of desire: we recoil with loathing from the painful, crave the pleasurable, and remain indifferent to the neutral. Desire represents the re-entry of mind into the cycle. In dependence on our experience arises mental volition. Our experience in the world is thus the basis for new reactions of mind.

The wheel turns on again as our minds set up the conditions for future experiences of the world. Those mental reactions are part of a pattern of ignorance-based *karma* we are creating in this life. That present *karma* then conditions, in a general way, the nature of our psychophysical organism and our experience in the life that follows. There is thus a continuous dialectic between mind and experience: mental volitions condition future experiences—which are then the basis for further mental reactions.

Although external conditions have a very powerful determining effect upon the mind, nonetheless it is capable of rising above its circumstances—no spiritual life would be possible if it were not. Indeed, the spiritual life consists in taking one's conditions, both inner and outer, and rising beyond them in a truly creative act: the act of Going for Refuge. However, even Going for Refuge is initially dependent on the context in which it arises. It is only on the upper reaches of the Spiral Path that external factors cease to shape the mind.

The implications of these theoretical considerations are very important indeed. They provide the basic grounds for the formation of a spiritual movement such as the FWBO and, more far-reaching still, for the extension of Buddhism into the social, economic, and political spheres. The essential point is that we must constantly remember the effect that our environment has upon us.

> It's not just a question of altering the individual's mental state. One must
> see that an individual's growth and development depend not just on
> that individual's own effort, but on the circumstances and conditions
> under which he or she lives. So you have to give some direct attention to
> them as well.[361]

So significant are circumstances and conditions that changing one's environment can itself be a major method of personal development.

> It needs to be emphasised and brought to people's attention that it
> sometimes isn't all that difficult to bring about a change in your mind—
> you can do it simply by changing your living conditions. Your way of
> life is therefore very important and should be given serious attention if
> you are serious about improving your mental states.[362]

The individual cannot, however, rest with altering his or her own immediate environment, for that environment exists within a broader field of social, economic, and political influences. That immediate environment is strongly affected by the larger world around it. If for no other reason than the interests of our own development, we must ultimately address society as a whole, seeking to transform it so that it becomes more supportive of spiritual endeavour.

> One of the reasons why we want to set up a 'New Society', why we want
> to transform the world, is to make it easier to lead a spiritual life. In
> other words, we want to set up a social structure within which it is easier
> to develop certain states of consciousness.[363]

Once again, though hints and clues abound in the scriptures, Sangharakshita has had to piece together the social principles of Buddhism for himself. The modern Buddhist world offers no theoretical model for the extension of spiritual life into the collective dimension. Basic Buddhist principles have not yet been systematically applied to the world of today, so different from the agrarian economies and monarchical states in which Buddhism has largely been transmitted to the present. The Buddha himself does not anywhere discuss these issues in a form that would be recognisable to us, accustomed as we are to sophisticated political theory that explores exhaustively the role of the citizen in the state. In the Buddha's teaching of the Noble Eightfold Path, which is his most comprehensive account of the path, the fifth 'limb', Right Livelihood, contains the 'political' dimension of his teaching. Here, he simply enjoins restraint from means of livelihood that trade in violence, dishonesty, or negative mental states.

In his own commentary on the Buddha's Noble Eightfold Path, Sangharakshita entitles his discussion of Right Livelihood 'the ideal society', since he sees this teaching, for all its scantiness, as embodying the principle of social transformation.[364] He argues that the Buddha could not have said more on the matter. At that time in India, the city had not developed as a political institution and therefore there could be no citizen—and therefore no theory of citizenship. The dominant political force of the day was a form of monarchy that allowed no elective power to the subject and gave no scope for political expression. The older tribal oligarchic republics, whose system the Buddha seems to have favoured, were gradually being swallowed up by these newer and more aggressive kingdoms. Similarly, the caste system prevented the formation of a common political community.

> The political community was subdivided into castes and you lived your life within your caste. There wasn't a wider political framework within which you lived, as there was in the case of the Greeks and the Romans.[365]

The fact that monarchy and caste system did not permit the development of political activity is not perhaps the most fundamental reason why the Buddha developed no systematic theory of social transformation along modern lines. There was not only no opportunity for political activity, there was very little need. The one great social evil of his time, the caste system, which was then just beginning to establish itself, he did attack openly, frequently, and remorselessly. He used penetrating logic, gentle irony, and sometimes outright ridicule to expose the absurdity and injustice of brahmanical claims. That aside—and caste was certainly not at that time the terrible social blight it later became—the society in which he lived and taught did not stand in such need of transformation as does our own. It was much simpler and much healthier.

> The world in which we live makes it much more difficult to lead the spiritual life than did the world in which the Buddha lived. One gets the impression that, in the Buddha's day, the main obstacle was just one's family responsibilities. But nowadays, if the family was the only obstacle, we would be having a very easy time![366]

If the king would govern according to the moral law and the people live a moral life, then a perfect society would come automatically into existence. The Buddha therefore emphasised personal moral conduct, especially in the sphere of economic activity through his teaching of Right

Livelihood. He vigorously exhorted all he met to live by the precepts and not to engage in means of livelihood that harmed others. For the kings, he upheld the ideal of the *dharmarāja*.

> *Dharma* means truth, righteousness, reality. *Rāja* means king, or even government. Thus, the ideal of the *dharmarāja* represents the ideal of government by righteousness: the ideal that even in political affairs ethical and spiritual considerations and values should be paramount. It represents the idea that politics should not just be a cockpit of rival interests and factions, not just a question of manipulation and string-pulling, but that one should try to see the ethical and spiritual principles involved, and apply these to this aspect of one's collective existence.[367]

The righteous king should uphold the moral precepts and encourage his subjects to practise them. 'This is, in essence, what the transformation of the world consists in.'[368]

The Buddha encouraged the transformation of society by attacking the caste system, by exhorting people to practise the precepts and Right Livelihood, and by urging the king to be a *dharmarāja*. He also established a model society in the midst of the wider society. He founded a sangha or order, which he intended as 'an anticipation, in miniature, of what society as a whole could be like further on in the course of human evolution'.[369] Not only was it a blueprint for the future but it was a base from which the rest of society could be transformed.

> You could say that the Buddha saw the society of the future in terms of the Sangha, because presumably he wanted the Sangha to grow. The Sangha was the Buddha's New Society, existing in the midst of the old society, and gradually taking it over, or at least influencing it very powerfully—which in India it did for some centuries.[370]

Sangharakshita thus sees in the Buddha's own teaching and activity a definite economic, social, and political programme, appropriate to the Buddha's own times. That programme aimed ultimately at completely transforming society according to moral principles and the needs of the developing individual. This is the essence of Sangharakshita's own vision of social transformation. Basing himself on the principles established by the Buddha, he has developed a vision of the collective dimension of spiritual life that takes into account the far more complex nature of the modern world. His social, economic, and political ideas are therefore completely traditional, representing a modern application of the Buddha's principles rather than a modernist interpretation of them.

> I think, in all my expositions of Buddhism, I have been very little influenced by non-Buddhist or secular thought. I have just pondered on the implications of the Buddhist teachings themselves.[371]

Before we examine his ideas in greater detail, we must look again at the reasons why the developing individual must consider not only the transformation of self but the transformation of world. We have already seen that we must, out of self-interest, try to change that environment because of the influence that the environment has on our minds.

> We cannot ignore the social dimension—this is one of the things I have emphasised from the very beginning of the FWBO. Inasmuch as the world acts upon you, it is in your interest that it does so in a helpful rather than in a harmful way. That means you have an interest in the particular way in which 'worldly' affairs are organised or run. If you are living in an 'unideal' community or state, it is going to have an unfortunate affect on you. You therefore have an interest in the creation of an ideal state or community.[372]

However, concern for social transformation runs deeper in Buddhism than this. Although Going for Refuge is the act of an individual, it is not an individualistic act. Integral to Going for Refuge is an empathy with other living creatures. This is a natural faculty of a truly human consciousness and is experienced ever more profoundly as that consciousness evolves. In the Mahāyāna tradition, this altruistic dimension of Going for Refuge finds its ideal expression in the Bodhisattva. The Bodhisattva transcends the distinction between self and other, no longer identifying exclusively with the subjective pole of experience. In other words, the Bodhisattva is not attached to self or is not selfish, feeling as much for other beings as for himself. The Bodhisattva's mind is almost unimaginable to us, since it contains none of the automatic self reference we ourselves experience—at the same time it is not self-denying in a neurotic sense. The Bodhisattva naturally and healthily empathises with all life, and spontaneously acts to relieve suffering wherever it is encountered. That state of mind finds its manifestation at every stage of spiritual life in an ever-deepening recognition that self and other are completely interdependent. We cannot go for Refuge alone. We are bound up with the entire universe.

> Without the idea of the New Society—without the idea of transforming world as well as self—our Going for Refuge is in danger of becoming an individualistic affair and, to that extent, in danger of being not truly a Going for Refuge at all.[373]

Concern with the society that surrounds us is an integral aspect of spiritual life. We must attend to it because we cannot but feel for others who are struggling in a society very often inimical to a decent human life, let alone a spiritual one. Indeed, this empathy extends beyond other human beings and is the basis for a 'Buddhist environmentalism'. One who goes for Refuge cannot observe the despoiling of nature without doing something to prevent it. Sangharakshita himself, when he first returned to England in 1964, organised a lecture on the environment by Rachel Carson, the author of *Silent Spring* and one of the first to draw attention to the terrible effects that man's actions were having on nature. Since then he has had little time to work in this field himself but he would like to see some of his disciples becoming more active in working to make people more ecologically aware.

Although concern for the society that surrounds us is integral to spiritual life, we should not think that members of the spiritual community are *'obliged* to do anything at all for the world'. Whatever they may choose to do, they do freely. They do it as an aspect of their own spiritual development and as a natural expression of Going for Refuge in its altruistic dimension.

> The Spiritual Community does not have to justify its existence to the
> world. It does not have to show that it brings about social and economic
> improvements, that it is helpful to the government or the administration.
> It does not have to show that it benefits the world *in a worldly sense.*[374]

Modern secular society does not generally recognise, as most traditional societies have done, that man exists for some higher spiritual purpose. There is therefore a constant pressure on members of the spiritual community to justify themselves in secular terms. Many Christians have fallen prey to this demand. In some traditionally Buddhist countries too, Buddhist monks and nuns have succumbed, seeking a new role for themselves through political and social involvement because they have lost their real, spiritual purpose.

For members of the spiritual community, their primary contribution and responsibility to the world is to keep the spiritual community in existence.

> It is good for the world that such a thing as the Spiritual Community
> should simply be there, good that there should be people around who
> are dedicated to the spiritual life, dedicated to the development of skilful
> states of mind.[375]

Whatever contribution they make beyond this is an overflowing of their own spiritual experience and not the fulfilment of any obligation to society.

Sangharakshita's discussion of the social dimension of Buddhism hinges upon a few key terms, emerging out of his idea of the Higher Evolution. As we have seen (pages 78 and 118), the unit of the Lower Evolution is the species. Individual organisms do not evolve by themselves: the whole species moves forward through the interaction of tiny mutations with the natural environment taking place over vast periods. In the Higher Evolution, the individual is the one who evolves—and the individual is the self-aware being who has consciously undertaken his or her own further development. To become an individual one has to differentiate oneself from the 'group' in which one has been immersed. The group is the human equivalent of the herd or pack. It is one or other of the collectivities in which those members of the human race who are not individuals gather for mutual security and to which they subordinate their identity. The 'world' consists of a complex interweaving of the many existing groups: race, nation, sex, class, age group, profession, football club, family—even religion. Members of the group relate to each other solely

> on the basis of a common need (economic, or political, or psychological,
> or sexual) or on the basis of competition, not to say conflict.[376]

Since it sees security lying only in conformity, the group usually opposes the emergence of the individual. To that extent, the group is the enemy of the individual.

Though the Higher Evolution is undertaken by the individual, he or she is not completely isolated. The individual functions within the context of the spiritual community.

> The Spiritual Community is a voluntary association of free individuals
> who have come together on account of a common commitment to a
> common ideal: a commitment to what we call the Three Jewels.[377]

The spiritual community exists on several different levels, corresponding to the levels of commitment or Going for Refuge. The spiritual community, in its fullest sense, consists of all whose Going for Refuge is Real: in other words, it consists of those who have entered upon the transcendental path. At the broadest level, the spiritual community consists of all those who go for Refuge to any extent at all. When individuals who go for Refuge Effectively come together, however, they form a spiritual community in its most practical sense—they form an order. It is in this sense that Sangharakshita most commonly uses the term spiritual community and that it should be understood in what follows.

Sangharakshita points out that between the group and the spiritual community there is an inevitable tension. The group constantly seeks to reabsorb the spiritual community: for if the group is the enemy of the individual, it is even more the enemy of the community of individuals, by whom it is even more threatened. From its own side, the spiritual community is always in danger of dissolving into the group. Many of its members, not being Stream Entrants, will still be subject to the 'gravitational pull' of the Conditioned. They will all too easily fall away from the spiritual path if they do not have supportive conditions. However, the spiritual community is not merely passive in relation to the group, trying to protect itself from it. It actively seeks to expand itself by encouraging members of the group to become individuals and thus make the transition to the spiritual community. It also seeks to transform the group, so that it functions more in accordance with moral principles and in support of those who wish to develop as individuals.

In his lecture, 'A Vision of History', Sangharakshita interprets human history as the struggle between the group and the spiritual community.[378] He shows how one spiritual community after another has emerged from the group and then been reabsorbed into it. Some have broken free again under new spiritual inspiration, as has the Buddhist sangha through the centuries. Some have been obliterated completely, as were the Cathars of thirteenth century Languedoc. That struggle, he says, is now more intense than ever, since the group has become more complex and pervasive. Few traditional forms of spiritual community have stood up well to the transition to the modern era, and many new attempts have not prospered for lack of clarity of purpose. Sangharakshita has drawn some lessons from the experience of modern Utopian movements, particularly those in America during the last century:

> The message that emerges most clearly is that in order to have a spiritual community you have got to have a common spiritual vision. If you have got a lot of individualists, all following their own ideas and going their own way, you can't possibly have a spiritual community. Another reason for the break-up of many of the communities was that the male/female question was not resolved. There were many tensions on that score. It also emerges that some of these communities developed quite successful business enterprises, which ended up absorbing all the energies of the people involved. The spiritual communities became, sometimes officially and legally, business corporations—one or two of which still continue. And the whole spiritual community side of things was lost. Broadly they all failed because there was no common way of life; no common spiritual practice; no real emphasis on individual growth and development and helping one another to grow and evolve; and no emphasis on the community as a situation with a structure that helps the individual to evolve.[379]

In principle at least, the Western Buddhist Order does not share these weaknesses—Sangharakshita sees the Order as 'the spiritual community in a particularly pure and uncompromising form'.[380] It continues the battle of all genuine spiritual communities down the ages to remain free from the group and to transform it into the spiritual community.

The group and the spiritual community both try to absorb each other. Members of the spiritual community try to transform the group in two senses. Their ultimate aim is to turn the entire group into the spiritual community, and they therefore seek to expand the spiritual community in the midst of the group. In pursuit of that ultimate Goal, they also try to bring the group, *qua* group, into alignment with the spiritual community. They try to bring the ideal of the *dharmarāja*, the government of righteousness, into reality, so that the group is pervaded by the influence of moral principles and supports the leading of the spiritual life. The group transformed in this way Sangharakshita calls the 'positive group'. Such a positive group can only come into existence when there is a community of individuals, in Sangharakshita's special sense of the term, at its heart. These individuals are able to influence group members to act in a moral way and to honour and aid those who wish to lead a spiritual life. It should be noted that they influence group members by persuasion and example alone—the positive group can never be established by coercion or violence.

There is thus an ideal progression: the spiritual community forms in the midst of the group, which is at this stage inimical to it; gradually the influence of the spiritual community pervades the surrounding society, transforming it into a positive group; finally, the spiritual community transforms even the positive group into the spiritual community, and the perfect society has become a living reality. This ideal progression has, however, never been achieved. The group is very strong and pervasive. It not only surrounds the spiritual community but is potentially in its midst: those members of the spiritual community who are not Stream Entrants are, as we have seen, but a step away from the group and can easily fall back into its ways. Nonetheless, the task of each and every member of the spiritual community is not ended until the ideal society has been brought into existence.

Sangharakshita has borrowed the term 'New Society' for the society that comes into being when the spiritual community has transformed the group into the positive group. However, the New Society in this sense can only be provisional. There must be a constant effort to complete the transformation by encouraging every member to move toward true individuality. Then the New Society would be coextensive with the spiritual community itself. The old society is, of course, the society formed by the group and is more or less inimical to spiritual life. The extent of the opposition between the old society and the New is, perhaps, easy to underestimate.

> I feel that we will gradually realise more and more clearly how *totally* we
> [in the FWBO] are in opposition to our environment and the way in
> which society at large thinks. Yes, totally. It's as though we represent a
> completely new beginning in just about every way.[381]

During the first of the three phases in the progressive establishment of
the ideal society, the spiritual community exists in the midst of the old
society. Its task then is to form around it a 'New Society in miniature'—or
a series of New Societies in miniature. Within the limits imposed by the
existence of the old society, environments must be created that encourage
and support those living and working within them to develop as individuals. These proto-New Societies have a threefold purpose. First,
they provide the best possible settings under prevailing circumstances
for the development of the individual. In them, members of the spiritual
community are able to influence those members of the positive group
connected with them to become individuals and to join the spiritual
community. Then, the small-scale New Societies are a model of what
society as a whole could be like. This will help to motivate other people
to transform their own environments in a similar way: a single living
example is worth a thousand theoretical discussions. Finally, the New
Societies provide the necessary support for those of their members who
are going out into the old society to transform it. They use the New
Society

> as a sort of base from which we sally forth into the old society to spread
> our ideas and plant little outposts of a nucleus of a New Society.[382]

This base is indispensable for most people.

> You can get so easily lost in the world, and influenced, carried away,
> submerged by the world, even while you are trying to help it. One finds
> lots of very well meaning social workers, reformers, and people of that
> sort who in the end are swallowed up by it. They just sink into the
> morass: society is too much for them. You need to operate from a basis of
> strength.[383]

Though the New Society may act as a base from which some people go
out to transform the old, others may spend long periods completely
immersed in the New Society. Such people may be engaged in full-time
meditation or study and can be

> a sort of powerhouse or inspiration for those who are operating outside.
> Maybe sometimes they can see things more clearly than you who are
> working directly at transforming the old society can because you are
> immersed in the old society. Maybe you would need to turn to them
> sometimes for guidance and inspiration.[384]

This phase of creating small pockets of the New Society in the midst of the old is the one we presently find ourselves in. Nowhere in the world does there exist a true positive group, coextensive with society as a whole—although there have been such societies in limited areas in the past: perhaps in the India of the Emperor Aśoka, for instance, or in medieval Tibet. Sangharakshita has therefore seen his primary 'political' task as the establishment of a spiritual community and then the creation of those pockets of the New Society. This is the significance of the movement and Order he has founded.

> It is as a nucleus of a New Society that the Friends of the Western
> Buddhist Order offers itself—a nucleus of which the Order is the central
> and most essential part.[385]

From that nucleus, members of the Order try to draw members of the old society into the New. At the same time, they try to transform the old society as a whole so that it will become the New Society.

> It is with such an end in view that the FWBO has established, and
> continues to expand, that network of centres, communities, and
> team-based Right Livelihood businesses which constitute the nucleus of
> what it calls the New Society or, in more traditional terms, the Kingdom
> of the Dharma.[386]

The triad of public Dharma centre, residential community, and team-based Right Livelihood business provides a radical alternative to the three most basic elements of most people's lives: family, work, and leisure activities. Sangharakshita describes the residential community as offering a radical alternative to the family in general, but especially to the family in the form in which it is frequently found today:

> the claustrophobic, neurotic, nuclear family consisting of the
> monogamous couple with one or two children, car, television set, dog,
> cat, and budgerigar.[387]

Community members live together because they share a common spiritual ideal rather than because they belong to the same blood-family —the basic unit of the group. The team-based Right Livelihood business is a radical alternative to work:

> By work one means wage slavery or salary servitude and the earning of
> money in ways that are harmful to oneself and which exploit others.[388]

The Right Livelihood business is based not simply on the profit motive but on moral principles, spiritual friendship, and the desire to contribute to the expansion of the New Society. The Dharma centre presents a radical alternative to leisure activities:

> By leisure activities one means activities which simply enable us to pass
> the time, to forget about work, maybe forget about the family too, and
> maybe even forget about ourselves.[389]

A Dharma centre is the meeting point for members of the spiritual
community and positive group within its area. People come together at
the centre to participate in activities that assist the developing individual
and promote the harmony of the spiritual community: learning about the
Dharma, practising meditation, celebrating Buddhist festivals, and engaging in meaningful cultural activities.

Dharma centre, residential community, and Right Livelihood business
together form an entirely new way of life. They are the heart of the 'New
Societies in miniature' that members of the Order are forming in various
parts of the world. They are also the basis for other alternative institutions
such as educational establishments, organisations engaged in social welfare projects, and cultural ventures of various kinds. All aspects of a full
and healthy human life will ultimately have to be included.

As well as presenting the outlines of a radical alternative to existing
social forms, this triad forms a basis for the transformation of the old
society in all its aspects: social, economic, and political. We shall therefore
now consider Sangharakshita's ideas on social transformation under
each of these three aspects. We will both examine transformation within
the 'small-scale' New Societies and the wider project of transforming
society as a whole.

### SOCIAL TRANSFORMATION

The social transformation of the old society into the New consists in
people ceasing to relate to each other as group members and beginning
to relate as individuals. Each will see every other primarily as a human
being rather than as the member of a particular sex, family, age, class or
caste, tribe, nation, or race. The spiritual community exemplifies this
social transformation in its purest form. Its members have come together
out of a common desire to develop as individuals, rather than from any
group interest, such as blood-relationship. At its best, there are no barriers
based on group attitudes between members of the spiritual community.
At the very least, all will be making systematic efforts to surmount
whatever barriers there may be.

Illustrating this principle, the Western Buddhist Order consists of
members from many different social backgrounds, nationalities, and
races. This diversity itself offers a spiritual practice: each Order member

must make a very considerable effort to overcome his or her conditioned attitudes and prejudices. Each must relate to all others simply as individuals who are Going for Refuge.

> Certainly, within the Order, the individual should be paramount. That someone came originally from a particular social group, nationality, or caste has no relevance whatever within the Order—except to the extent that it may help you understand someone inasmuch as he may still be under the influence of the situation from which he came.[390]

The same principle applies to the social transformation of the old society. Members of the New Society should work to break down barriers between people outside the spiritual community as well as within it. In the first place, this means simply relating to others as individuals, whether they are really individuals or not.

> If one wants to break down class [and other] distinctions, one must do what the Buddha in effect said in connection with the caste system: relate to other people just as individuals. In communicating with them you should not see them in terms of any group to which they may happen to belong. You should try to see the person in front of you and try to relate to the incipient individuality that is in him. If you do that on a sufficiently wide scale, class and every other kind of group barrier will be broken down.[391]

This personal effort to break down barriers through one's own communication outside the spiritual community is not enough. It must inevitably be supplemented by work to break down social barriers enshrined in group attitudes or embodied in legislation. This requires some involvement in political activity—and we shall be examining that in more detail later. One point should be made clear now, however. In one's efforts to break down social barriers, one may find oneself allied with people from outside the spiritual community. Here one must be very careful, for they may have their own ideological agendas: Feminist, Marxist, 'New Right', etc. One may agree with their immediate intentions, but their underlying motivation may be completely different, even inimical, to one's own.

> It is not on general ideological grounds one is trying to break down class barriers, etc. What one is really trying to do is to relate to other people as individuals[392]

—and to enable them to relate to each other as individuals, too.

Sangharakshita has been careful to distance himself from ideologies that are, in a famous Buddhist phrase, 'near enemies' of the Dharma—seeking similar immediate social objectives but for very different underlying reasons.* Thus he is fully in sympathy with those women who truly wish to relate as individuals rather than merely as women— but he has little time for much feminist ideology. He is careful to speak in Buddhist terms rather than the terms of modern social and political ideology with its long list of isms: racism, sexism, ageism, etc.

> As Buddhists we don't really need to think in terms of these isms at all. We have got a better and much more beautiful vocabulary that deals with these same human problems. For instance, we have the beautiful word 'mettā'. You develop mettā towards all living beings. And 'all' means all, so you don't have to specify age, sex, class, or race: you just treat all you meet with mettā. So let us discuss problems in Buddhistic terms, rather than in terms borrowed from modern ideologies and attitudes that are really quite alien, even inimical, to the spirit of the Dharma and that, more often than not, lead to the very sort of conflict they are meant to overcome.[393]

One of the most basic terms of modern political ideology is 'human rights'. The various isms are usually considered unacceptable by these ideologies because they are infringements of the individual's rights. Sangharakshita, however, argues that the assertion of 'rights' exacerbates social conflict, rather than helping to resolve it. While he in no way condones prejudice against people on the grounds of their sex, race, or age, he argues that the pursuit of rights enhances the view, so central to Western thought, of the individual as separate and isolated from others.[394] Western political systems ultimately derive from the Christian belief in the metaphysical existence of 'separate, mutually exclusive ego-entities' that are significant in themselves. They therefore 'all insist on the intrinsic reasonableness of clamorous agitation for rights'—and therefore lead to conflict, both within the individual and within society.

Buddhism sees all things and beings as interconnected, as having no ultimately separable existence. This enables an appreciation of the individual in society, not as an isolated unit, but as being bound into a network of social relationships. We can therefore view each such relationship either in terms of what is due to us or what we owe to the other: in

---

* The terms 'far enemy' and 'near enemy' are used in connection with the cultivation of the *brahma-vihāras*, the positive spiritual emotions of mettā etc. The far enemy of mettā is hatred; the near enemy is *pema*, 'sticky affection' or romantic attachment. It is an enemy because it is not selfless as is mettā. It is a near enemy because it has a superficial resemblance to mettā, in so far as there is an apparent concern and interest in the object of attraction. See *A Survey of Buddhism*, pp.182–3.

terms of rights or of duties. When we think of our rights, we see only what is due to us. When we think of our duties we acknowledge what we owe and therefore see ourselves set in a web of social relationships. Rather than thinking of claiming our rights, we should do our duty. Society is not an uneasy compromise between competing rights but a harmony of complementary duties: 'Duties are co-operative, rights competitive.' Since all members of society stand in relation to each other, if all do their duty all will get their rights.

> The remedy for any injustice or inequality in human relationships, whether domestic, social, civic, political, cultural, racial, or religious, is not an insistence upon the rights of one party, but on the duties of the other.[395]

This does not mean that those against whom there is prejudice should simply submit to the way they are treated. Sangharakshita's work among the ex-Untouchables of India is testament to his belief that no individuals or groups of individuals should be subjected to social prejudice. However, they can best free themselves from that oppression, first, by seeing themselves as equal members of society with all others, and then by demanding that others do their duty by treating them as such—especially, in India, in accordance with the constitution of the Republic. Sangharakshita's work among the ex-Untouchables is also proof that caste has no place in genuine Buddhism—although unfortunately it has crept into Sri Lankan Buddhism, which has a *nikāya* of the monastic order reserved for members of a particular high caste. The notion of 'duty' as Sangharakshita uses it has nothing to do with the Hindu notion of *dharma* or caste duty. As the Buddha made clear, Buddhism has no place for any such system of hereditary social inequality.

The term 'duty' is not a very popular one in modern society, because it has the connotation of something imposed upon one from without. But, to Sangharakshita,

> From a Buddhist point of view, your duty is what you impose upon yourself. It is what you see as incumbent upon yourself in view of the principles in which you believe, and the situation in which you find yourself.[396]

Even at the most basic level, no human society is possible unless most of its members value that society, if only for protection and convenience. In valuing it, they impose upon themselves certain duties to their fellow citizens. The awakening of the future citizen to this awareness should be a basic aim of education.

A major function of any society is to provide mutual aid and security, as well as to fulfil more intangible social needs. In traditional societies, the extended family and local community form the primary welfare unit. In many modern countries the state replaces their functions, although it cannot replace their provision of acceptance and emotional bonding. Since the individual has left the group he or she can rely on neither the family nor the state to provide either material or social welfare. From now on, that support must come ultimately from the spiritual community. It will be given out of the immediate and natural sympathy of one member of the community for another. Breaking down barriers means sympathising with others and responding to their needs, in as far as one is able. Out of their deep empathy for one another, members of the spiritual community will help each other in whatever way they can. They will give practical aid, emotional support, and spiritual guidance. Sangharakshita very strongly emphasises this point:

> The responsibility for the care of each member rests on the entire
> spiritual community. Ultimately, all are responsible for each, and each is
> responsible for all to the extent of his strength. Otherwise there can be no
> spiritual community.[397]

Within the spiritual community this care for the welfare of all should be a natural expression of *kalyāṇa mitratā*, of spiritual friendship. Once society has been transformed into the New Society, that spirit of mutual helpfulness will permeate the entire population. Yet, how are members of the New Societies in miniature to relate to the social problems that surround them while the old society still exists? They will feel for the sufferings of those who do not have the positive facilities they themselves enjoy. They will be very aware of the many material and social problems in the wider society around them. However, they will have limited time and energy immediately available to help resolve those problems, and they must therefore think very carefully about how they use their resources. The primary work must always be the encouragement of group members to become individuals and to follow the path of the Higher Evolution.

> I am certainly all in favour of people trying to improve the worldly lot of
> others. However, the preaching of the Dharma has priority. There are
> many people engaged in trying to improve people's worldly lot and
> comparatively few in teaching the Dharma. Anyway, it is the Dharma in
> the long run that is going to make things better—not only in a spiritual
> sense but even in a worldly way.[398]

Sangharakshita therefore argues that, unless one has a definite vocation for social work, one should concentrate on teaching the Dharma or on helping others to do so. Material and social problems will only finally disappear when there is a New Society, for in that New Society each member will care for everyone else and resources will be distributed equitably, according to need. The New Society will only come into being when there are sufficient individuals within it to transform the group into the positive group. It is the Dharma that enables people to develop as individuals, and it is individuals who form the spiritual community, and it is the spiritual community that transforms the group into the positive group—and thereby establishes the New Society within which material and social problems will be spontaneously resolved. Therefore, 'a little Dharma teaching goes a long way.'[399]

Nonetheless he does consider that members of the spiritual community should engage in some welfare work. In some very poor countries, it is very difficult for people to develop as individuals because of the over-whelming pressure of material needs. Those needs must be alleviated to some extent while the Dharma is being taught. Sangharakshita has therefore encouraged his disciples to establish social welfare projects among the ex-Untouchables of India. A charity, the Karuna Trust, has been set up in Britain to raise funds in the West for this work. In India another charity, Bahujan Hitay, administers a number of welfare projects in several Indian states: primary health-care, basic education pro-grammes, and hostels for young students from the villages.

He envisages that his disciples will also undertake such work in the West.

> In the West people are much more in need of spiritual help than material. Nonetheless, I think we should broaden our approach. Our big centres and large groupings of Order members should be concerned not just with conducting meditation classes and giving lectures. They should also do some—for want of a better term—social work in the neighbourhood, say with old or deprived people of one kind or another. I am not thinking of anything very high-powered, but more in terms of personal contact and personal help, in one's spare time.[400]

The spiritual community, once it has established a 'small-scale' New Society in any particular area, should start to have an impact on the old society that immediately surrounds it. This will, in the first place, help to enhance conditions within the New Society—since it is still affected by the old. It will also be a direct expression of concern, even of compassion—an expression of the altruistic dimension of Going for Refuge. Unless the New Society starts to influence its environment in this way, it will be increasingly isolated and therefore increasingly vulnerable.

One of the most effective ways of transforming society is through the education of its future members. The FWBO has done little work yet in this field, although Sangharakshita envisages that there will be residential communities in which adults and children live together, as well as schools run on Buddhist principles. The movement is much more broadly based in India, and there Sangharakshita has given some consideration to this subject. In 1982, he set out his basic philosophy of education in a lecture, 'Buddhism and Education,' given at Dr Ambedkar's Siddharth College in Bombay. He distinguishes three broad purposes of education.

> The first purpose of education is to enable the individual to take his place as a functioning, responsible member of the wider society to which he belongs.[401]

This consists essentially in teaching the growing child to live with others, respecting their feelings. In instilling this lesson a middle way must be followed. One must neither be too easy going so that the child never grows out of its 'basic raw egotism' nor be so strict as to crush all energy and initiative. This education should start at home when the child is very young. At school and university, students should first be taught their 'rights and duties as citizens belonging to a particular political and social community'. But eventually they should learn to think of themselves as world citizens and to accept their responsibilities for the environment.

'The second purpose of education is to give [the individual] the knowledge and skills that will enable him to earn his living.'[402] There should be a variety of possible courses of education that allow for the individual talents and preferences of the various students. In considering what course to follow, students should also take into account the needs of society for particular kinds of workers. From the Buddhist perspective, the most important point is that individuals should have the knowledge and skills necessary for them to earn their living according to the principles of Right Livelihood.

'The third purpose of education is to help [the individual] to develop as an individual human being.'[403] For Buddhism, this is the deepest and most important dimension of the subject. Development should be all-round, including all aspects of the personality. First, the body should be strong and healthy through games and sports. If it is not, ill-health will prevent the individual from making the best of his or her life and work. Then the intellect should be developed. Sangharakshita was at pains to point out to his Indian audience that intellectual development does not simply mean cramming with facts and then regurgitating them at examination time without understanding—a curse of the Indian education system. While it is important to learn facts, one must also learn to reflect upon them and come to one's own independent understanding of them. As a citizen, one will, for instance, need to think for oneself so that one can distinguish truth from fiction in such matters as advertising and electioneering.

The emotions should be educated too, especially through 'ordinary human friendship'. In friendship one can communicate one's feelings, so that they are not bottled up but can rather unfold and flower. The appreciation of classical music and of poetry also helps educate the emotions. Fourthly there is aesthetic and artistic education—which is closely connected with emotional education. This means not only learning to appreciate the fine arts, but beauty in general—and learning to take responsibility for our environment so that it is clean and tidy, as well as beautiful and inspiring. Then there is ethics. Students should be educated in 'respect for the feelings and the convenience of others'. Truthfulness is a vital part of ethical training—elsewhere Sangharakshita says that human society is ultimately impossible without truthfulness. Ethical education is not merely a matter of learning to refrain from doing harm, it also consists in taking responsibility for one's surroundings and in taking initiative in helping others.

The final aspect of education is spiritual. Sangharakshita says that this does not consist in teaching the tenets of a particular religion—although this may help to provide a basis.

> To be paradoxical, one could say that religion cannot be taught, it can
> only be caught. You have to catch the spirit of religion, and you can do
> this through the influence of other people.[404]

In other words, one 'catches' religion through *kalyāṇa mitratā*. A growing individual needs contact with someone more developed than themselves so that he or she can imbibe the spirit of a higher stage of human evolution.

Actually, in the first place, young people simply need contact with sympathetic older people who have greater human experience than they have, let alone any higher spiritual experience. Sangharakshita therefore emphasises the principle of *kalyāṇa mitratā* in its most general form. The whole process of education depends upon positive contact with someone older and more experienced. In modern education systems there is less and less human contact between teacher and pupil. Indeed, in Western society generally there is a growing 'generation gap'. Many young people are not on close or positive terms with any older people, including their parents. Sangharakshita has, incidentally, emphasised to his disciples that they should make an effort to be on good terms with their own parents. Without compromising their commitment to spiritual life, they should try to cultivate positive and friendly relations, even if deep communication does not seem possible. Within the New Society itself there should be no generation gap. Young people should know people older and more experienced than themselves to whom they can turn for advice. They should, therefore, have positive human relations with their parents, their teachers, and others. More especially, they should have access to some who are members of the spiritual community, leading a full time spiritual life. From them they can learn what it is to go for Refuge to the Buddha, Dharma, and Sangha.

Education can be viewed from another point of view. The populace at large needs to be educated in certain basic principles. Although the primary educational work must always be the direct teaching of the Dharma in order to help people become individuals, there are broader issues through which the Dharma can be approached on a wider platform.

> If we try to reach out to a wider audience we should deal perhaps with
> questions like 'What use are you going to make of your leisure?' Forget
> about Buddhism, for the time being, and say, 'Look, here you are with
> more money and leisure than your ancestors ever had. Do you really
> think that you are making use of it in a way that is worthy of a human
> being? If not, why not? What use should you make of it?' Raise all these
> very general, very fundamental questions—and then perhaps bring in
> meditation and Buddhism.[405]

In this way, the spiritual community will begin to create the conditions for the transformation of the group into the positive group.

## ECONOMIC TRANSFORMATION

We must now look at the transformation of the economic aspect of society. In the first place, we must recognise that the kind of work we do and the conditions under which we do it have a strong effect upon us.

> Since it occupies the greater part of our waking life, our livelihood will
> obviously have an important effect on our whole being. I do not think
> we always realize this. But if you do something for seven or eight hours
> a day, five days a week, fifty weeks a year, and if you do this for twenty,
> thirty, or forty years, it is not surprising if it leaves a mark on you.[406]

Sangharakshita considers it of crucial importance that those who wish to develop spiritually attend to their means of livelihood. The first consideration here is that the work one does should be ethical. It should involve one in no violence to other living creatures, whether directly or indirectly. It should not exploit others, playing on their weaknesses and negative states of mind. It should not lead one to act dishonestly.

However, the matter goes much further than this. The context within which one works will, for most people, make the difference between work being an unfortunate necessity and it being an indirect method of raising consciousness. One's work could be an essential part of one's spiritual practice. To integrate work fully into spiritual life, the FWBO has evolved an entirely new kind of working situation: the 'team-based Right Livelihood business'. The function of these ventures is

> first of all, to provide workers in the business with their material needs;
> then to provide a situation within which the workers can experience
> spiritual friendship in a way that will conduce to their spiritual growth;
> and thirdly, to make a surplus that can be given to the centre with which
> the business is connected or to some other Dharmic cause.[407]

Sangharakshita sees the Right Livelihood business essentially as 'the spiritual community at work', and therefore functioning primarily on the basis of *kalyāṇa mitratā*. The usual division of the work-force into workers and managers does not apply: in reality all are workers and there is none of the classic confrontation of 'front office' with 'shop-floor' of conventional working life. People will take different areas of responsibility within the business, according to ability and inclination. Some may be responsible for management and will be allowed to make the necessary management decisions. However, everyone shares a basic responsibility for the venture. Workers are not paid—rather, do not pay themselves— according to the job they do, but in relation to their particular circumstances and needs: the managing director might therefore receive less than a warehouseman, if the latter, for instance, had a family to provide for.

The making of a financial surplus is an essential aspect of the business. However, the quality of relationships between workers and the effectiveness of the working situation as a means of raising awareness is of primary importance. The business activity itself offers workers the opportunity to work on themselves spiritually. By co-operating together in their work, they can deepen their spiritual friendships with each other. By openly confronting difficulties as they arise, they can overcome conditioned patterns that stand in the way of personal effectiveness. They can take practical steps in self-transcendence by collectively giving away the money they have made—in traditional Buddhist terms, they can practise *dāna* or generosity, an important spiritual quality. Since they collectively take responsibility for the business, there can be no question of exploitation.

One of the most important functions of these businesses is to give the New Society a degree of independence from the old. Sangharakshita considers that many of the problems of traditional Buddhist monastic sanghas arise because monks and nuns have often been almost entirely dependent on alms from those outside the spiritual community. They are then under strong pressure to conform to the worldly expectations of their supporters. This results in much hypocrisy and compromise, frequently almost eradicating any trace of genuine spiritual commitment.

> It is not easy to continue to depend on the existing society for your support and at the same time to point out that society's faults. This is one reason why I emphasised, at the beginning of the FWBO, that we should be financially self-supporting. That is one of the relevances of the Right Livelihood businesses. We should not be dependent upon the support of rich people, because, as the proverb says, he who pays the piper calls the tune.[408]

Many will be unable or unwilling to work in the team-based Right Livelihood businesses—which are very difficult to set up and demand a high level of spiritual commitment. Sangharakshita even considers it of benefit that some members of the New Society have jobs outside it. He recommends, however, that anyone with such work lives in a residential community so that they have access to regular spiritual support. In the first place, those working outside the New Society can often earn money for use within it—if they are living in a community they will probably need less money for themselves than would someone living in a conventional family setting. What is more important, they can act as a kind of link between the New Society and the old: influencing those with whom they work and bringing contacts and experience into the New Society. Work done outside the New Society should still be Right Livelihood, in the sense of being ethical and not standing in the way of the worker's development.

Starting from the Buddha's own teaching of Right Livelihood, Sangharakshita offers guidelines for deciding what work one should and should not do. The best kind of livelihood is a vocation:

> a means of livelihood which is directly related to what one considers of ultimate importance in one's life.[409]

It is, of course, very rare to be paid to do what one most deeply wants to do and most people will not have this opportunity. For those whose work does not have a vocational element, there are four categories of occupations to be considered.

> Firstly there are those which, like working in a slaughterhouse, cannot be right under any circumstances. Secondly there are those which are not wrong in the obvious way that the first type are, but which definitely increase people's greed. Such occupations include working in the advertising industry, and producing luxury goods that people do not really need and have to be persuaded they want. Thirdly there are those occupations which can constitute Perfect Livelihood if one makes an effort. For example you might be a clerk working in the office of a firm that produces some quite good and necessary article, such as bread. If you work honestly and conscientiously at your job you can make it a form of Right Livelihood, even if not of Perfect Livelihood. Fourthly there are those occupations which do not involve undue mental strain.[410]

This fourth category indicates that, even if an occupation is ethically sound, it may still not be Right Livelihood, in the full sense. It may, for instance, subject one to such strain, because of anxiety or excessive mental activity, that one is unable to meditate.

Those who are working at a vocation are unlikely to be concerned about how much time they spend at work. A Right Livelihood business can also be considered as a vocation since workers have joined it because they believe in its objectives. They will therefore work as much as is required to fulfil those objectives—in the early stages of establishing some businesses, workers have worked very long hours indeed. For those not in these situations, Sangharakshita recommends they work as little as possible. They will then be free to devote more time to spiritual practice and to helping the growth of the New Society.

So far, while the discussion has been confined to matters of personal livelihood, the principles have been reasonably clear—although it may be very difficult for any particular individual to find work that is really Right Livelihood. When we come to consider the transformation of the economic life of society as a whole, the issues become more obscure. Modern economies are now extraordinarily intricate, depending on a vast range of factors, including psychological ones. State finance ministers and experienced economists seldom seem able to predict what is going to happen in the economy with any great accuracy. Into that complex global economic network every one of us is inextricably linked. It is probably not possible to dissociate ourselves altogether from direct or indirect involvement in some activities that we might consider unskilful. For instance, part of the taxes we pay to the state is used for weapons of war, and the banks in which we keep our money lend it to companies engaged in the arms trade or selling tobacco.

As far as we can, we should withdraw from those aspects of the economy we know to be unskilful. For instance we should try not to invest our money where we know it will be used for unethical purposes. Sangharakshita is keen that some research is done into finance in the modern economy.

> I have been asking some of our friends who are involved in Right Livelihood businesses to give attention to the whole question of how economics and money work in our society. In England recently there have been very big financial scandals. We can't ignore these things; we have to try to understand them.[411]

Once we have a clearer understanding we will be in a better position to make ethical decisions, withdrawing if possible from those aspects of the economy that are corrupt.

In addition, he argues that we should not use products that we know cause pollution or that harm others. We should avoid simply wasting resources:

> One can certainly make an unambiguous start by taking a stand against the production of luxury items—things that we clearly don't need. First, one should not use them oneself. Then one should discourage people who are in contact with the movement from using them.[412]

To give an example, he himself always discourages women in the movement from using cosmetics. In general he encourages people to live a simple life, in which they restrict their needs as much as possible—without thereby condemning themselves to squalor or deprivation of necessities. The simple life is an important weapon in the transformation of society, since it cuts down on demand and works against the prevailing idea that we should be consuming more and more as each year goes by. By living a simple life one will either need to spend less time earning money to pay for one's consumption or else will have money to spare for Dharmic purposes. Finally, living a simple life helps to overcome the neurotic craving so prevalent in our consumer society.

One of the most complex problems in assessing the complex modern economy is evaluating the place of industrialisation and technology. Sangharakshita is unwilling to commit himself prematurely as to whether or not they are harmful or beneficial as a whole. Nor is he willing to predict what place they might have in the New Society of the future. Temperamentally, his inclinations are against industrial development but he does not fall back into pastoral romanticism. He recognises that, for many people, technology and industrialisation have brought a very definite amelioration of life. A clear example of this is the improvement he has seen in the lives of his ex-Untouchable friends, as India has developed industrially over the last decades. He therefore thinks that some serious and thorough investigation needs to be done before we accept or reject these developments.

> There are undoubted harms as a result of industrialisation, but there are also undoubted benefits for many people. So one has to weigh the one against the other. One has to ask oneself: Is it possible to limit industrialisation so that it works for the benefit of humanity and not the opposite? Or is it intrinsically so harmful that it represents a retrograde step in the development of humanity, a step which we have to retrace?[413]

We have to be aware that were we to decide that industrialisation was a retrograde step we would have to return to an agricultural economy that had its own evils. Would we *really* be prepared to 'go back to the land'?

Sangharakshita offers few answers to these broader questions—because there cannot yet be answers. Members of the spiritual community must transform their own economic lives. They must create alternative ways of working and withdraw from those aspects of the economy that are obviously unskilful. Gradually their understanding of the economic system of the old society will grow, in the light of their experience of Right Livelihood in the small-scale New Societies. They will be able to draw more and more public attention to what is unskilful and encourage and applaud what is skilful. Slowly, very slowly, the economic life of the old society could change into an entirely new pattern that provides everyone with their material necessities while supporting their spiritual development.

## POLITICAL TRANSFORMATION

We come now to the political aspects of the transformation of society. Sangharakshita says that politics 'is about who possesses the power to coerce, or who coerces whom'.[414] We must therefore explore how power functions, if at all, within the New Society, as well as how those within the New Society are to relate to power in the old society: What are the politics of the New Society? What involvement are the members of the New Society to have in the politics of the old?

Power in this context is 'the capacity to coerce, whether directly or indirectly, physically or psychologically'.[415] One person acquires the capacity to coerce others either because they fear him personally or because he has been invested with power by an institution. In the latter case he exercises institutional or political power over others by virtue of the position he holds and the authority it confers upon him.

> The [political] power he exercises is not his own power: it belongs to his office; and this office or position is created by the particular group or organization to which he belongs. That power therefore belongs to the group.[416]

Here a person does not have power as an individual but as the representative of the group; the individual, as an individual, has nothing to do with this sort of power. Since the spiritual community consists of individuals in free association with one another, political power, authority, and office have no place within it. Power of this kind belongs to the group and without it the group cannot exist. Sangharakshita is careful to point out that such power is not necessarily a bad thing, so long as it is confined to the group and subordinated to moral principles. Indeed, the group depends on such power to provide security and order for its members.

In Sangharakshita's terminology the group functions according to the 'power mode', relations within it being essentially based on power in the sense of the capacity to coerce. Within the spiritual community the principle that governs relations is the 'love mode' or 'mettā mode'. People relate to each other on the basis of positive emotion: not only mettā, but *karuṇā* or compassion, *muditā* or sympathetic joy, and *upekṣā* or peace or equanimity, as well as *śraddhā* or faith and devotion.

> We could say that *all* these sublime, uplifting, inspiring positive emotions constitute the principle that governs the spiritual community.[417]

The spiritual community must, however, be governed by some higher principle still. There must be a metaphysical or transcendental dimension, for 'it is only *that* dimension that can permanently sustain the spiritual community'. That dimension is the *bodhicitta* or 'cosmic will to Enlightenment', the urge to perpetual self-transcendence, 'reflected in the hearts and minds of all those individuals who make up the spiritual community'.[418] For the spiritual community to be a spiritual community at all, every member must be activated to some extent by a state of consciousness that goes beyond the personal.

Since there is no political or manipulative power within the spiritual community, there is no politics. No one coerces anyone else so there is no need to have structures for the equitable distribution of power and to safeguard the rights of the individual. The functioning of the spiritual community cannot really be analysed in the terms of conventional political theory. However, Sangharakshita says that 'In some respects we [in the Order] are hierarchical, in some respects we are democratic.'[419] The Order is democratic in that every Order member tries to act as an individual and as an individual takes personal responsibility for the spiritual community as a whole, to the best of his or her ability. In any situation where Order members are working or living together, everyone's views are taken into consideration and an effort is always made to achieve a consensus. If it is not possible to come to a decision upon which everyone agrees then usually the matter is dropped.

The spiritual community is hierarchical in that all members accept that there are people at different stages of development within it. Each will be prepared to accept the greater experience and maturity of some others, whom they will look to as *kalyāṇa mitras* and teachers, sources of guidance and instruction. However, *kalyāṇa mitras* and teachers will be looked to not by virtue of any position they may occupy. Experience will have shown them to be worthy of respect. Thus hierarchy within the spiritual community is based on the spirit of *kalyāṇa mitratā*—of loving respect, one might say—while hierarchy within the group is based on position and the capacity to coerce. Sangharakshita usually refers to hierarchy within the spiritual community as 'spiritual hierarchy' to distinguish it from the hierarchy of power.

Within the spiritual community there are certain responsibilities to be carried out: for instance, the training, selection, and especially the acceptance of new Order members. All members of the spiritual community can contribute something to these processes. However, to carry them out in full demands particular qualities that only the more experienced members will have developed. They will therefore be called upon to fulfil these responsibilities by virtue of their individual merits. They do so in their own individual capacity, not acting as representatives of the Order as a whole. One individual cannot represent another—only a group can be represented. Ultimately they alone must make any decisions connected with their responsibility—having listened to the views of other Order members and taken into account the effect their decisions have on the whole Order. This is a very important principle within the spiritual community and it has wider application. Those who carry a particular responsibility should be free to make the decisions it requires. Thus a group of Order members running a centre must make the decisions connected with that centre. No one who does not share that work with them can impose decisions upon them—although, of course, they may seek advice and guidance from people whose experience they respect. For this reason, all FWBO centres are legally autonomous. There is no 'head office' issuing them with directives. The unity of the movement comes from the fact that those who run the centres are all members of a single spiritual community.

The hierarchy of responsibility cannot be forced upon the spiritual community: it must be freely accepted by all members out of their respect for those who fulfil the greater duties—otherwise the spiritual hierarchy would actually be a hierarchy of power. However, there is no question of democracy in the ordinary sense: responsibility is not handed over by election. Only representatives can be appointed by election: and only a group can be represented, not an individual or community of individuals. Those who already carry out a responsibility will have the responsibility of finding others to whom they can hand it on. The handing on of responsibility and the carrying out of responsibility must all be conducted within a context of positive emotion, of trust, and particularly of *kalyāṇa mitratā*—if not, the spiritual community would simply be functioning as a group.

The first and greatest responsibility is that of actually starting the spiritual community. The hierarchy of responsibility emanates from a single point—from the individual or individuals who take that initial responsibility. Their recognition that others are effectively Going for Refuge is what first brings the spiritual community into being. It is they who must hand on responsibility for 'witnessing' or recognising the Effective Going for Refuge of new members in the ceremony of ordination—as well as the other duties that require spiritual maturity. It is they who are, at the outset, the principal unifying factor in the spiritual community.

Sangharakshita considers that the constitution of the monastic sangha founded by the Buddha did not sufficiently take into account the unifying influence of the founder. The Buddha disclaimed leadership of the sangha. He devolved the acceptance of new members upon groups of five or ten monks, presided over by an elder of at least ten years' standing. Responsibility was thus handed over on the basis of simple seniority in the Order. While one would expect that many elders would have the necessary individual qualities to carry out that responsibility, it is certainly not guaranteed. A quite different approach is needed that allows for the reality of the founder's position.

> The Buddha denied that he led the sangha. But that can't be taken literally, because the Buddha's word was law for all the *bhikkhus*, who are frequently represented in the Pali Canon as saying, in effect, 'The Buddha is our authority.' We find the Buddha invariably laying down the Vinaya rules. He never asked the opinion of the *bhikkhus*; nothing was ever put to a vote; he didn't even have referenda. The Buddha just

laid down Vinaya rules as he thought best, he was the supreme
authority. So during the Buddha's lifetime, the sangha was held together
by the Buddha.[420]

When the Buddha died, no successor was recognised, so there was no
comparable figure to hold the sangha together. Some individual monks
took initiative by calling large meetings of elders in order to maintain
some unity. Later the custom grew for monarchs to appoint *sangharājas*
or heads of the sangha, because they wanted to deal with a single figure
rather than the monks and nuns as a mass. In this way, the sangha fell
either into a kind of anarchy with individual groups simply going their
own way, or into authoritarianism under a highly centralised leadership,
usually sanctioned by the civil power.

Sangharakshita believes that neither of these alternatives is healthy,
and that the spiritual community must follow a middle way between
them. Both individual autonomy, on the one hand, and harmony and
co-operation, on the other, are of the essence of spiritual life. Both must
therefore be guaranteed within the spiritual community. However,

it is not very easy to ensure the one without detriment to the other. It's
very easy to get people working together and to ensure harmony
through a highly authoritarian regime and structure, but that would be
against the principle of individual autonomy. It is also quite easy to
ensure individual autonomy by not having any sort of structure, but
then you can't achieve co-operation and harmony. So you've got to do
justice to both of these. You have to try to keep to a middle path.[421]

When the spiritual community is quite small, it is relatively simple to
maintain both aspects spontaneously. When it begins to grow, some more
definite organisation is required to preserve that middle path. Sangharakshita has not yet completed the framing of a constitution for the
Western Buddhist Order, although the broad outlines are drawn. Individual autonomy is fostered by the autonomy of the local chapters, to
one of which each Order member belongs. Each chapter is entirely
responsible for its own affairs.

Harmony and co-operation are ensured by a number of unifying
factors. All Order members come together regularly in groupings of
several chapters—biennially in international conventions. There are also
regular meetings at a regional, national, and international level of those
who carry particular responsibilities at a local level: Chapter Convenors,
Mitra Convenors, and Chairmen and Presidents of centres. Sangharakshita is gradually handing over his remaining responsibilities as head
of the Order to a small group of senior Order members whom he is
confident will be able to continue his work and collectively replace him

as a principal unifying factor in the spiritual community. He is still considering, at the time of writing, whether a further unifying factor is needed in the person of a permanent Head of the Order to replace him.

We have seen that the New Society emerges when a spiritual community has a decisive influence upon a group, so that it becomes a positive group, functioning according to ethical principles and in support of the developing individual. Despite the influence of the spiritual community, the positive group is nonetheless still a group, and it can always slip away from the influence of the spiritual community. It can easily revert to the power mode—for in the positive group the power mode is merely held in temporary abeyance by the influence of the spiritual community's mettā. Members of the spiritual community must therefore make sure that they retain ultimate legal control over the primary institutions of the New Society. As far as they can, they should function in accordance with the love mode within the positive group, influencing by argument, persuasion, and example rather than by coercion. However, they must be able to use legal power if necessary to prevent the centres, communities, or businesses from being appropriated for group ends rather than for those of the spiritual community.

Members of the spiritual community must clearly be always very watchful that they have sufficient influence within the positive group to prevent it from degenerating into a mere group. Here there is a question of strategy: making sure that there are sufficient members of the spiritual community to exert an uplifting influence on the positive group. The required ratio can, of course, never be calculated as a fixed mathematical proportion—for it will depend on the individuals concerned and the circumstances in which they find themselves. A particularly dangerous time, from this point of view, is when the New Society is in a phase of rapid growth, for expansion can easily outrun the influence of the spiritual community.

Individuals within the spiritual community relate to the positive group that surrounds them on the basis of the love mode. However, they keep power in reserve where control of the basic institutions of the New Society is concerned. The power mode can only be completely abandoned in relation to others who have abandoned it—that is within the spiritual community. In the group outside the New Society, members of the spiritual community will find themselves relating to people who see them in terms of power—for the group member can only see the member of the spiritual community as another member of the group—or as the member of another group. At times, members of the spiritual community will be forced to defend themselves, their institutions, and their work against the attacks of group members. In other words, they will have to resort to power. That power should always be used, Sangharakshita argues, in subordination to the love mode. It should be minimal, sufficient simply to achieve its end of defending the New Society, and untainted by hatred or revenge. In a country in which there genuinely is justice, power should be used in accordance with the law.

Clearly the 'political' task of the individual is to end politics by transforming the group, which functions according to the power mode, into the spiritual community, which is governed by mettā. First, this means transforming a small section of the group into a positive group. Spiritual community and positive group together will form New Societies in miniature in the midst of the old. Gradually the New Society must be expanded until it becomes co-extensive with society as a whole.

> I do not want to see little pockets of Buddhism here and there with the remainder of society completely unchanged. I don't want there to be just little Buddhist oases in the midst of the desert of secular life. I want them to spread and to influence their surroundings in a positive way.[422]

If society is to be transformed into the New Society, it must be engaged with directly and actively, to some extent on its own terms. Simply waiting for people to come to Buddhist centres to learn meditation will never reach more than a tiny percentage of the population. Members of the spiritual community must begin to influence society on the most basic level, spreading ideas that will gradually transform the way people look at their lives. They must also start to engage with the actual machinery of government. They must use that machinery to change society so it will support an ethical life and the following of the spiritual path. Only by their direct involvement in political life will society as a whole move in the direction of the New Society.

In a sense, any member of a modern state has no option but to be involved in political life. The state considers one a citizen whether one likes it or not.

> You don't have a choice whether to be a citizen or not. You are in a sense forced to participate by the state. For instance, if you live under a parliamentary democracy, you have a vote. You exercise your political power by not voting as much as by voting, because your not voting may contribute to the success or failure of a particular candidate. So you cannot escape from exercising power within that system, regardless of your personal wishes.[423]

As a stark illustration of this truth, a neo-Fascist candidate has, at the time of writing, just been elected a councillor in one of London's boroughs by a majority of just one vote. Though not voting might still be one's option, one must be aware of it as an *active* decision. So all-embracing is the modern state that this same principle applies in many other fields. Even by not participating one participates—and thus has an influence. Members of the spiritual community, therefore, must acknowledge their citizenship and the duties inherent in it. They must exercise that citizenship actively, as a contribution to the creation of the New Society.

Many influenced by the ideas of the 'alternative movement' in the West are very reluctant to have any political involvement at all. Sangharakshita considers this a great weakness: 'We can't leave it to the politicians.'[424] Many Western Buddhists have also rejected politics. Quite a number have been severely disillusioned by previous political involvement, often of a radical kind: Marxist, Feminist, or 'gay rights'. However, Sangharakshita considers that a more basic reason for the rejection of politics is the increasing 'privatisation' of life. In traditional societies, individual members would naturally participate in the public life of their community. With the increasing scale and complexity of modern nations, it is very difficult to experience oneself as part of the community as a whole. This leads people to retreat into purely private interests and concerns—into 'private life'. Many who become interested in religion do so partly in retreat from the public arena.

Sangharakshita regards this as very unhealthy and strongly encourages his disciples to engage constructively in their own societies. Few have done so yet—partly because so much energy has been needed to build the basic institutions of the New Society. The political dimension of social transformation has not, therefore, been worked out in any detail—Sangharakshita says that many of his disciples in the West 'politically are babies'.[425] In India, where the Buddhist movement has grown out of the fight for social justice, Order members are, by contrast, politically quite mature. Despite the movement's relative lack of political experience, Sangharakshita has himself explored many of the principles of political involvement by members of the spiritual community.

Politics is about power and is therefore a difficult and dangerous business. In engaging in politics one will be in contact with people who are interested in power, many for quite ignoble reasons. There will therefore be a danger of becoming enmeshed in a world that gradually seduces one away from one's fundamental purpose. Sangharakshita, therefore, recommends that Order members who engage in such activities firmly link themselves into the New Society in other ways: for instance, by living in a residential community and keeping in close contact with Order members who are working more definitely within the New Society. Furthermore he believes that political involvement should be confined to a level where party politics can be avoided. He considers that political parties, with their demand for loyalty, are usually simply another manifestation of the group.

> I think it is not in the interests of the public that one identifies oneself with a particular party, whether that party is right or wrong, so as to carry it into power.[426]

Political involvement is therefore, at this stage, only really possible on the lowest level, certainly in Britain.

> What I have encouraged is participating on the lowest level of government, where there is the closest personal contact and where party politics does not enter much: such as the election of local councils in England—not the big national elections.[427]

Another reason for confining political activity to this level is that most issues dealt with there are relatively simple. It will be much easier to see directly the effects of political decisions—and therefore to assess whether one is doing harm or good. On the larger scale of national and international politics, issues are so complex that one can do a great deal of harm while trying to do good. Sangharakshita warns members of the spiritual community to beware of naïve idealism, especially in political affairs.

> Good intentions are not enough, sincerity is not enough, idealism is not enough. There must be an intelligent understanding of the situation, there must be a grasp of facts. A lot of harm is done in the world by misguided idealists.[428]

In his own discussions of political matters, he is always ready to admit the limitations of his own knowledge of the facts and is very reluctant to make uninformed pronouncements.

The naïve idealism of the alternative movement's 'political babies' often results in their wholesale rejection of government and state— leading them either to retreat into private life, simply evading the state as far as possible, or to engage in revolutionary activity. Sangharakshita sees clearly the difficulties of being subject to a state that is neither entirely moral nor supportive of spiritual life. Nonetheless, he considers that stability and order are a necessary basis for human life—and especially for the existence of the spiritual community. The individual must therefore be very careful not to undermine unnecessarily the basic framework of society, either by withdrawing support from it or by actively working against it.

> Law and order cannot but be an advantage to you as an individual
> because you live under the protection of that system.[429]

Rejection of government and state contributes to a breakdown of the
fabric of society.

> It isn't in anyone's interests that there should be social and political
> confusion and chaos or a breakdown of law and order. It's almost certain
> to make the situation worse in the long run rather than better.[430]

The individual should therefore give broad support to the government
in its efforts to provide security and order for society. This includes
acceptance that a certain degree of force is necessary to the state to control
those who act against the general interest.

> It would seem that there always will be a minority of people in society
> who will try to harm others. The majority will therefore need to invoke
> force, at least to restrain them from their anti-social conduct. I don't
> think one can get around that.[431]

A problem arises, of course, when the individual finds that he is
required to obey laws that he considers to be immoral. Sangharakshita
points out that in this situation there is a choice of two evils: acquiescing
in an immoral action or undermining the structure of society.

> I think that, as far as one possibly can, one should avoid coming into
> conflict with the laws of the land. I think one should permit oneself to
> come into conflict with them only if a very serious and vital Buddhist
> principle is involved; not if it is just a matter of your personal
> convenience or liking or disliking.[432]

He cites the example of being conscripted in a country that does not
accept conscientious objection. If one felt strongly that one could not
support violence by doing military service one could only refuse to serve
and take the consequences. One might be tempted to avoid the conflict
by lying—but that too has wider implications, particularly if one lies in
a court of law or other such public situation.

> From a Buddhist point of view, to lie in court is the most serious form of
> lying, because this undermines the whole basis of society. This is
> mentioned again and again in the Pali texts. If there cannot be mutual
> trust, the whole basis of civilised life is undermined.[433]

In some circumstances, of course, one might conclude that lying was the
lesser of evils—for instance, if doing so saved someone's life. However,
one would need to be aware of the price being paid for that life.

Sangharakshita has serious doubts about civil disobedience as a valid
means of bringing about social change. Not obeying laws that one does
not believe in may have disastrous consequences.

> In acting against a particular state on account of laws with which you
> don't agree, you have to be very careful that you do not in the end do

more harm than good. If we do take the law into our own hands because
of what we believe, anybody can do that on the basis of what *they*
believe. In that way you end up with a sort of free-for-all in which might
is right—and you could be back in a worse state than you were in the
first place. So I think you should weigh that very, very seriously.
Societies like Nazi Germany are relatively exceptional. A society or a
government would have to be very corrupt indeed for one to be justified
in opposing it by nonlegal means.[434]

He questions whether Gandhi's civil disobedience movement against
British imperial rule may not have complicated the process of British
withdrawal—they were clearly going anyway and simply went with
unseemly haste, leaving the disastrous bloodshed of partition. More
seriously still, Gandhi's use of civil disobedience has embedded in Indian
political life the idea that it is right to disobey a law with which you do
not agree. In this way it has probably contributed to the considerable
problems of law and order in independent India.

If one does come to the conclusion that the state is so corrupt that one
cannot obey its laws at all, one puts oneself in a position of outlawry. One
is then in 'a state of war with your own state'[435]—the position of the
terrorist. This is a very difficult and unfortunate situation to be in, because
one would have no community—and no opportunity to affect a community positively. One would have come to the conclusion that a descent
into complete social chaos and the creation of a new order within that
chaos was better than the existing corruption. However, revolutions are
usually accompanied by much bloodshed and suffering, and they are
often succeeded by regimes as harsh and corrupt as those they replace—
indeed, often more so. The present system would, therefore, have to be
very corrupt indeed to justify putting oneself at war with society.

The old society is not ideal and must be transformed into the New.
Nonetheless, members of the spiritual community must recognise that
the existence of any society at all represents some degree of good.

For human life to go on at all, there has to be some sort of positive social
framework. It's very difficult, by the very nature of society, to conceive of
a society that, while remaining a society, is unmitigatedly evil. That
would entail envisaging that everybody in that society was
unmitigatedly evil.[436]

The very existence of a society already implies an element of communication and co-operation, even if only for mutual security and even if
underlain by the power mode. The ordering of social, economic, and
political relationships under the rule of law, however corrupt and vicious,
is a move away from complete egoism and the opposition of each human
being to every other. While distancing himself as much as possible from

corruption and immorality, the individual must encourage the positive trends that are inherent in the nature of human society. The individual, as an aspect of his own development, wants to improve society, so that it supports his own spiritual efforts and those of other individuals—as well as providing a decent and just life for all its members. He therefore needs to have a constructive relationship with society, enabling him to influence it.

The need to preserve stability and order in society does not mean that one should simply accept the *status quo*. Injustices must be reformed and an effort must be made to transform the old society gradually into the New. However,

> One would be well advised not to adopt an attitude of premature
> hostility towards society or hostility over issues where hostility isn't
> called for. There can perhaps be selective hostility but, so far as possible,
> that hostility should find expression through the recognised channels—
> legal agitation etc.[437]

That 'selective hostility' means condemning the injustices of governments and other institutions without necessarily condemning the institutions themselves. It means pressing for the reform of those injustices, using the well-developed channels available in a modern democracy.

> Governments, at least in democratic countries, depend upon votes. They
> will do something if they realise that a sufficient number of people are
> not going to give their vote to a party that does not have as part of its
> platform the reforms you want to bring about.[438]

Members of the spiritual community should therefore join with others who wish to bring about change on particular issues: for instance, the arms trade, or the pollution of the environment. Once more, they must be very clear as to what they are doing. They must ensure that they are in possession of the facts and that they are not being used by those they ally themselves with for some ulterior motive—for political groups of all ideological colours cynically manipulate current issues, such as racism, as vehicles for their own political intentions.

Where local issues are concerned, it is usually relatively easy to see both the ends one is trying to achieve and the means to those ends. On the bigger scale of national and international politics, issues are much more complex. It may be possible to know only in a very general way what it is that one wants to achieve. Sangharakshita believes that it is for these general objectives that one should lobby: telling the government what it is that one wants them to do but leaving them to decide how best to do it. For instance, he believes that nuclear weapons are incompatible with the long term survival of the human race—if they exist, eventually they will be used. He therefore considers that citizens should put pressure on their governments to work with other governments to abolish nuclear weapons. This, he says, should be the present priority of all governments throughout the world.

> You can present a united front with regard to ends. Everybody agrees that nuclear weapons should be abolished. The only agencies that can do that are the agencies that have them: governments. You can put pressure on your government to take steps, honestly and effectively, to get together with other governments with a view to abolishing nuclear weapons. But I think it a bit premature to tell the assembled governments what steps they should take, because it will be a very complicated business, and interest will have to be weighed against interest. You as an individual—and a very, very amateur individual at that, knowing very little of the facts even in your own country—cannot work out a policy which you then insist that everybody should adopt.[439]

He believes that too often in political matters people with the same objectives become polarised in disputes about means—for instance, about whether nuclear weapons should be abolished unilaterally or multilaterally. Actually, most people are not in a position to know what the best means are and should simply combine to pursue their common objective. Again, naïve idealism can do more harm than good.

Sangharakshita believes that individuals in the spiritual community should support genuine democracy. Although the modern liberal democracy is profoundly secular, it does contain elements that ultimately imply spiritual ideals. Indeed, Sangharakshita argues that the secular nature of modern society itself implies a spiritual ideal. Pluralism, the allowance of different religious and cultural possibilities within a single society, is often thought of as a compromise. It is seen as a way of avoiding conflict and bloodshed after a supposedly desirable cultural homogeneity has been lost. Sangharakshita however considers that pluralism in society is an important positive principle. Firstly, it makes it possible to function as a Buddhist. In a pluralist society, Buddhists have the freedom to establish those small-scale New Societies, to spread Buddhist ideas and to try to transform the whole of society into the New Society. At the same time, the Buddhist is not subject to persecution by other beliefs. One is even free to disagree with other religions, openly and publicly. Buddhists should remember that it is not many years since it would have been impossible for them to practise the Dharma openly in the West. They should also realise that there are still states in which, for instance, a Muslim is not permitted to convert to Buddhism or any other religion and Buddhist activities are severely curbed, if not prohibited.

More importantly, pluralism—or secularism—implies the acceptance of certain ethical values: the spirit of tolerance and the freedom of the individual to decide his own beliefs. These are values central to Buddhism. Fundamentally, the principle of secularism is

> The principle that a human being is first and foremost a human being ... only secondly a Hindu, only secondly a Muslim, Christian etc. If we accept that we are first and foremost human beings then we can relate to others as human beings. We can treat one another as human beings, live together as human beings. Regardless of whether we are Hindu, Muslim, etc., we can live together in the same state.[440]

Secularism implies therefore that 'religion is made for man, not man for religion' and that it exists to make him a better human being—in Buddhist terms to make him a Buddha. This essentially humanistic attitude is not shared by all religions. Christianity, Islam, and Hinduism, for instance, all regard one as a Christian, a Muslim, or a Hindu before one is a human being. When these religions have each had power in a state they have used it to enforce their view of one as a member of their particular religion before one is a human being. The secular state forces these religions to change if they are to coexist with other religions. For Buddhism there is no such problem.

> Indeed, Buddhism flourishes in the secular state. This is because Buddhism always puts man first and religion afterwards. According to Buddhism, the Dharma is simply the means of human development.[441]

The fact that the principles of pluralism are shared by society as a whole is very important indeed.

> I think Buddhists everywhere should support pluralism, should support tolerance, should support democracy in the real sense—not just demagoguery, but the genuine acceptance of the fact that every individual in a society has, to the measure of his ability, some responsibility for the running of that society.[442]

Sangharakshita argues that the state should become fully and completely pluralistic: for instance, the Church of England should be disestablished, and all mention of God should be removed from the American Constitution and from the Republic's insignia. Not only is he critical of the vestiges of Christian ascendency in Western democracies, but he is very much against the idea of a 'Buddhist nation', such as exists in Sri Lanka and Thailand. He wrote a damning review of *The Heritage of the Bhikkhu* in which the 'political *bhikkhu*' Walpola Rahula, gave expression to the common view amongst Sri Lankan Buddhists that Buddhism was, and should be, the national religion of their country.[443] It is, of course, this attitude that has led to the violent insurgency of the Hindu Tamils.

[Walpola Rahula] refers with approval to the ancient Sinhalese idea that a Sinhalese had to be a Buddhist! This is surely a complete denial of the individual's freedom to follow the religion of his own choice, and as such a complete negation of both the spirit and the letter of the Buddha's teaching. One cannot be a Buddhist unless one is free not to be a Buddhist—unless one is free to be a Christian, or a Muslim, or a tree-worshipper, or anything else one wants to be. What Walpola Rahula in effect does is to turn Buddhism from a universal religion into an ethnic religion, surely the worst of all betrayals, the worst of all perversions, of a teaching that stressed above all others the responsibility of the individual for his own development.[444]

Of course, the attempt to turn the whole of society into the New Society means that ultimately one is trying to create what would cease to be a pluralist society—in the sense that everyone would be a Buddhist. However, it would still be pluralist in principle because everyone would be free to be anything other than a Buddhist if they wanted. If they were not free to be anything else, they would not be free to be Buddhists. Pluralism, thus, gives expression to principles at the heart of Buddhism. Unlike the monotheistic religions, which accept pluralism largely because they are forced to, Buddhism fully supports its adoption by modern democracies. It is a foreshadowing in the old society of the tolerance and freedom of the New. Indeed, the notion of pluralism offers a language for the transmission within society of Buddhist ideas.

We shouldn't necessarily be in a hurry to suggest that society at large follow Buddhist ethical principles. I think it is sufficient, for the time being, if we point out the very definite ethical ideal involved in pluralism, and see it in positive as well as negative and restrictive terms. It is not simply that pluralism prevents us from bashing each other's heads in—it provides us with a basis for co-operation. To have a friendly and co-operative attitude towards people of a different way of thinking is certainly not inconsistent with Buddhism, though it might well be inconsistent with certain other faiths and ideologies. In other words, indirectly, by promoting pluralism, you are in fact, though to a limited extent perhaps, promoting Buddhism.[445]

In these many different ways, the individuals in the spiritual community seek to expand the New Societies in miniature so that they become coextensive with society as a whole. Eventually, within the context of a democratic state, they hope to gain political power. They can then govern according to moral principles and the needs of the developing individual.

> But persuasion must be the keynote. You can't really dragoon people
> into being more truly moral, because morality is essentially a matter of
> individual attitude.[446]

Even though one aim of members of the spiritual community is thus to
gain power in the state, Sangharakshita points out that they cannot
confine themselves to converting just a single nation into a New Society.

> You've got to think in terms of the whole world. Suppose one state is
> organised as an ideal state: what if it's attacked by the others, who don't
> like ideal states? Suppose the fact that it is an ideal state has left it
> defenceless, it might soon be overrun. This kind of thinking would lead
> one in the direction of the formation of an ideal *world* state—or
> non-state.[447]

Essentially, Sangharakshita conceives of the Buddhist life as implying
the effort, not merely to transform oneself, but to transform the whole
world into an ideal society. He is reluctant to say what that world will be
like and he has no blueprint for its future constitution or government.

> I think, if society managed to become an ideal society, it would in the
> process work that one out for itself. It is very difficult to predict in
> advance. There could be a number of possible forms of government for
> an ideal society, depending on local conditions, even local temperament,
> local tradition, local history. Perhaps there is not any one absolutely best
> form of government for everybody.[448]

People in any given area would presumably need some 'machinery of
co-operation', but what that might be we cannot imagine. For an ideal
society to have come into existence human beings as a whole would have
to change almost beyond recognition. In the course of that change many
new possibilities would have arisen. There would probably be wonderful
technological developments. People generally might have new mental
powers and abilities that might make external forms of organisation
completely unnecessary.

The nearest we can get to what such an ideal world would be like is on
the plane of archetypal imagination. Sangharakshita points out that the
'Pure Lands', described in some Mahāyāna scriptures, are the archetypes
of the perfect society:

> A Pure Land … is a place, a world, a plane of existence, where there is no
> pain, no suffering, no misery, no separation, no bereavement, no loss of
> any kind. It is a place where there is no old age, no sickness, and no
> death. It is a place of perfect peace in which there is no conflict, no war,
> no battle, nor even any misunderstanding—it is as perfect and happy as
> that! These great Mahāyāna sūtras also tell us that the Pure Land or
> Happy Land is a place where there is no distinction of male and female,
> and where no one ever has to do any work. Food and clothing appear of
> their own accord whenever they are needed. In the Pure Land no one

has anything to do except sit on their golden or purple or blue lotus at the feet of the Buddha and listen to his exposition of the Dharma.[449]

From the lofty heights of the vision of Pure Land, we return to the harsh realities of the modern situation. It is, however, a penetrating look at that situation that provides Sangharakshita with his motivation to change society.

Reflecting upon the evils of life in a more concrete sociopolitical sense doesn't incite me to emancipate myself from it all. It incites me to try to create a viable alternative in the form of a whole movement, a whole New Society, within which there will be the possibility of a more decent human life—leaving aside anything spiritual! I won't say it makes me feel disillusioned that things go on in society as they do, it just makes me feel angry, and therefore all the more determined to create a better alternative.

My ultimate conclusion is that that alternative can be created only on the basis of definite spiritual values espoused by the individual, and by individuals working together as individuals to create a whole new spiritual community, and a New Society beyond that.

Those of us who do manage to live largely within the FWBO, we at least have a happy, meaningful, and creative life, compared with the lives of a lot of people outside. And this is why we want to expand it. We want it to become available to more and more people, because we see how rotten it is to live in the way that some people have to live. As individuals they are not strong enough to change things by themselves. But if they came across an alternative like the FWBO they would be open to it and would benefit from it very greatly.[450]

*Chapter Ten*

# THE MAKING OF A NEW BUDDHIST CULTURE

*Talkative one morning, the Cypriot barber*
*Asked me what I did for a living.*
*'Write,' I replied, not feeling*
*Particularly communicative. 'You write!*
*What do you write?' 'I write poetry.'*

*Ah, delight of the suspended scissors, exhilaration*
*Of the raised comb! 'You write*
*Poetry!'*
*   In depths of the mirror behind him*
*Athenian walls standing intact,*
*Long-haired warriors spared for great verses.*[451]

IF AND WHEN THE NEW SOCIETY finally comes into existence, it will consist not simply of new institutions: most significantly, it will consist of new individuals. Those new individuals in that New Society are almost unimaginable to us. They will have an entirely different way of experiencing the world and of interacting with it. The evolution to a New Society will have been accompanied by the development of new modes of perception. Things will literally not look the same, since they will have a different meaning and will find their place within a new scale of values. The souls of men will be different: their psyches will be structured in a new way that will give them different dreams and make them see a new significance in every object. Every detail of life, no matter how trivial or lofty, will be affected by the new consciousness of the true individuals by whom the New Society will be kept in being. There will be a new culture, emanating principally from the spiritual community at the heart of the positive group. Everything in that culture will support, encourage, and inspire the individual to follow the spiritual path.

'Culture' is a rather imprecise but compendious term. It refers first to the totality of ideas and beliefs, manners and customs, tastes and values that give a people their distinctive character. Culture, in this sense, is the broad influence of society, playing upon the individual and helping to shape his or her ways of experiencing and acting. It is the medium in which the individual psyche grows. The transformation of society is thus dependent on the transformation of culture as a whole. The culture of the old society must be replaced by the culture of the New. Clearly the relationship between culture and spiritual life is therefore of the foremost importance. This is, Sangharakshita says, 'a topic that has preoccupied me for almost as long as I have been a Buddhist'.[452] He has long wanted to write systematically on the relationship between Buddhism and culture, but has not yet had the opportunity. However, throughout his writings, lectures, and seminars are references to the subject, from which the outlines of his thinking can be discerned.

'Culture' can also refer to what is but an aspect of culture in the broad sense already given: put simply, it is the arts. The relationship between the arts and Buddhism is a topic that has also preoccupied Sangharakshita for many years. He has, indeed, wrestled very personally with whether there can be any such relationship. Fortunately, quite early in his Buddhist career, he did write about Buddhism and Art, setting forth perhaps one of his most original ideas.[453] Sangharakshita's life has been closely bound up with the question of culture, in both senses. He has crossed from one culture to another—and back again, carrying riches from the East to the West. From a very early age he has also found deep inspiration in the arts, and he has written poetry since he was twelve years old. We will now briefly explore Sangharakshita's 'cultural biography' as a background to his ideas.

The culture of working-class South London, into which he was born, was certainly not marked by any great knowledge or appreciation of philosophy, literature, painting, or the other arts. Nonetheless, his parents and close relatives were upright and kindly people, and his father had strong aspirations to higher culture. Indeed, he once told his son that he had always wanted to be a writer. Accordingly, when the young Dennis began to show interest in literature and painting, he found support and encouragement at home, if not understanding and companionship. His real introduction to higher culture came through reading Harmsworth's

*Children's Encyclopaedia,* while he was confined to bed between the ages of eight and ten. From the pages of that work

> the harvest of the ages was gathered unto me for the making of the bread that would keep my soul alive. The body was forgotten, and my imagination, now possessed of 'infinite riches in a little room', rejoiced in the freedom of all the heavens of the spirit.[454]

Art, literature, and history were the subjects to which he returned most frequently: especially art, represented in the encyclopaedia by plates, many in colour, of the greatest painting and sculpture of the West.

> Though every picture gave me pleasure, I admired most of all the works of the Renaissance artists, especially the deific sublimity of Michelangelo and the dancing delicacy of Botticelli.[455]

Once he was released from his bed, this intense love of art naturally led to him drawing and painting for himself, concentrating especially on historical themes. Meanwhile, he was reading, devouring with rare precocity the great literature of the English language. Receiving a copy of Milton's *Paradise Lost* as a Christmas present in his thirteenth year, he swung 'almost violently' from art to literature.

> That morning I had the greatest poetic experience of my life. If it was the reading of Spenser that made a poet of Keats, it was that apocalypse of Miltonic sublimity that made of me, from that day onwards, if not a poet yet at least a modest practitioner of the art of verse.[456]

He immediately began an epic of his own, the first of many poems he has written at every period of his life. He 'read, admired, and imitated' many other poets, though for many years Milton and Dante Gabriel Rossetti were his favourites. Prose, too, was not neglected: he wrote some short stories and articles—and a life of the Buddha.

Although one or two teachers gave him some guidance and encouragement, his education was largely his own. He relied on public libraries as his principal source of material—although he also began to haunt the second-hand bookshops and soon amassed a considerable library. He worked steadily through the classics of literature and philosophy, finding his own way across the highways and byways of European culture. By the time he was fifteen he was reading very diversely: Plato and Dr Johnson, Aeschylus and Sir Thomas Browne, Diderot and Ariosto. He kept a record of his reading in thick ledgers, which he filled also with passages that had particularly struck him and with his own comments upon each work. At this point it occurred to him that he need not confine himself to the literature of Europe.

> From that day there grew upon me the conviction, afterwards immovably implanted in the centre of my consciousness, that

regionalism or nationalism in literature or art, philosophy or religion, is
an anachronism.... The true citizen of the world should aim at a broad
acquaintance with all that is best in the whole cultural and spiritual
heritage of mankind.[457]

He launched himself upon the classics of the East. He was led to Madame
Blavatsky's *Isis Unveiled* and the discovery that he was not a Christian—
which in turn led to the *Diamond Sūtra* and the *Sūtra of Hui-neng* and the
discovery that he was a Buddhist. Here art borders on religion; and we
need pursue that progression no further since we have already followed
it to the present day.

While his interest in Buddhism was developing, he did not neglect art.
He continued to write poetry and, in his eighteenth year, he completed a
novel—apparently rather in the style of D.H. Lawrence and unfortunately now lost. At this time music became 'an addiction'.

Bach's *Toccata and Fugue in D Minor*, which seemingly explores the
heights and depths of the universe, occupied in my experience of music
a place analogous to that of *Paradise Lost* in my experience of poetry.
Stunned, overwhelmed, annihilated by those majestic chords, I went
about for several days in a kind of waking trance.[458]

Drama too received his devotions and, under the tutelage of his section
head at the London County Council where he worked, he sampled the
theatres of wartime London.

The army restricted his cultural activities somewhat, although he never
ceased to write poetry and to read widely. In India, Sri Lanka, and
Singapore, he had the opportunity to become acquainted with new
cultures. No doubt very unusually for a British soldier in the East, he
made friends among the peoples of those countries. Indeed, his memoirs
shows him to have a rare capacity to connect with people from all sorts
of backgrounds in all sorts of situations. When he finally discharged
himself from the army he began, consciously and deliberately, to discard
his European identity. He dressed in Indian style, cooked and ate Indian
food, and followed Indian customs in daily life. He learnt to speak Hindi,
and later Nepali. For some eighteen years, Sangharakshita cut himself off
from his Western background, meeting few Westerners. He did not,
however, cut himself off from Western culture in the narrower sense of
its literature and thought, and he continued to read extensively and to
write in English.

Whether he should write poetry at all, however, became a pressing
question as he devoted himself ever more deeply to the Buddhist life. The
period of his stay with Bhikkhu Jagdish Kashyap, in 1949, at the latter's
*vihara* in the Benares Hindu University, brought out into the open what

he later described as 'a conflict in my interests, perhaps a conflict in my nature itself'.[459] It was, he says, a conflict between Sangharakshita I and Sangharakshita II:

> Sangharakshita I wanted to enjoy the beauties of nature, to read and to write poetry, to listen to music, to look at paintings and sculpture, to experience emotion, to lie in bed and dream, to see places, to meet people. Sangharakshita II wanted to realize the truth, to read and write philosophy, to observe the precepts, to get up early and meditate, to mortify the flesh, to fast and pray.[460]

Now one would be victorious and now the other. During his wanderings in South India, Sangharakshita II had been supreme. Indeed, he had almost entirely suppressed his counterpart, believing that poetry and art were obstacles on the path to liberation. Now Sangharakshita I demanded an equal place. The struggle grew more intense—at one point, under the influence of Sangharakshita II, he even burned all the poems he had written since his arrival in India.

Resolution finally came shortly after he had settled in Kalimpong. He had started tutorial classes in English Literature for members of the Young Men's Buddhist Association of Kalimpong. Having dictated the paraphrases of poems that they required for examination purposes, he would begin to explore the verses in greater depth, trying

> to communicate to them something of the real meaning of the poem as the expression of an intense emotional and intellectual experience—an experience that was of universal significance and value.... One day, when the class was particularly attentive, and I was feeling more than usually inspired, I was explaining the last verse of Shelley's 'The Cloud', and discovering in it greater and greater depths of meaning, when suddenly I realized *I was teaching the students Buddhism*. It was not that I had forgotten about the poem I was supposed to be explaining, and had unconsciously slipped into teaching Buddhism instead. In explaining the poem I *was* teaching Buddhism. This could only mean that at a certain level of experience poetry and Buddhism—poetry and the Dharma—were the same thing. There was a sense in which Beauty *was* Truth, and Truth Beauty, and even if this was *not* all that I needed to know on earth it had at least become clear to me that my interest in poetry was not incompatible with the spiritual life, as I had sometimes felt, or had been made to feel, but that the two things were complementary aspects of the same process of higher human development.[461]

In this way the conflict between Sangharakshita I and Sangharakshita II was largely resolved: witnessing the birth, perhaps, of Sangharakshita III, who united 'beauty and truth, poetry and philosophy, spontaneity and discipline'.[462] Art, or at least an aspect of art, has the same goal as true religion. Sangharakshita gave expression to this insight in several articles, written from this time on, outlining what he called the 'religion of art'.[463]

Important reinforcement of this resolution came from his first meeting with Lama Govinda, a well-known German scholar and writer on Buddhism. Lama Govinda not only had an understanding of the nature of the Dharma that came close to Sangharakshita's own, but he was also an artist: he was both a poet and a painter of no small repute. The convergence between them went deeper still.

> For him as for me the painting of pictures and the writing of poems was an integral part of the spiritual life itself. The relation between Buddhism and the spiritual life, on the one hand, and literature and the fine arts, on the other, was not, therefore, one that was merely external, as between different material objects. On the contrary, there was a deep inner connection between them. For this reason there could be no question of the cultivation of literature and the fine arts being inconsistent with the practice of Buddhism and the living of the spiritual life, as I had for a time supposed (or had been led to suppose), much less still of the one being actually inimical to the other.[464]

Because of his long study of Tibetan Buddhist art in its many forms, Lama Govinda had, at that time, a much clearer understanding of this crucial truth. He had especially a profound appreciation of the relation between art and meditation.

With few others was Sangharakshita able to share his realisation of the deep inner connection between art and spiritual life. Nonetheless, he freely explored that connection for himself. He continued writing poetry, as well as a few short stories. Limited though he was by his meagre finances and the availability in India of books in English, he read as widely as he could. He had little contact with Western visual arts and none with Western classical music—indeed, little either with their Indian counterparts. Visual beauty was, however, certainly not lacking from his life. Kalimpong, facing the dazzling snow-peaks of the Himalayas to the north, is an exceptionally beautiful place.

> I was deeply affected by my surroundings. They stimulated and inspired me.... I was inspired by the bamboos and the orchids, by the haze-softened foothills, gashed red here and there by the landslides, by the changing cloud formations, by the breadth and blueness of the sky. Above all I was inspired by the snows.[465]

No doubt exploration of the visionary world of Tibetan Buddhist art also fed his aesthetic sense, as he came to know it more deeply. It went, of course, much further than that. Here was an art that directly served a spiritual purpose. Indeed, the images, symbols, and myths depicted in

Tibetan Buddhist art made an enormous impact on Sangharakshita, as he gradually came into deeper and deeper contact with them. When he first saw a colossal statue of Padmasambhava, or Guru Rimpoche, perhaps the most important figure in Tibetan Buddhism, he became 'conscious of a spiritual presence that had in fact been with me all the time'.

> Though I had never seen the figure of Padmasambhava before, it was familiar to me in a way that no other figure on earth was familiar: familiar and fascinating. It was familiar as my own self, yet at the same time infinitely mysterious, infinitely wonderful, and infinitely inspiring. Familiar, mysterious, wonderful, and inspiring it was to remain. Indeed, from then on the figure of the Precious Guru—Guru Rimpoche—was to occupy a permanent place in my inner spiritual world.[466]

When he visited a Tibetan temple with Lama Govinda and his wife, Li Gotami, he heard for the first time the mantras of Śākyamuni and Padmasambhava, which

> not only sounded strangely familiar but also set up reverberations that made themselves felt in the remotest corners of my being.[467]

Gradually, the immense spiritual riches of Tibetan Buddhism were opened to him as he came to know some of the leading lamas. From a few of these he took initiation and he meditated upon the archetypal Buddhas and Bodhisattvas to whom they had introduced him. As he says, from the point of receiving initiation his whole spiritual life was guided from that higher dimension embodied by these visionary figures.

Sangharakshita was extraordinarily fortunate to live in Kalimpong at this time. Already permeated by the influence of Tibetan culture, it became one of the main centres for Tibetan refugees as they fled the Chinese seizure of their country. He was able to watch one of the last completely traditional cultures in the world as it began to shatter before the onslaughts of communism and consumerism: twin aspects of the modern world. Like medieval Europe, Tibet was, practically until 1956, a culture in which religion permeated every aspect of human life. Although it had its corruptions and deficiencies, it was a very beautiful culture, which fully supported the following of the spiritual life. But it was doomed. Though it had much to offer the modern world by way of spiritual vitality and diversity of teachings, the Buddhist culture of old Tibet could not be sustained. Nor could it be bodily transplanted into a new and very different era.

The England to which Sangharakshita returned in 1964 was very different to the one he had left in 1944. It was Harold Wilson's England, in which burned what the Prime Minister called the 'white heat of technology'. Sangharakshita had to get used to tape-recorders and television sets, launderettes and supermarkets. He had to accustom himself to the greater affluence and the greater informality. For him the most significant aspect of his return was reconnecting with the culture that had led him to the Dharma. He could, for instance, participate in aspects of Western art he had been unable to pursue in India: he could again enjoy concerts, opera, theatre, and art galleries. He was able to discover the cinema, which till his return he had not realised could be an art-form. More significantly, he could reconnect with his deeper cultural roots. In 1966 he spent two months driving through Italy and Greece with a friend, visiting the places from which Western culture had sprung and in which its renaissance had taken place. This journey was very significant indeed for him. He had never been to continental Europe before and he now saw for the first time many of the paintings, sculptures, and buildings that he knew so well from the colour plates of Harmsworth's *Children's Encyclopaedia*. The catacombs at Rome made a powerful impression upon him, perhaps for their archetypal associations, and he was also particularly struck by the Byzantine mosaics of Ravenna and the archaic sculpture at Olympia. The trip was his real home-coming and proved a source of deep inspiration.

From the earliest days of the FWBO's foundation, Sangharakshita included the arts in its activities. In the first year or so, poetry readings were a frequent feature and he founded a drama group, reading some of W.B. Yeats's Noh-inspired plays. He has consistently encouraged the poets, painters, or sculptors among his disciples to continue with their work, and he takes a keen interest in the making of Buddha images and the design of shrines. More recently, arts centres and arts events have been established under his inspiration, in which the arts can be both enjoyed and pursued. He urges his Western students to study seriously their own higher culture, as much as they do traditional expressions of the Dharma. In these many ways he has tried to stimulate the development of a new Buddhist culture and to promote the religion of art. He has himself continued to write poetry down to the present—one of his most frequent modes of public communication, these days, being the reading of his own verse. He has continued to explore the arts in their many facets, throughout the very demanding years of the establishment of the new Buddhist movement.

Perhaps most importantly of all, he has evolved a body of teachings that provides a theoretical underpinning for the inclusion of culture in spiritual life. It is these ideas we will now examine. We must first look at Sangharakshita's view of the nature of the individual. Then we will explore the relationship between the Dharma and culture in the broadest sense. Finally, we will take up Sangharakshita's notion of the religion of art.

## THE PSYCHOLOGY OF SPIRITUAL LIFE

To understand the relationship between culture and spiritual life we must first have an understanding of the human psyche in all its depth and breadth—for culture touches on the innermost recesses of our being. However, we cannot understand the human psyche unless we understand the context in which it is set: before we can have an adequate psychology, we must have a comprehensive cosmology—for our understanding of the meaning of the individual is largely determined by our understanding of the nature of the universe. Here we come to one of modern Buddhism's central problems. From the time of the Buddha onwards, Buddhism has taken for granted a cosmology that includes many different dimensions of being and consciousness, existing parallel to one another and to some extent overlapping. Beings are born and reborn within these dimensions in accordance with their past deeds, under the principle of *karma*. Thus the earliest scriptures show the Buddha moving amid his human disciples, at the same time surrounded by beings belonging to other dimensions, angelic and also demonic. Though these beings are invisible to the fleshly eye, the Buddha and his more psychically gifted disciples could perceive and communicate with them. Some of them even became his disciples.

Here immediately is a clash of cultures. Western materialism, having chased away the angels and devils of Christianity and deconstructed its heaven and hell, cannot accept the existence of other planes of reality. Many modern Buddhists find traditional Buddhist beliefs in other worlds and other beings too much at odds with their own sceptical conditioning. At best, they reduce the gods and spirits to psychological allegories. At worst, they simply ignore them as primitive survivals that mar the rational purity of the teaching: sometimes translators have simply written them out of the scriptures. However, the opposite danger is just as prevalent. Some Western Buddhists, very literalistically, simply swallow whole one or other Eastern culture with all its cosmological and other beliefs, making no distinction between the basic teachings of Buddhism and the superstitions of that culture.

Sangharakshita favours neither reductionism nor literalism. Reductionism is widespread, particularly among scholars of Buddhism

—as well as rationalistic Western Buddhists. Many Westerners approaching Buddhism distinguish between the factual and mythic elements in the Buddha's biography, for instance.

> Now, this is all right so far as it goes, but most of them go a step further, and start indulging in value judgements, saying that only the historical facts—or what they consider the historical facts—are valuable and relevant. As for the myths and legends, all the poetry of the account, they usually see this as mere fiction, and therefore to be discarded as completely worthless.[468]

Sangharakshita considers this a grave error, since it limits Buddhism's appeal simply to the intellect. Buddhists who fall into this error fail to realise that it is not the intellect that moves us: below the surface of man's rational, conceptual mind are the 'vast unplumbed depths' of the non-rational, unconscious mind that is by far the larger part of his total psyche.

> In order to appeal to the whole man, it isn't enough to appeal just to the conscious, rational intelligence that floats upon the surface. We have to appeal to something more, and this means that we have to speak an entirely different language than the language of concepts, of abstract thought; we have to speak the language of images, of concrete form. If we want to reach this nonrational part of the human psyche, we have to use the language of poetry, of myth, of legend.[469]

Reductionism is not confined simply to the complete dismissal of the mythic elements. Some Buddhists and commentators on Buddhism assign the poetry, myth, and legend a definite but limited importance. Often under the influence of a superficial reading of Jungian analytical psychology, they 'interpret' the symbols and myths, thereby once more reducing them to level of the mundane intellect.

> There are lots of books about symbols written by all sorts of academics, but very often they don't seem to have much feeling. They're just academic compilations, explaining them away or pointing out parallels in other mythological systems. Really they are not talking about symbols at all. A symbol is something you respond to. First, an image appears— let's not even call it a symbol at this stage, because already you'd be introducing an element of intellectual interpretation. That image may mean something to you, strike a chord or set up a resonance in you. And that may set off all sorts of repercussions within you. Then it is a symbol for you.[470]

The literalist takes all the mythological details of one Eastern Buddhist culture or another as historically true: for instance, that the world is literally arranged around the cosmic mountain, Sumeru, or that chanting the mantra of Avalokiteśvara will literally save one from shipwreck and other disasters. This not only often clashes with the observable facts of everyday experience, but also perpetuates an unthinking and super-stitious state of mind, seeking security in simplistic certainties. Some-times people have rejected the credulity of their Christian background only to adopt what for them demands an even greater credulity—the superstitions of an alien culture.

To make clear the middle way between literalism and reductionism, Sangharakshita distinguishes two kinds of truth:

> There is what we call scientific truth, the truth of concepts, of reasoning;
> and in addition to this—some would even say, above this—there is what
> we may call poetic truth, or truth of the imagination, of the intuition.
> Both are at least equally important. The latter kind of truth is manifested,
> or revealed, in what we call myths and legends, as well as in works of
> art, in symbolic ritual, and also quite importantly in dreams.[471]

Reductionism accepts only scientific truth. The traditional cultures that the literalists accept so uncritically seldom clearly distinguish the two kinds of truth, often presenting mythic truth as factual. Furthermore, those traditional cultures contain not only mythic truth dressed as fact, but mere superstition, which is neither mythic truth nor scientific.

> There are some statements in traditional Buddhism which we can accept
> quite literally, others which it seems are meant to be taken
> metaphorically or symbolically, others which seem to be the result of
> popular belief and are just plain wrong. We have to try to sort out which
> is which.[472]

Modern Buddhists have a great deal of work to do, sifting through the nonhistorical material they have inherited from Eastern Buddhist tradi-tions. They must sort out what does actually represent the truth of imagination from what is simply the superstition of a particular culture.

Sangharakshita himself accepts the traditional teaching on rebirth and the 'existence' of other worlds with the beings who occupy them. These other worlds at least 'exist' in the sense that this world exists.

> The [different] realms are not to be regarded simply as representations or
> concretisations of subjective states experienced by human beings in this
> world. This world of human beings exists as a realm, the animal realm
> exists, the preta realm exists, the asura realm exists, the hell realm exists,
> and the worlds of the gods also exist. All exist in the same sense—so that
> if one is real or actual the others are real or actual: if one is not real or
> actual the others are not real or actual. The degree of reality, so to speak,
> that attaches to one attaches to all.[473]

This, of course, begs the much larger question of what one means by 'exist'. Here very important and complex philosophical issues are touched upon, issues that we will not now explore. Suffice it to say that existence and non-existence are, for Buddhism, both conceptual categories that do not correspond to any ultimate reality.

> Inasmuch as they arise in dependence on conditions phenomena can be described neither as existent nor as non-existent: they are *śūnya*, empty of self-nature.... Following the Middle Path in metaphysics consists [among other things] in understanding that reality is not to be expressed in terms of existence and non-existence.[474]

The important practical outcome of this metaphysical insight is that none of the various kinds of perceptual situation in which one can find oneself has existential priority over any other. Dreams, meditations, visions, and 'ordinary' waking experiences are all equally valid as perceptual situations. None of the different worlds or realms is any more or less real than any other. We cannot entirely reduce either our dreams or the realms of the gods to side-effects of waking experience. We must take each perceptual situation on its own terms—for one can go for Refuge—or even gain Enlightenment—in every situation.

Sangharakshita's assertion that each of these realms has the same degree of reality comes not only from his confidence in the Buddha and his understanding of his teaching, but from his own visionary experience. He describes, for instance, how he felt the presence of the 'Four Great Kings', guardians of the universe in the Indian Buddhist tradition, whilst he was preparing a series of lectures in which he touched on the cosmological function of the Four Kings.

> I didn't have the impression that my experience of them was purely subjective. I certainly had the impression that they did in some sense exist objectively, though obviously I can offer no proof of that. But that was certainly my feeling or my experience.[475]

He has had several similar experiences: for instance, on another occasion, he had a striking vision of *pretas* or hungry ghosts, a class of being who objectify a mental state of neurotic craving.

> Having finished my meditation, I opened my eyes to find myself surrounded by seven or eight tall black figures.... They were six or seven feet tall, naked, and as it were tubular in shape, being uniformly not more than ten or twelve inches wide. What was more remarkable still, each of the figures possessed a pair of enormous white saucer eyes, and with these eyes they were looking down at me. Their whole appearance and attitude, but particularly their eyes, were expressive of an indescribable mournfulness, of an infinite hopelessness and sadness such as I had never seen, and which I had never imagined could exist.[476]

After a while they simply disappeared. Again, the figures seemed to him entirely objective.

Sangharakshita thus accepts the basic Buddhist teaching that there are layers and dimensions within reality. Each layer or dimension has both a subjective and an objective pole: a consciousness and a world or realm. Consciousness and world are simply two aspects of a single dimension: consciousness corresponds to world, and world to consciousness. There are multiple worlds, 'existing' side by side, accessible to the consciousnesses that correspond to them and thereby take birth within them. These worlds are arranged hierarchically: each successive world is more refined and happy than the last, corresponding to the varying degrees of refinement of the consciousnesses of which they are the counterpart. Human consciousness is axial in the cosmological system. A human being is capable, within this life, of traversing the entire range of consciousness, temporarily entering all the different realms. Sometimes this 'psychic fluidity' appears apparently spontaneously; sometimes it will result from the systematic evolution of consciousness, particularly through meditation.

A psychology of spiritual life must therefore take into account the infinite possibilities inherent in consciousness. Effectively, different psychologies will be required for the lower states and for the higher. The lower realms in the Buddhist schema—the realms of demons, *pretas* or hungry ghosts, animals, and *asuras* or jealous gods—require a psychopathology. They are the objectifications of intensely painful states of mind: respectively, of hatred, craving, closed-minded ignorance, and envy. Essentially these are each extreme distortions of the self-awareness that characterises the human state. Human beings experience these states in milder forms—and it is these that modern human psychology is concerned with healing. Sangharakshita believes that help in unravelling the complex knots in many modern Westerners' psyches may be found in some current systems of psychology and psychotherapy. He is inclined to no particular psychological ideology and approaches such matters pragmatically. Several Order members have training in psychotherapy or psychology and Sangharakshita has encouraged them to use their skills to help people in the movement who cannot sort out their mental difficulties in any other way. However, he is very wary of the popularised psychology that is so common, especially among people involved with Buddhism.

> Over the last few years I've started getting really quite fed up with
> psychology. I'm not talking about psychology as a science, but this very
> subjective, self-psychoanalytic approach to the spiritual life itself,
> looking at it in a psychological way, using psychological terminology. It

seems to me more and more that the traditional approach is so much more effective and meaningful. I'd like to see less emphasis on a psychological approach and more on a truly Dharmic approach.[477]

He considers that many psychological problems have a spiritual root, in so far as the personality is constructed on an unwholesome basis: for instance, on some Christian beliefs such as original sin and eternal damnation. Apart from the most deeply buried mental problems, he is confident that most psychological difficulties can be resolved through spiritual practice within the positive context of the New Society. Deep friendship is, particularly, a powerful healer of psychological wounds.

However, the most significant aspect of the psychology of spiritual life concerns the higher possibilities of consciousness: those that lie beyond the human world, not below it as do the *duggati* or 'states of woe'. In traditional Buddhist cosmology, beyond the human realm stretch layer upon layer of ever more refined, subtle, and beautiful worlds. These are the heavens of the *devas* or gods, corresponding to the superconscious states experienced in meditation. Sangharakshita translates *rūpa-loka* and *arūpa-loka*, the Pali and Sanskrit collective words for these higher dimensions, as the worlds or planes of 'archetypal form' and of 'extremely subtle archetypal form'. These worlds are not experienced with the gross physical senses but with the subtle inner or visionary senses. The objects of these senses are similarly not gross physical objects but subtle archetypal images. These forms are archetypal in the sense that they pertain to a much deeper level of psychic functioning. Our minds normally operate at a quite superficial level, caught up with the sensuous appearances of things as objects existing independently of us. We relate to them in terms of the benefit or harm they may bring to us as ego-entities, missing the deeper patterns and structures that impart a far richer significance to our experience. In meditation we may enter upon the *rūpa-* or *arūpa-lokas* and experience the subtle archetypal forms that convey that deeper level of meaning.

Sangharakshita uses the term 'archetype' initially somewhat in the sense given it by C.G. Jung, the founder of Analytical Psychology. Jung discovered that many of his patients' dreams reproduced themes revealed in mythologies and religions throughout the world. He concluded that there are archetypes, basic psychic patterns common to all humanity, patterns that are expressed in the myths and religions of whole communities and in the dreams and creative works of individuals. The same archetype expresses itself in quite different forms through different cultures and individuals. For instance, the angel is the expression within the Christian tradition of an archetype represented in Buddhism by the images of the *deva* and the Bodhisattva. However, Sangharakshita carries the meaning of 'archetype' much further than does Jung.

> The Buddhist may well feel that the image of the Bodhisattva is the embodiment *par excellence* of the particular archetype in question. Indeed, he may feel that the archetype of which the Bodhisattva is the embodiment, and which the image of the Angel reflects in a different cultural context and on a lower spiritual level, is in fact nothing less that the Archetype of Enlightenment, as it may be termed, and as such immeasurably transcends the archetypes that were the subject of Jung's discoveries. This of course implies an enlargement of the meaning of the term 'archetype' far beyond the significance it possesses for any current system of psychology.[478]

In Sangharakshita's thinking, the archetypes ultimately exist on the transcendental level, only fully realised in Enlightenment. They express themselves on lower and lower levels within the planes of archetypal form, manifesting as the subtle sensuous experience of visions and some dreams. These visionary dimensions of archetypal experience are the worlds of the gods. The archetypes finally emerge within our world of sensuous experience as the myths and symbols of human cultures.

Although the different realms, planes, or worlds are spoken of as discrete from each other, they are all part of the same reality. Rather than being sharply differentiated from each other like steps in a staircase, they shade one into the other like the colours of a spectrum. All are latent within the individual consciousness. Indeed, in a sense, we exist on all those levels all the time. Sangharakshita explains this using the analogy of the dream state. Though we are usually largely unconscious of these other dimensions, nonetheless they are acting upon us, helping to shape our experience, just as last night's dream leaves a lingering impression that persists throughout the day.

> When we are in the dream state, we exist, one might say, in the dream realm. But what happens when we wake up? We are not conscious of the dream state, but has that dream state ceased to exist? Are not those emotions we experienced in the dream state continuing until we descend into that dream state again? Isn't it like a sort of subterranean river that we descend into from time to time through a hole in the ground? It is flowing there all the time [whether you are in it or not]. So, in a sense, you are all the time living in that dream realm. You've only got to extend that to the realm of archetypal experience. You are, in a sense, existing in the realm of archetypal reality all the time.[479]

While we are unconscious of these other dimensions acting upon us, we can only function in a divided way: reason split from emotion, conscious mind separated from unconscious. This is particularly evident in our spiritual lives: we often quite clearly know what we should do—but we cannot always bring ourselves to do it.

> We may say that we 'know' something, but we know it only with the conscious mind, with the rational part of ourselves. We know it theoretically, intellectually, abstractly. But we must recollect that man is not just his conscious mind. He is not all reason—though he may like to think he is. There is another part of us, a much larger part than we care to admit, which is no less important than our reason. This part is made up of instinct, of emotion, of volition, and is more unconscious than conscious. And this wider, deeper, and no less important part of ourselves is not touched at all by our rational or intellectual knowledge, but goes its own way, as it were dragging the mental part, still protesting, along with it.[480]

Although Sangharakshita emphasises the limitations of the rational mind, he insists that it is nonetheless very important to us as human beings. Reason is the basis for our civilised interaction with each other—and is an essential basis for that supra-rational *vipaśyanā* that carries us on to the transcendental path: we gain Insight by focusing attention upon the real nature of things, by means of one or other formulation of the teaching. Most people, Sangharakshita says rather ironically, have yet to develop a rational mind! However, the rational mind is not the whole of us and ultimately must be transcended by some more integral faculty.

Once we enter upon the archetypal planes—once we enter the *dhyānas*, to use the terminology of meditation—reason and emotion begin to unite. They are drawn together and transcended by the arising of a new and higher faculty.

> The conflict between head and heart, reason and emotion, conscious and unconscious mind, can be resolved only by the emergence of a higher faculty, wherein the light of reason and the warmth of emotion are not only fused but raised to the highest possible degree of intensity.[481]

The faculty that emerges is what Sangharakshita terms the 'imagination', borrowing from S.T. Coleridge, or the 'imaginal faculty'. This faculty is closely connected with *śraddhā*, usually translated as 'faith', that intuitive response to the ideal that leads one to set out on the path. Primarily, imagination is the faculty whereby we perceive the images through which the archetypes express themselves—here 'images' can be understood as the objects of any of the senses. The archetypes express themselves on different levels, corresponding to the different realms of the gods.

> This in turn implies a stratification, in the sense of an arrangement in a progressive, hierarchical order, of the faculty by which the images

themselves are perceived, or rather, a stratification of the successive
stages of its unfoldment or manifestation.[482]

Sangharakshita says that we should not take the term 'faculty' too
literally. Imagination is not one more faculty among others, like reason
or hearing. It merely appears as a faculty to us because in us it is in such
a rudimentary stage of development.

> The imaginal faculty is, in reality, the man himself, because when one
> truly perceives an image one perceives it with the whole of oneself, or
> with one's whole being. When one truly perceives an image, therefore,
> one is transported to the world to which that image belongs and
> becomes, if only for the time being, an inhabitant of that world. In other
> words, truly to perceive an image means to become an image, so that
> when one speaks of the imagination, or the imaginal faculty, what one is
> really speaking of is *image perceiving image*.[483]

We are the imagination. Our spiritual life, from this point of view,
consists in awakening the imaginal faculty—or awakening to the
imaginal faculty. Sangharakshita says that part of the predicament of
modern man is that he has no word for this faculty. He does not know it
exists. He does not know that imagination is what he truly is. Identifying
it as a valid means of cognition is a first step to awakening it. Once we
have begun to awaken the faculty, we will begin to unify all our energies
within it—and will be able to live out our true meaning and purpose. By
uniting on higher and higher levels with the images by which the
archetypes express themselves, we will be led ultimately to perceive the
truth. At this point imagination becomes identical with *prajñā* or Wisdom.

> Imagination in the highest sense apprehends *śūnyatā* or truth in the
> highest sense, through the medium of form—that is to say beauty in the
> highest sense. It apprehends truth and beauty together.[484]

The metaphor of ascent through higher and higher levels—or, it could
as well be, descent into greater and greater depths—is not to be taken too
literally. Indeed, we must be careful not to take literally much that we
have explored and will explore in this chapter. Something is being
communicated that cannot be fully and adequately expressed in words—
or certainly not in words understood as communicating a 'scientific'
truth. If we do not understand this point we will severely misunderstand
some of Sangharakshita's ideas.

> People tend to think very literalistically and what I call linearly about
> individual development and spiritual life. It has to be made much more
> multidimensional and much less pinned down to specific definable
> ideas. It shouldn't be too graspable—one would be justified in becoming

suspicious if it became too graspable. In a sense, it shouldn't be too clear.[485]

In the end there cannot really be a full and adequate psychology of spiritual life—or of human life, in general—since consciousness cannot be reduced to concepts. Something about our human existence always goes beyond our intellectual understanding. Sangharakshita has explored various ideas concerning the nature of spiritual life—such as the idea of the imagination—without ever fully tying them into a complete system of thought. This is not accidental. These ideas are not meant to be explanations of a philosophical-cum-scientific kind. They are not metaphysics but rather poetic metaphors that express and illuminate an aspect of spiritual experience.

Sangharakshita sees that Buddhist philosophy generally is of two kinds. The first offers a rigorous rational critique of reason itself, demonstrating that truth cannot ultimately be conveyed in words and concepts. The Mādhyamaka system, stemming from the great Nāgārjuna, is the finest flowering of this branch of philosophy. This approach has the danger that, in destroying all intellectual structures, it leaves a subtle impression of negation: instead of perceiving that reality transcends all explanations, one feels that there is only a meaningless void. The other kind, represented particularly by the Yogācāra, attempts to communicate in words and concepts spiritual experiences that belong to a higher level. There is a problem with this approach too. All too easily, the words and concepts that have been used to form poetic metaphors are fitted into a metaphysical system and interpreted as describing and explaining the nature of reality. Any such description cannot but be false, since it limits and therefore distorts the fullness of things. Sangharakshita considers that one must use something of each approach, according to circumstances and need, being very aware of what it is that one is trying to do by using them.

In expounding his psychology of spiritual life, Sangharakshita uses another important cluster of metaphors to counteract a literalistically linear interpretation of spiritual development. Instead of thinking of ourselves as consciously driving our own ascent up a slope, we can think that something is unfolding itself through us.

> If one studies one's own life one may see not just a constant repetition of
> one particular pattern or one particular theme, but the unfolding of a
> certain meaning. It is as though one's whole life in its different stages
> constitutes a working out of that meaning.[486]

It is as though there is a seed or germ, existing on a higher and more subtle plane, whose attempt to grow and flower is the course of our lives. That seed could also be thought of as a pattern or blueprint that shapes the unfolding of our lives—just as an architect's blueprint shapes the construction of a building. Sangharakshita refers to this seed, pattern, or blueprint as the 'gestalt'. He uses the word gestalt here in his own special sense to mean a whole, existing outside time, that unfolds itself in time. He draws an analogy with the way Mozart composed music. Apparently he would 'hear' a complete piece as a whole in a single moment: he would then write out the music as a series of notes played one after the other in a linear temporal sequence.

> It is as though our gestalt is us, as we exist already completed, in a
> manner of speaking, outside time, and our life consists in living that out
> in time.[487]

This does not mean that every person's life is inevitably manifesting more and more of the gestalt. Sometimes factors, both internal and external, check its unfoldment or lead it to unfold itself in a distorted, crude, or unskilful manner. Nor does this metaphor imply a deterministic fatalism—that there is some force shaping our lives that we must simply fall in with.

Usually we are only vaguely aware of this unfolding pattern, perhaps only perceiving it to some extent as we look back over the years. In retrospect, our lives do not appear completely random: things have happened to us according to a pattern that we can dimly perceive. We find, for instance, that at a certain appropriate moment we came across a particular book, or met a particular person; and that encounter helped us to unfold our lives more fully. At the time we might not have really known why we read the book or why we were attracted to the person. But, without our being fully conscious of it, we were trying to express something in our lives. That book or person was what we needed to do so more effectively.

Sangharakshita speaks of the gestalt as 'the reflection of the *dharmakāya* in the individual'[488]—the *dharmakāya* being, briefly, the ultimate nature of things. As we have already seen, we exist on many levels, including, in a sense, the ultimate level. All those levels are acting upon us and influencing us on the level of ordinary, time-bound, human consciousness—though much of the time we can escape or distort their influence. Spiritual life consists in allowing that pattern, which is the reflection in us of the *dharmakāya*, to be the dominant power within our lives.

Sangharakshita has also spoken of this pattern as the 'personal myth'. Each of us exists on the higher, mythic dimension and has a spiritual or mythic history with which we are not usually in contact. 'We are spiritual beings, with a spiritual destiny.' Nonetheless, that myth does affect us, being the deepest theme and dynamic of our lives. We can live that myth out in a very limited and distorted way or we can live it out on the most sublime and exalted plane. Whether we can live out that personal myth more fully to some extent depends on external factors. If we live, for instance, in a rigidly materialistic setting, without higher cultural influence, we do not have the materials with which to work out that myth on a higher level.

Once more we see that the conditions that surround us are crucial in determining our spiritual development. What we need is a 'public myth' that gives the space and context for our personal myth to unfold more fully. The public myth does not replace or absorb the private myth. It provides the setting for its more adequate expression and for its alignment with the personal myths of others. Clearly it is the function of the New Society to provide such a public myth. The culture of the New Society is one that gives the developing individual all encouragement. In the New Society the private myths of individuals find the corresponding public myth that gives them the context and the freedom to reveal themselves more fully, on a deeper and more subtle level.

All this is, of course, open to much misunderstanding. Again, Sangharakshita warns that it is meant to be taken as poetic metaphor, not to be understood literally as science or metaphysics.

> I'm only trying to underline the point that you are trying to work out an ideal in your life or as your spiritual life. It's much more than a purely rational process. Much deeper forces and factors have to be involved to make it really meaningful and effective and for you really to get anywhere. More creative forces have to be involved.[489]

The metaphors of gestalt and myth arise out of his reflection on spiritual life and are ways of trying to communicate something of the nature of spiritual experience. Sangharakshita says that the course of his own life has 'been determined by impulse and intuition rather than by reason and logic'.[490] As we have quoted elsewhere, he understands even his own work of founding the Order and movement in these terms:

> There are times when I am dimly aware of a vast, overshadowing Consciousness that has, through me, founded the Order and set in motion our whole Movement.[491]

## A NEW BUDDHIST CULTURE

From the point of view of our present exploration, the function of culture within the New Society is to express the public myth within which the individual can work out his or her personal myth. Every artefact, action, and institution in that New Society is endowed with a deeper significance, so that all supports and encourages spiritual life. Every feature of life strikes resonances with the deeper levels of the individual's being. Spiritual life is not presented in a rational form alone, but through powerful images that really are symbols, echoing profoundly within the individual psyche, calling us to a higher destiny. This kind of culture is very difficult to imagine since our own Western culture is so far from it. Ours is probably the first truly secular culture, in which the spiritual order has very little public place. Perhaps every other civilisation has, to a greater or lesser extent, corresponded to what Sangharakshita, in an early work, termed 'Traditional', in which

> every branch of knowledge, and every kind of activity, is integrated with conceptions of a metaphysical order. Every aspect of life, even the lowest and most mundane, is given a transcendental orientation which enables it to function, in a general way, as a support, if not for the actual living of the spiritual life, then at least for a more or less constant awareness of the existence of spiritual values.[492]

Our modern civilization suffers from the 'progressive dissociation of more and more activities of life from the unifying and integrating dominance of Tradition'.[493] In particular, 'religion'—perhaps better, spiritual life—has become simply a department of life, which as a whole is overwhelmingly secular and materialistic. Western culture is breaking ever more decisively from its traditional roots and losing ever more rapidly a sense of a higher order of reality that permeates and unifies every aspect.

Western culture's break with 'Tradition' is manifest in its alienation from nature. Because of Christianity's historical hostility to the folk religions it replaced, Western man has lost a healthy 'pagan' relationship with the natural world. The early Church set out systematically to extirpate animistic beliefs and practices. Protestantism carried the process yet further—it is only in the Catholic Mediterranean countries that pagan features have survived to any significant extent. Science has completed the task of destruction. The loss of its pagan roots has grave consequences for Western civilisation: further evolution is dependent on a healthy and integrated self-awareness, not one cut off from the most basic forces of life. Though pagan religion represents a quite low level of human culture on the whole, Sangharakshita considers that for Buddhism to flourish in the West there must be something of a pagan revival. That revival is not, however, to be constituted by the self-conscious recreation of ancient rites, such as the neo-pagan 'Druids' perform annually at Stonehenge. To be truly pagan is to sense nature as peopled with living forces, animating every stream or tree or mountain. The pagan is not a mere romantic, however: paganism engenders a realistic but positive relationship with the forces of nature.

> So you've got to work at both ends: at the one end you've got to work at trying to be more and more of an individual, imbued with spiritual values, and at the other end you've got to work at being a happy and healthy pagan. Paganism is a good foundation for being a Buddhist.[494]

Western culture has lost the traditional integration of spiritual principles with ordinary life and is alienated from nature. It is broken in other senses too. It has been under the influence of a religion that Sangharakshita considers to be crude and degenerate in many ways.

> In fact it is not Western culture that is in a state of decay so much as Western religion. By this I do not mean that Christianity is in state of decay (though it may be, on its own terms), but rather that traditional Christianity is itself a state of decay.[495]

It is in the midst of that decay that Western Buddhists have to go for Refuge to the Buddha, Dharma, and Sangha.

Broken though the traditional culture of the West largely is, the New Society cannot be created simply by importing an Eastern Buddhist culture—since that Eastern culture will have very little appeal to the psychic depths of Westerners. We must therefore distinguish the essential principles of the Dharma from the cultural forms through which they are expressed. What can be brought from the East are those spiritual principles, not the manners and customs of oriental culture. Indeed, some features of traditional 'Buddhist' cultures will not conduce to Higher Evolution at all, whether in their own setting or any other: Sangharakshita cites the very high incidence of prostitution in Thailand, tacitly supported by the monks.[496]

> It is not enough simply to transplant Buddhism to this country. Buddhism must also become acclimatized here, and the Buddhism that will become acclimatized here is the Buddhism that is a matter of universally valid spiritual principles, not the 'exotic Buddhism' that is largely a matter of eastern 'Buddhist' culture and which attracts those who … hunger for the exotic.[497]

Western Buddhists have, as yet, effectively no culture of their own. They must therefore create one for themselves—a culture that will truly support the Higher Evolution of the individual. They must recognise, however, that it will probably take centuries for a distinctive new Western Buddhist culture to emerge. When it does so, it will probably have three main sources:

> It will be the product of (i) the interaction between Western Buddhists
> and the traditional Eastern Buddhist cultures, especially as represented
> by their literature and fine arts, (ii) the interaction between Western
> Buddhists and elements of Western folk and high culture (though not, I
> think, mass culture, now rapidly becoming worldwide), and (iii) the
> inspiration Western Buddhists derive from their personal experience of
> the Dharma, especially their experience of meditation.[498]

The new Buddhist culture 'will be the product of the interaction between Western Buddhists and the traditional Eastern Buddhist cultures,
especially as represented by their literature and fine arts'. While not
accepting oriental culture undigested, Western Buddhists cannot simply
cut themselves off from it and ignore it. Buddhism does come to them
from the East, mediated by the cultures of the East. They are going to be
'interacting' with those cultures to some extent and are bound to be
influenced by what is best and most beautiful in them. Western Buddhists
should not be troubled by this. Cultures have always influenced one
another: Sangharakshita often points out that Christianity is an oriental
religion and that European culture has absorbed from it many features
of ancient Jewish culture.

Further, that new Buddhist culture will be the product of 'the interaction between Western Buddhists and elements of Western folk and high
culture'. There are certainly many features of the high culture of the West
that could be of value to Buddhists.

> We shall have to establish, wherever possible, connections between
> Buddhist ideas and concepts of Western origin, as I have done in the case
> of the Buddhist idea of conditionality, mundane and transcendental, and
> the Western concept of evolution. We shall have to be able to recognize
> the Buddhistic nature of some of the insights of Western philosophers,
> poets, novelists, and dramatists.[499]

Indeed, he argues that modern education increasingly neglects the classics of our culture, so that those insights are becoming less accessible.
Furthermore, the traditional vocabulary of Western high culture is not
being learned. Since many people do not know the Greek myths or the
Bible stories that are the subject-matter of many works of art, they are cut
off from the greater part of what is valuable in their cultural heritage. He
strongly encourages his disciples to educate themselves in the best of
Western civilisation.

Sangharakshita has also done much to make links with elements in
Western culture that could be sources of Buddhistic insight and inspiration. Besides studying works of literature with various people, he has, for
instance, written articles on the Cathars and on William Blake. He has

been studying some of the 'alternative traditions' of Western civilisation, pointing out that Christianity is far from being the West's only religious tradition.

> Besides the traditions of classical antiquity, such as Mithraism, Gnosticism, Hermeticism, and Neoplatonism in its more religious aspect, there are Alchemy, Theosophy, Rosicrucianism, and Freemasonry. There are, in fact, all the various alternative traditions of the West which, after surviving 'underground' in an attenuated form, or being reconstituted from the remains that became available at the time of the Renaissance, have come to constitute an increasingly serious challenge to Christianity.[500]

Some features of these traditions may provide the Western Buddhist with sources of insight. Since he was fifteen, Sangharakshita has been studying Neoplatonism, which he considers to be

> the major spiritual tradition of the West, just as Buddhism is the major spiritual tradition of the East, and Buddhists can no more afford to ignore Neoplatonism than Neoplatonists (should there be any left) can afford to ignore Buddhism.[501]

Indeed, having read all the major surviving texts of Neoplatonism, he has come to the conclusion that

> such affinities as exist between Buddhism and the religious traditions of the West are to be found in Neoplatonism rather than in Christianity.[502]

He has long projected a paper on the subject of Buddhism and Neoplatonism, but yet feels he has more study and more thinking to do.

At times, Buddhists may even find themselves drawn to works of art depicting Christian images, for instance certain Italian Renaissance paintings of angels or saints. This will be the case where those images

> are Christian images only in the sense that in them an archetype which is of universal significance and value has been clothed in a Christian, Italian, Renaissance form—even in a form peculiar to a particular artist.... What the Buddhist is drawn to is not so much the Christian form of the image as the archetype of which that image is the embodiment.[503]

Sangharakshita has made this point clear in an exploration of the image of St Jerome in his cave—an image to which he found himself particularly attracted when he saw it represented in a number of paintings on his first visit to Italy in 1966. After examining all the elements of the image, he avers that it depicts

> man as a spiritual being who, in the shadow of time and death, strives to fathom the mystery of existence.[504]

Sangharakshita predicts that the final source of the Western Buddhist culture of the future will be 'the inspiration Western Buddhists derive from their personal experience of the Dharma, especially their experience of meditation'. Personal experience of the Dharma means a direct glimpse of its truths, not as intellectual postulates but as immediate intuition. It is a direct meeting of the individual imagination with reality, unmediated by concepts. As the Dharma impresses itself upon the psyches of Westerners they will begin to express the Dharma in all their activity. Their words and deeds, inspired by the Dharma, will contribute to a Western Buddhist culture.

That meeting with the Dharma is the purpose of the Buddhist life, but it is not at all easy to achieve. Between the archetype of Enlightenment and our present experience is a vast gulf. This is the principal work of spiritual life: bringing our total being up to the level of our highest aspiration, bringing all the uncharted depths of the non-rational mind behind our spiritual quest, finding 'emotional equivalents for our intellectual understanding'.[505] We have to proceed by small stages.

> We have to establish all sorts of intermediate links from the things that
> we actually do *feel*, however crude they may be, to more refined things,
> which eventually link up with the archetypal, or the ideal, and make it
> more real to us.[506]

This means finding intermediaries to which we can respond: for instance, poetry or classical music that might lead us to the yet more refined inner experiences of meditation. It requires us to build up associations with the ideal in terms of our own personal experience. We must find links within our own culture that can draw our feelings upwards towards the Dharma itself. We must engage our imaginal faculties with images that lead us upwards towards the archetypal realms.

A Western Buddhist culture will emerge as Western Buddhists cultivate their imaginal faculties so that they experience the archetypes on ever more sublime levels. They will experience the archetypes that, by their very nature, transcend time and place; but they will experience those archetypes as expressed in images that are particular to them—and to their culture. Although this work will take place in all aspects of the Buddhist's life, it will be pursued particularly in meditation. It will be in meditation that aspiration and present experience will be united in the uplifted imagination. Thus it will especially be the experience of meditation that will be a source of the new Buddhist culture. Those images perceived directly by the meditator will be painted or sculpted by the artist, described by the poet, hymned by the musician—and a new Buddhist culture will have come into being.

## THE RELIGION OF ART

A new Western Buddhist culture will then have, as one of its sources, 'the interaction between Western Buddhists and elements of Western folk and high culture'. As we have seen, Christianity itself will probably feature little in such an interaction: for so decayed has Christianity become, or such a state of decay *is* Christianity, that it has virtually ceased to have any real spiritual vitality.

> So much is this the case that for the last few hundred years it is secular literature, secular art, secular music, and secular philosophy that have been the principal bearers of spiritual values in the West, not religion, even though the old Christian forms and symbols have continued to be made use of to some extent.[507]

High culture can, it seems, be a medium for spiritual values: 'art and religion overlap'. This is an important point for Western Buddhists, for they may discover in art a source of spiritual nourishment. In addition, they may find a point of contact with those who, while having no time for religion because of their experience of Christianity, may be attracted to spiritual values as expressed in art.

> It might be possible, by developing the implications of that part of art which is also a province of religion, to promote a way of life dedicated to the realization of values in a manner attractive to those who are only repelled when it is presented to them from a formally religious point of view. It might even be possible to inaugurate for such people a Religion of Art.[508]

From the outset it should be clear that, in talking about a religion of art, Sangharakshita is not referring to that refined sensualism represented, for instance, by the Aesthetic Movement of the late nineteenth century— to those who regard 'works of art as an amusement' or employ them 'merely as a means of egoistic pleasure'.

> The Religion of Art, on the contrary, views the creation and enjoyment of paintings, musical compositions, and poems as primarily a means of liberation from the egoistic life and looks upon Beauty as one of the three great initiators into the mysteries of the life of egolessness.[509]

The Religion of Art has as its aim the goal of all true religion: the transcending of self in the experience of egolessness. There are three principal routes to that end: through Truth, Goodness, or Beauty—the philosophic, ethical, or aesthetic lives. The Religion of Art approaches egolessness through the 'gate which is called Beautiful'.

This aspect of spiritual life in general, and Buddhism in particular, is not often brought out. Indeed, some have argued that Buddhism eschews the appreciation of beauty altogether—citing such meditation practices as the *aśubha-bhāvanā*, 'the cultivation of [the perception of] ugliness'. This technique does not, however, imply that everything is inherently ugly in an ordinary sense. It is intended as a specific antidote to a specific spiritual disease: excessive sensuous craving. It is prescribed therefore for those whose attachment to sense objects is so strong that they cannot enter the *dhyānas*. Their attention needs to be drawn to the unattractive side of life, since they are so habitually inclined to see, and cling to, the attractive. Again some argue that Buddhism definitely rejects aesthetic appreciation since one of its basic insights is that all conditioned things are *aśubha*—impure or ugly. However,

> When Buddhism insists that all conditioned things are *aśubha*, it does not mean that we have to regard a flower, for instance, as essentially ugly, but only that in comparison with the beauties of a higher plane of reality those of a lower plane are insignificant.[510]

We will only be able to perceive conditioned things as *aśubha* when we have experienced the Unconditioned. Then we will really see the *śubha*, which is

> pure Beauty in the Platonic and Neoplatonic sense of something shining in a world of its own above and beyond concrete things, which are termed beautiful only so far as they participate in its perfection.[511]

From the realm of ordinary sensuous experience to that Absolute Beauty lies a whole hierarchy of aesthetic experience. Each higher level participates to a greater and greater extent in the perfection of Pure Beauty.

The Buddha clearly appreciated even the mundane beauty of the natural world, as Sangharakshita illustrates in *The Religion of Art* with quotations from the Pali Canon, and is seen encouraging the poetic gifts of his disciples.[512] Indeed, through the ages, Buddhism has inspired many very beautiful cultures of a very high level indeed. This is not adventitious. Truly to be influenced by the Dharma is to be ever more open to the influence of beauty. The true Buddhist's every word and action will express beauty and he or she will be inspired to embody beauty through creative activity. Furthermore, neglect of this side of life cannot but lead to spiritual stagnation, since there is nothing for the higher emotions to respond to. Sangharakshita considers that the failure to appreciate the aesthetic and emotional sides of Buddhism is one of the major reasons for the 'spiritually moribund condition of most parts of the Theravāda Buddhist world today'.[513]

The Religion of Art is the ascent, by means of artistic creation and appreciation, of the hierarchy of beauty until that Pure Beauty of the Unconditioned is experienced—that experience being identical with the experience of egolessness, by whichever of the three great routes it is approached. However, not all that goes by the name of art is part of the Religion of Art.

> Much conventionally religious art, particularly Christian art, is not religious art in the sense that we have defined the term because it not only fails to induce the experience of egolessness, but even positively strengthens the ego-sense.[514]

Sangharakshita distinguishes between conventional religion and essential religion: conventional religion being religious in form but not in content, essential religion being that which conduces to egolessness. Art too can be distinguished in the same way: there is art that strengthens and art that weakens the ego-sense. We can then discern four categories of art: (i) that which is conventionally religious, in the sense that it depicts the images of a particular religion, and at the same time is itself truly religious in that it leads towards the experience of egolessness; (ii) that which is not conventionally religious yet leads towards egolessness; (iii) that which is conventionally religious but does not lead towards egolessness; (iv) and that which is neither conventionally religious nor leads towards egolessness. In speaking of the Religion of Art, Sangharakshita is primarily concerned with the second type of art: art that has no religious content but is nonetheless essentially religious, in that it leads to the goal of all true religion.

Art is concerned with outlines, colours, masses, words, and sounds, which the artist 'subdues and adapts to his creative purpose'.

> These sensuously given elements the painter, sculptor, poet, and musician organize into formal relations which, by some mysterious resonance of the human spirit, are capable of imparting a pleasure more intense and rare than that given by sensuous experiences which have not been so organized.[515]

But art is not simply a means to pleasure. It is also communication. Art communicates to his audience values the artist has himself already attained. Members of the audience

> are first of all startled into an enhanced awareness of life by the impact of a sensibility infinitely more refined and powerful than their own, and then confronted with the terrible necessity of renouncing their old self and transforming it into a new personality by the assimilation of a wholly unfamiliar experience.[516]

Thus Sangharakshita arrives at a definition of art:

> Art is the organization of sensuous impressions into pleasurable formal relations that express the artist's sensibility and communicate to his audience a sense of values that can transform their lives.[517]

The transformation that takes place is in the direction of egolessness. To understand this better we must explore a little what egolessness means. The Buddha's insight into the nature of reality showed him that all things arise in dependence on conditions. He saw reality as one vast process of becoming, with no fixed and isolated entities, immune from the law of change. There are no substances that stand behind the accidents of experience. In particular, there is no unchanging soul. Behind the flow of bodily and mental events, there is no fixed self or ego, separate from everything else and capable of ordering our lives independent of conditions. Human individuality too is a flow of conditions, physical and mental. Egolessness is not the loss of ego: it is the acceptance of the principle of conditioned co-production and therefore the realisation of the limitations of clinging to the ego. The realisation of egolessness brings with it the dropping of all barriers and an awareness of identity with all things. No longer will one be defending one's fragile sense of identity against the threat of new experience.

> Selfishness is simply unwillingness to face new experiences. A radically
> new experience which we cannot weave into the pattern of our life
> demands the changing of the pattern and the working out of a fresh
> design in which it can form a part. The ego resists the onrush of new
> experiences because of the changes they involve; for a change in
> experience means a modification of existence; and though, in relation to
> the new life, such a modification is a birth, in relation to the old life, to
> the ego, it is in fact a death. Unselfishness, on the other hand, is an
> openness to new experiences, a willingness to die for the sake of being
> born anew.[518]

The artist possesses from his birth an extraordinary capacity to face new experience—new, not in the sense of not being previously experienced by him, but 'the absolute newness of a symphony by Beethoven or a sonnet by Keats'.[519]

> 'New' is not necessarily the opposite of 'old'. It can also indicate that
> which does not really belong to the temporal order and which is,
> therefore, neither old nor new. Thus it is possible to distinguish between
> the vertically new and the horizontally new, as we may term them, the
> vertically new being that which has no connection with time but which
> irrupts into, or manifests within, the temporal process, from another
> dimension, while the horizontally new is simply that which is
> unprecedented in time.[520]

The artist plunges again and again beyond his own limits of experience, exploring ever wider horizons. In particular, those horizons are the horizons of beauty. By this means he approaches closer and closer to egolessness.

> The Religion of Art may therefore be defined as conscious surrender to
> the Beautiful, especially as manifested in poetry, music, and the visual

arts, as a means of breaking up established egocentric patterns of
behaviour and protracting one's experience along the line of egolessness
into the starry depths of Reality.[521]

In so far as the artist is developing in egolessness, he also becomes more
moral. He has learnt to go out of himself into the lives of others and
therefore cannot harm them. The conventional image of the artist as
immoral arises for three reasons. Firstly, many immoral 'artists' are not
artists in the sense comprehended in Sangharakshita's definition of the
religion of art—they are producing art that is either conventionally
religious without being essentially so, or else neither conventionally nor
essentially religious. Moreover,

> Unlike the religious ascesis of the Buddhist devotee, the aesthetic ascesis
> of even the truest artist is rarely a conscious process, so that a fall from
> egolessness, and the consequent performance of an immoral action, is
> more to be expected of him than his fellow-pilgrim on the parallel path
> of goodness.[522]

Finally, true artists may appear immoral but only because they often
'substitute a finer morality of their own for the grosser moralities of the
crowd'.[523]

The Religion of Art has not only its active but its passive votaries. The
art-lover too is led towards egolessness by his or her appreciation of
works of art. That appreciation will have practical consequences. Art-
lovers will learn to distinguish good art from bad and will banish all bad
art from their surroundings—as much as they would cease from immoral
behaviour. They will make their houses beautiful inside and out and will
do what they can to beautify their neighbourhoods. Incidentally, Sangharakshita comments that one of the duties of the state is to provide a
beautiful environment for its citizens—and this reminds us that the New
Society will be beautiful. Finally art-lovers will take as much opportunity
as they can to experience the beauties of nature. Those who are affected
at all deeply by art will be compelled to create for themselves. They will
of course express their aesthetic sensibility in the details of ordinary life,
but they will also begin to paint or write or compose for themselves. Thus,
however inferior their works may be, they will begin to experience to an
even greater extent the breaking down of the ego through the Religion of
Art.

The immediate benefits of the Religion of Art, both for the artist and
the art lover, consist

> in the broadening of their sympathies, in the enrichment and refinement
> of their experience, and in the uplifting of their transformed personality
> to new heights of being.[524]

The function of art is to stretch the mind beyond its usual rigid bound-aries. Since the experience of art is bound up with the experience of pleasure, it is, for many, a far more enticing route to egolessness than that of morality or even philosophy: 'A single smile of Beauty can bring about greater transformations of character than all the frowns of Righteousness'.[525]

Art also has a social benefit. It engages the emotions, refining them and directing them to a higher level. If those emotions are not engaged and refined they will seek some cruder outlet: often in uncontrolled lust and in violence. Much violence and delinquency among young people, Sangharakshita argues, has its roots in a lack of satisfying emotional outlets. It is certainly one responsibility of education to educate the emotions so that they have healthy and creative means of expression.

> Not the smallest part of the value of the Religion of Art is that it restores
> our individual and social life to order by giving work to our
> unemployed affections, transforming them from not only lazy and
> yawning, but positively dangerous, drones into 'singing masons
> building roofs of gold'—the million-tiled golden roofs of the Temple of
> Beauty.[526]

Sangharakshita argues that art has a vital part to play in man's spiritual future.

> Despite its present undeveloped condition the Religion of Art is
> peculiarly fitted to produce, in these troublous days, a kind of character,
> a type of spiritual personality, which will be the living embodiment of
> the fact that Religion and Art are in essence one, and that Beauty is not
> merely Truth, but Goodness as well.[527]

In the increasing emotional sterility of modern times, the spiritual life needs a new and stronger stimulus. The realms of imagination are no longer represented to us in the details of daily life. We have no public myth that can encourage us to live out our personal myth. Art appeals directly to the deeper emotions, it appeals to the imagination, to the mythic. It deals in the stuff of our own culture and the stuff of our own psyches. Through art, as well as through meditation and other aspects of spiritual life, we can breathe back life into the broken images of Western civilisation—which are also the broken images of our own imaginations.

The comprehensiveness of Sangharakshita's vision is, perhaps, shown nowhere more strikingly than in his understanding of the place of art and culture in spiritual life. Sangharakshita's thinking is dazzlingly lucid and he has presented the Buddhist teaching with great penetration and insight. But it is not enough to be clear, one must be moved. He sees that spiritual life, and the future of Buddhism in the West, depends upon a revival of the imagination and a reconnection with our inner mythic roots. Only then will we have the power to translate clear teachings into the renewal of ourselves and of our world.

*Chapter Eleven*

# A NEW VOICE

WE HAVE NOW EXPLORED SANGHARAKSHITA'S leading ideas, as communicated in his writings and in his lectures and seminars. There is however a crucial dimension to his thinking that we have not explored in much detail: that which is embodied in the new Buddhist movement he has created. The movement itself is as much a communication of his ideas as his books, lectures, or seminars.

> Instead of only embodying my ideas in abstract form in a book, I have been able to embody them in concrete form, to some extent, in a living movement—which I think actually is better. The movement is the continuation of my thoughts as they began in *A Survey of Buddhism* and *The Three Jewels*. It's not enough to look at the things I've written since then, one has to look at the FWBO if one wants to see what I really think or feel about things in any way.[528]

Indeed, if one wants to get to know Sangharakshita more deeply one must get to know the movement he has founded.

> I don't make a hard and fast distinction between myself and the movement, because the movement is an extension of me or an embodiment of some part of me—though only in a sense, of course: I do not mean that the movement belongs to me or anything like that. I feel that whatever is done for the movement, for instance, is in a sense done for me.[529]

Sangharakshita's role as the founder of a new Buddhist movement makes it hard finally to assess him and his thinking. The founder of a new movement is making a bid for history. He intends his work to affect future generations. In a sense only history will be able to judge him. Not only that, but as the founder of a new movement he is perforce a curiously ambiguous character, since he belongs neither to the old Buddhist world in which he began his career nor in the new Buddhist world he has attempted to create. Sangharakshita himself is very conscious of his ambiguity.

> I don't fully belong to the old dispensation, and I don't fully belong to the new: I am half way between—I form a sort of bridge. So I'm in a more difficult position than both those who follow the old dispensation and those who follow the new dispensation. Those who follow the new dispensation, by being part of the Order or the FWBO, are in the fortunate position of having got the principles of spiritual life right from the very beginning, whereas I had to work things out for myself. I have to hover uneasily between the two: there is no alternative, that is just my *karma*, good, bad, or indifferent—that is just part of my history. In some ways my position is ambiguous, especially in the eyes of Buddhists outside our movement. I quite understand that. I can't blame them for regarding my position as ambiguous, because I started off as something they could recognise, and I seem to have changed into something they can't quite recognise.[530]

If Sangharakshita is to be assessed it is as a transitional figure who has attempted the renewal of the Buddhist tradition. His claim is to have discerned the unity of Buddhism in basic principles that can be recognised most clearly especially in the Buddha's own historical teachings. He has communicated those essential principles principally by creating a new Buddhist movement that draws on the entire Buddhist tradition. That movement is the response of those principles to the radically new conditions of the modern world—conditions that affect the Eastern world now as much as they do the Western. Those new conditions have demanded a new beginning—and it is a new beginning that Sangharakshita has created, certainly for his own disciples, perhaps for many other Buddhists too, who may draw on his insights without ever directly joining his movement. Surely his thought and his action will have a profound influence on the future of Buddhism.

Sangharakshita has, throughout his life as a Buddhist, striven to bring about the renewal of Buddhism throughout the world, both in its old heartlands and in the new world of the West. He has founded an Order and a movement. He has taught the Dharma through many different media. He has given himself continuously to many people, both on the public platform and in intense personal communication. Still he strives to communicate his vision of the true individual in the New Society. That is the whole meaning and purpose of his life. The work is never finished and he is continuously unfolding his vision more fully. This introduction to his life and thought can only show a glimpse of what he has already achieved: it cannot hope to hint at what is to come.

Though he has communicated so much and so effectively, he has much more to say. However, he feels keenly the inadequacy of the media he has so far used to convey truths that belong to a dimension beyond ordinary intellectual understanding. He would like to find a new medium of communication altogether through which to speak of new things—new in the sense of vertically new: 'that which has no connection with time but which irrupts into, or manifests within, the temporal process'.[531] In the future, perhaps he will speak to us with a new voice.

*I should like to speak*
*With a new voice, speak*
*Like Adam in the Garden, speak*
*Like the Rishis of old, announcing*
*In strong jubilant voices the Sun*
*Moon Stars Dawn Winds Fire*
*Storm and above all the god-given*
*Intoxicating ecstatic*
*Soma, speak*
*Like divine men celebrating*
*The divine cosmos with divine names.*
*I should like to speak*
*With a new voice, telling*
*The new things that I know, chanting*
*In incomparable rhythms*
*New things to new men, singing*
*The new horizon, the new vision*
*The new dawn, the new day.*
*I should like to use*
*New words, use*
*Words pristine, primeval, words*
*Pure and bright as snow-crystals, words*
*Resonant, expressive, creative,*
*Such as, breathed to music, built Ilion.*
*(The old words*
*Are too tired soiled stale lifeless.)*
*New words*
*Come to me from the stars*
*From your eyes from*

*Space*
*New words vibrant, radiant, able to utter*
*The new me, able*
*To build for new*
*Men a new world.*[532]

Let us hope that we can hear him.

# References

1  *Peace is a Fire*, p.99.
2  *The Enchanted Heart*, p.v.

## Chapter One

3  'Stanzas' 1967, from *The Enchanted Heart*, p.103.
4  *My Relation to the Order*, p.22.
5  Ibid., pp.26–7.
6  *The History of My Going for Refuge*, pp.18–9.

## Chapter Two

7   From 'The Buddha' 1961, *The Enchanted Heart*, p.97.
8   *Learning to Walk*, p.118.
9   D.P. Lingwood, 'The Unity of Buddhism', *The Middle Way*, May–June 1944, p.4.
10  *Learning to Walk*, p.68
11  Ibid., p.91.
12  Ibid., p.103.
13  'My Life and Mission, and the Teaching of Dr Ambedkar', *Dhammamegha* no.17, p.4.
14  *The History of My Going for Refuge*, p.71.
15  Triyana Vardhana Vihara, Kalimpong, *Report, 2501–2506BE (1957–1962)*, p.4.
16  Ibid., p.30.
17  *A Survey of Buddhism*, p.5.
18  *Majjhima-Nikāya* I.135, trans. F.L.Woodward (amended) from *Some Sayings* of the Buddha, Buddhist Society, London 1973, p.212.
19  *A Survey of Buddhism*, p.229.
20  *Vinaya* ii, 258, trans. F.L. Woodward (amended) in *Some Sayings of the* Buddha, op. cit., p.186.
21  *A Survey of Buddhism*, p.228.
22  From discussion at Aryaloka Retreat Center, USA, 1993.

23  From discussion on Sangharakshita's lectures, 'Creative Symbols of the Tantric Path to Enlightenment'.

24  Sangharakshita recommends Paul Williams, *Mahayana Buddhism*, Routledge, London and New York 1989, as bringing the historical details of *A Survey of Buddhism* up to date.

25  *A Survey of Buddhism*, p.206.

26  Ibid., pp.207–8.

27  Ibid., p.325.

28  From discussion on Sangharakshita's lectures on 'The Higher Evolution of Man'.

29  Ibid.

30  Ibid.

31  Ibid.

32  *Alternative Traditions*, p.124.

33  *Wisdom Beyond Words*, p.10.

34  *A Survey of Buddhism*, p.247.

35  From discussion on Sangharakshita's lectures on 'Creative Symbols of the Tantric Path to Enlightenment'.

36  *Wisdom Beyond Words*, p.104.

37  *A Survey of Buddhism*, p.327.

38  *Wisdom Beyond Words*, p.105.

39  From discussion at Aryaloka Retreat Center, 1993.

40  From a seminar on *The Precepts of the Gurus*.

41  *A Survey of Buddhism*, p.427.

42  From discussion at Aryaloka Retreat Center, 1993.

43  Ibid.

44  From discussion with Order members at the London Buddhist Centre, 1990.

45  From discussion at Aryaloka Retreat Center, 1993.

46  From discussion on Sangharakshita's lectures on 'Creative Symbols of the Tantric Path to Enlightenment'.

47  Ibid.

48  Ibid.

49  Ibid.

50  *A Survey of Buddhism*, p.276.

51  *The Meaning of Orthodoxy in Buddhism*, p.32.

52  Ibid., p.15.

53  *The FWBO and 'Protestant Buddhism'*, p.57.

54  *The Ten Pillars of Buddhism*, p.7.

55  *New Currents in Western Buddhism*, p.64.

56  Ibid., p.64.

57  The Islamic Foundation, Leicester 1980.

58  'The Nature of Buddhist Tolerance', in *Crossing the Stream*, p.170.

59  *The History of My Going for Refuge*, p.125.

60  Refer to taped lecture no.174: 'Sangharakshita on his Eight Main Teachers'.

61  See Vessantara, *A Guide to the Bodhisattvas*, Windhorse Publications, Cambridge 2008.

CHAPTER THREE

62 'Life is King' 1970, in *The Enchanted Heart*, p.115.

63 *The Buddhist*, Colombo, 1950; reprinted as 'Buddhism as Philosophy and as Religion', *Dhammamegha* no.9.

64 Ibid., p.3.

65 *Vinaya*, I.3–4, trans. Hermann Oldenburg, *Buddha*, p.120; also at *Majjhima-Nikāya*, I,167 etc.

66 *Majjhima-Nikāya*, II.32, *Saṁyutta-Nikāya*, II.28, etc.

67 *A Survey of Buddhism*, p.109.

68 Ibid., p.114.

69 Ibid., p.114.

70 Ibid., p.114.

71 Ibid., p.248.

72 Ibid., p.249.

73 For a fuller exposition of this important teaching see *A Survey of Buddhism*, pp.126–134; *The Three Jewels*, pp.76–8; also Alex Kennedy (Dharmachari Subhuti), *The Buddhist Vision*, Rider, London 1985, pp.80–112.

74 *Saṁyutta-Nikāya* ii.3.

75 *The Birth of Indian Psychology and its Development in Buddhism*, Oriental Reprint Books, Delhi 1978, p.354.

76 For Mrs Rhys Davids's comments see *The Book of the Kindred Sayings* Part II, Pali Text Society, London 1982, p.viii. For the positive *nidānas* see *Saṁyutta-Nikāya* ii, 30ff.; also *Aṅguttara-Nikāya* V, 1–6, 311–15.

77 Dr B.M. Barua, 'Buddhism as Personal Religion', *Maha Bodhi Journal* vol.52, p.62; and in *Ceylon Lectures*, Calcutta 1945.

78 *Cūḷavedalla Sutta*, *Majjhima-Nikāya* I, 299.

79 *A Survey of Buddhism*, p.141.

80 Ibid., p.109.

81 Ibid., p.336.

82 Ibid., p.336.

83 Ibid., p.161.

84 Ibid., p.336.

85 Ibid., p.336.

86 'Buddhism as Philosophy and as Religion', *Dhammamegha* no.9, p.14.

87 *Vision and Transformation*, p.36.

88 *Mind—Reactive and Creative*, p.3.

89 Ibid., p.7.

90 Ibid., p.7.

91 Ibid., p.8.

92 *A Survey of Buddhism*, p.92.

93 From discussion during the 1985 men's ordination course in Tuscany.

94 Ibid.

95 Ibid.

96 See *Udāna* I.i–x.

97 *The FWBO and 'Protestant Buddhism'*, p.184.

98  Vinaya-Piṭaka, *Mahāvagga* I, 5.10, trans. I.B. Horner (amended) from *The Book of the Discipline* vol.IV, Pali Text Society, London 1982, p.9.

99  From a seminar on *The Precepts of the Gurus*.

100  *The FWBO and 'Protestant Buddhism'*, p.182.

## CHAPTER FOUR

101  'Secret Wings' 1948, from *The Enchanted Heart*, p.16.

102  *The History of My Going for Refuge*, p.42.

103  *Facing Mount Kanchenjunga*, pp.370–1.

104  *A Guide to the Buddhist Path*, p.111.

105  Ibid., p.110.

106  *Dhammapada*, 188–9, trans. Sangharakshita.

107  *Dhammapada*, 190–2, trans. Sangharakshita.

108  *The Three Jewels*, p.x.

109  *Going for Refuge*, pp.11–12.

110  Ibid., p.13.

111  Ibid., p.13.

112  Ibid., p.13.

113  Ibid., pp.9–10.

114  Ibid., p.11.

115  *A Guide to the Buddhist Path*, p.111.

116  From discussion on Sangharakshita's lectures on 'Creative Symbols of the Tantric Path to Enlightenment'.

117  Ibid.

118  *The History of My Going for Refuge*, p.42.

119  *The Ten Pillars of Buddhism*, p.15.

120  *The History of My Going for Refuge*, p.99.

121  Ibid., p.99; *Going for Refuge*, pp.22–4.

122  *The History of My Going for Refuge*, p.101.

123  Ibid., p.101.

124  From discussion with Order members at the London Buddhist Centre, 1990.

125  From discussion on Sangharakshita's lectures on 'Creative Symbols of the Tantric Path to Enlightenment'.

126  Ibid.

127  From discussion during the 1982 men's ordination course in Tuscany.

128  From discussion on Sangharakshita's lectures on 'Creative Symbols of the Tantric Path to Enlightenment'.

129  *The History of My Going for Refuge*, p.104.

130  Ibid., p.104.

131  From discussion with Order members at the London Buddhist Centre, 1990.

132  *The History of My Going for Refuge*, pp.92–9.

133  *The Priceless Jewel*, p.155.

134  *The Three Jewels*, p.96.

135  *A Guide to the Buddhist Path*, p.95.

136 From discussion on Sangharakshita's lectures on 'Creative Symbols of the Tantric Path to Enlightenment'.
137 *The Priceless Jewel*, p.152.
138 Ibid., p.152.
139 Ibid., p.151.
140 Ibid., p.152.
141 Ibid., p.152.
142 *The History of My Going for Refuge*, p.103.
143 From discussion on Sangharakshita's lectures on 'Creative Symbols of the Tantric Path to Enlightenment'.
144 From discussion during the 1985 men's ordination course in Tuscany.
145 *The History of My Going for Refuge*, p.99.
146 *The Priceless Jewel*, p.154.
147 *The History of My Going for Refuge*, p.103.

## Chapter Five

148 'The Sangha' 1956, from *The Enchanted Heart*, p.89.
149 *A Guide to the Buddhist Path*, p.105.
150 From a seminar on Michael Carrithers, *The Forest Monks of Sri Lanka*.
151 *The Three Jewels*, pp.225–6.
152 *Dhammapada*, 142.
153 *The Three Jewels*, p.226.
154 *Anguttara-Nikaya* II, 1, vii.
155 From a seminar on Michael Carrithers, *The Forest Monks of Sri Lanka*.
156 Ibid.
157 Ibid.
158 Ibid.
159 *The History of My Going for Refuge*, p.88.
160 *Forty-Three Years Ago*, p.35.
161 From a seminar on Michael Carrithers, *The Forest Monks of Sri Lanka*.
162 'The Bodhisattva Ideal', in *Mitrata* no.57, p.11.
163 *Forty-Three Years Ago*, p.9.
164 Ibid., p.9.
165 Ibid., p.9.
166 *Facing Mount Kanchenjunga*, p.117.
167 *Forty-Three Years Ago*, p.11.
168 *The Ten Pillars of Buddhism*, p.49.
169 *The Priceless Jewel*, p.155.
170 Ibid., p.155.
171 *Peace is a Fire*, p.95.
172 'The True Individual', *Mitrata* no.17, p.6.
173 Ibid., p.7.
174 *New Currents in Western Buddhism*, pp.21–2.
175 Ibid., p.24.
176 *The Priceless Jewel*, p.155.

177 P.A. Mellor, 'Protestant Buddhism', in *Religion*, Lancaster University, January 1991, p.80.

178 *The FWBO and 'Protestant Buddhism'*, p.34.

179 *New Currents in Western Buddhism*, pp.40–1.

180 *The Three Jewels*, p.151.

181 *Human Enlightenment*, p.74.

182 *Peace is a Fire*, p.69.

183 From 'Fifteen Points for New—and Old—Order Members'.

184 *Human Enlightenment*, p.81.

185 'Stream Entry: The Point of No Return', taped lecture no.80 in the series 'The Higher Evolution of Man'; also *The Meaning of Conversion in Buddhism*, p.46.

186 *Human Enlightenment*, p.81

187 *Facing Mount Kanchenjunga*, p.269.

188 *A Guide to the Buddhist Path*, p.109.

189 *The History of My Going for Refuge*, p.88.

190 *Dhammapada*, 168–169.

191 *Buddhism and the West*, p.19.

192 Ibid., p.19.

193 Ibid., p.20.

194 *The Endlessly Fascinating Cry*, p.27.

CHAPTER SIX

195 'Nalanda Revisited' 1956, from *The Enchanted Heart*, p.79.

196 *The Ten Pillars of Buddhism*, p.42.

197 Ibid., p.42.

198 *Vision and Transformation*, p.80.

199 Ibid., p.81.

200 *The Priceless Jewel*, p.107.

201 *Brāhmajāla Sutta, Dīgha-Nikāya* 1.5–7.

202 *The Priceless Jewel*, p.100.

203 *Vision and Transformation*, p.82.

204 *The Priceless Jewel*, p.20.

205 *Mahāparinibbāna Sutta, Dīgha-Nikāya*.

206 *The Priceless Jewel*, p.22.

207 *A Survey of Buddhism*, pp.159–163.

208 *Saṁyutta-Nikāya* V.xii.

209 *A Survey of Buddhism*, p.161.

210 Ibid., p.162.

211 Ibid., p.163.

212 Ibid., p.167.

213 *Vision and Transformation*, p.84.

214 *The Ten Pillars of Buddhism*, p.42.

215 Ibid., p.15.

216 Ibid., p.18.

217 Ibid., p.37.

218 For sources see Ibid., p.45.

219 Ibid., p.33.

220 Ibid., pp.19–30.

221 Ibid., p.56.

222 Ibid., p.57.

223 Ibid., p.57.

224 Ibid., p.58.

225 *Matthew* 7:12—which finds its exact equivalent in *Dhammapada*, vv.129–130.

226 *The Ten Pillars of Buddhism*, p.60.

227 *The Priceless Jewel*, p.128.

228 *The Ten Pillars of Buddhism*, p.61.

229 Ibid., p.62.

230 Ibid., p.65.

231 Ibid., p.66.

232 Ibid., p.75.

233 Ibid., p.77.

234 Ibid., p.82.

235 Ibid., p.84.

236 Ibid., p.48.

237 Ibid., p.89.

238 Ibid., p.89.

239 Ibid., p.92.

240 Ibid., p.93.

241 Ibid., p.94.

242 Ibid., p.95.

243 Ibid., p.98.

244 Subhuti, *What is the Order?*, Padmaloka Books, 1989, pp.x–1.

245 *Forty-Three Years Ago*, p.42.

246 Ibid., p.42.

247 Ibid., p.45.

248 Ibid., p.45.

249 Ibid., p.46.

250 Ibid., p.47.

251 Ibid., p.47.

252 Ibid., p.48.

253 Ibid., p.48.

254 Ibid., p.49.

## Chapter Seven

255 'Forgive Me if I Have Stained...' 1951, from *The Enchanted Heart*, p.47.

256 See taped lecture no.89, 'The Individual and the Spiritual Community'.

257 *Saṁyutta-Nikāya* V,2.

258 *Pali–English Dictionary*, Pali Text Society, London, 1979.

259 'Is a Guru Necessary?', taped lecture no.90.

260 *The History of My Going for Refuge*, p.78.

261 'Is a Guru Necessary?', taped lecture no.90.

262  *A Guide to the Buddhist Path*, p.118.
263  *The Buddha's Victory*, p.71
264  Ibid., p.71.
265  Ibid., p.68.
266  Ibid., p.71.
267  Ibid., p.76.
268  Refer to 'Fidelity', taped lecture no.153.
269  From a seminar on the *Sigālovāda Sutta*.
270  Ibid.
271  *The History of My Going for Refuge*, p.88.
272  *My Relation to the Order*, p.13.
273  From a seminar on the *Sigālovāda Sutta*.
274  'Buddhism, Sex, and Spiritual Life,' *Golden Drum* no.6, p.12.
275  *The Ten Pillars of Buddhism*, p.73.
276  Ibid., p.73.
277  Ibid., p.73.
278  *Travel Letters*, p.71.
279  *Travel Letters*, pp.71–2.
280  *The Ten Pillars of Buddhism*, p.74.
281  'Buddhism, Sex, and Spiritual Life', *Golden Drum* no.6, p.10
282  Ibid., p.10.
283  Ibid., p.8.
284  *Alternative Traditions*, p.180.
285  Ibid., p.180.
286  'Buddhism, Sex, and Spiritual Life,' *Golden Drum* no.6, p.10.
287  From discussion with Order members at the London Buddhist Centre, 1990.
288  Ibid.
289  From a seminar on the *Parābhava Sutta*, 1982.
290  From a seminar on the *Sigālovāda Sutta*.

## CHAPTER EIGHT

291  'Meditation' 1947, from *The Enchanted Heart*, p.5.
292  *A Survey of Buddhism*, p.288.
293  *The Thousand-Petalled Lotus*, p.10.
294  From a seminar on Michael Carrithers, *The Forest Monks of Sri Lanka*.
295  *Human Enlightenment*, p.45.
296  Ibid., p.46.
297  Ibid., p.49.
298  From a seminar on Michael Carrithers, *The Forest Monks of Sri Lanka*.
299  *Vision and Transformation*, p.135.
300  Ibid., p.138.
301  Ibid., p.142.
302  Ibid., p.144.
303  *A Guide to the Buddhist Path*, p.170.
304  Ibid., p.171.

305  Ibid., p.173.
306  Ibid., p.173
307  *The Way to Wisdom*, p.83.
308  From a seminar on Michael Carrithers, *The Forest Monks of Sri Lanka*.
309  *Human Enlightenment*, p.70.
310  *Learning to Walk*, p.156.
311  *The Thousand-Petalled Lotus*, p.27.
312  From a seminar on Michael Carrithers, *The Forest Monks of Sri Lanka*.
313  *The Thousand-Petalled Lotus*, pp.302–309.
314  Tape-recorded interview with the author, 1989.
315  *Human Enlightenment*, pp.51–2.
316  Ibid., p.58.
317  *A Guide to the Buddhist Path*, p.178,
318  From a seminar on Michael Carrithers, *The Forest Monks of Sri Lanka*.
319  *Guide to the Buddhist Path*, p.132.
320  *The Way to Wisdom*, p.121.
321  'Dhyana for Beginners', in *A Buddhist Bible*, ed. Dwight Goddard, Beacon Press, Boston 1970, p.493.
322  See *A Survey of Buddhism*, p.xiii.
323  Thich Nhat Hanh, *Breathe! You Are Alive*, Rider, London 1992, p.20.
324  From a seminar on Michael Carrithers, *The Forest Monks of Sri Lanka*.
325  Ibid.
326  *A Guide to the Buddhist Path*, pp.129–134.
327  Ibid., p.131.
328  From a seminar on Michael Carrithers, *The Forest Monks of Sri Lanka*.
329  Ibid.
330  Ibid.
331  From a seminar on the *Mettā Sutta*.
332  *A Guide to the Buddhist Path*, p.161.
333  Ibid., p.161.
334  Ibid., p.161.
335  *Peace is a Fire*, p.111.
336  *A Guide to the Buddhist Path*, p.161.
337  From discussion during the 1982 men's ordination course in Tuscany.
338  *The Three Jewels*, p.140.
339  *A Guide to the Buddhist Path*, p.162.
340  Ibid., p.165.
341  From *Mahāyānasūtralaṇkāra* XVI, 23, quoted in Gampopa, *The Jewel Ornament of Liberation*, trans. H.V. Guenther, Rider, London 1959, p.182.
342  *The Way to Wisdom*, pp.68–9.
343  *Mitrata* no.9, p.3.
344  From a seminar on 'Milarepa's First Meeting with Rechungpa'.
345  *The Way to Wisdom*, pp.55–6.
346  *My Relation to the Order*, p.27.
347  *Travel Letters*, p.i.
348  *My Relation to the Order*, p.28.

349  *The Way to Wisdom*, p.9.

350  *A Survey of Buddhism*, p.312.

351  *A Guide to the Buddhist Path*, p.95.

352  *A Survey of Buddhism*, p.317.

353  *Learning to Walk*, p.59.

354  *The Thousand-Petalled Lotus*, p.11.

355  Ibid., p.18.

356  Private correspondence with the author, November 1993.

## CHAPTER NINE

357  'Four Gifts' 1975, from *The Enchanted Heart*, p.125.

358  From discussion on 'The Buddha's Noble Eightfold Path', 1985.

359  From discussion during the 1982 men's ordination course in Tuscany.

360  Ibid.

361  Ibid.

362  From a seminar on Michael Carrithers, *The Forest Monks of Sri Lanka*.

363  Ibid.

364  From discussion during the 1982 men's ordination course in Tuscany.

365  Ibid.

366  From discussion during the 1985 men's ordination course in Tuscany.

367  *Vision and Transformation*, p.97.

368  From discussion during the 1982 men's ordination course in Tuscany.

369  *Vision and Transformation*, p.109.

370  From discussion during the 1982 men's ordination course in Tuscany.

371  From discussion on 'The Buddha's Noble Eightfold Path', 1985.

372  From discussion during the 1982 men's ordination course in Tuscany.

373  *My Relation to the Order*, p.13.

374  *Human Enlightenment*, p.73.

375  Ibid., p.73.

376  *A Guide to the Buddhist Path*, p.115.

377  *Human Enlightenment*, p.66.

378  'A Vision of History,' taped lecture no.136.

379  From discussion during the 1982 men's ordination course in Tuscany.

380  'A Vision of History', taped lecture no.136.

381  From the seminar on 'The Chapter of the Snake' of the *Sutta Nipāta*, 1975.

382  From discussion during the 1982 men's ordination course in Tuscany.

383  Ibid.

384  Ibid.

385  *A Guide to the Buddhist Path*, p.115.

386  *The FWBO and Protestant Buddhism*, p.145.

387  'Authority and the Individual in the New Society', *Dhammamegha* no.28, p.4.

388  Ibid., p.4.

389  Ibid., p.4.

390  From discussion during the 1982 men's ordination course in Tuscany.

391  Ibid.

392  Ibid.
393  In concluding remarks to a talk by Subhuti, published as *Are There Ethics in the Order?*, Padmaloka Books, 1990.
394  'Rights and Duties' in *Crossing the Stream*, pp.40–5.
395  Ibid., p.44.
396  From discussion during the 1987 men's ordination course at Guhyaloka in Spain.
397  *The Buddha's Victory*, p.76.
398  From discussion during the 1987 men's ordination course at Guhyaloka in Spain.
399  Ibid.
400  From discussion during the 1985 men's ordination course in Tuscany.
401  'Buddhism and Education', *Dhammamegha* no.22, p.7.
402  Ibid., p.9.
403  Ibid., p.11.
404  Ibid., p.17.
405  From discussion during the 1982 men's ordination course in Tuscany.
406  *Vision and Transformation*, p.101.
407  From discussion during the 1987 men's ordination course at Guhyaloka in Spain.
408  From discussion during the 1982 men's ordination course in Tuscany.
409  *Vision and Transformation*, p.107.
410  Ibid., p.106.
411  From an interview by Martin Baumann and Christian von Somm for *Spirita—Zeitschrift für Religionswissenschaft*, Berlin, September 1992.
412  From discussion during the 1982 men's ordination course in Tuscany.
413  Ibid.
414  'Authority and the Individual in the New Society', *Dhammamegha* no.28, p.12.
415  Ibid., p.12.
416  Ibid., p.12.
417  Ibid., p.19.
418  Ibid., p.19.
419  From an interview by Martin Baumann and Christian von Somm for *Spirita—Zeitschrift für Religionswissenschaft*, Berlin, September 1992.
420  From a seminar on Michael Carrithers, *The Forest Monks of Sri Lanka*.
421  Ibid.
422  From an interview with Martin Baumann and Christian von Somm for *Spirita—Zeitschrift für Religionswissenschaft*, Berlin, September 1992.
423  From discussion during the 1982 men's ordination course in Tuscany.
424  From an interview with Martin Baumann and Christian von Somm for *Spirita—Zeitschrift für Religionswissenschaft*, Berlin, September 1992.
425  Ibid.
426  From a seminar on Al-Ghazālī, *The Duties of Brotherhood in Islam*.
427  From an interview with Martin Baumann and Christian von Somm for *Spirita—Zeitschrift für Religionswissenschaft*, Berlin, September 1992.

**428** From a seminar on Al-Ghazālī, *The Duties of Brotherhood in Islam*.

**429** Ibid.

**430** Ibid.

**431** From discussion during the 1982 men's ordination course in Tuscany.

**432** From discussion during the 1987 men's ordination course at Guhyaloka in Spain.

**433** From a seminar on Al-Ghazālī, *The Duties of Brotherhood in Islam*.

**434** Ibid.

**435** Ibid.

**436** Ibid.

**437** Ibid.

**438** Ibid.

**439** Ibid.

**440** 'Religion and Secularism', *Dhammamegha* no.11, p.9.

**441** Ibid., p.15.

**442** From discussion on 'The Buddha's Noble Eightfold Path', 1985.

**443** 'Religio-Nationalism in Sri Lanka', in *Alternative Traditions*, pp.69–91.

**444** Ibid., p.84.

**445** From discussion on 'The Buddha's Noble Eightfold Path', 1985.

**446** From discussion during the 1987 men's ordination course at Guhyaloka in Spain.

**447** From discussion during the 1982 men's ordination course in Tuscany.

**448** From discussion on 'The Buddha's Noble Eightfold Path', 1985.

**449** *Vision and Transformation*, pp.94–5.

**450** From a seminar on *The Precepts of the Gurus*, Part 3.

## CHAPTER TEN

**451** 'At the Barber's' 1970, from *The Enchanted Heart*, p.118.

**452** *The FWBO and 'Protestant Buddhism'*, p.139.

**453** See *The Religion of Art*.

**454** *Learning to Walk*, p.39.

**455** Ibid., pp.40–1.

**456** Ibid., p.56.

**457** Ibid., p.88.

**458** Ibid., p.102.

**459** *The Thousand-Petalled Lotus*, p.291.

**460** Ibid., p.292.

**461** *Facing Mount Kanchenjunga*, p.84.

**462** *The Thousand-Petalled Lotus*, p.292.

**463** Collected in *The Religion of Art*.

**464** *Facing Mount Kanchenjunga*, p.271.

**465** Ibid., p.473.

**466** Ibid., p.100.

**467** Ibid., p.279.

**468** *A Guide to the Buddhist Path*, p.40.

**469** Ibid., p.39.

470 From discussion during the 1981 men's ordination course in Tuscany.
471 *A Guide to the Buddhist Path*, p.40.
472 From discussion during the 1985 men's ordination course in Tuscany.
473 Ibid.
474 *A Survey of Buddhism*, p.161.
475 From discussion during the 1985 men's ordination course in Tuscany.
476 *The Thousand-Petalled Lotus*, pp.170–1.
477 From discussion during the 1981 men's ordination course in Tuscany.
478 *The Priceless Jewel*, p.56.
479 From discussion on the *Vimalakīrti Nirdeśa*.
480 *Vision and Transformation*, p.35.
481 *The Essence of Zen*, p.73.
482 *The Priceless Jewel*, p.56.
483 Ibid., p.57.
484 From discussion on *The Buddha's Law Among the Birds*, during the 1982 men's ordination course in Tuscany.
485 From discussion on *Milarepa's First Meeting with Rechungpa*.
486 Ibid.
487 Ibid.
488 Ibid.
489 Ibid.
490 *The History of My Going for Refuge*, pp.18–19.
491 *My Relation to the Order*, p.28.
492 *A Survey of Buddhism*, pp.45–6.
493 Ibid., p.45.
494 From a seminar on *The Precepts of the Gurus*.
495 *The FWBO and 'Protestant Buddhism'*, p.175.
496 Ibid., p.129.
497 Ibid., p.160.
498 Ibid., p.144.
499 *Buddhism and the West*, p.12.
500 *The FWBO and 'Protestant Buddhism'*, p.16.
501 *My Relation to the Order*, p.35.
502 *The FWBO and 'Protestant Buddhism'*, p.16.
503 *The Priceless Jewel*, p.55.
504 Ibid., p.91.
505 *Vision and Transformation*, p.36.
506 From discussion on the *Kālāma Sutta*.
507 *The FWBO and 'Protestant Buddhism'*, p.175.
508 *The Religion of Art*, p.61.
509 Ibid., p.64.
510 *The Three Jewels*, p.85.
511 Ibid., p.85.
512 *The Religion of Art*, pp.43–52.
513 *The Three Jewels*, p.87.
514 *The Religion of Art*, p.81.

515  Ibid., pp.82–3.
516  Ibid., p.84.
517  Ibid., pp.84–5.
518  Ibid., p.87.
519  Ibid., p.93.
520  *The FWBO and 'Protestant Buddhism'*, p.79.
521  *The Religion of Art*, p.93.
522  Ibid., pp.100–1.
523  Ibid., p.101.
524  Ibid., p.110.
525  Ibid., p.112.
526  Ibid., p.119.
527  Ibid., p.121.

## CHAPTER ELEVEN

528  From discussion on 'Aspects of the Higher Evolution of the Individual'.
529  Ibid.
530  From a seminar on Michael Carrithers, *The Forest Monks of Sri Lanka*.
531  *The FWBO and 'Protestant Buddhism'*, p.79.
532  'New' 1969, from *The Enchanted Heart'*, p.110.

# BIBLIOGRAPHY

Works by Sangharakshita referred to in the text:

*A Guide to the Buddhist Path*, Windhorse, Glasgow 1990.
*A Survey of Buddhism*, seventh edition, Windhorse, Glasgow 1993.
*Alternative Traditions*, Windhorse, Glasgow 1986.
*Buddhism and the West: The Integration of Buddhism into Western Society*, Windhorse, Glasgow 1992.
*Crossing the Stream*, Windhorse, Glasgow 1987.
*Facing Mount Kanchenjunga*, Windhorse, London 1991.
*Forty-Three Years Ago: Reflections on my Bhikkhu Ordination*, Windhorse, Glasgow 1993.
*Going for Refuge*, Windhorse, Glasgow 1983.
*Human Enlightenment*, third edition, Windhorse, Glasgow 1993.
*Learning to Walk*, Windhorse, Glasgow 1990.
*The Meaning of Conversion in Buddhism*, Windhorse, Birmingham 1994.
*Mind—Reactive and Creative*, third edition, Windhorse, London 1977.
*My Relation to the Order*, Windhorse, Glasgow 1990.
*New Currents in Western Buddhism*, Windhorse, Glasgow 1990.
*Peace is a Fire*, Windhorse, London 1979.
*The Buddha's Victory*, Windhorse, Glasgow 1991.
*The Enchanted Heart: Poems 1946–1976*, Ola Leaves, Norwich 1978.
*The Endlessly Fascinating Cry: An Exploration of the Bodhicaryavatara*, FWBO, 1977.
*The Essence of Zen*, fourth edition, Windhorse, Glasgow 1992.
*The Eternal Legacy*, Tharpa, London 1985.
*The FWBO and 'Protestant Buddhism': An Affirmation and a Protest*, Windhorse, Glasgow 1992.
*The History of My Going for Refuge*, Windhorse, Glasgow 1988.
*The Meaning of Orthodoxy in Buddhism*, Windhorse, Glasgow 1987.
*The Religion of Art*, Windhorse, Glasgow 1988.
*The Ten Pillars of Buddhism*, second edition, Windhorse, Glasgow 1985.

*The Thousand-Petalled Lotus*, Alan Sutton, Gloucester 1988.

*The Three Jewels: An Introduction to Buddhism*, Windhorse, Glasgow 1991.

*The Way to Wisdom: An Exploration of the Five Spiritual Faculties*, Windhorse, Glasgow 1984.

*Travel Letters*, Windhorse, Glasgow 1985.

*Vision and Transformation*, Windhorse, Glasgow 1990.

*Wisdom Beyond Words: Sense and Non-Sense in the Buddhist Prajnaparamita Tradition*, Windhorse, Glasgow 1993.

Most of these books are available from Windhorse Publications,
38 Newmarket Road, Cambridge, CB5 8DT, UK

They are also usually on sale at all FWBO centres. For addresses contact:
The London Buddhist Centre, 51 Roman Road, London, E2 0HU, UK.
Telephone: 020 8981 1225/0845 458 4716.

Quotations from seminars and discussions are taken from the unedited transcripts. These can usually be consulted at FWBO centres. I have given no publication details of the texts on which the seminars and discussions are based, since these are only referred to so as to identify the source of the quotation.

References to Sangharakshita's taped lectures give the number in the Dharmachakra Tapes 1992 catalogue. The tapes can be obtained from: Dharmachakra Tapes, PO Box 50, Cambridge, CB1 3AG, UK.

# Recommended Reading and Listening

This work offers an overview of Sangharakshita's life and work. The reader who wishes to study Sangharakshita's thought more systematically could read the following works as background to each chapter.

## Introductions to Buddhism

Chris Pauling, *Introducing Buddhism*, second edition, Windhorse, Glasgow 1993.
Sangharakshita, *A Guide to the Buddhist Path*, Windhorse, Glasgow 1990.
Sangharakshita, *The Three Jewels*, Windhorse, Glasgow 1991.
Sangharakshita, *Vision and Transformation*, Windhorse, Glasgow 1990.
Sangharakshita, *Who is the Buddha?*, Windhorse, Birmingham 1994.

## Chapter 1: The Translator

Sangharakshita, *Learning to Walk*, Windhorse, Glasgow 1990.
Sangharakshita, *The Thousand-Petalled Lotus*, Alan Sutton, Gloucester 1988.
Sangharakshita, *Facing Mount Kanchenjunga*, Windhorse, London 1991.
Sangharakshita, *The Enchanted Heart: Poems 1946–1976*, Ola Leaves, Norwich 1978.
Terry Pilchick, *Jai Bhim! Dispatches from a Peaceful Revolution*, Windhorse, Glasgow 1988.

## Chapter 2: The Unity of Buddhism

Sangharakshita, *A Survey of Buddhism*, seventh edition, Windhorse, Glasgow 1993.
Sangharakshita, *The Eternal Legacy*, Tharpa, London 1985.
Sangharakshita, *The Meaning of Orthodoxy in Buddhism*, Windhorse, Glasgow 1987.

## Chapter 3: The Metaphysical Principle

Sangharakshita, *Mind—Reactive and Creative*, Windhorse, London 1977.

Sangharakshita, 'The Bodhisattva Principle' in *The Priceless Jewel*, Windhorse, Glasgow 1993.

Alex Kennedy (Dharmachari Subhuti), *The Buddhist Vision*, Rider, London 1992.

Sangharakshita, 'The Higher Evolution of Man', taped lectures 75–82, Dharmachakra, Cambridge 1969.

Sangharakshita, 'Aspects of the Higher Evolution of the Individual', taped lectures 83–90, Dharmachakra, Cambridge 1970.

CHAPTER 4: GOING FOR REFUGE

Sangharakshita, *Going for Refuge*, Windhorse, Glasgow 1983.

Sangharakshita, *The History of My Going for Refuge*, Windhorse, Glasgow 1988.

Sangharakshita, *The Meaning of Conversion in Buddhism*, Windhorse, Birmingham 1994.

CHAPTER 5: SANGHA

Sangharakshita, *Forty-Three Years Ago: Reflections on my Bhikkhu Ordination*, Windhorse, Glasgow 1993.

Sangharakshita, *New Currents in Western Buddhism*, Windhorse, Glasgow 1990.

CHAPTER 6: THE FUNDAMENTAL CODE OF ETHICS

Sangharakshita, *The Ten Pillars of Buddhism*, second edition, Windhorse, Glasgow 1985.

Sangharakshita, 'Aspects of Buddhist Morality' and 'Buddhism and Blasphemy' in *The Priceless Jewel*, Windhorse, Glasgow 1993.

CHAPTER 7: SPIRITUAL FRIENDSHIP

Sangharakshita, *The Buddha's Victory*, Windhorse, Glasgow 1991.

CHAPTER 8: A SYSTEM OF SPIRITUAL DISCIPLINE

Sangharakshita, *Human Enlightenment*, third edition, Windhorse, Glasgow 1993.

Kamalashila, *Meditation: The Buddhist Way of Tranquillity and Insight*, Windhorse, Glasgow 1992.

CHAPTER 9: THE NEW SOCIETY

Dharmachari Subhuti, *Buddhism for Today: A Portrait of a New Buddhist Movement*, Windhorse, Glasgow 1988.

Sangharakshita, 'Buddhism, World Peace, and Nuclear War', in *The Priceless Jewel*, Windhorse, Glasgow 1993.

CHAPTER 10: THE MAKING OF A NEW BUDDHIST CULTURE

Sangharakshita, *Alternative Traditions*, Windhorse, Glasgow 1986.

Sangharakshita, *Buddhism and the West: The Integration of Buddhism into Western Society*, Windhorse, Glasgow 1992.

Sangharakshita, 'St Jerome Revisited' and 'The Journey to Il Convento' in *The Priceless Jewel*, Windhorse, Glasgow 1993.

Sangharakshita, *The FWBO and 'Protestant Buddhism': An Affirmation and a Protest*, Windhorse, Glasgow 1992.

Sangharakshita, *The Religion of Art*, Windhorse, Glasgow 1988.

## CHAPTER 11: A NEW VOICE

Sangharakshita, *My Relation to the Order*, Windhorse, Glasgow 1990.

# INDEX

The Windhorse symbolizes the energy of the enlightened mind carrying the Three Jewels —the Buddha, the Dharma, and the Sangha—to all sentient beings.

Buddhism is one of the fastest growing spiritual traditions in the Western world. Throughout its 2,500-year history, it has always succeeded in adapting its mode of expression to suit whatever culture it has encountered.

Windhorse Publications aims to continue this tradition as Buddhism comes to the West. Today's Westerners are heirs to the entire Buddhist tradition, free to draw instruction and inspiration from all the many schools and branches. Windhorse publishes works by authors who not only understand the Buddhist tradition but are also familiar with Western culture and the Western mind.

For orders and catalogues contact
WINDHORSE PUBLICATIONS
38 NEWMARKET ROAD
CAMBRIDGE
CB5 8DT
UK

Windhorse Publications is an arm of the Friends of the Western Buddhist Order, which has more than forty centres on four continents. Through these centres, members of the Western Buddhist Order offer regular programmes of events for the general public and for more experienced students. These include meditation classes, public talks, study on Buddhist themes and texts, and 'bodywork' classes such as t'ai chi, yoga, and massage. The FWBO also runs several retreat centres and the Karuna Trust, a fundraising charity that supports social welfare projects in the slums and villages of India.

Many FWBO centres have residential spiritual communities and ethical businesses associated with them. Arts activities are encouraged too, as is the development of strong bonds of friendship between people who share the same ideals. In this way the FWBO is developing a unique approach to Buddhism, not simply as a set of techniques, less still as an exotic cultural interest, but as a creatively directed way of life for people living in the modern world.

If you would like more information about the FWBO please write to the
LONDON BUDDHIST CENTRE
51 ROMAN ROAD
LONDON
E2 OHU
UK